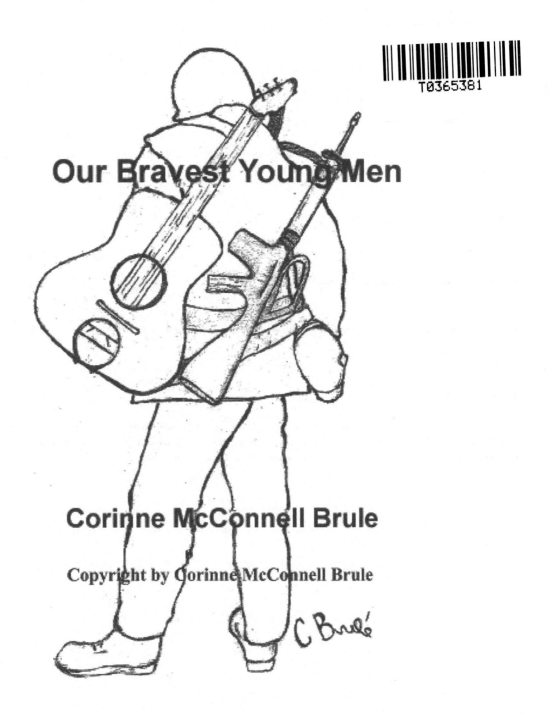

Our Bravest Young Men

Corinne McConnell Brule

Copyright by Corinne McConnell Brule

AuthorHouse™ LLC
1663 Liberty Drive
Bloomington, IN 47403
www.authorhouse.com
Phone: 1-800-839-8640

Published by AuthorHouse   12/12/2013

ISBN: 978-1-4817-5671-6 (sc)

Library of Congress Control Number: 2013909683

Any people depicted in stock imagery provided by Thinkstock are models, and such images are being used for illustrative purposes only.
Certain stock imagery © Thinkstock.

This book is printed on acid-free paper.

Because of the dynamic nature of the Internet, any web addresses or links contained in this book may have changed since publication and may no longer be valid. The views expressed in this work are solely those of the author and do not necessarily reflect the views of the publisher, and the publisher hereby disclaims any responsibility for them.

Preface

This book was written to entertain the
reader, to make him laugh, to make him cry and to
make him think about the Vietnam War. I am a
contemporary of the Vietnam War. It was my war in
my time and it is still my war. This was a war I
was against throughout its course except for its
first year. This book does not try to change ideas
about the Vietnam War or any war. It does try to
tell the reader to try for diplomacy, first,
before sending young men out in arms. The title of
this book was derived from the first few lines of
Robert F. Kennedy's Vietnam War Speech that he
gave in California on March 24, 1968. And the
purpose of this political, historical novel is to
give a message about the Vietnam War—-actually it
is to give a message about all war—-that war is
grievous--and with this, the Vietnam War.What
about the Soldiers who were drafted and did not
want to fight in this war? This story is based on
that Soldier and on all Soldiers who fought in the
Vietnam War. With this novel, I try to give my
message to my country--to my fellow citizens--
about war especially about our Vietnam War. But
most importantly this novel was written as my
tribute to the Soldiers, who fought in the Vietnam
War--especially to the-over 58,000 Soldiers whose
voices have been silenced forever for that war!
All of the Soldiers are Our Bravest Young Men.

This book is not controversial as always has
been with the topic of the Vietnam War but it does
note well that it is truly tragic for a human
being to lose his life like this whether one
agrees that it is a-horrible-loss-of-life or
whether one believes in something else. This is
for the reader to judge for himself and *for* our
country—-the U.S.A.--to judge for itself. But we
all do agree to fight for our great country for
justice and for self defense.

So that it is not confusing to the reader,
inside quotes (single quotes) have been used in

the dialogue quotes. This was done because I have included many well-known quotations within the story dialogue. I dedicate this book to my family--to my husband, Albert Harper, for his immense support, for giving me some valuable ideas on using my computer and for his help with the photography. And I also dedicate this book to my son Chris, Dr. Harper, for his designing and formatting the book covers, his critiques of my paintings, his Photo Shop computer skills, his help with the photography; Dobrosia S.; Adam H.; Dr. Mike Kaczor, MD; Dr. E. Chan, MA, CPA, MD; Dr. R. Carlino, MD; S. Wiktor, J. Desch; Dr. M. Josefksi MD, Dr. Louise-Marie Johnson, MD; Dr. Kenneth Johnson, MD, Edward Sheriff Curtis total talent and Poznan University of Medical Sciences. And I thank J. Trumps and R. Mackey and Fred for their helpful tips on the computer. And I also thank Florence Alonzo, D. Higgens, Cassidy T., E. Belcher, T. Mendoza, Amy T., Angel R., JM Kane, J. Raven, M. Alvarado, S. Cabading, Beth & Steve Dutschmann and Houbre Pascal for their help. I dedicate this book to my daughter Candice who helped me find some music that I have chosen in this book and also for her part our painting for the back cover of Book II, the Dying Marine and also to Blize B., Jaden B., Ginger B., Shelly Jane B., Kenneth B. and Peter Flores. And I thank Dr. Bernard Bihari MD, Dr. Clay Hammett, Pharm D., Dr. W. Chapman MD., K.M. Pritchett and Mr. Salim Francis. My family has backed me up with their extreme patience while waiting for me to write this book. My family did this by making their own meals, by eating *TV Dinners,* by eating snacks for meals, and by doing things for themselves that ordinarily I would have been able to do *for* them--but most importantly--by doing things that ordinarily I would have been able to do *with* them. I thank my father Elmo Alfred Brule Jr. also known as Al Brule a well known American commercial art painter, 1940-1965 and a fine arts painter, 1966-1999. Also I thank his supporting wife Fern and daughter Cecilia of many years. A painting of his commissioned by the Boys Club of America was presented to the Kennedy White House where it hangs. And Al Brule's original oil painting, In Defiance of Kings hung in the White House in

Washington, D.C. and was presented there`for the
American Bicentenial. And I thank the Benjamin Art
Gallary, Washington County Museum of Fine Arts,
Williamson Art and Antiques and many others for
showing his work. And I thank his friends Mr. and
Mrs. J. Thomson, R&K Stevens, Mr. S. Strong, J&M.
Hixon, B&J Kalmar and Mr. and Mrs. George and Ruth
Rudisill, LollyB.Decker my dear mother Betty Ruth
McConnell and my great stepfather Roy E. Kenner. I
thank my husband's parents Robert E. Harper for
his support and who served in WWII in the U.S.
Army Eighth Air Force as an English French
interpreter at the Casablanca Conference for
President Franklin Roosevelt, Prime Minister
Winston Churchill, General De Gaull and General
Henri Giraud. I thank his mother Margarita Lopez-
Bermejo de Harper for her support in my life.
Also, I thank my brother, Alfred and his family;
my sisters Rochelle and her family, Kalianne H.
and Lynne for her pure musical genius and my
cousin Bette Jane. I also thank NO KILL NATION and
PETA. I thank my freshman college English teacher
for assigning me a book to read called English
2000, Joseph C. Blumenthal, circa 1964 which was a
programmed-learning-English grammar book. It was
assigned to me to read at Rockland Community
College. I thank Mr. and Mrs. R. Freilich for
their help in my life. I thank Mr. and Mrs. Moss,
Hilton and Highland Real Estate, Mr. Richard
Maslan. Also I thank Colonel J. Strang and Colonel
C. Brown for our interesting conversations about
Vietnam. My pets have all been good companions
through the years and to name them, my Gopher
Tortoise, Desert Tortoise, Rufus, Missy, Licorice,
Nifty, KD, Rainey, Yo-Yo, Auggie, Febe, Olivia,
Jodi, Sandi, Scampy, Buffy, Kitty, Hermis,
Trooper, Jake, Dulcie, Rubin, Raven, Rainey,
Skippy, Felix, Precious, Preciousesness, Smokey,
Red, Dusty, Pepper, Breezy, Misty, Cupcake, Smokey
II, Emma, Finnegan, Murphy,Duke, Maggie Pepsi,
Coco, Ferrel, Charlie, Molly, Blondie, Peg, Latte,
and Fluffum, Auggie & Scoopy.
   And also finally I thank little Benji and
Breezy

Corinne McConnell Brule, BA History, Arizona
State University

Contents

Our Bravest Young Men
Volume II

Introduction

Our Bravest Young Men

Volume II

This is the continuation of the political, historical novel, Volume I, with Sp4c. Peter McConnell, a college student who was drafted into the Vietnam War. He has been drafted with his childhood friend Sp4c. Guy Von Bexin. And upon induction they decide to join the Army Rangers Special Forces, Long Range Reconnaissance Patrol (LRRPs). Sp4c. Peter McConnell is married to Sherry who is pregnant with his child and he goes to war in Vietnam.

And Peter's battle buddies, Sp4c. Mc (Chris) Davison had been attending San Diego State University as an art major until his grades dropped and then he was drafted as a Soldier in the Army in the Vietnam War then he joined the Special Forces. Another friend/*battle buddy*, Sp4c. John Kelsey, is pro war and he has volunteered to join the Army Special Forces, LuRRPs to serve his country. Sp4c. Dion Johnson, a World Cup holder in track and field was drafted into the Army. He is an Army Soldier--Special Forces--in the Vietnam War and is not happy with this war. Sp4c. Joel Hammerstein was a pre-medical student who fell ill with mononucleosis, dropped out of college, was drafted and then volunteered to be a Sniper with the Army Special Forces--LuRRPs. Sp4c. Buzz Brule was a former pre-medical student in college, was drafted and joined the Army Special Forces in Vietnam. He is fed up with the war and discusses his negative feelings about the war throughout the books. These Soldiers are not happy with this war and complain most of the time with their many discussions in dialogue, covering the political issues and strategic military issues of the Vietnam War. One opinion is that, had President

John F. Kennedy not been tragically killed, the U.S. would never have become militarily involved in Vietnam.

And now in Part II of *Our Bravest Young Men*, the lead characters, Sp4c. Peter McConnell and Sp4c. Buzz Brule continue to discuss the political and military ramifications of the Vietnam War. The Soldiers take a journey to Qui Nhon for R&R where Mc (Chris) meets a beautiful woman. And a new character is introduced--Sp4c. Joe Wolfing--who is a young naive surfer from Malibu. He has also been drafted into the Vietnam War and has joined the Special Forces LuRRPs. These Soldiers also discuss President Abraham Lincoln, slavery and the Civil War. Sp4c. McConnell and his Battle Buddies attend pre-mission briefings for a mission on Mt. Dong Ap Bia (Hamburger Hill/Hill 937). The Soldiers *rif* Mt. Dong Ap Bia and then go to battle. [Note: with chapters 18-23 in Volume II the characters' *points of argument* are fictitious with the battlefield plans, strategy and military operations with the Battle of Hamburger Hill but are based on the actual historical events of the Vietnam War.

With both books a different format is presented by combining much dialogue with political discussions/conversations and some descriptive prose. All of the historical and political information presented in the dialogues are historical facts from the Vietnam War and the prose is descriptive of Vietnam. Historical and political quotes are noted with singular quotation marks around them.

The information for the songs--the song writers, the artists/singers/musicians, the song lyrics and the record labels--was searched through Wikipedia.org., other internet-lyric sources and from my own music files and record collection.

Our Bravest Young Men, Volume II

Chapter 1

Peter Talks About Presidential

Advisors, Politics then Back to Base and R&R

Peter, Buzz, Mc, Joel, John, Dion and Guy are ordered to their much deserved R&R to Vung Tau. Once again they find themselves in their military convoy on their way for R&R. It seems to be the most reasonable thing to do. Peter's mind is set on Sherry again.

As the monsoon storm darkens, there begins a few hard drops of rain ... and then a refreshing tropical breeze blows hard past their faces. Peter knows this is going to be *the storm of storms*--making it night with a dense cover of low hanging clouds. With Peter's mind on Sherry, Peter tells Guy, "I wish that I could see Sherry again. Her photo is all I have of her now. [He takes out her photo and looks at it.]. I carry her photo everywhere with me. She is beautiful and I can't wait for our child."

Then Peter's mind snaps back to reality with their new destination. The Soldiers arrive in Vung Tau. This city looks different from anything they have ever seen before. Mc says, "I don't like this hole. It is the hole of holes. Some want to call it Dodge City because it looks just like a city out of the old American West with the swinging saloon doors and with everything a Western movie has. This is shit with all these crazies playin' cowboy." [Everyone laughs.]. Buzz remarks, "Boy these guys are really playing their games of 'Cowboys and Indians.' No wonder they want to stay here and fight. They are reliving all of the Westerns they grew up on and saw on TV--all of the John Wayne western movies and more. They are having way too much fun here to stop this now—-reliving their childhood fantasies. Is this a return back to the *Old West* for these Soldiers or isn't it? Guy says, "Yes, this is a game some of our Soldiers are playing but not all of them are playing it." Peter says, "It is 'Cowboys and Indians?' Guy, do you remember the cowboy Hopalong Cassidy--Hoppy shooting-it-up in those fabulous movies of his? We played that game out there on the grounds of our Little Red School House when we were kids--remember? It was a lot of fun. I was John Wayne and Hoppy and you were the bad guy, sometimes? Don't you remember, Guy? And as they rode off into the sunset there was always a happy ending. That was a long time ago." Guy does not answer for fear of

the sadness it would evoke in himself and in Peter but
everyone is laughing. Buzz says jokingly, "Yeah Guy is
always the bad guy--not just sometimes. No I am just kidding
with you Guy." Buzz then says angrily, "No really, they do
have a lot of nerve sending us out here into a hell-hole
like this western cowboy town for our R&R?" (rest and
relaxation). [Peter, Guy and Mc laugh.]. Mc then asks Buzz,
"Ah, you don't want to play *Cowboys and Indians*, anyway, do
ya', Buzz?" Buzz says, "How do you know? These streets
resemble an old western mining town in early America.
Actually this town of mud and dirt could be from anywhere
out of the Old American West." Mc says wisely, "Yeah, but
there is one difference, this town does not have the gold."
Buzz says, "Yeah, but it sure is costing our country a lot
of gold." [Everyone laughs and with Peter the laughter is
non-stop.]. Peter then says to Buzz, "Man you are funny."
Peter is happy for the moment with not much of a care on his
mind. Guy says, "No, I already played these games back in
grade school. As I was telling Peter, I really don't care
about reliving those games anymore. I guess I got it out of
my system way back *when* a long time ago. It was a long time
ago with this childhood wonder but I just do not want to
bring this 'wonder' back into my life if it means going to
war and dying for it!" Buzz then says, "Yes, I guess you are
right. I don't want to bring this *wonder* back into my life
either if it means going to war for the allure of it and
dying for something of which I am not too terribly sure
about. This town now, here, in Vietnam for us Americans is
really reliving the *old west*." Guy then says, "This country
is back several centuries behind us anyway." Buzz says,
"Yeah, no joke but this Dodge-City stuff was done for the
benefit of our Soldiers." Mc says, "Yeah, you are the
knowledgeable one--great man--smart man. Yes, it is done for
our Soldiers. Did you expect anything different here in
'Nam? Let's try to get us out of this hole, now." Buzz says,
"How do you want me to do that 'big boy'--click my heels
together like Judy Garland did in The Wizard of Oz or what?"
Mc then says, "Yeah, do what you want to do but you really
don't look anything like Judy Garland and also, believe it
or not, this is not The Wizard of Oz ... but I wish it was."
Buzz says, "Yeah, unfortunately, I know it is not and I wish
it was too. And if it was The Wizard of Oz, and I could play
the Tin Soldier ... then ..." Mc interrupts, "Yeah, you got
that one right. You look real tinny and you are real tinny
in the brain. You do look like the Tin Soldier--yeah real
tinny!" [Peter laughs non-stop.]. Peter then says these wise
words, "But really these Vietnamese are kicking our ass all

over this damn place--big time--and the Tin Soldier in The Wizard of OZ did not get his ass kicked by the Vietnamese. He had it better than any of us out here have it, so please don't scoff the Tin Soldier, now. The Tin Soldier was lucky [Everyone laughs.]. All he needed was a little TLC and a little oilin.' We sure ain't gettin' any of that around here." [Everyone laughs and Peter laughs the most. Peter is happy.]. Buzz then quips in a quick last one and says, "Oh bright idea, Pete. Since you opened your big mouth about oilin', why don't you oil me a little bit, then?" [Everyone laughs.]. Peter turns around and says to Buzz, "Oh shut the f*ck up, man would you? I'm sick of your raunchy mouth, already yet. I ain't no queer. I have heard enough of your mouth for one lifetime, so shut up. Hasn't someone else around here ever accused you before of having too much *mouth*, already yet?" Buzz responds, "No I don't have too much mouth. And oilin'--that ain't bad?! What's wrong with some oilin', Pete? Joel then says, "Oh you guys sound like a bunch of ignorant ass holes. Your heads are not screwed on too tightly. And in the meantime we are tearing this poor country into pieces while we are all laughing and joking here." Joel now laughs at Buzz but brings up a good point and says, "Yeah, look at what these warring factions are doing—-the Communists and the non Communists--to the indigenous peoples all over this country. We are tearing them out of their jungle homelands and resettling them in make-shift refugee camps and killing them off. We are using them and then disposing of them anyway we so desire. They are our pawns in our game." Guy says, "Yes, they are pawns and we are doing everything you have said. Yes, what we do in Vietnam is best for us—-the U.S. If these people get some *left-overs* after all this destruction in the windfall, they are doing real well. It is done not with deliberate intention of harm but it is done in complete wonton disregard for the wants and needs of these people—-no more no less." Peter then says, "No, we are not that bad." John says, "Yeah, Peter is right. We must think of how we can win this war. All these people really want here is, Democracy and freedom. We will get it for them. [Soldiers' Code] 'My sacrifice is your comfort.'" Mc chimes in sarcastically, "You really think so? That's news about *their* comfort and don't be so sure of it." Buzz agreeing with Mc for once, "You really think so? I think I get your drift. But it is not *comfort* to be displaced from their homes and put into refugee camps and forced to live in a country of terror. That is not *comfort*!" Buzz then says most sincerely to all of this political talk "Gee, you know somethin,' I really

wish I could make everybody in this world happy, but I
can't. But you know something--if I could, I would! Peter
then pats Buzz on the back several times and says, "You know
what, Buzz ... I really believe you would!" Joel asks
wisely, "Yeah, are you sure that freedom, then, is what
these people really want here? And ... 'It is very hard for
local people to accept any foreigners who say they are
fighting for our freedom,'" [as said by Gen. Azizudin
Wardak, provincial police chief, U.S. war in Afghanistan,
2009]. Joel continues, "I mean a freedom to live as a
displaced person in a refugee camp? 'For them the
[Communist] Taliban regime was awful, but perpetual war may
be worse,'" [as said by Nicholas Kristof—editorial--2010
U.S. War in Afghanistan]. Is that the freedom they want?
Don't they want to return to their villages of ancestral
heritage or even have a united country once again? 'May they
be able to forgive us for what we have done to them, may we
begin to heal and may we live in peace from here till
eternity,'" [S. Acheson U.S. Army Veteran Iraq 2012]. John
says, "'We're here to protect the [Vietnamese] Afghan
people. And we're here to protect them from everything that
can hurt them. ...,'" [as said by Gen. McChrystal 2009 war
in Afghanistan]. Peter says, "Yes, but these people want
their village-lives back and live in peace. They want to
live in peace ... on their own terms—-not as America wants
them to live it." John says, "Yes, that makes some sense
since you mentioned it like that but now we need to save
these people from Communism, we must save Vietnam for
Democracy." John now starts ideas and discussions about U.S.
war policies, "But Nixon was on the right track with his
bombing of Hanoi and the mining of Haiphong Harbor and with
his Linebacker I and Linebacker II Campaigns. A former U.S.
Aid to President Johnson said 'Linebacker had a greater
impact in its first four months than Rolling Thunder had in
four years,' [historian and writer Dale Andrade]. 'Nixon's
bombing of North Vietnam and the unprecedented air support
given to the South Vietnamese Army dealt a devastating blow
to the offensive,'"[Andrade]. "Peter says to that, "Nixon
tried to cut-off overland supply routes between China and
North Vietnam." Mc changes the subject, "But the problem is
that Trail scoots all the way through Laos and back into
Vietnam—-yeah--this neutrality and the trail? We sign a
neutrality treaty with our enemy before we go to war with
them—-I mean smart-—real smart--isn't it? Now, isn't that
the way to go—-sign a non-aggression pack and then go to war
with them? This gave us 'Restrictive rules of engagement
[and] forbade U.S. ground units from entering Laos, and it

4

also even prevented air controllers from coordinating tactical air strikes.' And again, our commanders were angry when an 'American fighter jet ... bombed a group of Taliban fighters ... and Afghan civilians,'" [as said by Byron York reporter 2009]. Buzz then says, "Yeah that is a bummer--not real smart. Our troops are going to pay for that. It will be the American Soldier who will pay with his life with too many rules of restrictive engagement." Peter says, "With the Laotian Border, yeah our border with 'Laos is a long open flank ... which may soon be an open base for the Viet Cong operations,' [as said by the chief of the Interagency Vietnam Task Force during the young Kennedy Administration]. How can we fight a war like this?" Buzz responds emphatically, "No we really just got to-get-the-hell-out, that's all. It's like this. [As said to Joe Galloway, newspaper commentator/reporter, 2006, about U.S. war with Iraq], 'There may be fifty ways to leave your lover, but there is only one way to leave Iraq [Vietnam]: load our people on their trucks and Bradley's and Humvee's [and troop transporters] and head for the border. Now.' [And with another war in Afghanistan said by George F. Will]: 'Genius said de Gaulle, recalling Bismarck's decision to halt German forces short of Paris in 1870, sometimes consists of knowing when to stop. Genius is not required to recognize that in Afghanistan [Vietnam], when means *now*, before more American valor [...] is squandered.'" Buzz continues and brings up another topic, "And what about head counts--live or dead? Our commanders don't even have a *live count* on our enemy? Don't you think we should have an idea on our enemy numbers on how many troops? I think our commanders want to fight this war to show the world that we can win this war. Our commanders believe they cannot lose this war or any war." Mc agrees, "Yes, totally, they are all damn good commanders but they believe they can win this war even when their hands are tied by civilian advisors and the politicians in Washington. But also it goes the other way. Washington has been told exaggerations by our military commanders that made our progress with this war seem to look good--as if we were winning--and it became a vicious circle. Nobody ever imagined in their wildest imagination that the war would go this badly for us." Peter then changes back to the neutrality issue, "But the real problem is President Kennedy got us tied into a policy of neutrality with South Vietnam's neighbors. In Geneva at the multilateral negotiations over Laos and we signed the Geneva Peace Accord. With these neutral neighbors the enemy keeps coming across the borders. He keeps infiltrating enemy material and manpower into South

Vietnam. [Said by Bill O'Reilly about the American War with Iraq 2009], 'No matter how many engagements are won, there will always be more fanatical killers coming across the border.'" Mc then says, "President Kennedy's Secretary of State Dean Rusk said, '(...) we wanted an agreement that produced a neutral but independent Laos, an *island of peace* in Southeast Asia that would be a buffer zone.' That was the objective but in the end it hurt us." Buzz says so wisely, "Even the JCS of the Kennedy administration knew these borders would pose some serious problems whether they were neutral or not. 'The JCS concluded that Hanoi would probably not relax its Viet Cong campaign to any significant extent and would intensify their efforts to establish a secure route for motor vehicle traffic into the South and increase harassment and ambush and guerrilla attacks and the neutralization of Laos would not significantly reduce Communist infiltration of men and equipment from North into South Vietnam through Laos.'" Peter changes the subject, "Yes that is true but with all this bottom line President Kennedy believed that the Indo-China states were pawns of the international mega powers and perhaps neutrality would help them in choosing their own fate. This is why we signed the Neutrality Agreement." Peter now talks Imperialism with this idea and quotes President Kennedy, "'The Indo China States are puppet states, French principalities with great resources but as typical examples of empire and colonialism as can be found anywhere. To check the southern drive of Communism makes sense but not only through reliance on the force of arms. The task is rather to build a strong native non-Communist sentiment within these areas and rely on that spearhead of defense. To do this apart from and in defiance of innately nationalistic arms spells foredoomed failure.' He had the right idea. He never wanted U.S. arms/military involvement except to be advisors in South Vietnam. In the beginning of Kennedy's administration his political advisors Maxwell Taylor, Edward Lansdale and Walt Rostow sent 8,000 troops to South Vietnam but only for help in controlling the floods and farmlands, not for self defense." Guy says, "Yes, and President Kennedy had a pretty good idea about what he wanted in South Vietnam and he did not want to commit our troops. His advisors had all the ideas on how to win the war but bottom line. They were Hawks. But Kennedy in his heart did not want U.S. combat troops in Vietnam. He sent troops as aids and advisors to help the South Vietnamese people in their self-defense but not to fight the war for them." Mc has another idea, "But we should be committed all the way with our troops and with our country backing us or get out.

And neither President Johnson nor President Kennedy is committed to Vietnam." Peter adds, "This is quite true because [said by John Prados historian and writer], 'George Ball (senior diplomatic advisor) and Robert McNamara agreed on one thing: Lyndon Johnson far from a confident war-maker, was agonized and uncertain. LBJ could have gone either way. But the evident worsening of the situation in Vietnam seemed to require some decision, and McNamara's management style created an appetite for options. The situation was *ripe* for men of ideas.'" Buzz says, "Hey President Johnson was scared silly of China. President Johnson '(...) could not face the thought of being regarded as the first President in U.S. History to lose a war.'" Guy says, "Nobody could agree on what course to take." Buzz says, "Foreign policy on Vietnam was ambivalent. One day the Hawks in Washington make decisions on foreign policy and the next day the government leans toward the Doves. Nobody in Washington could agree on anything. But one thing for sure--the Soldier was expendable." Guy then says, "Yeah, and Walt Rostow made the Rostow Thesis which said, that insurgency would work if there were limited gradual military actions put on the population with some political and economic pressures. U.S. Advisors in Washington saw the war could be won in villages of the South but not by '*force majeure*'. So this was one theory. But Walt Rostow (National Security Advisor) and General Maxwell Taylor (presidential advisor) both always wanted U.S. military control in Laos from the very beginning and they were leery of the SEATO Plan 5 (Southeastern Asia Treaty Organization/multinational army), of which Kennedy had agreed to. But for Vietnam, General Taylor believed [The Blood Road by John Prados], that 'the immediate military danger to Vietnam as well as to its neighbors derives from the continued infiltration from the North into the Laotian Panhandle and over the western border of Vietnam.' Everyone in Washington has his theory but the problem ... no one could come to a unanimous agreement or solution to the problem." But we still continue to fight this war with all of these different theories for winning with no general agreement. Taylor believed that SEATO should have put troops in Laos, Mekong Valley and the Thai Border to prevent a Communist take-over and infiltration. And Laos was a major infiltration point for enemy men and materials into South Vietnam and we should do something to stop it. Taylor also believed that we should launch air attacks against targets in Northern Laos and Northern Vietnam and launch offensive guerrilla operations." Mc says, "Taylor and Rostow knew from the beginning the constant infiltration and that the international military occupation to these areas was crucial. These guys believed, then, in an international military occupation as well. This was another theory. Everyone had his idea on how to win this war."

Buzz talks about another theory, [As said by Rostow and quoted in The Blood Road], "'The battle of South Vietnam hangs in the balance.' Yeah, I guess they knew it."

Peter then brings in another point of view, "But as for the Prime Minister of North Vietnam, Pham Van Dong ... he wanted a 'just solution' which meant a united Vietnam and a U.S. withdrawal, [as said in The Blood Road by Prados]; and, also Walt Rostow wanted the US occupation of lower Laos if it meant prevention of a more protracted war later. Maybe that would have been an answer to this. But Walt Rostow (National Security Advisor) believed if we did get our forces into Lower Laos, we could help slow the Chinese and the North Vietnamese conventional forces. Thus, this is another theory on how to win." Peter adds another idea now [from The Blood Road], "However, President Kennedy demanded realism and accuracy. President Kennedy did not believe in keeping our U.S. airfields in Lower Laos and that the poor military situation in lower Laos was a situation that U.S. troops would not be able to deal with it. This was the President's theory." Mc says, "But bottom line, we should have listened. Prime Minister Van Dong said at the very beginning, at a conference in Hanoi in 1964 with a U.S. spokesman/diplomat that should there be a military confrontation with the U.S. Van Dong said, 'We shall win.' And said by Mao Zedong Chinese Statesman, 'All counter revolutionary wars are unjust, all revolutionary wars are just.' We should have known." Dion adds a good point, "Well, Ho knew way back in the fall of 1965. He said, in an interview with an Australian journalist, Wilfred Burchett, in response to the question what would happen if America invaded Vietnam, 'The idea reminds me of a fox with one foot caught in a trap.' 'He starts leaping about trying to get out and—pouf—he gets a second one in another trap.'" Dion continues, "The reporter asks the same question of General Giap and he answered, 'Let them try! We would welcome them where we can get at them with modern weapons. But they will also find themselves caught up in a People's War. The whole people are united as they were under our ancestors, and invaders will find every village a hornet's nest.'" Peter then says, "But we knew their strategy. Rostow warned President Johnson in a memorandum in June 1964 that Mao's basic doctrine has always been, 'when the enemy advances, withdraw; when the enemy weakens, attack.'" Peter continues [said in The Blood Road], "Walt Rostow in this memorandum to President Johnson went on to say further, 'must be your judgment that war must be faced if necessary.' But again the President was afraid of China and Russia. President Johnson said, 'Our goals in Vietnam are limited (...). (...). I want to keep them that way.' Walt Rostow thought this was a bad idea—-yet another theory." Mc says next, "Bottom line to all of this it seems President Johnson did no want to commit our country militarily with a full scale war. Johnson was never sure what he wanted to do. He tried to pass-the-buck with this statement by saying, [as said in The Blood Road], 'During my first year in the White House no formal proposal for an air campaign against North Vietnam ever came to me as the agreed suggestion of my principle advisors.'" Mc continues, "I don't know, maybe President Johnson wanted to blame someone else for his not having decided himself on an effective war strategy or commitment to Vietnam." Buzz adds, "But President Johnson was committed to finding some solution. I will admit." John then says, "Yes, but our President will not make a commitment." Mc continues again, "If we are going fight we got to commit *all the way* or not at all. Now only as it is, we are committing our troops to slaughter." Peter then says, "Yeah, even Walt Rostow still insisted from the very beginning of this war, that we must fight it at a 100% commitment. Our Soldiers are committing their lives 100% for this war. How much more do you want the Soldier commit? Our military commanders have to do the job and our country has to back-up us all. If our Soldier is willing to commit at 100%, then so should our country." Guy changes the subject and adds one more thing that should have been done before sending troops into Vietnam, "Walt Rostow said that we should hold and recapture the panhandle of Laos from Thakhek to the southern frontier with Thailand and should be done with both Vietnamese and US forces. He believed that idea to be the solution to winning this war—-yet another theory!" Buzz then says jokingly, "Yeah, we should do the strategy that Civil War General Nathan Bedford suggested, 'Get there firstest with the moistest.'" [Everyone laughs.]. Guy says lastly about the many theories to winning the war, "Everybody in Washington had has own theory for victory in Vietnam and I believe Kennedy was definitely influenced by the above mentioned policies/theories of Taylor, Rostow and Lansdale." Peter continues again, "Yes and we need someone in Washington to make-up his mind to fight this war." Buzz agrees, "Yeah, these are the killing fields. I do believe that death has become a way of life in here Vietnam. Why do our young men want to get themselves into a mess like this? Our _bravest young men_ are committing their lives to something they are not too sure about doing. Here _our bravest young men_ are fighting Communism. But in Washington they are making détentes with the Chinese--the very people who are selling the armaments to Hanoi? What is this? We must ask questions. But most importantly, bottom line ... we must ask ourselves, why do we fight this war? When the Soldier goes to battle he should be sure that his country is willing to back him, has a sound strategy and has exhausted all means of diplomacy." Guy then asks, "But the President is not sure--can't these guys make up their minds? And then Guy brings in a new idea, "I think also if we are going to fight this war ... let us protect our borders--and all borders." Mc then says "Yeah, again, about the borders ... our men in Washington had another idea with Rostow-Taylor and Lansdale about protecting the borders in Vietnam. To do this was to occupy lower Laos and defend with military action against the DRV (Democratic Republic of Vietnam)—which yet was another theory." Buzz then interjects and changes the subject with, "Oh, yeah! Let's protect our borders no matter where--here--there--everywhere. And look at the North—South Korean border, 'the most heavily armed border in the world.' '(...) the Korean War ended nearly 60 years ago. Hundreds of thousands of troops stand ready on both sides of the border zone, which is littered with land mines and encased in razor wire.'" Guy changes the idea again to guerrilla warfare now, "But the real problem is here and now in fighting this war in Vietnam, we are not ready to fight a guerrilla war. Our Soldiers and the South Vietnamese Army are prepared and trained to fight a conventional war but not a protracted guerrilla war." Guy continues, "For one thing, I am not a military strategist but for starters, we need to use our superior air power. President Johnson's Rolling Thunder is not enough to stop the enemy. He is afraid of Russia and China." Buzz then says, "But not really because in April 1965 at the meeting of the Joint Chiefs of Staff 'the ground rules for the war in Vietnam were set. The conference also set basic outlines for Rolling Thunder: The DRV was to be coerced by an air campaign whose purpose was _not_ primarily to inflict damage.' How can you win a war like that? As I said before, Nixon had it right. If President Nixon had been in office at the onset of the war, we may have won. As Sir Robert Thompson, a British advisor to Vietnam once said, 'In my view on December 30, 1972 after 11 days of those B-52 attacks on Hanoi area, you (U.S.) had won the war, it was

all over. They had fired 1242 SAM's. They had none left and
what would have come over land from China would be a mere
trickle. They and their whole rear base at that point would
be at your mercy. They would have taken terms. And that is
why of course, you actually got a peace agreement (...).'"
Buzz says his bit and resolutely so, "Really, bottom line to
this is, "I believe that Kennedy and Johnson inherited
something they did not want from the Eisenhower
Administration and they got stuck in it—-no more no less.
This is why President Johnson was unsure and uncommitted
with this war. It was neither Kennedy nor Johnson who wanted
this war--and never wanted it from *Day One*. All that Johnson
wanted as President was to pass his civil rights bills into
laws that will give equality for our citizens at home. He
did not want Vietnam!" Buzz suggests again, "This is why it
is difficult with the transformation of power from one party
administration to the next. There is the *carry-over* of
policies from the former administration to the incumbent."
Buzz changes back to bombing, "But most important is to do
heavy bombing to our enemy. This is essential in our winning
this war. I don't like it but it wins wars. Peter says,
"Bombing, though, is indiscriminate." Buzz says again, "Yeah
but ... yeah that is our advantage however wrong it is. This
bombing strategy is to our advantage in any war and it has
to be done if we want to win this war." Guy says, "No, the
bombing is OK because according to the original Linebacker
directive [under President Nixon] the planners insisted, 'It
is essential that the strike forces exercise care in weapons
selection to minimize civilian casualties.' I mean if we are
going to fight, we have to fight with some of this strategy
but avoid civilian death." Guy adds more, "And with
Linebacker II President Nixon made it clear that all
targets—-military and economic would be sought in the
bombing. His bombing disrupted the enemy's rail traffic
systems and the enemy's electric power generating systems.
The bombing also reduced enemy oil supplies and some of
their industrial capability. And civilian casualties had
been greatly exaggerated but the cost in American lives was
high with 15 B-52s lost because of the surface to air
missiles of the North Vietnamese. And Guy continues,
"President Nixon forbade the bombing of dams because
civilian casualties would be high. In fact with the
President Nixon Administration, 'claim that strict rules of
engagement' were used with 'pinpoint bombing'. An Hanoi
journalist 'confirmed the raid's accuracy noting that
although many press reports left *the impression Hanoi had
suffered badly in the war ... in fact the city is hardly*

touched.'" Peter says, "Nixon told his Joint Chiefs of Staff that 'This is your chance to use military power to win this war.' President Nixon said, to his Chiefs of Staff Admiral Thomas Moore, 'I don't want anymore of this crap about the fact that we couldn't hit this target or that one, this is your chance to use your military power to win this war and if you don't, I'll hold you responsible.' Bottom line, Nixon tried a strategy that worked with our airpower. I mean, I can honestly say, we are in this mess and let's get out as best as we can. Military historian, S. L. A. Marshall, said Nixon's move with Linebacker 'was the boldest action taken by an American war president in this century.'" Buzz then says, "Amen to that." Guy says next, "Yeah, everybody criticized Nixon but his bombing campaigns were the only thing that threw the war into our favor. It was our superior air power that did it for us. Then Hanoi said, 'The Americans struck our strategic and military targets and they were successful. In four years of air war under Johnson, the Americans had not achieved the type of results that were achieved during only one month under Nixon.'" Buzz says again, "Amen to that." Mc says, "U.S. ground troops need all the help we can get from the air." Buzz changes the subject, "Each military branch has its own defense; and, General Clay has the job of keeping it all coordinated for us. The Army has our helicopters, the Marines have their Air Wings and our Navy has their Route Pack System for Vietnam. With aircraft defense, these aircraft provide air support for our ground troops."

Mc then begins his long list, "American AGM-28 B, McDonnell ADM-20 hound dogs Quail, SA-2 Surface to Air Missile, LTV A-7D Corsair II, General Dynamics F-111A, T-28 B Trojan, Douglas A-IE Skyraider, Cessna YA-37-A Dragonfly, Martin EB-57B Canberra, Northrop YF-5A Skoshi Tiger, Cessna 0-IG, Cessna O-2A Skymaster, North American Rockwell OV-10A Bronco, Kaman HH-43B Huskie, Douglas B-26K Sikorsky CH-3E, Helio 4-10-D Super Courier." He continues, "U.S. Air Force B-57 Canberra bombers, with five main types of helicopters in the U.S. Army: UH, UH-1 Hueys (utility), AH, AH-1 Cobra (attack),OH, OH-6 Cayuse (observation/Reconnaissance), CH, CH-47 Chinook (cargo) and HH (heavy) used in transport." Mc continues, "As far as the helicopter is concerned, the Army gave them names which gave them three different uses such as: Dusters (Medivac) medical evacuation, Slicks—troop transport, and UH-1B Gunships or heavily armed Hogs w/70 mm rocket, 7.62 mm multi-barrel Miniguns and grenade launchers--armed Hueys. Each mission usually had four helicopters. Some were heavily armed such as the Gunships, Hogs, Cobras and the slick (slick floors) used for troop transport, and a Medivac/Duster or a backup/rescue ship." Guy then says, "Also for air support, Bell 'Huey' helicopters, Bell Huey UH-IP Iroquois, Beech QU-22-B, Marine Cobra carriers and fighters, AH-1B was an attack helicopter and the ground Soldier's best friend. I can honestly say these flying marvels help us to fight this damn war."

Guy starts *his* list, "... such as the Teledyne Ryan AQMM-34L Firebee, Douglas RB-66-B Destroyer, Lockheed EC-121D Constellation, Republic F105s F-4 phantom cockpit, AH-1G helicopter, H-H 53 Jolly Green Giants/helicopters, Fairchild C-123 provider aircraft (photo aircraft), Reconnaissance ECU, AC-47 Gunships, AC-119 Stinger Gunships, American AC-130H Spectra Gunships (air *RECONs*, coordinated air support systems, Combat Skyspots (high-tech equipment), jet bombers with laser guided bombs, tactical air strikes), FAC's (Forward Air Controllers)prop-driven and prop-driven A-IH Skyraiders, A-4 Skyhawk light weight carrier attack planes, A-6 Intruders carrier bombers, Cessna A0-1 Bird Dogs, F-100 Super Saber fighter planes, A-1H or A-1E Skyraider Gunship, AI Sandys and Mistys F-105s and F-100s, and F-105 Thunderchief fighter planes. There were both fighters and bombers, A-IE fighter-bombers, RF-101Cs, McDonnell Douglas Air Force RF-4C/D Phantom II, coordinated navel and air gunfire for ground support from warships stationed off the coast (ANGLICO), F-4 Phantom II carrier and land based fighter planes, A-4, EB-66 radar surveillance plane, Air Cavalry Huey IB attack helicopters, AH-IG Cobras, AH-IE attack helicopters, jet bombers with laser-guided bombs, America C-130 aircraft air drops and photo planes, Navy AC Corsairs, A-7 II attack planes, South Vietnamese AI-E and A-IH Skyraiders, FAC spotters with visual Reconnaissance, Ground Radar Air Delivery Systems (GRADS), U-2 aerial photography, intelligence air is unmanned drones, U2 and SR-71 strategic Reconnaissance, forward air controlled-assisted strike system (Jolly Ho), ravens (Tiger Hound FAC's), Air Force C-7A De Havilland Caribou cargo planes, C-5 Galaxy cargo planes, B130 Hercules cargo planes, C-141 Starlifter cargo planes, F-8 Crusader carrier fighters and others such as Mark I PBR's." And Guy finishes it there.

Peter then says, "Our ground war with the Cavalry is great but is not used often in combat in Vietnam with our Big Bertha tanks with 81 mm mortar which were M48 tanks, M46s, M47s, M-60s, M113s with many types variants of these models. We also have 'Dusters' (M-42A1) with twin 40 mm guns and Gun Trucks, Quads and Minis of these are (Quad 50's). And you know our Naval Gunfire Support Units on naval destroyers and on cruisers were armed with 5"/38 or 5"/54 guns provided armed support for our land troops." Mc says, "Yeah but President Johnson won't have enough air support for us. He's afraid of what China and Russia might do." Now Buzz brings other ideas for thought with anger, "And please don't walk away from the ground well earned by blood--ever again." Peter then says, "Yeah, I wish there was something I could do but no one will listen to me—-no one. We all left behind ... someone back in the world. I just hope that we can make it back there to see them all again--Sherry, my child--my Mom--my Dad. I did not realize how much my life back home meant to me until it was taken away and also because other people have decided on a fate for me because of their fear of Communism. Suppose my life is taken away from me on a battlefield somewhere in this distant land; then there would be no worry of Communism for me anymore except that my family and my countrymen back home would cry for me and they would hope that I knew of the *freedom* I was fighting for in Vietnam." Buzz says, "Yes, death is a way of life here in Vietnam but let us try not to be a part of it and *sobeit*. *Nuf* said of this talk. It is what it is! Let's get some girls because my girl back home wrote me a *Dear John Letter* like the song by Ferlin Husky and Jean Shepard and Before the Next Teardrops Fall, (Ben Peters &Vivian Keith), [ABC-Dot.]. And Freddy Fender. '*If he brings you happiness, Then I wish you both the best...*'"

Peter now starts a long list of songs, "Yeah, you get one of those *Dear John Letters* after all the good is gone like the song by Conway Twitty, After All the Good is Gone and George Jones, You've Become My Everything, Loving You Beats All I've Ever Seen, Yes, I Know Why, He Stopped Loving Her Today, Garage Sale Today." Buzz then says his list: "Don Rich, Wayne Wilson, Leave Me Something to Remember You By; Jim Glaser, Woman, Woman; Wayne Kemp, I Turn My Mind on You, Did We Have to Come This Far, I Sure Need Her Now, [manycam.com], Alcohol of Fame; Vernon Oxford, Move To Town in the Fall, This Woman is Mine, Blanket of Stars, (CoolymicJukeboxCountryPete); Since I Met You Baby, I Almost Lost My Mind, Ivory Joe Hunter, [Atlantic Records] or Sony James; Bobby Darin, Mack the Knife; Floyd Cramer, You Win Again; Johnny Mathis; Ray Coniff; Yvon Collette—Nevada, Just When I Needed You; Rheal LeBlanc, Blue Christmas Tree, Il Faut Pardoner, La Vie N'est Pas Fini, (lyricFind, leoslyrics); Peter boasts more lists, "Father of Country Music, Hank Williams or Conway Twitty his Twitty Bird Band

(Decca)sing Hank Williams' Wedding Bells, You Win Again, Cold, Cold Heart, I Can't Help It, They'll Never Take Her Love From Me, Your Cheatin' Heart; Conway Twitty or George Jones, Window Up Above; George Jones, I've Got to Get Used to Being Lonely; Keith Whitley, I Never Go Around Mirrors "Live" [You Tube, RCA, BNA], (Lefty Frizzel and Sanger Shafer). Conway Twitty--his singing style-—his band—-his music--It's Only Make Believe," (Jack Nance, Twitty). Then Guy brags more about the best and explains more music, "There's Doo Wop, the Nashville Sound, Country, Honky Tonk, Countrypolitan and Bakersfield Sound--the sound of Buck Owens and Don Rich, I Can't Stop, I Don't Hear You—-the best. And also Twitty is the best." Mc agrees, "He's the best—-Harold Jenkins--Conway Twitty is great." Peter has another long list of greats: "Yeah, *my* song-—that is *our* song—-Sherry's and my songs--our favorite--Just Someone I Used to Know Dolly Parton &Porter Wagoner written Cowboy Jack Clement. More of Sherry's and my favorite songs: Tammy Wynette & Ray Lynam, 'Til a Tear Becomes a Rose; George Jones, Walk Through This World With Me [YoutubeDoowop, live]; Wayne Kemp, Harlan County, Yellow Pages, We're Waking a Sleeping Memory, One Time Too Many, (QWJS Classic Country); Temptations, with Bruce Willis Under the Boardwalk (Youtube); Desmond Dekker-Aces, Tips of My Fingers; Roy Orbison, Crying, Running Scared, [Monument]—TCB Band, Bruce Springsteen, Hardin, Burton, Scheff, Tutt, Pretty Woman, Only The Lonely [HBO, Virgin Records, Eaglevision,); Hank Williams or Bruce Springsteen, Wedding Bells; Jeanie Pruett, Satin Sheets; Del Reeves, The Only Girl I Can't Forget; Waylon Jennings, Amanda, Luckenback Texas, Looking for a Feeling, Turn Back the Years; Jennings &Jesse Colter, Storms Never Last; Bob Wills; Johnny Rodriguez, Pass Me By; Byrds— Roger McGuinn, Turn, Turn, Turn, (Pete Seeger), M. Lowe; Kris Kristofferson, Waylon Jennings, Willie Nelson, Johnny Cash, Highwaymen, Help Me Make It Through the Night; For the Good Times, (Kris Kristofferson); Five Satins, In the Still of the Night; Lloyd Price, Just Because, Personality; Dells, Oh What a Night; Seekers, I'll Never Find Another You; Sheb Wooley; Toby Keith, American Soldier; Sam the Sham and the Pharaohs, Wooly Bully; Dick Dale; Dickey Lee; Roy Drusky; Supersonics, Guitar Boogie; ? And The Mysterians, 96 Tears; Mike Kogel-Los Bravos, Black is Black; Zombies, She's Not There; Bobby Gentry, Ode to Billy Joe; Ronettes, Be My Baby; Joe Sun, Old Flame; Cascades, Rhythm of the Rain; Jody Reynolds, Endless Sleep; Johnny Cash, Ballad of the Teenage Queen; Johnny Rivers, Mountain of Love, Poor Side of Town; Temptations, My Girl; Moe Bandy, I Just Started Hatin'

Cheatin' Songs Today, Here I Am and Drunk Again, It Was Always So Easy to Find an Unhappy Woman, (YouTube); Charley Pride, Chrystal Chandelier, You Win Again, (YouTube), My Eyes Can Only See As Far As You; (Naomi Martin, Jimmy Payne, Jerry Bradley); Tom T. Hall, Old Side of Town (YouTube); Hank Snow; Leroy Van Dyke, Just Walk On By; Roy Clark, Yesterday When I Was Young, Malaguena; Don Cherry, Band of Gold (YouTube); Conway Twitty and the Twitty Bird Band, Fifteen Years Ago, Hello Darlin', Almost Persuaded; Buck Owens/Buckaroos, Rich, Dole Holly, Tom Brumley, Pierce, Cantu, Maness, Wiggins, Crying Time, Act Naturally, Foolin' Around, Wham Bam, My Heart Skips a Beat, Open Up Your Heart, Loves Gonna Live Here, Tiger by the Tail, Long Lonely Nights, Memphis Tennessee, (YouTube); Jerry Lee Lewis or Johnny Rodriguez, Jealous Heart; Joe Carson or Bobby Helms, Fraulein; Victor Wood, Crying Time; Righteous Brothers, You've Lost That Lovin' Feelin', Philip Spector--sound; Dixie Cups, Chapel of Love; Jim Ed Brown &Helen Cornelius, I Don't Wanna Have to Marry You; Jim Ed Brown-Browns, Three Bells, Old Lamplighter; Buck Owens, Dwight Yoakam, Streets of Bakersfield, Turn it On; Joe Barry, I'm A Fool to Care; (YouTube) George Jones, Melba Montgomery, We Must Have Been Out Of Our Mind; George Jones, A Bridal's Bouquet, Big Fool of the Year, I've Been Known to Cry, She Thinks I Still Care; George Jones & Johnny Paycheck, Love Bug; Johnny Paycheck, AKA Donald Lytle, Take This Job and Shove It, (David Allen Coe), Old Violin, She' All I Got, YouTube); Paycheck's promoters—-Billy Sherrill, Nick Hunter (CBS), Buddy Killern, Aubry Mayhew; groups--Cowsills, Flower Girl; Left Banke, Walk Away Renee [YouTube]; B. J. Thomas, Raindrops Keep Fallin' (promoter Larry Butler); Sandy Posey, Born a Woman; Ivory Jo Hunter, Since I Met You Baby; Shirelles, Will You Still Love Me Tomorrow, LiveDooWop; Penguins-Duncan, Madison, Saulsberry, Jones, Earth Angel (YouTube); Robert Mitchum, Little Ol' Wine Drinker Me; Tommy Overstreet, Easy Lovin; Hank Locklin, Please Help Me I'm Falling; Teddy Bears, To Know Him is to Love Him; MelloKings, Tonight Tonight, Herald Records, Dick Levister, Billy Myles; Danny &The Juniors, At The Hop, liveYouTube; Lorrie Morgan, Picture of Me Without You; Whitley/Morgan, 'Til A Tear Becomes A Rose; (Rice); Jack Greene, There Goes My Everything, (Dallas Frazier); Ned Miller, Mona Lisa; Darrell McCall, Dreams of a Dreamer; Curtis Potter, Undo the Wrong; Bob Marley &the Wailers, Go Tell it on the Mountain; A. Albert, D. Mahony, L. Silvestri, R. Vaccaro-Four Aces or Andy Williams Love is a Many Splendored Thing (Sammy Fain, Paul Francis Webster), Moon River; Mack Johnson Jr., Today I

Started Loving You Again; Neverly Brothers, (Giragosian, Gigstad), You Never Can Tell," [YouTube]. Peter then says, "I love Sherry and I wish we were together again--can't wait until I get back to the World to see Sherry again. I'm always waiting for her letters--like in this song. ... *Today I Got a Letter from Someone.* You know who." Buzz says, "Yes, I can guess who you got a letter from today. I hope I find *my Sherry* somewhere here in Vietnam. Oh shucks, I know you got *your Sherry* but maybe I'll find a girl from around here somewhere somehow. These dames are good looking dames." Mc says, "You told me you don't like Chinks but Buzz that is all you are going to find here. You're fighting them one minute and making love with them the next. Man that makes a lot of sense. Buzz, make up your mind, would yuh?" Buzz responds, "You're right, Mc, but my love is for my girl back home but she wants to leave me. Before nothing else mattered in this world except her—-nothing--her beautiful face-her beautiful eyes--her sweet smile ... and her perfect body. I gave her everything she wanted--a nice house--a nice car-- security. And in exchange, she gave me her beauty, her love, her sex, her intellect, and one day maybe--our child. She was somethin' else. As my mouth touched hers, my hands went to her perfect body and then I was out of control. I loved and lusted for her. She told me she loved me too. I would do anything for her-—to please her in anyway that I could--and because of that she loved and lusted for me. She loved me. ... I loved her but I guess it was the distance that drove us apart. We got lost Somewhere Between or Dreams of a Dreamer Gone Blind. We had nothing left between us anymore except for a lot of space and Vietnam. We drifted apart. That ain't going to hold nothing together, is it? When I lost interest, she lost interest. I lost interest in her looks—-her body--and when I lost interest, I didn't care anymore. And when I didn't care anymore, she didn't care. And so she took off. There was really nothing left for her anymore. Emotionally we could not connect. So now this relationship ain't possibly going to happen for us anymore-- not in this lifetime. Bottom line, if the sex is gone, I am gone and when I am gone she is gone and that is the story of love." Buzz continues, "So for me, when there is no sex or lust, it is hard for love and when two souls do not connect, there is no long-term sex. And all that is left is the fast, short-time stuff--the stuff that has no depth or has any meaning for me in my life. I guess we did not connect anymore in anyway—-anywhere--even at home. It's like the song by The Highwaymen--Waylon Jennings and Willie Nelson, Mamas Don't Let Your Babies Grow Up to be Cowboys (Ed Bruce,

Patsy Bruce), [United Artists]--these words ... *When you're at home you're always alone even with someone you love* or Making Believe, (Jimmy Work) or Conway Twitty, Georgia Keeps Pulling on My Ring (Timothy Marshall; David Wilkins); Conway Twitty/Loretta Lynn. Isn't that right? Maybe someday it will work out—-maybe—someday—-sometime—-somehow. I don't know. So it all has to go together in love and lust, Mc and Peter. Do you guys want another lesson on love? Peter is good at being in love--I mean with his Sherry and all. He is getting two letters from her everyday. That must mean somethin', right? But that is kinda what I want to find here in Vietnam—-love and lust." Buzz turns to look at Peter. Peter did not respond but in his *heart of hearts*, Peter knows and he agrees. Peter just says, "Let's turn around and go back home." The Soldiers all agree. They turn on the radio and hear their Rock n' Roll once again all the way back to base. Peter continues, "Sherry and I like these songs together, "Sincerely, Moonglows, (Fugua; Freed); RCA, Champion, Chess, Chance, Lana, Times Square, Crimson, YouTube(Doo Wop), Harvey Fugua, Bobby Lester, P. Barnes, P. Graves, B. Johnson-Moonglows; Floyd Cramer, Vaya Con Dias (Larry Russell, Inez James, Buddy Pepper); Ray Peterson, Corinna Corinna; Ralph Mooney, There Goes My Everything; Shep-Limelites, Daddy's Home; Doug Supernaw/Anderson, I Would Have Loved You All Night Long (G. Martin); Arlo West, End Not in Sight; Jim Lowe, Green Door; Somerville, Reed, Kowalski, Levitt—Diamonds, Little Darlin' Little Darlin' (Maurice Williams, David Carroll),(YouTube); Earl Lewis/Channels, That's My Desire (Helmy Kresa &Carroll Loveday), The Closer You Are (You Tube); Suggins Bros; John LeMaster; Walter Stettner; John Hughey; Lloyd Green; Don Williams, Some Broken Hearts, Amanda; Susan Raye, LA International Airport; Brad Paisley, Trace Adkins, Same Ol' Me; Conway Twitty, The Image of Me (Wayne Kemp); (LiveYouTube); Sammy Kershaw, You're Still On My Mind; Gene Watson, Dreams of a Dreamer Gone Blind, Love in a Hot Afternoon, (V. Matthews; K. Westbury), Got No Reason Now for Going Home (Johnny Russell), Nothing Sure Looked Good on You (Jim Rushing), Its Not Love (Ross Lynch), (YouTube); Bobby Bare; Dwight Yoakam, Today I Started Loving You Again, It Won't Hurt(You Tube); Johnny Paycheck/Lytle, A-11(Hilltop); Box Tops Cry Like a Baby; Yardbirds, For Your Love; Carl Perkins, Blue Sued Shoes; Ben E. King, Stand by Me; Fleetwoods; Mr. Blue; Orioles, Crying in the Chapel; Mike Johnson; Joe Jones; Jimmy Charles, A Million to One; Silhouettes, Get a Job (YouTube); David Allen Coe, Face to Face; John Hartford, Fraulein; Jimmy Clanton, Just a Dream;

18

Kenny Chesney I Always Get Lucky; Earnest Ashworth; Crests; Metallics; Billy Bland; Rivingtons, Papa Oom Mow Mow; Larry Verne; Ketty Lester; Angels; Ronnie Dove, One Kiss For Old Times Sake; Beatles, Something; Joe Barry, I'm A Fool to Care (Jin Records); Elegants, Little Star; Jack Scott, My True Love; Tony Orlando or Billy Fury, Halfway to Paradise; Maurice Williams-Zodiacs, Stay; Cadillacs, Gloria; Simon &Garfunkel, Sound of Silence (P. Simon), [Columbia]. Music is a necessity we can't live without." Before the Soldiers get back to their base in the heavy downpour, on a rough muddy road through the dense dark jungle, they come across a small wood shack ... and up above the door a white hand-painted sign reads with intent ... 'Boom-Boom Girls." Buzz says, "As I was telling you, Peter ... my girl back in the World, just broke off with me. Let me venture in-there to pay her a good visit?" Peter says, "I don't care what you do. You got the bucks to give her; it is your damn business. It's like life ... we give 'em the bucks and they give us the f*cks. She won't give you any love without some bucks. But just remember, you can't buy love. There are a lot of things that the dollar will buy you but it won't buy you love, Buzz." Mc pipes in a good one, "Yes but it sure can help." Peter then says, "I just want to get back to Sherry. That's all I care about." Buzz hops out of the jeep--says, "Pick me up later and then begins to think about the things he likes the best such as his favorite song. He begins to whistle the song as he starts towards the shack while another downpour begins. Now Buzz is eager to enter inside. Buzz enters the shack hoping to find love and he then gives her the money she needs to live her life.

She introduces herself with, "Hello, my name is Rita after the American actress--Rita Hayworth." Buzz hopes to find love that will last a lifetime but in his heart-of-hearts, he knows it won't. It may but probably won't. She smiles at him, grabs him by the hand, takes his money, and leads him to the bed. She undresses under the sheets. Buzz says, "You know I am here with you now--loving you but tomorrow I will be out there in that damn jungle trying to kill your brother--maybe your father. Does this make any sense to you?"

He is hoping to get some understanding and some sympathy from her. He talks to her because he tries for a connection of the minds--more than what bodily flesh can do.

Rita answers, "I don't know what you wan' Soldier. You give me money and I give you sex, right? You wan' talk, now?"

19

Buzz says, "No, I talk enough and I complain enough and I don't want to talk anymore, here, tonight."

He realizes that she is just another dumb head. He was looking for more than sex but he remembers as Peter said, *You can't buy love.*

He undresses and joins her under the sheets in pure carnal pleasure--first with a caress across her thighs--then to her back side--then to her breasts.

Buzz says to her, "You are not what I want but you are still all that I have."

Before he knew it, he released himself with her.

"Is that all you wan', Soldier?" says Rita.

Buzz says, "Yes, this is all I want from you, for now. Goodbye, Rita. I hope this money feeds your kids tonight." He walks out the door and does not look back. He jumps quickly into the waiting jeep with Peter and the guys. Buzz says, "Ah women, they are all the same everywhere in this world. Can't live with 'em' and can't live without 'em.'" [Everyone laughs.]. All he could think of was the song Can I Sleep in Your Arms Tonight, Mister, Jeanie Selly.

They drive into Da Nang and then back to Camp Eagle. The sky grows midnight dark in day and ... boom ... thunder sounds with a massive deluge of rain. Nature is echoing its anger with loud cracks of thunder and threatening streaks of lightening. As Buzz listens to the thunder, he says, "The wrath of God pails in comparison to that of man." Peter says sadly, "Yeah, Buzz you are right but God has a plan for us all. I just wish I knew how Vietnam fits into his grand-scheme-of-things with all of us. And his plan for me and why am I here now?" It is wet everywhere as the jeep slips and slides in the mud to a fast and slippery stop. The Soldiers become drenched with God's-gift-to-earth. They bolt-out quickly. Peter steps out and feels the ground slip-out from under him. The Soldier's feet sink ankle-deep into the mud slipping and sliding in the wet-soaked ground. They finally get into the safely of their make-shift home--their haven-of-peace. Inside their door, there is some relief from the wet but still it follows them inside on their clothes and with the mud on their boots. They deal with it quickly and can't wait until they get into their warm beds for some relief from the wet, the damp and the cold. The Soldiers shed their wet uniforms and drop to their beds. When the Soldiers finally lose their boots and their helmets, they feel immediate relief of their weight and of the responsibility they bore. Peter says to Guy, "This is it.

This is all we have--our place here and now." Buzz says, "You think so. I hope not. I want to get back to the world-- see it all, feel it all, do it *all* and *be* it *all*." Mc says, "Yeah, you wanna feel it all especially if it is wearing a skirt and female." Peter lays back and he unfolds his color photo of Sherry and sets it out on the table and looks at her very lovingly. He thinks sadly about Sherry and *how much he needs and wants her now--to be with her in flesh and in mind--and to hold her close to him in a very loving embrace.* Buzz says, "You are lucky, Peter, that you have such a deep connection with Sherry. I envy you. She loves you for who you are. You have a spiritual connection with her that can't be exchanged with anything else in this world. There are three things in life, and one is love. Yes, three things ∴ happiness, love and money—in that order--what degree of love, what type of love, how much money, what type of money?" Mc says irrelevantly, "Green I hope." Buzz says. "Yes if you are American. And happiness is most important— yes." Then Mc reaches over to turn on a black and silver transistor radio--turns the dial for some music with its large knob for volume and a red dial knob for the station- marker which moves across the radio to mark the station. It brings music to their room. "Listen to this. I love this stuff," says Mc. Peter says, "Man, that's my stuff-—the best! This song plays on their radio by the Dells with this most beautiful song, Oh What a Night, (Junior; Funches), [Vee-Jay Records]. *Oh, What A Night*: *Oh what a night, to love you dear, Oh what a night, to hold you near, Oh what a night, to squeeze you dear.* Peter thinks about Sherry.

Again there is the sound of the hard rain hitting their metal roof. Suddenly the air becomes cooler when the downpour ends ... but still the air is heavy and smells damp. Suddenly to the Soldier's delight, a soft gentle breeze blows-in through their open window. Theirs is a small dark room ... lit by a lamp that sits best at the corner of a wooden ammo box. Ahh, the Soldiers fall into their slumber and are temporarily gone from the disturbing reality of their lives. The drops of rain are ceaseless and spell- binding hitting hard and fast but cannot prevent the sleepers from their pulling-slumber.

Buzz does not fall asleep right-away but lies alone with his thoughts of the day. He hoped maybe he could have found a connection with Rita but it did not work-out that way; so, he falls into a mindless sleep with a void set deep in his heart.

Chapter 2

R&R, Going to Qui Nhon and Thoughts

Peter, Buzz, Guy and Mc head eastward toward the city
of Qui Nhon and Going Up Country, Canned Heat for some R&R
via an American military jeep. They should have been
convoyed-out but chose not to. Peter keeps thinking about
his beautiful Sherry and wishes he could see her beautiful
face just one more time but knows it will not be too much
longer and he will be back home with her again. He wants to
hold his new son so very much. But now he has a job to do--
to fight. He must defend his country as he has been asked to
do. He also thinks about the ideas that Vietnamese Colonel
had suggested--about how important it is to stop the enemy
from infiltrating into South Vietnam through the Trail and
into the A Shau Valley. This infiltration through the A Shau
Valley primarily has to stop if the U.S. wants to win this
war.

Now it is the heart of the monsoon season and in their
open jeep convertible, the Soldiers began to feel the sky
fall down upon them as hard drops of rain and they raise the
convertible top that keeps the comfort of *the dry* inside.
The air is heavy with moisture but relief is felt
immediately with *the dry* and refreshing breeze coming-in
through their open windows and blowing gently past their
faces ... sending-in more cool relief. And still ... wafts
of a cool gentle breeze comes-in with the omnipresent sweet
smell of tropical blooms but also with the ever present and
ever so unrelenting odor of decaying flesh.

Peter wonders. ... *What flesh is this? Whose flesh?
Whose flesh might this be--an unclaimed American dead, a
Vietnamese dead--the rotting carcass of an animal?*

He wonders. It is on his mind. This thought can't leave
his mind. He keeps thinking about it. This odor brings to
him a very strange feeling of dread. All he can do now is
wonder about it. Peter cannot believe that the smell of
death could stretch so far--mile after mile, after mile,
after mile--no end to the odor of death. *How could there be
so much of it,* he wonders again? He thinks about death,
smells it, and wonders about it some more but he knows that
death is as much a part of life as life is a part of itself.
He knows of the death in this war. This is a country of
death. Death is a way of life here. And he thinks of the
futility of it all. There seems to be no purpose to any of

this--especially for the young Soldiers losing their lives every day.

And now the dark bilious clouds are moving inward on light winds still waiting to shed their glory from the heavens above. They hover above impatiently as if they can't wait any longer to rain-down to tell their side of this sad story. As Peter turns the corner onto the long-stretch of his narrow dusty trail, he is smacked suddenly by a beautiful panoramic view of the South China Sea bordered by a palm-tree forest. The sea is spotted with white-caps in its dark-blue-mood day. And there lies a white-sand beach of tall spindly palms with fronds that move lightly in the gentle breeze. And Peter's dusty trail holds back tall stands of elephant grass that move wistfully to the command of a gentle breeze. And as Peter passes by ... it seems to be saying, "We will forever hold it a mystery our contents herein."

Peter asks Buzz, "Have you ever wondered about death since you worked with it so much in the hospitals back there in the World?"

Buzz responds to Peter's question about death, "Yes, I have wondered a lot about it. We will all have it coming to us one day but how or when is the mystery. But it will come and we hope ... late in our lives and painless, if anything. I have seen it happen to my loved ones, my friends, my enemies and strangers. It is the same for all--all over. It is death. It takes our loved ones away. We watch-on helplessly and ever so hopelessly as the dying inexorably slip-away from our grasp and into the depths of another realm. We can't hold on even though we want to ... so desperately. It is a certain outcome--forever and final--the end of life--gone from us forever--for an eternity--from all that we know ... forever ... and forever leaving us with a void ... way too great ... death."

Mc says, "Boy that is some pretty heavy stuff, Buzz."

"Yeah it sure is," says Guy. "Let's go," says Peter.

They want to hold on tightly and ever so tightly to their *present* so they can have a chance to grab for their *future* but they know it is not theirs to decide.

And the down-pour begins.

23

Chapter 3
Qui Nhon

The Soldiers arrive in this seaside town of Qui Nhon listening to a song by the great Hank Williams. This town is a bright dusty little Vietnamese shanty town but with a huge American military base. This city is carried out into the sea on a long peninsula which provides a good port for U.S. Navy ships.

This sun-drenched town sits at the edge of the sea with a tall massive mountain towering close behind. The sun is bright and intense through the haze. Brightly washed clothes hang on clothes lines outside small shacks constructed from pieces of everything—-wood, corrugated steel, tin plates, chicken wire, pieces of glass and *throw-aways* from something else that had another seemingly more important use.

Parked in front of a shanty is an old American car from a time before--from a bygone era--another place far away—-a time long ago--but now it is a most valued and highly cherished possession for someone. And further on down the road, moving along--a moped, an Army Jeep, a bicycle, a Citroen car and a lambretta--on a street of big steel buildings built by the Americans—-yes by the Americans.

Signs posted about are in English, some are in French and some are in Vietnamese. And the guys are looking for some much needed drink, food and rest. And as they step inside the cool shade of the tavern; all they could think about now was shedding their jeep and the *fatigue* of the long trip they left behind.

"I am so pissed at this shit. This is not a place to take R&R. It is hot, dirty and dusty and there is nothing here. There is nothing in this hole for me," says Mc.

Buzz then says, "What did you expect—the Rex Hotel? Yeah, this is the song I think of by Freddy Fender, <u>Wasted Days &Wasted Nights</u>," (Duncan, Meaux, Fender), [ABC-DOT Records].

Wasted Days and Wasted Nights.

Wasted days and wasted nights,

I have left for you behind.

Inside the cool dark tavern, they hear Vietnamese spoken all about. This chatter makes no sense to them but they hope for some words in English to come their way. As they walk to the bar, Peter asks, "Do you have a coke to drink? We are thirsty and we are famished."

A very friendly middle-age Vietnamese woman, who is a waitress, serves each of them a bottle of coke at the bar. It is iced-cold and Peter loves that. He picks it up before she could put it down and it went to his mouth before he could say *thanks*. She saw their thirst and did not answer Peter's questions or start small-talk until all they downed most of their cold drinks.

The Vietnamese woman says, "We don't have a menu but we can give you "Today's Special," *Plat de Jour*, which is *Pho* [*phir*] and *Cha Gio*."

"Oh I love that stuff," says Guy, [trying to be a connoisseur in Vietnam].

Buzz then says, "That's queer. How do you know about that stuff? You don't know what that shit is, do you? You are just playin' the connoisseur-role for this Vietnamese woman, here. And anyway, aren't you sick of rice by now? You have been here all this time, and you are not sick of rice yet-- good for you boy? Just give me my cooked spinach with a little unsalted butter and some lemon juice—that's what food is really all about ... and what about sardines?" And even my beer does not have to be cold—-really! [Buzz pats him on the back.]

"I love this stuff," says Guy.

Buzz then says rather rudely to Guy, "Just hope it ain't made with dog meat."

"Shut up, Buzz. I am sick of you," says Guy.

Mc then says angrily, "Where do we get some brew around here? I am not wasting any more of my time trying to get what I want--some beer and a good lay. You know what I mean. I am sick of 'Nam." [Everyone laughs.]

Guy says, "Don't act like a jerk. They know what you are saying and what you want, but don't make a fool-out-of-yourself in here. Mc, play the dignified role, for once, and you will be treated better."

Then says Mc looking around, "Yeah, what do these assholes want from me--my life? I know what I want now. I have been out there riding in that hot, dusty jeep for four hours just to get to a hole like this for R&R—-no way, man? Hey, what do they want from me and what can I get around here in this dirt shit-hole? I am willing to throw my life out into the bowels of hell where it may end and I still can't get shit around here? What is this? [Everyone laughs hysterically. The laughter continues.]. What do they have in here--in this hole for me? There is nothing for me, here. Where are the women? Yeah, sex--that is what life is all about. Where's the sex? And I can't find it or get any of it around here? I am willing to give my life away and ..."

Mc could not finish his words before a beautiful woman walks over and places her lips on his. "Shut up, American. I will give you what you want—-whatever you want.

Mc then says to her, "'*I thought I've never seen a girl like you in here before. My thoughts were running wild and free as I watched you tonight,'"* [Conway Twitty, I've Already Loved You in My Mind, (Twitty), [MCA], [Electra, MGM Decca, Sun].

Music is playing on the jukebox but Mc does not get up to dance this time. He loves her presence.

Mc stays with her and listens to the music.

The other Soldiers finish their meals and crash-out but Mc is with her for the entire night.

She is what he wants--a beautiful female at his side. He thinks to himself, *Oh how I need her in my life. How I want her in my life. I hope it works for us tonight. She is most beautiful. I need her desperately-—her love, her beauty and her support.* "What's your name?" "CaLu ... let's go somewhere together where we can be all alone," she says. Mc says, "I'd love that truly. You are most beautiful." The two go up to their room at the Inn. They get undressed and enter their bed together underneath the sheets. She takes his hand, holds it and squeezes it ... while she places her lips gently on his. Then he pulls her body close to his in a most passionate intense love-embrace. He says to her ... "You are what I want in my life and you are what I need most desperately. You have a beautiful body and I love it." She loves his words and she brushes her lips over his body to show her love, her sensuality, her respect, her compassion and her understanding for a lonely Soldier and for a man she loves.

For him the smell of her perfume drives him crazy as he pulls her body close to his in a rough but gentle embrace. "You smell so good." Then he makes their souls connect. They love in a most intense and warm embrace that seems to stop the world for a moment. These two are closer than any two humans could be in any way. They now find the love and the comfort they both need and want in each other's arms. He caresses her, holds her tightly and so closely with his strong arms--with all his love in this world. Then he says to her, "You know Calu, you are everything I ever dreamed about in my life and to have you with me always. I love you so much. You feel so good." He loves her body ... and he loves to hear her most beautiful words, begging him for more. He is overjoyed with the love she has for him. Their love for each other brings so much happiness-and-joy to their hearts. She feels the love that she needs and wants from him. She adores him. He too wants her beauty that brings him so much happiness with her beautiful love. This is what he deserves and this is what he finally gets.

Mc says to her most passionately, "Oh ... Calu ... what a wonderful thing ... to be in love! I have waited for you for so long ... for this. 'You made love so good, for so long.'"

[Conway Twitty's song, Don't Take it Away.]

He knows she is permanent and forever. It has to be. He tells her, "I will be back for you!" "I know you will," she says.

Chapter 4

Story of Interrogation

The next morning, the guys all go downstairs to the bar for some needed breakfast chow except for Mc.

"Yeah, we were tired and we got our needed sleep. But we have to move on now," says Guy.

Buzz asks, "Where is Mc?"

Guy answers, "Oh, he is still in *Seventh Heaven* with that woman he met in here last night."

Buzz then says, "Well let's wait or do we go up there and get him, but I hate to be the one to spoil his fun? He can't just get up and leave her now. He has got to say good-bye to her. Give him some time." Peter says, "OK. We will do that. I know how he feels because I can still see Sherry in my mind's eye as if it were yesterday. I just want to hold her in my arms one more time. I miss her and can't wait to be with her and our new baby again."

Then Peter jumps back to the real world of Vietnam and his world in Qui Nhon as he steps outside into a bright hot day. Peter is squinting from the brightness of the mid-afternoon sun. The bright light momentarily blinds him. Peter turns back around and glances back to the inside of the soft blue-lit barroom and sees his friends engrossed in rapid conversation. And Peter then goes back inside again to join in on the conversation--back into the darkness and security of this cool-lit sanctuary--inside the bar room. There is a small fan placed at the end of the bar which keeps the comfort level tolerable. The only light is from a small lantern and a blue neon light sign hanging on the wall above the bar. These Soldiers are on their R&R for fun but hate the unknown of this new town. This is a new town and this is not rest and relaxation for these Soldiers. His mind drifts off to a wonderful thought of a faraway place of being alone with Sherry and holding her close in the intense moment of making love with her on a beach somewhere. But now Peter is here in this place-—this strange town-—but hopes to be back home one day soon. This place is strange and different from anything he has ever known before from back home in Haverstraw. Peter even feels more at home back at his military base at Camp Eagle--even though he hates the place so much. But here in Qui Nhon, he does feel foreign in a foreign land. But now it is truly such a relief to still be with his friends on R&R. He knows that whatever they are doing or wherever they are going now, they are all doing it together as a team. As he walks back into the bar he caught a hold of the conversation Buzz, Guy and Mc are having with an attractive middle-aged Vietnamese woman but her face shows that her life has been hard. She is well dressed and presents an air of certain dignity but now is extremely distraught over something that she is explaining to Buzz, Mc and Guy. Peter steps over to them and asks, "What is wrong?"

Mc introduces the woman and Peter, "Oh this is our buddy Sp4c. Peter McConnell--another *mucker*," The Vietnamese woman continues her story, "My grandmother had been a patriot her entire life. She loved her country for all of her 70 years of life. She lived with her son—-my dad--in Saigon who taught classes at the University in Saigon. She loved her country and talked one day of seeing her country as a united Vietnam once again. She was tired of seeing so many of our people suffering and living in the misery of war with lost families. I told her that *one day you will get into trouble if you keep talking this way*. Last week a couple of men broke-down the door to her home and stole her in the secrete-of-darkness. They were driving a black unmarked car. One witness—-*a passer by*--said it may have been a CIA car? Maybe they were part of the Phoenix Program which is supposed to crush the Viet Cong infrastructure which is controlled through CORDS and is part of the U.S. pacification program run by the CIA? 'Operation Phoenix was a military intelligence and internal security coordination program designed by the U.S. Intelligence Agency during the Vietnam War. The program was designed to identify and neutralize—capture; induce to surrender; kill or otherwise disrupt—the civilian infrastructure supporting the Vietnam insurgency or Viet Cong.' Or maybe it is a result of your new military policy under General Creighton Abrams, the new Commander of MACV or from a policy of 'search and destroy' or the policy of 'strategic hamlets' which means your government is trying to establish population security for Vietnam. But she was just a person. My grandmother was taken—just taken because she loved her country. She was being a person in love with her country. We combed all of Saigon for her. We searched everywhere for her. She was a Vietnamese—-not a North Vietnamese nor a South Vietnamese but a Vietnamese living her life in her country that she loved so much. The Americans believed she might have known something but really she was a victim and became an enemy in her own country. We never saw her again." The Vietnamese woman continues her sad story, "But my uncle who also works at the university said he heard that the Americans and my

government do kidnap people and hold them captive for
interrogation if they think they are spies for the Viet Cong
or the North Vietnamese. She was not and wanted to live her
life in peace in her country like anyone else anywhere else
in this world. Later someone here in Saigon told my uncle
that an old woman was being held captive in a house
somewhere in Saigon. She fit my grandmother's description.
The witness said she heard a lot of horrible screams coming
from the house. Another witness said they kept her from
water long enough to try to break her with the heat--an old
woman? On the third day she was weak and incoherent. They
could not get information from her. She could not tell them
anything because she knew nothing. There was an electric
light in her room and the interrogators used it on her. She
screamed horrifically. As her condition weakened, her
screams became weaker and weaker. And after four days, she
succumbed. But ... why ... why ...?" Buzz says, "I'll try to
tell you. You know with the Phoenix Program, 40,000 people
in Vietnam were routed-out and killed. That does not sound
too hospitable now does it all for the name of freedom? I
don't know. Maybe there is something wrong with me, but it
does not sound good, Peter, Mc, Guy?" Mc answers, "I can't
believe--we--the U.S.A. does this in this day-and-age in a
country like this to save the world?" Buzz says, "Hell,
yeah. It's not right. I guess Henry Kissinger is right when
he said, 'What political leaders decide, intelligence
services tend to seek to justify.' I tell you one thing for
sure. This place is a complete *waste* for us all--like the
song by Freddy Fender, Wasted Days and Wasted Nights. Here
in Vietnam there is a lot of misery and suffering. Why can't
we just get out of here and let this place for these people
to decide what they want to do with their lives for
themselves? We cannot police this entire world over. It
cannot be done as much as we wish that it could be done.
It's just impossible and impractical to monitor and control
this entire world over. We can't do it! We try and we think
we are doing right but we can't even stop the misery that is
happening even in our own country so why go look for
somebody else's misery to stop? I don't know!" Peter cannot
believe this story. He actually feels numb from it and
thinks to himself about all that Sherry has said to him so
many times before about this war and what would she think of
this horrific story about this old woman?" Guy quite
appropriately says, "Yeah, but in other places, it is far
worse but that does not mean interrogation with torture is
right. Still two wrongs don't make a right. Maybe a spy, but
that is no excuse for torture." [Talk about torture ... one

30

of the worst acts of genocide in this century happened in
the Pol Pot and Kang Ket Lew regimes. They with others--had
exterminated 20% of Cambodia's population with torture and
systematic extermination of millions.]. [From another war
before ... Himmler's reasoning for extermination and torture
was as he said with this quote in Poznan in 1943: "Nature is
cruel therefore we are also entitled to be cruel," (YouTube,
September 2010).]. "Totally, I agree, says Peter. You are
right but the issue with all of this ... still remains....
We just don't belong here in Southeast Asia." Buzz says,
"Yeah, Peter, sending Americans out here in this far off
jungle to die truly boggles my mind." They all hop back into
the familiarity of their jeep. Peter wants to forget this
sad story here and he could do this—-totally--by tuning on
to the U.S.-base-radio station. This song played: The Closer
You Are, [Whirling Disk, Soul Jam], Lewis; Brown; Aziz;
Rivera III; Coleman.]. As Peter turns on the radio he says,
"Earl Lewis and the Channels are great. His lead falsetto is
harmonized with his back-up vocals and complemented
beautifully with the bass voice of Jack Brown. No one can
hold a candle to them! The Closer You Are by Earl Lewis and
the Channels, *When I first saw you, I did adore you...*"
Peter decides to drive along the coast to finish their R&R
south towards Tam Ky. Peter says, "You know, Guy, I would
never have thought in my wildest dreams that such a place as
this ever existed on this planet earth—-or anywhere--and
that such a thing could ever happen that so involved our own
country. You know all I really ever knew my whole life was
Spring Valley, Haverstraw, Suffern, Stony Point, Nyack, West
Nyack, Nanuet, Pearl River, Congers, Ramapo and Nyack--you
know Rockland County, New York. And of course the best--New
York City. And New Jersey with Paramus and Woodcliff Lake
are great. I was happy--so happy then—-there--with Sherry--
my folks--my family. I remember when I took Sherry out to
Requa Lake on our first date--she was so beautiful--her
beautiful face and her beautiful body. Over there, we danced
while they played Rock 'n Roll songs in their dance
entertainment room at the lake. We danced. Boy did we dance.
It was a large covered indoor-outdoor room with a wooden
dance floor open on all sides. The music and the acoustics
were perfect." Peter continues, "I remember dancing to Alley
Oop by The Hollywood Argyles, Gary Paxton," [Capitol
Records], (Dallas Frazier), (Dahlheimer; Gracy; Kowalczyk;
Taylor). *(Alley Oop, oop, oop-oop), (Alley Oop, oop, oop-
oop), There's a man in the funny papers we all know...*

Peter continues, "As she watched me dance I was really
acting like a big shot for Sherry--showing off. I was

showing-off my dance moves for her. I was pure carnal with
my high stepping dance moves ... ride 'em daddy, ride 'em,
hippsville." [They laugh.]. "And we danced the slow dance
with Shep and the Limelights. Man, I love her so much. She
looked so beautiful. I was high stepping with the 'Slop'.
That is what we called it—-the 'Slop.' I mean that is what
it was--real sloppy. Sherry thought I was great." [They
laugh, but not really.]. Guy laughs and says, "It was a
whole world-away and I remember Brenda Lee and Bobby Helms
with Jingle Bell Rock? And we also danced the 'Watusi' to
Runaway by Del Shannon (Shannon; Crook), [Big Top]. We
danced the 'Cha, Cha' to Little Star by the Elegants and the
'Stroll' song, (Brook Benton) to the dance`The Stroll by The
Diamonds." [Popular Line Dance of 1950's. Two lines of
dancers, men on one side, women on the other, face each
other, moving in place to the music. Each paired couple then
steps out and does a more elaborate footwork dance between
the rows of dancers. Come, let's stroll, Stroll across the
floor.]. Peter continues, "Yeah, "The slop we could dance
any old way—-no special dance moves. We just did the slop.
My specialty was not any other dances but the 'Slop' and the
'Mash Potatoes.' Guy adds these dances to the conversation,
"I remember the dances called the 'Mash Potatoes,' 'the
Stroll,'(Dick Clark), 'the Locomotion,' the 'Swim,' the
'Hully Gully,' the 'Fish,' the 'Bop,' the 'Franklin,' the
'Watusi,' the 'Twist,' the 'Jitterbug Stroll,' the 'Jerk,'
the 'Locomotion,' the 'Ding-A-Ling,' the 'Shake,' the
'Shimmy,' the 'Pony, and the 'Boog-A-Loo' but the 'Slop' is
my favorite. And To Sir With Love, LuLu, {D. Black; M.
London); Floyd Cramer, Last Date, Cold, Cold Heart, Release
Me; Johnny Horton, Battle New Orleans (Jimmy Driftwood),
Mansion You Stole; Don Rich, Out of My Mind; Leonard Cohen,
Tennessee Waltz (Pee Wee King, Redd Stewart, J.Marshal);
Little Jimmy Dickens, Bird of Paradise; Johnny &Joe (Johnny
Richardson &Joe Rivers), Over the Mountain Across the Sea,
(Rex Garvin), (Milt Grant Show),(Youtube); Jimmy Beaumont-
Skyliners, Since I Don't Have You; Brady Clark, Frauline;
Toys, Lovers Concerto; Johnny Maestro; Skeeter Davis, Last
Date, Crying Time, The End of the World;; Vince Gill,
Loretta Lynn, Table for Two; Buck Owens &Don Rich, Don't Let
Her Know; Elvis Presley, From a Jack to a King, Sweet
Caroline, One Night (D. Bartholomew, P. King, A. Steinman),
[RCA]; Wilma L. Cooper, Mac Wiseman, Tramp on the Street
(Cole); Chuck Willis; Brook Benton, It's Just a Matter of
Time; J&B Purify; Rheba McIntire; Freddie Scott, Hey Girl;
T. Graham Brown, Tell It Like It Used To Be; Gary Puckett,
(Ralph Emery Nashville Now), Woman Woman; Roy Head, Shindig,

YouTube: (Jimmy Fortune, Your Sweet Love; Balfa Brothers, Dewey Balfa, Marc Savoy; Johnny Western, Paladin; Buddy Randell—Knickerbockers, Lies; Marv Johnson, You Got What It Takes; Suspicion, Terry Stafford; Ally Harron &Marian Curry; Chantels-Arlene Smith, S. Goring, R. Minus, L. Harris, J.L. Jackson, A. Smith, Maybe; Dubs, Blandon, Still, Carlisle, Gardner, Grate, Could This Be Magic; Dan Helms; James Segrest; Jonathan Edwards; Chris Hillman; Conway Twitty or Jeff Newman, Last Date (Cramer, Twitty), Danny Boy; Blue Grass Boys; Blossoms; Henry Sahilatua, Tantowi Yahya &Friends, Blue Eyes Crying, (YouTube); Henson Cargill, Skip a Rope (Jack Moran, Glenn Tubb); Searchers, Needles and Pins; Bell Notes, I've Had It; Pozo Seco Singers, Don Williams, Time (Michael Merchant); Joe South, Games People Play; Teddy Redell; Leland Martin; Johnny Ace, Pledging My Love; Tommy Collins/Sipes, High on a Hilltop; Buckinghams, Kind of a Drag; EDU Schalk; Oscar Rexhauser; Ray Charles, You Don't Know Me, I Cant Sop Loving You; Johnny PayCheck, I Wish My Mind Would Stay Out of This, (Country Social-Mathis Bros, Danny Williams), (Charlie Justice, Sonny Curtis), Just Between You and Me (McKeehan; Leimmerman), Sleep With Her Memory Every Night, Feel Like Cryin'; Gene Hughes-Casinos, Gene Hughes, Ron Hughes, Pete Bolton, Joe Patterson, Tom Mathews, Bob Armstrong, Mickey Denton, Bob Smith, Dave TrathanBill Hawkins, Ray White Then You Can Tell Me Goodbye (You Tube) "Live", DooWopPBSShow (Fraternity Records), (John D. Loudermilk); Bill Ferguson—Country River Band; Fenders, Mule Skinner Blues; Johnny &Hurricanes, Red River Rock," (Johnny Paris, Paul Tesluk, Dave Yorko, Butch Mattice, Bill Savich). Peter says, "Yeah, the 'Slop' and the 'Mash Potatoes' are the best." Peter thinking quite nostalgically says sadly, "Yeah, Guy, it sure was good memories and I want to go back to it all. I wish we could turn back the hands of time. You know, I do wish that to happen more than anything else in this world. If only we could turn back the hands of time but we can't and sobeit." "Not to change the subject or anything but all of us guys are going to get Article 15 thrown at our faces for going out without a military escort and if we don't get out of here soon," says Mc.

"I'm boogying out of here! That's the word," says Buzz.

"What word?" says Peter.

"That's it. If we want Quang Ngai or Phu Cat, we have to get there now, yeah. Let's go," says Mc.

"Let's go. Let's get there convoy style," says Mc.

Buzz repeats again, "That is the word."

Chapter 5

Going to Phu Cat and Talking about

President Lincoln

They begin their drive to fire base Phu Cat. And all Mc could talk about was his new love, how much he loves her and that he must find her again somewhere in Vietnam before he does anything else in this world. With this thought, this came to his mind, the Ronettes, <u>Be My Baby</u> (P. Spector, J. Barry, E. Greenwich), [Philles Records].

The night we met

I know I needed you so

and if I had the chance, I'd never let you go...

But now they are on their way into a military base.

"Didn't you make arrangements to get into Phu Cat, Mc?" asks Buzz.

"No I did not," says Mc.

He continues, "Well we need armed military escort and it looks like we are on our own in our military jeep again out here in this damn jungle."

Peter comes to this American town called Phu Cat. This is a real American town. This is a town built of the Americans, by the Americans and for the Americans. One could hear the constant screams of jets flying overhead with their take-offs and landings. It looks American and sounds American. It is American. This fire base was built by the Americans and it commands everything in its sight and far beyond. This American town with large modern buildings on wide paved streets is an anomaly set in the stone-age Vietnam of thatched huts on narrow dirt roads.

This airbase town seems to be saying, *Hey, I am American and I am the boss; you just shut your mouth and do what I tell you to do. You listen and you obey my orders. I'm built here--and here I will stay, whether you want me to stay or whether you want me to go. I do what I want.*

The Soldiers eat some grub at the mess hall--something good—-something different? No, it isn't different. It is sliced roast beef again. The Soldiers are very hungry and Peter says, "Man, the only thing I want to do around here is eat." [They laugh.]. Buzz says, "Something has to go down now, Buddies. We have been having too good of a time here in 'Nam. I mean Mc finding his girl...

and ..." Mc cuts-off Buzz, "But I will find her again in all
of this madness. I will scope every woman who passes by me,
until I find her again." Buzz smart-mouths with, "Ah, you
always look at every dame who passes by you, anyway, so what
difference does it make?" And Mc says to Buzz, "I hate this
hole more than you do now, buddy. You have turned me into a
believer-of-hate, Buzz. It is the same old hole. Each town
looks exactly the same." Buzz then says, "Oh quit your shit.
After all you should not be the one complaining. You found
your girl in this place and you laid her here."

Mc then plants his fist onto Buzz's nose. Buzz then
says, "Hey don't break it. I need this thing for the 'right
look' under my helmet. See?" [He is pointing to his nose and
holding up his helmet.]. Buzz continues, "I mean, how would
this helmet *look* without a nose under it? Come on Mc, wake
up, boy,—think! How would this helmet *look*? [Everyone
laughs.]. Oh, and, by the way, just in case you didn't know,
besides *the look*, I also need this nose for breathing? I
can't do much fighting out there if I cannot breathe through
my nose ... right? I know no one else cares about my nose
except for me but believe it or not, Uncle Sam also cares
very much for my nose as long as he can use it to shoot a
gun and fight somewhere. You see basically, without my nose,
I can't breathe and when I can't breathe, I can't fight this
damn war for him. Or maybe *he* will care about my nose just
long enough until he puts me into a body bag--probably? What
do you think? I am right on that one?!" Mc says, "Yeah, man
I think you are hella right on that one--maybe." Buzz
continues on his angry tangent, "If I am not young, healthy
and of course breathing what good am I going to be out there
in the jungle--on the battlefield--somewhere in Vietnam,
what? So, Mc, don't try to break my nose, into the hospital
and off the battlefield, OK? You just might get me out of
this hole with that one. Then if I am out of this war-game,
then what'll I do? Well, I'll tell you what, Mc, you will be
thrown into the brig and you'll be out, too. [Everyone
laughs.]. Then there will be two less viable bodies to fight
this damn war--to defend our homeland. Is that what you
want? Thanks but no thanks. I don't want a broken nose, OK,
Mc?" Buzz is very bitter and very angry with everything and
everyone around him. He then turns to Peter and asks him,
"Are you still crying for your old lady?" [Everyone laughs,
and laughs, ha, ha, ha.]. Mc then butts in with, "Oh let him
alone. Don't bug Peter, Buzz. He loves her."

The Soldiers walk-out of the cool sanctuary of the mess hall
in Phu Cat--out into the steaming hot tropical air. They get

into their jeep and head for another small town nearby. The Soldiers arrive in town, stay the night at the small cozy Three Teardrops Tavern (Jim Reeves song, Blue Side of Lonesome). They get up the next day and step outside. It is midday in their monsoon water-filled world with dark clouds pressing hard into the sky which suddenly bursts-out with cool massive downpours. As the Soldiers take a dash to their jeep, Buzz says, "Boy this rain cools it down fast. Come on Peter--run. Let's get out of this wet mess." They get into the comfort of their dry covered jeep. Peter then says, "Yeah it rains like this in the summers back East in Spring Valley New York. I never really try to get caught in the rain unless I am with Sherry and she is wearing a white blouse. [Everyone laughs.]. One time Sherry and I did get caught in the rain and she was wearing a white blouse. And as her blouse got wetter, it became more transparent. She is all about pizzazz. She looked real sexy after her hair got straight from the rain. Man, I love Sherry. Reminds me of the song by Toussaint McCall, Nothing Takes the Place of You (Patrick Robinson, Toiussaint McCall), [Ronn Record]. And then we headed right to my house where she changed her clothes." Buzz rudely wisecracks-in with, "Her hair was not the only thing that got straight, was it ... or wet?" [Everyone laughs.]. Mc now adds his smart-ass bit with, "Did you change her clothes for her?" [Everyone laughs.]. Buzz asks smartly, "Did she dry her hair?" Peter says, "Oh shut up you idiot. I don't remember if she did but I do remember a lot of other stuff and you'll never guess what we did, idiot. Shall I tell you or shall I leave it up to your great imagination because I know you can dream real well--I mean *dream* real well." [Everyone laughs.]. Buzz adds, "Hey that's my man, Peter. Put that idiot, Mc, in his place."

Peter continues with his list of songs, "My feelings for Sherry are like the song, Ed Townsend, For Your Love (Townsend); Faron Young, He Stopped Loving Her Today, Sweet Dreams (Don Gibson), Hello Walls, Wine Me Up Again; Tommy McClain, Sweet Dreams, [ACE]; Barbara Lynn, You'll Lose a Good Thing (Barbara Lynn Ozen); Robin Luke, Susie; Dion DiMucci, Abraham, Martin &John (David Holler); Bellamy Brothers, Let Your Love Flow (Larry Williams); Kathy Young-Innocents; Merle Haggard, Oakie From Muskogee; Heather Myles, Brantley Kearns, No One Will Ever Know; Willie Nelson, Blue Eyes Cryin'in the Rain, (Fred Rose); Ralph Stanley, All I Ever Loved Was You; Beau Brummels; John Anderson, Would You Catch a Falling Star; Joe Dowell, Wooden Heart; Bobby Mackey; Archies; Little Dippers, Forever; Corsairs, Smokey Places (Riesenfeld; Zamechik; Spector); Dan

Paisley; Beachley; M. Paisley; Lundy; Eldreth; Mobley;
Delaney; Meek-Southern Grass, Room Over Mine (Eddie Noack);
Mick Flavin, Table in the Corner (Twitty), [Prism] or Conway
Twitty; Il Divo; Ricky Nelson, Burton, Fools Rush In; Marty
Robbins, Long, Long Ago (Thomas H. Bayley), El Paso and Red
River Valley; Foster &Allen; Roger Whittaker; Chris Isaak
&Stevie Nicks, Red River Valley; Jimmy Jones, Handyman;
Texas Tornados, Doug Sahm, Augie Meyers, Freddy Fender,
Flaco Jimenez, Kevin West, Jorge Diaz, Anybody Going to San
Antone?; Sir Douglas Quintet, Sahm, Meyers, Barber, Perez,
Morin, Kagan, Stallings (Meaux), Who Were You Thinking Of?
(BBC) (YouTube); Brian Mallery; Jody Nix; Tommy Emanuel;
Frank Vignola; JC Honeycut; Mark O'Conner; Tex Ritter, High
Noon, (Dimitri Tiomki); Craig Morgan, When a Man Can't Get A
Woman Off His Mind, (Bill Anderson); Freddie Hart, Easy
Lovin'; George McCormick, My Shoes Keep Walking Back to You;
J. Frazier-Impalas, Sorry (Zwirn; Giosasi); Dion & The
Belmonts; Mickey Dunne, An Ciarraioch Mallaithe; Maureen
Hegarty; Ral Donner, You Don't Know What You Got (G. Burton,
P. Hampton); Harry Belafonte, Banana Boat; Fendermen, Mule
Skinner Blues; Hank Williams Jr. The Living Proof [Ronnie
Prophet Show, You Tube]; Clifton Chenier, Lafayette Waltz;
Heartbeats; Dee Clark, Raindrops; Delfonics; Lenny
Cocoa/Chimes; Pony-Tails; Gene Pitney; Ricky Van Shelton,
Rockin' Years; Kenny Rogers-First Edition, Ruby (Mel
Tillis); Ricky Skaggs, I'll Take the Blame (Ralph Stanley);
Mel Tillis, Veil of White Lace, Ruby, Coca Cola Cowboy; Anne
Murray, Snow Bird; Paul Anka, Oh Carol, Neil Sedaka; Frankie
Avalon; Jimmy Gallagher or Mara-The Passions; Classics;
Mystics; Chad &Jeremy, Summer Song; Peter and Gordon, World
Without Love, I Go To Pieces; Gerry &Pacemakers. Ferry Cross
the Mercy; Johnny-June Carter-Cash; Johnny Tillotson; Johnny
Preston; Bill Monroe, Blue Moon of Kentucky; Buck Owens,
Susan Raye, Somewhere Between, (Haggard); Scott &Gerald
Delhunty, J'ai Recu Une Rose; Carl Smith, There She Goes
(QWJS); Wanda Jackson, Right or Wrong, One Night With You;
Hank Williams, On Top of Old Smokey, Tramp on the Street;
Donna Fargo, Did We Have to Come This Far to Say Goodbye;
Dolly Parton, Raul Malo, Don't Let Me Cross Over; Sweet
Dreams, Crying, Its Now or Never; Bouchers,(Rotary de
Bouctouche); Dailey &Vincent, Is This How it Is; Perez
Prado, Patricia; Eddie Arnold, Make the World go Away; Bob
Dylan, Rainy Day Woman; Nat King Cole Mona Lisa, Misty;
George Morgan, Candy Kisses; Heidi Hague; Vern Gosdin, Lacey
Lynn, Must Be Out of Our Minds; Raymond Miller, Verre Sur la
Table; Richard Langelier, Unis Pour la Vie; Marcel Martel;
Webb Pierce; Chuck Jackson, Any Day Now; David Wills,

There's a Song on the Jukebox; Andy Tielman, Blue Byou (Christopher Hillman, Gram Parsons); Louis Cormier, Richard Bourque-Bluegrass Diamonds, Another Place Another Time, She's Walking Through My Memory; Merle Haggard, Mark Bryant Holding Things Together (Bob Totten, Merle Haggard); Paul Dwayne, Ensemble Pour Toujours, The Day You Said I Do, The Puzzle; Mike Sanyshyn, Cajun Fiddle, (Buck Owens), (Owens, Rich; Merritt, B.C.); Jeannie C. Riley, Harper Valley PTA, Rose Garden; Wendell Roach, Reserve One Table; Ray Price, Jealous Heart; Ricky Skaggs, Crying My Heart Out; Yvon Collette—Nevada, Tennessee Whiskey; Kendalls, Don't Let Me Cross Over, Making Believe; Jamey Johnson, For the Good Times; Freres Bessette; Hert LeBlanc, She Thinks I Still Care; Blue River, One Kiss Away; Danny Denise; Irvin Blais, L'Bum; Rheal LeBlanc, Au Paradi des Musiciens; Louis Cormier, Pourquoi Pleurs-Tu; John Conlee, Rose Colored Glasses; Kitty Wells; Stuart Hamblen, I Won't Go Hunting With You Jake; Jimmie Davis, You Are My Sunshine (Mitchell, Hood, Davis), Nobody's Darlin'; Harrell Perry, Can I Sleep in Your Arms Tonight-Lady, I Would Have Loved You all Night Long, The First Fall of Snow (YouTube)(TDP); Jimmy Clanton, Just a Dream; Charts; Danleers; Chords; Spidels; Chordettes; Safaris-Jimmy Stephen, Image of a Girl; Cleftones, Heart and Soul; George Lanius and Crescendos, Janice Green (YouTube), Oh Julie (Moffitt and Ball), (1958 Nasco, Scarlet, Guest Star, Top Label, Excello Records)(YouTube); Pascal Bessette, Croisier de L'Amour; Otis Williams/Charms; Classic Country QWJS; Harold Hutchens, Amber Martin, All I Have to Offer You is Me; Branson Music Factory; 5th Dimension, Aquarius; Amber Digby-Midnight Flyer, How You Drink the Wine; Marianne Faithfull, As Tears Go By; Billy Joe Shaver; Gogi Grant, Wayward Wind; Gale Storm Ivory Tower, Memories are Made of This, I Hear You Knocking; Neil Diamond; Canadian Grass Unit; Jim &Jesse; Adams &Gueli-Fireflies, You Were Mine (Gracalone); Jive Five; Chiffons; Cal Smith, Country Bumpkin; Justine Trevino; Vince Gill, Blue Eyes Crying in the Rain; Hank Thompson or Kitty Wells, Wild Side of Life, God Made Honkey Tonk Angels, (J. D. Miller, Carter, Warren); Connie Smith; Monotones, Book of Love; Dwight Yoakam, Heartaches by the Number, (live, YouTube), It Won't Hurt/Today I Started Loving You Again with lead guitarists, Josh Greene--great vocal harmony Eddie Perez; Johnny Preston, Running Bear; Jay and the Americans Cara Mia, She Cried; Hank Locklin, Send Me the Pillow; Travis &Bob; B. D'Andrea-Knockouts; Vaughn Monroe/Duane Eddy, Ghost Riders in the Sky; Nixon-Aquatones, You (D. Goddard); David Seville/Bagdasarian; Skip $Flip, It Was I; Chet Atkins, Mr.

Sandman; Roy Buchanan, <u>Sweet Dreams</u>; Johnny Smith, <u>Moonlight in Vermont</u>; Phil Phillips; George Strait; Mack Johnson Jr., <u>Today I Started Loving You Again</u> (You Tube), Merle Haggard/co-written-Bonnie Owens; Bo Diddley, <u>Bo Diddley</u> (Checker Records, YouTube, EaglerockTV); Chuck Berry, <u>You Never Can Tell</u>; Gary Stewart; Linda Ronstadt, <u>Blue Bayou</u>; Ink Spots; Tony Williams-The Platters, <u>Smoke Gets In Your Eyes</u>, (Otto Harbach, Jerome Kern), <u>Harbor Lights</u>, (Hugh Williams, Henryk Szpilman, Jimmy Kennedy). Mc is still angry with Buzz and suddenly turns around, tries to throw a punch at Buzz's gut but Peter blocks it in time before 'a connect.' Peter says, "Hey quit this shit you guys. Aren't we fighting the wrong people here by fightin' each other? We are supposed to fight Charlie. We will all be getting outta here and going home soon so don't worry and quit this shit." Mc says, "And yeah, I remember you need your nose to fight this war because your helmet would not look too good without your nose under it *and* you gotta breathe--right? That is why I punched for your gut this time." [Everyone laughs.]. Buzz says flippantly, "No my gut would be a pity to waste here in this fight with you. I may have to save my gut for the Cong to pummel some metal into it, right? No he will shoot for the heart like in the song <u>Desperado Love</u> (Garvin; Johns)-- Conway Twitty—yeah." As the Soldiers continue their drive along a lonely muddy pot-hole filled road, they hit the darkness of another sudden massive downpour. The Soldiers could see more ominous dark streaks of shedding showers with bolts of lightening out in the distant sky. The guys continue their drive on their muddy road through mazes of tall saw-tooth elephant grass that rise higher than a man's head. But as soon as Pete turns the corner, there is a panoramic view of shimmering glistening rice paddies as far as the eye can see. Peter says, "This place is beautiful and seems peaceful but it sees a lot of terror and destruction. This watery shimmering beauty fools you and there is so much poverty here with a lot of war-ridden misery. I never really knew what poverty meant until I saw this place. These people live for their rice and you take that away from them, they have nothing." Mc says, "That is why I don't like Agent Blue or Agent Orange." Guy says, "Yeah, and these people know how to live in order to survive. These people do not have much meat in their diet and don't need a variety of different types of foods every day. They just make due with what they have—-their rice. Maybe one—-maybe two bowls--of rice a day. Generally, it is sufficient for these people to sustain a long life." Buzz says, "No these people had meat here but they have hunted this place to-hell and now there is nothing-—no wild life left to hunt." Peter asks, "This rain is so very good for these people to grow their rice crops but how much more water can this ground take-up from these constant downpours?" Peter stops the jeep for a moment and says, "Man look at this place, how much more water-logged can a land get? If we stray off this road, we are sure to get caught in this watery mire forever." Mc cuts him off and says, "Don't stop this jeep, man. Keep it moving because I am afraid if you stop, we will get bogged-down in this mess. It's not grass. This grass or rice is growing in deep muddy water. This water-logged grass can fool you. This is not a lawn it is water with grass floatin' on it. This is not like Peter's New York where we can drive-up and park a car on the grass. It is all water, rice paddies, and mud." Buzz says, "But ... why do we have to destroy these peoples' rice fields—their life--with these chemicals? Do these people care about our freedom and our Democracy?" Peter says, "No, but I keep thinking about the little boy who lost his mother with the bombing and how he feels his sorrow. As Robert Kennedy said '(...) we must feel it (...).' What is wrong with us? We must all feel it!"

Just as Peter finished his words, the jeep gets mired down and stuck in the mud. The Soldiers step out to push the jeep but their feet just sink deeper and deeper into the mud. They quite futilely attempt to push the jeep out. Now, however, they are not too far from the Cambodian border and they want to get out of here fast but they are flooded in with mud everywhere. Buzz then says to Mc, "Man this was your responsibility to get us armored escort and you got us into this mess. We would not have been in this mess if you had planned something better." Mc suddenly says, "Hey, man, I can't take this shit. 'I'm ankling out of here.'" Mc is a little angry and jumps out of the jeep like an idiot and starts walking but does not get too far because his feet sink deep into the mud rising past the top of his boots. Buzz wise-cracks-in with, "Yeah, See You Later Alligator and go ahead, Mc, I know you are still chasing after CaLu but you won't get to her like that in this mud-hole, believe me, you won't." Mc says, "No, I know I will find her again. It is kinda like this song, If You Think Your Lonely, [Johnny PayCheck]. That's what it is. Or kinda like ... I held her right on The Tips of My Fingers, [Bill Anderson, Steve Wariner]. She's gone now." Peter says, "Oh, Buzz, shut up-- just let Mc love his girl. I know what it means to be in love. I know because I adore Sherry. Between a man and a woman, love is the greatest emotion on the planet." Mc turns around, in agreement and says, "I know love is the greatest.

And right now, I am not chasing CaLu. I am just trying to get my ass the-hell-out-of-here--just want the-hell-out-of-this-hole! So shut the hell up, would ya, Buzz?" Buzz says, "Yeah, "You are not the *Lone Ranger* about wantin' to-get-the-hell-out-of-this-hole." [Everyone laughs.].

Shining, glimmering sheets of water and more water that is stretching-out far and far beyond, but with nowhere to turn a jeep around. Pete suddenly guns the pedal-to-the-metal and the jeep bolts forward. Miraculously Pete is out and onto solid some ground. Sun light quickly becomes as bright now as it had darkened. The sun's reflective light shines brightly on the Soldiers as they laugh and laugh with joy. Now they laugh once again at each other's very silly jokes. They are ready to talk about something ... something special again. The landscape shows green rice plants stippling the watery landscape in beautiful shimmering reflections of green and sky blue ... far ... and far beyond. As the Soldiers drive onward, this scenery changes to high dry plateaus and then changes again to steep dark-green mountains at the Cambodian frontier. The Soldiers fear the danger of the border; so, they turn-around quickly and high-tail it back into the direction in which they came. As the Soldiers continue their drive, Buzz says, "You know, Peter, I keep thinking back to all the stuff that Lieutenant Colonel Holden Coneycutt had said to us--awhile ago--all those fine quotes from our great Presidents. Peter says, "Yes, with President Abraham Lincoln ... He was one of the greatest Presidents this country has ever had the privilege to be served by. It was another time—-another horrible war in our country--our own Civil War--but then much different but still yet much the same as here because *war is war* wherever it is in this world--in Vietnam or anywhere!" Peter interjects once again with this ... "Talk about *our* Civil War—-well, its cause was to free man. Our slavery was the most horrible epoch we ever had in our nation and in this world. Do you know how African slaves were used in Europe? Well, 'one of the main reasons Europeans bought slaves was to put them in their armies to fight wars,'" [said Professor Ralph S. Brax of Anne C. Bailey's book]. And 'Bailey identifies a direct connection between European warfare and intensity of slave traffic.' Buzz changes the subject, "And people would say, *it was the black man who sold himself into slavery with African slave trading* but the white race did the same." Peter responds with, "Yes—-the white man has also sold its race into slavery. And ecause the black man does this, that makes him a traitor but the white man is not? I don't get the reasoning. There isn't any." Mc says, "Lincoln

41

fought our war to free American men held in bondage. Lincoln
was a very just man." Mc now brings in another issue for
discussion with, "I do firmly believe that all African-
Americans of slave-decent should be financially *compensated
for* because of the horror they endured with slavery." But
then Mc contradicts himself, "But another thing, being black
American does not necessarily mean he has descended from
slavery. How can we compensate for everyone equally and
fairly? There will be no end to it all." Guy agrees, "True,
it is nearly impossible to trace decedents. But we should,
as a nation, continue to make our apologies--our President
on *each* Inauguration Day for the length of slavery in
America--make an apology to all of the descendents of those
who lived and suffered with slavery and who were kept in
bondage by it. Mc states, "We also did wrong to the American
Indians. Why not compensate for the American Indians? Buzz
agrees with understanding, "Yes, totally--why not as a
Nation make formal apologies to the American Indians for
every generation? I still can't help but think how could one
race do that kind of wrong to another race? I always hold a
reserve deep in my heart for our race for the wrong we did
to the black race. It stays in my heart. It was wrong no
matter what--any of this injustice. There is nothing more to
say. It was wrong. I can't forget it. Peter says, "But I
think that this nation has apologized adequately for the
horror of human bondage with our own Civil War--when our
country went to war with itself to free black Americans. And
our Civil War was a way of an apology with roughly 750,000
Americans killed and died (J. David Hacker, history
demographics professor, Binghamton University)--and also
with the addition of disease and guerrilla warfare on the
border-states--and 50,000 who became amputees? The American
Civil War killed so many and tore-apart families." Peter
thinks of music, "This all reminds me of my favorite song by
Norman Brahm, Rockhouse Mountain Dream about a Union Soldier
who was killed three days before the Civil War ended. This
soldier sang about his love and about coming home again with
these words: *Watch the mountain sunset, with its colors blue
and gold. They're the colors of peace, my lady. My lord I
miss her so. As I write this letter, the Rebel shells blast
all day. But I can feel the Rockhouse Mountain Breeze. As
our sparrow soars in May. She sings, brave young Soldier,
brave young Soldier soar home.*" Now Peter emphasizes this
fact, "We had to go to war with ourselves so people could be
free." Buzz agrees, "Yes, but look also at what this country
has done to the American Indians. This can be called a
national disgrace. Look ... we lied to the American Indians

and brutally treated them. We took them from their homelands
and threw them away." Guy asks, "Yeah, the American Indian
and the *Trail of Tears*? Look at that. ... *The Trail of
Tears*." Peter asks, "How could one do this to another?" Guy
explains, "Starting with the Europeans and finishing with
the American settlers, they were extraordinarily unfair to
the American Indians. This was a tragedy. True, the American
Indians did not need all of the land for themselves.
However, Indian land should never have been taken from them.
There should have been written contracts and honored
treaties between the invaders—settlers--and the American
Indians." Peter agreeing, "True and the United States left
these people with no land. We have disgraces in our history
and this is one." Buzz says truly, "We were wrong and I
disagree completely with John Wayne's belief that the
American Indians had too much land. John Wayne said, 'I
don't feel we did wrong in taking this great country away
from them [the American Indians]. There were great numbers
of people who needed land and the Indians were selfishly
trying to keep it for themselves.' Selfishly keep it for
themselves? But listen to what Chief Joseph, Chief of the
Nez Perce Indians and humanitarian/peacemaker said, 'Our
chiefs are killed. ... The little children are freezing to
death. My people ... have no blankets, no food ... my heart
is sick and sad ... I will fight no more forever.' Is this a
way to treat a people and take their land from them? You
can't walk into a country and take it from its occupants. It
doesn't matter how much land they have. I know the American
Settlers needed the land but taking it *carte blanche* was not
the way to do it? The American settlers should have tried to
work-out some formal agreement with the American Indians. We
should have made treaties and kept them. You can't uproot
people from their homeland and send them off somewhere. But
put our own history aside for now. Look at what *this world*
did to the Jews. In one area of the Ukraine, near 'Babi Yar,
a ravine outside the capital Kiev where the Nazis [with
collaborative effort] slaughtered some 34,000 Jews over two
days in September 1941 (...).' So many Jews were killed that
even places/towns on the map ceased to exist. Jews were told
to undress and lie in a trench face down and shot in the
back systematically in numbers by the hundreds and thousands
and millions—-killed because they were Jews!" Guy changes
now, "And look at to our citizens of Japanese decent in
World War II. But they were financially compensated for
later." Peter adds, "I think too in the end that this war in
Vietnam will one day be looked upon as another great tragedy
in our history." Guy agrees, "Yes, but slavery is the

greatest tragedy in our history." Mc agrees, "Yes!" Peter
changes the subject back to Soldiers and Lincoln, "Our great
President Abraham Lincoln spoke so beautifully of the fallen
in the Civil War--speaking at Gettysburg, Pennsylvania,
November 19, 1863 ... he said beautifully about the tragic
loss of life for such a noble cause. President Lincoln said-
-beyond what any words any human being could ever express--
about its nation's fallen Soldiers with Gettysburg Address:

'(...) that from these honored dead we take increased
devotion to the cause for which they gave the last full
measure of devotion--that we highly resolve that these dead
shall not have died in vain--that this nation, under God,
shall have a new birth of freedom--and that the government
of the people, by the people, for the people shall not
perish from the earth.'"

"What words--the finest words ever written," Buzz says.

Guy then says, "If it was not for President Lincoln we
would not be standing in America we know it today. Our
country was torn by a great difference--almost beyond any
hope of salvation. The issue was slavery. It hung on our
country like a horrible plague. The Missouri Compromise and
the Compromise of 1850 could not hold this country together
in any way as long as people were kept in human bondage.
Lincoln had seen American slaves chained on river flatboats
on his trips into New Orleans. This was one of Lincoln's
first experiences with the horror of slavery and it affected
him deeply." Buzz says so very wisely, "I can't believe that
one human could put another in the bondage of slavery like
this. I can't understand that slavery existed in our country
of the free. It is just truly an inconceivable thought to
me--totally." Mc agrees, "Yes--true." But Mc continues and
disagrees, "But we can't keep dwelling on it. We had our
Civil War and we had paid the price so dearly with the war
with ourselves. We have to move on now and support laws for
equality and Civil Rights," (1960's). Buzz agrees, "Yes,
that is true." Mc says, "We must now move on with laws that
support the rights of everybody." And Buzz being a music
fan, changes the subject now to music, "Yeah you know I love
music and I love the drums. Yeah, and the Blues music
originated with African Americans. I love the Blues. But
thinking of African-Americans with their living conditions,
I would also have the blues if I had to live as a slave.
Drums were outlawed in the south. What good is music without
the drums, yeah?" [They laugh.]. I love the Blues Music like
Son House and Buka White." And now Peter changes from music
to Lincoln's greatness, "And Lincoln was all greatness. He

44

was one of our greatest Presidents our country has ever known. He was destined for greatness from the moment he took his first breath in this world." Guy agrees, "Yes, you are absolutely right." Then Peter begins to explain Lincoln's greatness, "He was the greatest servant this country has ever had. And he gave speeches to show his appreciation for our troops—-always. He was grateful to the Soldier for their great sacrifice. He gave a speech to the One-Hundred-Sixty-Sixth Ohio Regiment in Washington, D.C. on August 22, 1864 and said this, 'The nation is worth fighting for, to serve such an estimable jewel.' He worked hard to try to save this nation with everything he had. When President Abraham Lincoln followed President James Buchanan in office seven states had already seceded from the Union to form the Confederate States of America with Jefferson Davis as President. President James Buchanan basically gave up hope on holding our country together and was waiting for his term to expire--with no hope. President Buchanan said that he would be the last President of the United States. Our Congress had no power to stop the rebellion. Our nation's federal army was totally unprepared for war and most people sympathized with the South. The North had 16,000 Soldiers that were not well organized under General Winfred Scott. The State militias were also in terrible shape and could not fight. The numbers of the army were not there to fight a civil war." Buzz then explains Lincoln's political predicament with the South, "President Lincoln inherited a country divided. He had two nations, in one, at fierce opposition with each other. Besides the Confederate South, he also had to deal with the Northern States of Abolitionists and the Southern-border states holding slaves." Peter then responds to Buzz's explanation with, "Yes, no doubt, our country was made great by a great man. Lincoln said in his <u>Inaugural Address</u> that the southern states would not be allowed to separate and that the issue of civil war was in the hands of the South. Lincoln said 'In seventy-two years since our first inauguration of President under our National Constitution (...). I now enter the (...) task for the brief constitutional term of four years, under great and peculiar difficulty. A disruption of the Federal Union, heretofore only menaced, is now formidably attempted.' Lincoln used full powers as President and created new powers never before used in order to save our country. Lincoln said that America '(...) a free Government, where everyman has a right to be equal with every other man.' He said to the South, 'In your hands, my dissatisfied fellow countrymen, and not in mine, is the momentous issue of civil war. The government will not assail you. You can have no conflict without being yourselves the aggressor. You have no oath registered in Heaven to destroy the government, while I shall have the most solemn one to preserve, protect and defend it.'" Mc asks most truly, "Yes, how much more greatness and devotion do we want for our nation from our great President?" Buzz being emphatic, "We had what we needed--a man like President Abraham Lincoln and at this time in our history. He knew there would be a great loss of life but he forced the issue of war with ourselves to save our country--to rid our country of slavery. But our country had skirmishes and always the border guerrilla wars." Now Guy talks, "Yes, President Lincoln did what was his only option for his country--and that was to go to war with itself in order to rid the country of slavery and to be united." Peter states emphatically, "He did what he knew he had to do to save his country. And for Lincoln slavery was evil. President Lincoln said this on his sixth debate with Stephen A. Douglas in Quincy, Illinois on October 13, 1858. His feelings about slavery were well put with, 'As I would not be a slave, so I would not be a master.' President Lincoln's feeling about democracy with slavery is so well said with this quote, 'This expresses my idea of democracy. Whatever differs from this, to the extent of the difference, is no democracy.' Then in a letter he wrote to Henry L. Pierce on April 1, 1859, he said this, 'This is a world of compensations; and he who would be no slave, must consent to have no slave. Those who deny freedom to others deserve it not for themselves; and, under a just God, can not long retain it.' Lincoln said 'I believe that our government cannot endure permanently half slave and half free.'" Guy then adds this idea, "From the very beginning, President Lincoln decided he had to be strong to save our nation. Since the firing on Fort Sumter by the South, President Lincoln issued a call for troops about ten times. He was the first President to enact conscription on August 4, 1862." Guy now explains the political policies that Lincoln had in office with slavery, "He issued proclamations to issue blockades of the Confederate states. He declared martial law--showing his strength--by suspending the Writ of Habeas Corpus and did not have the right to do so. Only Congress has that right. That made the U.S. a state of martial law in which the military could make arrests without specific charges. Lincoln used the 'Presidential War Powers.' This allowed future Presidents to follow the same actions if needed. His key advisors told him to capitulate with the South. He set a precedent. And he decided to re-supply Fort

Sumter rather than give-in to the South. The fact that the South fired first gave the President justification for strong action against the South. It was an act of war." Peter brings up an important point about Lincoln, "I believe his hate for slavery was a passion that ran deep in his soul as seen with his quote in Chicago on July 10, 1858. 'I have always hated slavery.'" Guy adds, "And he loved his country. Our country was a *house divided* and Lincoln so eloquently said, 'A house divided against itself cannot stand.'" Mc adds his piece, "President Lincoln said, 'Slavery is founded on the selfishness of man's nature--oppositions to it on his love of justice. These principles are in eternal antagonism; and when brought into collision so fiercely as slavery extensions brings them; shocks and throws and convulsions must ceaselessly follow.'" Guy says, "President Lincoln sent men off to battle—-to die--to save our nation. He wanted a united nation with freedom for all. President Lincoln took unprecedented powers of the Presidency with the determination to abolish slavery. He did not want to see a civil war and believed that 'The Civil War is a people's contest ... a struggle for maintaining in the world, that form and substance of government, whose leading objective is to elevate the condition of man.' That is what President Abraham Lincoln said—-and a civil war to elevate the condition of man. He hated slavery and he knew that war had to be." Now Peter says, "The American Civil War—a war with itself—-was the only way. Lincoln said these words about the war in his <u>Second Inaugural Address</u>: Peter takes out a small piece of paper written in Peter's handwriting and he reads Lincoln's words:

"'*With malice toward none; with charity for all; with firmness in the right, as God gave us to see the right, let us strive on to finish the work we are in to bind-up the nation's wounds; to care for him who shall have born the battle, and for his widow, and his orphan—-to do all which may achieve and cherish a just and lasting peace among ourselves and with all nations.'*"

Buzz says, "Amen to that. No greater words can be said by anybody." Peter says, "He knew our cause was just." Buzz says, "With our Generals, at times he grew quite frustrated and impatient with many of his generals with their slow progress with engaging the enemy. All of his Generals of the North were reluctant to engage the South. One time he told, General George McClellan, 'If you don't want to use the army, I should like to borrow it for awhile.'" [Everyone laughs.]. General Joe Hooker asked President Lincoln if rather than engaging the enemy in combat, if he could rather advance to the Confederate capitol of Richmond. President Lincoln's response to that was, 'I think Lee's army, not Richmond is your true objective point. ... Fight him when opportunity offers. If he stays where he is, fret him and fret him.'" Peter says, "Another time he told one of his advisors that, 'I am thinking of taking the field myself.' His generals used many excuses to avoid engaging the enemy such as inclement weather used by General Joe Hooker. President Lincoln said to this, 'The Army of the Potomac is stuck in the mud.' This he told to his secretary John Nicolay and another excuse this time used by General George McClellan was that his horses were worn out. President Lincoln said to him, 'I have read your dispatch about sore tongued and fatigued horses.' (Lincoln was an accomplished horseman.). 'Will you pardon me for asking what the horses of your army have done since the battle of Antietam that fatigues anything?'" Guy says next, "President Lincoln 'eased' many of these generals out of power because they would not engage the enemy as he wanted them to do. Another time he was very angered with General Meade--General of he Army of the Potomac. At the Union victory at the Battle of Gettysburg, Meade allowed General Robert E. Lee to escape across the Potomac and back into Virginia. Lincoln had hoped this would be the final battle of the war and was sorely disappointed with Mead." Buzz says, "I like this quote that President Lincoln said of General Meade. General Meade said '[We drove them from], our soil every vestige of the presence of the enemy.' When Lincoln read this telegram he yelled, 'Drive the invader from our soil?! My God is that all? The whole country is our soil.'" Mc says, "Yes, it took a lot of prodding by President Lincoln to convince his own generals to engage their troops to battle which would be fighting brother against brother." Peter then adds, "President Lincoln's strategy for winning the Civil War was in 'short-term goals or steps,'" [as`quoted from Don Phillips]. "'He [Pres. Lincoln] started first with blockading key southern ports, gaining control of the Mississippi River, and rebuilding and training the military,' {Don Phillips]. Peter says, "'He concentrated on the destruction of Lee's army as opposed to the capture of the Confederate capital.' He took one battle at a time. And General Robert E. Lee of the Confederate Army had a hard time wrestling with the idea of fighting brother against brother on the battlefield and found it difficult to accept as seen with this quote later in his military career, 'With all my devotion to the Union, and the feeling of loyalty and duty of an American Citizen, I have not been able to make up my mind to raise my hand against my relative, my children, my home. I have, therefore, resigned my commission in the army (...).' And, 'The war was an unnecessary condition of affairs, and might have been avoided if forbearance and wisdom had been practiced on both sides.'" And now Mc goes back to the subject of Lincoln's Generals, "President Lincoln was very tactful in the way he relieved his generals of their command if he didn't like them. He did this by changing their field of command usually and replaced them. Lincoln had to go through many generals to find the one he wanted and he found him with General Grant. He replaced or relieved from command: General Winfred Scott, General Irvin C. McDowell, General John C. Fremont, George B. McClellan, General Henry W. Halleck, General John A. McClernand, General William S. Rosecrans, General Ambrose Burnside and General Nathanial P. Banks. Then he finally found General Ulysses S. Grant to do the job. Grant did engage his troops with success. President Lincoln said of General Grant when critics urged his dismissal because of a rumor that he was drunk after the Battle of Shiloh, 'I can't spare this man. He fights.' Grant said 'The art of war is simple enough. Find out where your enemy is. Get at him as soon as you can. Strike him as hard as you can.' President Lincoln always wanted a military engagement from his Army Generals. He had to preserve the Union and eliminate the evil of slavery from his country. General Grant was President Lincoln's favorite General and most respected General who got results with the battles he had won against the South." Peter says, "I like this one, when General Grant was fighting with General Lee in the Wilderness Campaign, President Lincoln had not heard back for several days from the field. Lincoln said this of Grant, 'Grant has gone into the Wilderness, crawled in, drawn up the ladder and pulled in the hole after him, and I guess we'll have to wait till he comes out before we know just what he's up to.' President Lincoln's entire direction of the war was toward the freedom of slaves." Buzz says, "There was no bull shitting with Lincoln." [They laugh.]. Guy then says another quote from President Lincoln. "General Sheridan said to General Grant in a telegram, 'If the thing be pressed, I think Lee will surrender.' After reading the message, Lincoln replied, 'Let the thing be pressed.'" Buzz says, "President Lincoln saw Americans fighting against Americans as a lesser evil than human slavery. Men had to fight and die to free men's souls." Peter has another idea, "Anyway about our Civil War, Lincoln did say of slavery, 'I have often inquired of myself what great principle or idea

it was that kept this Confederacy [original colonies] so
long together ... but that sentiment in the <u>Declaration</u> <u>of</u>
<u>Independence</u> which gave liberty, not alone to the people of
this country, but I hope, to the world, for all future time
(...). If it cannot be saved upon that principle
[<u>Declaration</u> <u>of</u> <u>Independence</u>] it will be truly awful. But if
this country cannot be saved without giving up that
principle, [<u>Declaration</u> <u>of</u> <u>Independence</u>]. I was about to say
I would rather be assassinated on this spot than surrender
it.'" Peter brings in another war--with Vietnam, "Our own
countrymen are now loosing their lives here, in Vietnam to
fight for another man's freedom as we did with our Civil War
but here in Vietnam ... this is a different war." Mc
questions, "Well, it is different, true, but maybe the
Vietnamese people are fighting each other with their own
very real civil war for their freedom as we did?" Peter
says, "We don't know--maybe it is their own civil war and we
are fighting for their *freedom*. We should try to save
another country for freedom in any way we can but not *by or
on our own terms*. And as much as I love my country I don't
know if what we are doing here in Vietnam is good for these
people." Buzz says "Yeah, we can't fight for another's
freedom by invading the country and then removing its
government and call it freedom but I hope maybe this is the
way to do it. I don't know. I mean I love freedom more than
anybody else but is it for ourselves here in 'Nam that we
are fighting or is it freedom for the Vietnamese people? But
also how can we logistically fight the-world-over? For us
... we have just so many troops and material to stretch-out
to fight all over this entire world. We must be cautious. I
do understand these people here in Vietnam want their
freedom as Lincoln said but I don't know if they want it on
our terms with our freedom. Everyone wants freedom the-
world-over but each country wants freedom on its own terms--
not on our terms." Peter then says in disagreement, "But
what we do here in Vietnam is what Lincoln believed and
wanted for America during our Civil War--a war for freedom.
But here now in Vietnam and in the world, we set our goals
for freedom--yes. Mc says, "Yeah, but this entire world over
... we must fight for freedom? I have my doubts ... and for
Vietnam?" But Peter rationalizes, "Yes, maybe we fight for
freedom in Vietnam so that in the end we fight for our own
freedom *this world over*. 'This will not be quick, or easy.
But we must never forget: This is not a war of choice. This
is a war of necessity. ... This is fundamental to the
defense of our people,'" [as said by President Barak Obama
2009 Afghanistan War]. 'Yes military intervention should

defend national security interests' as said by The Heritage
Foundation but here in Vietnam it seems not to be so." Buzz
now says his *Sermon on the Mount*, "This is not self defense.
We are policing *this world over*. How can we police this
entire world over? Maybe attrition and the logistics of
fighting in Vietnam will make it difficult for our country
to fight the war? We fight and die for another country but
it may be a country that is idealistically different from
our own. Some people in this world don't see freedom as we
see it or as we want it? But better still if we are going to
fight let us use our superior military advantage--our
airpower which is one of our best advantages in war for
sure. Let's use it wherever we go." Peter insists, "Now here
in Vietnam we want this freedom for the entire world as
Lincoln wanted." Buzz busts in quite angrily at Peter and
says, "Yes, freedom for the entire world is a *tuff row to
hoe* when we have to go-it-alone in this world." Buzz adds,
"But I think what Lincoln wanted was freedom from slavery,
not freedom from Communism. There is a big difference." Guy
tries to calm Buzz's anger, "We must define the freedom we
are fighting and for whom we are fighting? What may be
freedom to Uncle Sam may not be freedom for a united
Vietnam. The people we are fighting-for here--what do they
want? Mc adds, "Yeah, Buzz, we must qualify our meaning of
freedom and principles of our government even though
President Lincoln believed freedom was for everyone." Buzz
says, "And yes, for us Americans, Lincoln believed in saving
freedom for our country. He had no choice but to take our
country to-war-with-itself to save it." Peter states this
fact, "Yes, war is about principle but let us be careful
before we shed blood. Each side of the argument sees it *only
his* way. With our own Civil War, Jefferson Davis tried hard
to avoid bloodshed. Jefferson Davis said, 'I worked night
and day for twelve years to prevent the war, but I could
not. The North was blind, would not let us govern ourselves,
and so the war came.' Lincoln was a man of principle and
shedding blood to rid our country of slavery was our
obligation. President Lincoln had to end slavery. The
Crittenden Compromise, Missouri Compromise and other
compromises were brought forth and rejected by President
James Buchanan and President Lincoln. Our country had its
back up against the wall. The problems were compromises and
the compromises did not provide principles by which the
South could deal." Peter explains, "Before President Lincoln
took office six states had seceded from the Union. Lincoln
knew nothing more could be done. War was inevitable. Lincoln
did not want civil war but Lincoln knew that war with itself

meant our county's only salvation." Guy states with the Civil War won, he wrote his appreciation to the mothers and the families of the fallen Soldiers. Now Guy takes out a paper from his pocket which he had copied from somewhere and shows how Lincoln appreciated all of the sacrifices that were made by our Soldiers to save this Union. Guy reads this letter of bereavement to a mother during the Civil War. Guy reads, "Let me read this to you:

Dear Madam,

I have shown in the files of the war department a Statement of the Adjunct General of Massachusetts that you are the mother of five sons who have died gloriously on the field of battle. I feel how weak and fruitless must be any words of mine which should attempt to beguile you from the grief of a loss so overwhelming. But I cannot refrain from tendering to you the consolation that may be found in the thanks of the Republic they died to save. I pray that our Heavenly Father may assuage the anguish of your bereavement and leave you only the cherished memory of the loved and lost, and the solemn pride that must be yours, to have laid so costly a sacrifice upon the alter of Freedom.

Yours, very sincerely and respectfully,

President Abraham Lincoln

Guy finishes with, "I can't imagine how deep this loss was to a mother. We are all very thankful to all mothers everywhere in this world in every war." Buzz says, "Now with Vietnam, we are getting more world freedom in this world but we are dividing our own country with this war in Vietnam. Mc says, "Our American freedom may not be something Vietnam can deal with right now. We must realize that our type of government might not be for everyone in this world even though we think it should be. And besides with all of this *freedom stuff*, Vietnam is really fighting its own civil war. We don't belong here in Vietnam or anywhere else fighting for another country's civil war. We are fighting to give this country a freedom that we choose for it—no more—no less. We are fighting a war that does not have to be fought." Peter then goes on a different tangent ... concerning the needy and hungry in America, "And besides don't we have enough problems of our own with our poor and hungry in America? We will fight for another country's freedom but what about our hungry at home ... that really gripes me. Let's take care of our own at home first, to try to give them freedom from hunger, want and poverty. That's the freedom I'm talkin' about." Buzz agrees, "Yeah, right on, Peter." Peter goes on, "In our country some people may be politically free, but they are not free from poverty. This is not freedom! They are poor. They are hungry. They are bound into poverty as a type of slavery. Then why should these poor care about the political freedoms of some country in this world? This does not make much sense. Being poor in America, is being helpless and sometimes homeless. Some people care but many do not care enough to be bothered." Buzz says, "Yeah, you know you are right with that idea." Peter continues, "We care but we only care enough not to be bothered by somebody else's problems. Who is going to help the poor and the sick in the United States of America—the richest nation in the world? Our government should try to guarantee something for our poor in our country. So why, then, are we spending billions of dollars somewhere else— with something else to fix--when we have our own hungry, poor and desperate in America? We are a country of freedom and Democracy. We fight for it anywhere in the world but we must take care of our poor at home first. We guaranteed political freedom in our Constitution so let's guarantee freedom from hunger as well. Sometimes humanity has to be legislated!" Buzz agreeing with Peter says, "This is what makes our Constitution so great ... it has *righted moral wrongs*. The Constitution is a document of mandated human rights and freedoms." Peter then adds, "Yes ... and we must be free from hunger. We must be free from need and hunger; and we must be free from tyranny as well ... both and all. And so as Americans we are free from political tyranny but we must be free from hunger!" Buzz agrees, "But it should be so--absolutely—especially for the richest nation in this world! Yes, if one is hungry, then freedom has no meaning." Peter states, "It's not just about *freedom*. It's about *hunger*. Do you think it is fair for a person to live his life in poverty and in hunger? Let us take care of our own at home first!"

Mc now goes back to our own Civil War. He says lastly, "Bottom line ... we fought our war for Americans. We fought our Civil War because slavery had to end for Americans. Buzz says, "Lincoln knew Americans had to die. But I wish we had another way! But maybe there is no other way. We all have our principles for which we are willing to die. And maybe it will always be this way."

Peter finishes it with, "But I don't know if there ever will be. I wish there was. Maybe we can try to find it. I know President Abraham Lincoln would want it that way."

Chapter 6

Meeting an American Lieutenant in the U.S. Army, a FAC's Pilot, an Air Force Fighter Pilot and onto Phu Cat, Pleiku and Qui Nhon

The next morning Peter, Buzz, Mc, Guy and John leave with the convoy in a troop transport carrier that is driven by Lieutenant Sherman, U.S. Army, from the battalion at Da Nang and are accompanied by Captain James Johnson from the U.S. Air Force a fighter pilot from Phu Cat in Binh Dinh Province, and Captain Richard Maslan a Forward Air Controller (FAC) from Phu Cat Air Force Base. It is much safer to travel in a convoy but the radio sings a song ... Brady Clark, I'd Like to Sleep 'Til I Get Over You.

Peter says to Buzz, "I keep thinking of that poor Vietnamese boy with his horrible plight--the nightmare we have made for him here in Vietnam--the tenuousness of his young life in this battle-stricken country we now have come to know as *our objective to resolve.*"

Buzz says with sadness, "But this is ... this poor boy's awful nightmare."

Mc says, "And it's ours."

Peter then says sadly, "Yeah, this place nobody would believe it if we went back to the world and told everybody. But I think of Sherry and our child when I heard that sad story from the poor Vietnamese boy. Boy, I tell ya' right now I would give anything to just talk with my Darlin' Sherry and to see her beautiful face. I want to hold her in my arms one more time!"

The convoy is headed to Phu Cat and then it will go on to Pleiku in an APC (Armored Personnel Carrier) with troops.

"Hello my name is Lieutenant James Sherman from the Fifth Infantry, Sixth Division. [The Soldiers salute.]

"Hello my name is Captain Richard Maslan from the FAC (Forward Air Controllers), Fast FAC'S, and Misty A Thunderchiefs from the 1,416th Tactical Fighter Squadron at Phu Cat Air base." [The Soldiers salute.]. Captain Johnson enters.

Sp4c. McConnell salutes and Captain Johnson salutes and says, "Captain Johnson U.S. Air Force."

Peter says as he salutes, "Good day, Gentlemen."

Captain Richard Maslan, Fast FAC's, says, "With the initiation of Commando Sabre Test Group, my career has changed. We now fly our single-engine F-100-F's and F-100-D's Fast FAC's which fly at 400-500 mph at altitude 3,000 5,000 feet. Now some of us are called Fast FAC's or Super FAC's. We fly the F-100-F's and some of us fly the slower 02A Skymaster, the North American Rockwell 011-10a Broncos or Cessna 0-1Gs Bird Dogs for our forward observation missions. We all go out there and hope we can help you Troopers on the ground."

He continues, "Our mission now is to fly North Vietnam and in so doing, try to stop the flow of supplies from North to South; locate and identify SAM sites, truck parks, fuel dumps and enemy convoys and then we call in the strike aircraft and direct the attack against the targets. FAC's radio call signs were every name in the book but now we are Fast FAC's and our radio call is Misty. What we do is we screech in real fast, mark our spot and we launch our marking smoke rockets and ask, *'Do you have my smoke?'* [or] *'Hit my smoke.'* (The spot the Fast FAC marked the bombers to hit.). "'Whenever a FAC located a mortar pit or anti-aircraft position, he dove his frail little Cessna airplane straight toward the ground, releasing white phosphorous rockets to mark the position for the attack aircraft.'"

Captain Richard Maslan continues, "We develop a sixth sense almost. We can see the slightest sign of enemy tracks on the ground as reflections of pools of water left in the mud from vehicles recently passed. And we can look for an ever so slight trace of steam/heat exhaust from a running engine. The NVA many times cut trees and their branches from one area of the jungle to camouflage another are where a gun turret or a vehicle may be hiding. And in this process, the leaves would wilt slightly but we, FAC pilots, can see the slight wilting of cut leaves in the foliage. We will mark these targets with a smoke bomb. We develop 'Misty' Eyes which means we can see what no other pilot can see."

Lieutenant Sherman adds another point, "We are going to send some of our troops into A Shau Valley to stop the infiltration through The Trail. With A Shau Valley, we can try to slow-down his advances into South Vietnam. The enemy infiltrates into the A Shau Valley from Laos and then finds his way onto our battlefields here in South Vietnam. We have to be ready to stop them.

Lt. Sherman continues, "You men know what I am all about and I am not going to repeat myself. Do you know what I mean, men?"

John says proudly with a salute, "Yes, nice to meet you."

"I am Sp4c. John Kelsey and 'ma' buddies are Sp4c. Peter McConnell, Sp4c. Buzz Brule, Sp4c. Guy Von Bexin and Sp4c. Chris 'Mc' Davison.

"Yes we do," says Sp4c. Peter McConnell and Sp4c. John Kelsey.

The Lieutenant says, "You guys could have gotten yourselves burnt-up real bad goin'-it-alone out here in this jungle. [Peter laughs.]. At least with this convoy you have some cover."

Peter says, "How do I say your name? Excuse me sir, but ..." [He is cut off by the Lieutenant.]. Lieutenant Sherman says emphatically, "Lieutenant Sherman ... S-H-E-R-M-A-N— understand?" [Buzz laughs to himself--thinks this is silly.]

Lt. Sherman says, "Well we have divided South Vietnam into four Corps or Tactical Zones of I, II, II, IV."

"I (eye) Corps is the furthest north; just below it is Corps II which is the Demilitarized Zone (DMZ); III Corps is the Central Highlands and IV Corps is the Mekong Delta and the southern most part of Vietnam."

He continues, "The eye corps ... I Corps is known as the 'Ring of Steel' which borders North Vietnam and which circles around to the northern Laotian Border. It is also known as the 'Blazing Front Line' because it bears the brunt of constant enemy pressure."

Captain Richard Maslan then says, "Or it is the 'Ring of Steel' because of its good defense. As Air Force pilots we have to cover six Route Packages. North Vietnam is divided geographically into six Route Packs. Route Packs 5&6 encompass Hanoi and Haiphong. Route Pack 1 covers the Southern panhandle of North Vietnam. It is the area most heavily defended because all enemy war supplies coming down the Ho Chi Minh Trail have to come through this area. Route Pack 2, 3, 4 covers the remainder of the country. But we are mostly in the *Steel Tiger* area of Laos and Route Pack 1."

Lieutenant Sherman then says, "Yes, you are right, Sp4c. McConnell, you would not be here in this war if you really did know what was going on here—what this war is about--would you? There is no way around this war. You guys have to fight it. 'The surest way to prevent war is not to fear it' as said by John Randolph," (actor).

Buzz says most truly, "I don't fear it. I just hate it. I just wish we all did!"

Peter then says, "Yeah, 'War that mad game the world loves to play,' as Jonathan Swift (Irish cleric, satirist, essayist, political pamphleteer and poet) said so well."

Guy then cynically adds his two cents with, "Yeah, it is a game alright at least we think it is."

Buzz adds, "Yeah ... but better still as asked by Leslie Parrish-Bach with her question, 'Suppose they gave a war and no one came?'"

Mc says, "No, it sure is something out here, in 'Nam. Will this madness ever end? I don't know. I just want to find my girl. I just want to find her somewhere—-somehow--in all of this madness and I will!"

Buzz says jokingly, "You are girl crazy. That's all. You don't care about war, peace or anything else but girls. The only peace you like is a piece of ..."

And Guy then cuts off Buzz's smart remark before Mc tries for a-connect with his fist for Buzz's face. But Mc does try for a karate chop to the jugular of Buzz's neck.

Buzz says smartly, "Hey, don't try that on my neck. I need this neck desperately to be Buzz because without my neck and all of its enervating arteries to nourish my brain, I can't be Buzz. My neck has the arteries I need—-the Carotid--that carries my blood to my brain and the veins—- the Jugular--that carries my blood away. My neck holds-on my head and I need my head for my brain--that too; so, please don't go for my neck. I am nothing without my neck." [They all laugh.]

Guy says, "Hey shut up you guys and have some respect for each other around here, would you?" [They are nervous about their upcoming mission.]

Mc answers that with, "I have just found a beautiful woman here in 'Nam who finally means everything to me. I found someone in my life who really means everything to me—- someone I found in this damn war. I just wish she was with me now, holding my hand."

Buzz laughs at him and says, "That's not all you wish she was holding. [Everyone laughs.]. You want her to hold your c*ck and maybe she ..." [He is cut off by Peter.]

Peter says, "Oh shut up. I don't want to hear about your c*ck and what it does in CaLu's hands." [Everyone laughs.]

Mc is now infuriated tries to slam his fist into Buzz's face but misses as Peter jumps in between the two of them to break-it-up as Guy holds Mc back. He says, "You know I have come to the conclusion that your problem is that you are real mad at the world."

Guy says, "Come on you guys. Quit it. There is no end to this madness here. We are not supposed to be fighting with each other like this."

Mc in a very conciliatory voice says, "Yeah, I know you are right and I am sorry, Buzz, for acting like that. I should not have acted that way. It is like my favorite saying, ha. *Sticks and stones will break my bones but words will never hurt me,* ha, ha, ha. I know words don't do the damage as much. It is the bad deeds and acts that do the harm, *sobeit.*"

Peter says next, "No! Let us forget the bad words and the bad deeds."

They all agree.

Lieutenant Sherman says, "You got it all right. Let's forget trying to fight each other. We got enough to fight here in Vietnam. This war is going to be with us for quite awhile."

Buzz says, "Yeah, it ain't 'goina' end anytime too terribly soon."

Lt. Sherman continues, "You know, I think about the reality of this quote as said by Robert Lynd--an Irish essayist and journalist--'The belief in the possibility of a short decisive war appears to be one of the most ancient and dangerous of human illusions.' We are not 'gettin' 'outta' here any time too soon because we have our job to do and that is to finish this Vietnam. We can't give in to the Communist. We have to finish this job and not settle for anything else no matter what. As Marcus Lulus Cicero (Roman orator, statesman, political theorist, lawyer and philosopher) said, 'An unjust peace is better than a just war.'"

Buzz says with some anger, "Yeah, I am disgusted with this mess, and this is true as Herbert Hoover said once, 'Older men declare war. But it is the youth who must fight and die.'"

Peter says, "You are not happy with this war as none of us are."

Lieutenant Sherman states truly, "I have worked my entire life to get to this rank and position in my division—my battalion--in this war at my base in Qui Nhon. This job is my whole life. I took my oath, 'I do solemnly swear (or affirm) that I will support and defend the Constitution of the United States against all enemies, foreign and domestic; that I will bear true faith and allegiance to the same and that I will obey the orders of the President of the United States and the orders of the officers appointed over me, according to regulations and the Uniform Code of Military Justice, So help me God.'"

Lieutenant Sherman continues, "My superiors are now asking me to produce numbers of enemy dead but my numbers don't seem to match with what I saw. My CO said to take the numbers that he gives me and to forget the rest. It was like this ... my CO asked me, *how many of our men died in battle yesterday*, and I told him *150 enemy-dead were counted, yesterday, sir.* Then he told me *that number is not correct.* But I insisted that my count *is correct* because I was out there myself and saw it. He insisted again, that *500 enemy dead was the correct count and to shut my mouth about it-- that the AVRN (South Vietnamese Army) and the GVN (Republic of South Vietnam) made the count and that their numbers are correct.* My Commander stated that *One reason I tell you this is that the AVRN does not always bring all of their Soldiers KIA back here to count and also the enemy, many times, carries his dead away; so, with this we cannot get an accurate count on any of it. It is for these reasons, they count better than we do--I say with sarcasm-understand,* said my CO? He continued *If you do not agree with me, things are going to change around here real fast being Lieutenant of C Company, so, shut up.* Lt. Sherman continues, "My CO (Commanding Officer) is even pissed-off with the press for the reporting of *wrong* casualty counts that favored the North Vietnamese. He told me that Ambassador Nolting is becoming more and more infuriated with the press lately-- especially with the Saigon Press--because they are reporting that the war is favoring the North Vietnamese."

Buzz then says, "We need journalists like UPI's Neil Sheehan; Tim O'Brian and AP's Malcolm Brown to question the news sources as Mailer; G. Emerson; Nicosia; Stacewicz; Moser; Cortright; Hunt; Palmer; others and photojournalists as Henri Huet; E. D. Reese; Nick Ut; H. Faas; O. Noonan Jr.; R. Pyle; K. Potter; K. Shimamoto; D. McCullin; H. Thanh My; Haughey and others to say about it. And yes, what we really need is an American journalist to speak out as did David

Halberstam [and as reported by Joe Galloway], 'the truth in
the face of official lies' when at a news briefing in Saigon
with the Saigon Press, with Two-Star General Richard
Stillwell, Halberstam confronted Stillwell about the
accuracy of the information that the American people were
getting. David Halberstam said to General Stillwell, 'Excuse
me, sir, but we are not your corporals and PFC's. We're here
because the New York Times, the United Press, the Associated
Press and Time magazines sent us here. And X number of
American helicopter pilots with gunners went into combat
today, risked their lives and I don't know how many millions
of dollars worth of gear. It was a very big battle. The
American people are entitled to know (...),'" [more about
it].

Peter says, "Yeah, there is no front in this war and
there is no accurate body count. There is no accurate number
of sorties for the U.S. Air Force which doesn't match-up."
Buzz then says jokingly, "What a revolting development this
is ... shiiit? I can't hang with it, man."

The Lieutenant did no hear this and now discusses
guerrilla warfare, "Yes, without front lines, the enemy is
using guerrilla tactics with a protracted guerrilla war. We
don't even know with who we are fighting, how many we are
fighting or the dead enemy count."

Mc asks, "The enemy is the National Liberation Front
(NLF)--the Vietcong, right?" Buzz answers, "Don't get those
letters mixed-up with the NFL" (the National Football
League). [Everyone laughs.]. It is a different game. Believe
me, a very different game but a better game. [Everyone
laughs.]

Mc says jokingly, "No, this war is kinda' like a
football game but more intense. It does get the *adrenalin
rush* going." Peter then brings up an important point, "But
most importantly, I think, we should know the numbers of
enemy troops we are fighting."

Then Captain Richard Maslan adds, "In our war with the
North Vietnamese Main Force (NVA) against us, the U.S. and
the South Vietnam's troops--the AVRN (South Vietnamese
Army)--we are fighting a war of attrition--more troops are
killed than can be replaced. About numbers, we never have
real numbers of enemy soldiers alive or of enemy dead."
Captain Maslan changes the subject, "We fight this war with
our forces that descend upon the enemy with helicopters
engage and then withdraw to seek-out other enemy forces
elsewhere. The advantage of doing this is for increased U.S.

mobility so we are not tied down to fixed locations. It is
very discouraging to fight a war like this because there are
no front lines there is no ground to win. We will liberate a
Vietnamese Village with this strategy but the problem is
that the next day we abandon it and allow the enemy to
return. [This same concern continues again with another war
in Afghanistan. "(...) Afghan leaders fear that the U.S. may
leave after their clearing operations are complete, allowing
Taliban forces to return."]. Maslan continues, "And these
people here in Vietnam--in these hamlets can't be loyal to
us. They have many spies who come into our bases as cooks,
maintenance, laundry workers etc. We cannot see our enemy
because we don't know who he is. The South Vietnamese
Villagers will appease anyone who is holding control of
their village. This war has no front line."

Guy adds, "And another thing, we don't bomb them in
places where it will work, such as their railroad stations,
utility power plants and that just does not make much
sense." Now Captain Johnson adds something to this
conversation, "But with air power, we are doing everything
we can to make it safer for our ground troops. I don't have
a good story for us either because we have a 22% shot-down
rate as fighter pilots. But our job is important in that we
do *prep* the terrain for our troops on the ground.

Lt. Sherman says to Captain Johnson, "We know you guys
are saving our asses. And on the ground what we do is fight
this war enough to demoralize the enemy but we need your
help with air support to win this war. For most of the time
the enemy is avoiding heavy contact with us in favor of
terrorism and ambush. Once you locate them with your FO
(Forward Observer) and your FAC's (Forward Air Controller)
and bomb the targets, then we can be more effective on the
ground."

Mc says, "But all of South Vietnam is a war arena with
shifting areas of combat. This is a war different from
anything that we have ever known before."

Lt. Sherman adds some important points, "When the NVA
and the VC initiate their offensive actions, they tend to
avoid the allied strong points and attack the weak spots.
They use these basic tactical operations, the raid, the
ambush, and the attack by fire. Their purpose is to inflict
high casualty rates, to destroy equipment, to disrupt
installations and to inflict psychological fear on to his
enemy. At the end of the battle, they carry away their dead
so we cannot count their casualties. Our enemy has his
battle strategies which are poor because he cannot hold

strategic points and they only hold Cambodia, Laos and North Vietnam because of its neutrality. They defend by evading. They tried to draw allies into traps and divert them from the larger unit that was nearby. There is a high casualty rate with the allies because of enemy sniper fire and the booby traps set throughout the jungle. But our forces have superior fire power and in order for the enemy to counter this, they mass attack and then withdraw before allies can react. They move fast and lightly. Every move is carefully planned. Many times they would bring their supplies in before battle and place them in position ahead of time on or near the battlefield such as food, weapons and medical supplies."

Buzz adds other information about the Easter Offensive, "On the other hand, later in this war, the enemy changed his strategy with the Easter Offensive with direct main force engagement and the use of heavy artillery."

Captain Johnson says, "Yes, that is true."

Lt. Sherman continues, "And our enemy always knows when air bombings are going to start. They just have to look at the clock. The bombing starts at the same time in the morning, off for lunch and home at 5:00 PM. And they know when to take shelter and avoid the bombings. Their success on the battlefield, to minimize their loss, is to disengage or to avoid the enemy--to avoid contact with the allied forces. Their withdrawal phase is just as important to them as combat action. They would counterattack only to disengage the troops. Our remedy for this is that we have to use maneuver warfare to work around their strategy. Maneuver warfare is:

'Maneuver warfare is when you try to defeat the enemy by shock and disruption. Methods of war stand on a continuum of maneuver warfare and attrition warfare. Maneuver warfare is best for militaries that are smaller, better trained and better prepared tactically. Maneuver warfare should be the strategy we choose if we want to fight this enemy successfully. With this type of warfare, we could use rapid movement to keep the enemy off balance. The Cavalry and mechanized vehicles make this type of warfare work better. And Methodical warfare is a war of attrition. One moves masses of men and materials against enemy strong points. What is important with this is to destroy infrastructure, kill in high numbers, take territory and destroy material. There is a very rigid central command. With maneuver warfare we have a local commander in control. There is an effort placed on taking control and attacking the enemy target, weaken fire support strength and attack their logistical bases.'"

Peter wants to sum it all up with this very fine quote, "No one really knows what this war is all about. But [as said by historian, writer, chemist and professor, John Prados], we are 'firing at faces in the rain at night.'" [Everyone laughs.]

Buzz then says rather appropriately, "That is most true! Yeah your right, Pete. It all sounds like we are 'firing at faces in the rain at night.' I could not have said it better than that myself." [They laugh.]

Buzz feels he wants to explain the Air Force, "The Air Force Soldiers have some of the best amenities in the military such as movie theaters, weight and workout rooms, TV every night, tennis courts, barbequed steaks and broiled lobster—sounds good for these guys in war."

John pipes in his remarks with, "Don't really try to knock these guys as they are saving our ground asses. We could not fight our battles here in Vietnam on the ground without their air support. I have a lot of respect for you men. You guys deserve it."

Captain Johnson adds ideas for the Air force, "We command the air but the U.S. Marine Corps, the Navy and the Army do their good share on the ground. The Army with its UH-1 Iroquois helicopter or AH-IB attack helicopter. The Huey offers excellent support for close air support for our ground troops. The C-130 Hercules of the USAF operated as a troop carrier and it was a good gunship that carried weapons for combat from the air such as 20 mm cannons and 7.62 Miniguns used for close air support, air interdiction and armed reconnaissance. These babies are known as our Gunships or attack helicopters and the Marines with their AH-IG, AH-IE Cobras. They were supportive in the Battle for Khe Sanh. The Air Force has its F-4 Phantoms, the A-6 Intruder, the F-105 Thunderchiefs and the B-52 Stratofortress. Enemy anti-aircraft defense systems are becoming a constant and increasing threat to our air systems. The F-105 Thunderchiefs now have the responsibility to take on the enemy by using anti-radar missiles and bombs. These pilots are known as the Wild Weasels and have the most dangerous assignments in the war. The Huey AH-IB attack helicopter provides close air support for our ground troops. Since battle lines are not clearly drawn, the Huey is also used for 'Search and Destroy' Missions to carry the fight to the enemy. 'The helicopter was used to hunt down enemy positions and eliminate them so U.S. ground forces could overrun their positions.' 'The AH-IB helicopter has become the ground Soldiers best friend during ground operations because it could extract Soldiers on the ground if it became untenable.' Squads of attack helicopters were also used to soften the ground before any large-scale ground operation."

Captain Johnson continues, "Another weapon used by the Marines was 'snake and nape'. "Snake was a 500 pound bomb that had the shape of a tail and had snake eyes. Nape was of course Napalm. The Marines work in teams with the use of the Hughes H-6 Cayuse known as the 'Loach' and the AH-1 Huey Cobra. They are a hunter/killer team. The 'Loach' would hunt/seek and the Cobra would kill. For Tactical Air lift we use the De Haviland C-7A and the Fairchild C123K Provider. The C-119 was known as the Flying Boxcar. It was used for cargo transport, paratrooper transport, mechanized equipment transport and it specialized in attacking targets on the Ho Chi Minh Trail. The B-52 known as the Stratofortress with model types A-H. They were very good at bombing enemy ground target in support of our ground troops. But don't get me wrong, the F-4C and the F-C, Phantom I and II does a damn good job too for support of our ground forces. The Hound Dog AGM-28B and the Quail ADM-20 also did their share of support. We got our Arc Light Boeing B-52D Stratofortress, the F-4 Phantom I and II, the Super Sabre F-100, the Douglas A-IE Skyraider, the Cessna YA-37A Dragonfly, the Martin EB-57B Canberra, and the Northrop YF-5A Skoshi Tiger."

Captain Johnson continues, "For 'search and rescue' and for the Trail we have the Douglas B-26K, the Sikorsky CH-3E, the Helio U-100 Super courier. The Bell UH-IP Iroquois, the beech QU-22B and the Kaman HH-43B. For Reconnaissance we used, Teledyne Ryan AQM-431 Firebee and the Douglas RB-66B destroyer. For command and control, we used the Lockheed EC-121D Constellation. The Navy has its equivalent known as the CH-46D Sea Knight helicopter. The USMC uses the CH 46E as an assault vehicle and as a troop transport. Now for the F4 Phantom fighter, we don't have privy to its sole use. Besides us in the U.S. Air Force, the Marines use it and the 'Thunderchiefs' and the Navy use it as the 'Blue Angeles.'"

Captain Richard Maslan begins to speak about the FAC's (Forward Air Controllers): I am not trying to brag but ours is the only job in the Air Force where a pilot can use his fighter, without a flight plan, go where we want at any altitude and at any speed. And we should get these privileges. We earned them. Our job is not easy and we have one of the highest mortality rates of any flying job in the war."

Captain Richard Maslan continues, "We Fast FAC's and FAC's try to make it good for you troops on the ground as we fly out every day in our single-engine F-100 Fast FACS at 400-450 knots at 4,500 feet but usually lower and jinking (zig-zagging/changing flight path) continuously every 5-7 seconds. We are exposed to gun-fire at the low altitudes (3,000 feet). It takes one second for the explosive rounds of an AAA (antiaircraft artillery) to reach us. We have to fly at a low altitude and at about 400 mph because the ground is a blur at speeds of 500 mph. We carry very little armament. We have two launching pods that contain seven white phosphorous marking rockets, (2 pods of 2.75 white phosphorous--Willie Peter) and two twenty mm cannons with 400 rounds of 20 mm ammunition that fire 3,000 rounds per minute. We carry 2x335 gallon fuel tanks smoke rockets. We mark areas on the ground for the fighter bombers of the U.S. Air Force with smoke rockets. We flew into Route Pack 1 and in Southern Laos called 'Commando Sabre Operation.' With our planes, we have a two seat F-100. I pilot and my back seat works the radios and carries the maps and a hand-held 35 mm camera with a telephoto lens. Our job is to spot and mark men and materials headed to South Vietnam. We try to stop the build-up of supplies—-trucks, tanks and armament. Most importantly we want to blow out the SAM's or the SA-2 missiles in this area. This build-up changes from day to day and each time we go out on a mission, we have to be briefed thoroughly on the new developments and the standing targets through maps and photos provided by intelligence. Much of this is information that we gather on our flights. But just before we head out into Laos and the North, we contact Airborne Battlefield Command and Control Center (ABCCC's) for last minute updated information. We will mark the target on our first cycle if a fighter is available. We can refuel over Laos or Thailand via the KC-135 tankers. If we see a downed aircraft, we will stay until an A-1 Sandy or a Jolly Green arrives for the rescue or if we see a target we will return again for a third or fourth cycle of the day. By the time I am done for the day, I have put in eight to ten hours in the air each day depending on my mission and my orders. If I see the enemy target, I come back to get him. While doing our job, we are faced with antiaircraft artillery (AAA) missiles, with those SA-2 SAM's (Surface-to-Air-Missals) and the 37 mm guns. This is our job to gather intelligence and to mark it. We mark it with a white phosphorous bomb--a smoke marker. If I see an enemy target,

I will mark it and take it out. We do RESCAP's (rescue attempts of downed airmen). This type of a rescue is very important to me. But one trip I got a radio call from a downed pilot. He was minutes from a garrison of Viet Cong. I called Sandys A-1s and Jolly Greens for Medivac. The downed pilot told me he could not walk because he had a broken leg but he was conscious. I figured we had to get to him before the Viet Cong got to him. The enemy was on his perimeter and we had to get to him first. 'The *downed pilot* radioed to me, *My jet was shot down and try to get me out of here now--as soon as you can.*' I radioed back and said, *Don't worry, help is on its way.* But no sooner had I said that and then I got hit by a 'barrage of flakbursts and 23 mm antiaircraft fire and one good hit nailed me straight with a 37 mm hit on my right wing and my fuel gage was showing empty'; so, it made me think that I got some hits on my tanks as well. But I did get his mark and radioed for a Medivac. I was able to pinpoint a location for extraction of the *downed pilot.* 'I radioed the *downed pilot* and told him to send a pencil-flare marker for the Jollys.' 'I egressed fast and as I looked over my left wing' I saw the enemy descending quickly upon our *downed pilot.* Jolly got in there but was under heavy enemy fire. 'The *downed pilot* radioed to the other pilots to *get the hell out.* The pilot threw him a life-line but he refused his tow for fear that the Jolly's safety would be compromised. He lost his life to save the life of the Jolly crew.' I thought to myself he could have grabbed onto his lifeline and in seconds he could have been pulled up and saved but it would have put the Jolly and its crew in harms' way. They did egress but very reluctantly so and not without some good cussing on the part of our *downed pilot* to tell us to *get the fuck out of here.* What a hero! He saved the Jolly and its crew as the barrage of incoming fire was unstoppable. ... And I made it back to base, 'landed with my crippled aircraft and I honestly don't know *how* or even *why* it stayed airborne' for as long as it did to take me to another day. As I walked away, I turned to look back over my left shoulder and looked toward the plane. I just saw a 'pile of badly twisted metal' sittin' on the tarmac behind me that had no resemblance to an aircraft and I wondered again, *how* and *why*? I asked this of myself, for <u>our bravest young man</u>—the *downed pilot*--who decided to take his own life--to save the lives of the rescue crew—his fellow Soldiers," [USAF Misty Pilots].

John says proudly, "I sure have a lot of respect for you and all your guys out there for putting your lives on-the-line for all of us." John changes the subject, "But the

66

important thing we must do is to get *intelligence*. Our
government is trying to get us more information about the
trail in 1964 Operation Trojan Horse got some photos on the
activity of the Trail by using U-2 planes to take
surveillance photos." And then there was Carmen Muscara a
young Army sergeant who received a commendation medal for
his role in interpreting photographs that showed that
Hanoi's troops were on the move but not much was done about
that information. I don't know what happened to that
information."

Buzz says, "With all of this information that we are
gathering, whatever happened to the White Paper that William
J. Jorden did for the State Department? Jorden was a former
journalist and expert on Vietnam. He discussed Hanoi's
support for the war and why Hanoi wanted to fight it? It was
an eight-part paper based on Hanoi's reasoning for the war.
Jorden also did research on the infiltration of men and
materials into Vietnam along the Trail coming in from the
surrounding border of Laos and Cambodia. But this important
and informative White Paper has sunk into oblivion. Jorden's
quote, 'movement by units occurs and appears to be on the
increase.' If enemy troops are on the increase, what makes
us think that the troops are going to slow down as they are
on the increase?"

[Jorden also said according to Historian John Prados
that Techepone is full of Viet Cong. He found the "presence
of the VPA 304th and 24th Divisions in the Route 9 Techepone
area" and the 325th Divisions just above the DMZ and
People's Army battalions in lower Laos. This White Paper
knew of enemy plans and presence. It was an excellent piece
of information about Hanoi's plan for the war. There was a
relative "lack of consensus that existed in 1961 which
became the first manifestation of Vietnam as a political
problem, one that mushroomed to threaten the very roots of
the American political system," (Prados).]

The convoy arrives where it takes the officers to their
destination in Phu Cat except for Lieutenant Sherman who
continues on to Qui Nhon and Pleiku with the convoy.
Peter's convoy continues-on in a different direction towards
the coast where the scenery starts to change.

The tan dry mountain plateaus change to deep palm
forests--the deep dark jungles that fringe glimmering rice
paddies—-truly God's beautiful gift to man. The Soldiers get
nearer to the coast and the landscape changes to tall
heavily forested dark green mountains that border an azure
blue sea. Then the rumbling a dark thunderous sky dares to

deliver its watery gift to the life below. And the ominous jungle takes issue with peace as it waits for life that offers itself so freely. The five Soldiers arrive back near Qui Nhon again and enter a cozy little tavern at the edge of the sea. Buzz then says, "Well it is not the Continental Palace in Saigon but it's just as good for me."

And the sea like a polished mirror glimmers in beauty. The five enter the tavern and greet the concierge at the front desk--a Vietnamese man gives them the keys to their room. The Soldiers walk to the edge of the sea and they attempt to forget.

Peter says looking out to the sea, "I may never see Sherry again ... maybe I won't." Peter then contradicts himself, "But I will. I know I will. I know I will be back with Sherry again and I will see my new son. You know why ... because I want it so badly. I want to go back home-- that's why!

Guy agrees, "You'll be back. You will see Sherry again because you have a new baby coming and your new baby must have a dad, so don't worry about that. You're here now to be a Soldier. Now you are a fine Soldier. Your time is not wasted here. You are learning a lot here in Vietnam--seeing this country. You can explain all of this to Sherry when you get back. But now ... I am sorry but ... we are here."

Peter agrees but he is not too sure about anything now and says, "Yeah, we are here." Guy responds with, "Everything will be fine--don't worry. You are a better Soldier than the rest of us. You will be back. Don't worry."

Peter explains to Guy, "Yeah but having a baby does not exclude me from becoming *statistic of war* here in Vietnam."

Guy reassures Peter, "Sherry needs you to take care of her and your new baby. You'll be O.K." Peter then says, "This place is a trap, Guy. How could our country do this to us? We are really just all *victims of circumstance.*" Guy says, "Yes, we are all *victims of circumstance* here in this war where so much has gone wrong for so many of these poor souls who have lost everything in this bottomless quagmire. Peter then asks, "But who really does care about any of this, anyway? The only one who really cares is Sherry." Buzz interrupts and says to Peter about this whole mess, "These *young naives* got themselves into this mess, but now realize that it is not quite what they thought it would be or what they thought they wanted of this war. And some did not want it at all. They were drafted! Man, I really *wantoutofit*. Ah, let's forget it and get some sleep."

68

The Troops go to their comfortable beds. The smell of the sea and the sound of waves crashing against the shore, attempts to lull their very tired minds and bodies to sleep but it cannot do that for Peter because Peter is still thinking. Peter is worried.

Buzz says sadly, "I feel sorry for all of these young Soldiers. They cannot get themselves out of here because they are committed. But as you said Peter, *who really cares?* Isn't this how this endless story goes--forever and forever, sobeit." Peter says surely, "We don't belong here."

Peter gets up to look out the window. He pulls back the curtain and says to Buzz as he looks out to the sea, "I wish that this was the ocean halfway across the world--on the Pacific Coast--by Malibu."

A tear could be seen rolling down Peter's cheek,

[A Tear Fell, Victor Wood, (Randolph Burton)]. Mc sees sadness here and tries to bring some humor for the moment, "This town looks just like the last one we were in and it ain't no West Coast, Californ-i-a, U.S.A.," [Johnny &Joe, Over the Mountain, Across the Sea].

Guy says, "With us--this story here--in this room could be repeated a-thousand-times-over by fellow Soldiers with *their melancholy dreams of home*." Buzz tries to cheer-up the group and says to Mc, "I know this ain't no Malibu but what were you expecting here in Vietnam--the Hollywood Bowl in *Californi* or some Heavenly Bodies, (Earl Thomas Conely, Elaine Lifton & Gloria Nissenson) at your doorstep--with some beautiful razzel-dazzle American sex goddess--peekin'-out 'round the corner just in-search for your ass? ... and your *oggling her down*--no. It ain't goina happen that way--no way Jose—not in this lifetime!"

[Everyone laughs.]

Peter lightens it up and jokes around some. Peter now asks with some humor, "You guys make me laugh with all this girl-stuff. Are you guys all still on the hunt for your perfect woman?" Mc answers, "No I have already found my true love here in Vietnam with CaLu. Now, I just have to find her again in all of this mess--in this hole. It should not be hard as this place does not have too much going-on for it anyway except that it's hell. And, yes, I want the Hollywood Bowl if it means getting out of this hell hole and back to the World." Guy changes the subject, "See those Phantoms way over there to the north sky? They are doing some bombing raids just past the DMZ Line."

Blazing fire with black smoke lash-out in furor with death and destruction for everything that lies in its path. The Phantoms have unleashed their weapons-of-destruction. Peter has such great pity for all those poor living souls nearby and underneath. The ground rumbles, moves and quakes with such ferocity that Peter says, "Absolutely nothing can survive under that path of terror. With each flash and rumble there is more and more dying. This is overkill. I do know one thing for sure, whoever lies in this path-of-terror and destruction is unprepared for it and is not expecting it. These poor souls are caught by total surprise! There is no time and there is no place for them to run. For those caught in it, I have such great pity on their poor trembling souls. These poor souls live the horror of it and feel agonizing death. Can't we have any pity on those who are caught in this path of terror? ... And for those who are not killed immediately by the bomb's impact, who are yet still living, will live their last moments of life in true horrible excruciating agonizing pain from massive bodily injuries--burnt and peeling flesh and broken bodies? How can this be done to so many in the name-of-freedom, *anywhere*? I guess it can. And more ... do we really want to be free and have to live like this? Maybe we do. I don't know."

Agreeing with Peter Buzz now says sadly, "No, they did not expect it to come; otherwise, they would have fled. They had no time to flee. They didn't stand a chance!"

Guy says now, "Yes, you are right. This is truly horrible. Everyone suffers here in this war. Nobody gets away. You know ... nobody gets away without suffering somehow—someway--here in this war. Who do we blame for this crazy mess? I don't know. You can't blame anyone in particular but you can blame everyone for allowing it!"

"Yes, it seems that way," says Peter.

Then these young Soldiers crash-out in this tavern near Qui Nhon by the sea, before they get to Pleiku, with no more to say or to think about, except for perhaps *the feel on the cheek* of a rolling tear or two—-sad!

Chapter 7

The Next Day--Political Discussions in a Tavern
Near Qui Nhon

The next day, Buzz wants to continue this political discussion about Vietnam and the Soldiers do so in a Tavern near Qui Nhon, "But we *can* blame our Government and our Commander-in Chief for this war," says Buzz.

Mc asks, "What can we do as a nation to fix this problem now? Maybe we should form a bipartisan Study Group to help us make an assessment about this war?"

Buzz then replies wisely with, "No as a nation we have made the decision about this war and we have agreed to it by voting our President into office. Yeah, President Truman said, 'The buck stops here.'" [They laugh.]

Peter expresses his ideas about Johnson's strategy, "President Johnson and advisors believe that this war can be won and our military commanders believe the same. President Johnson believes, in his heart that we are here in Vietnam to avoid a bigger and much more deadly confrontation with Russia and China."

Buzz asks sadly, "Yeah but this one is pretty deadly already is it not? But does President Johnson really believe that this war can be won as we are fighting it?"

Peter agreeing, "I guess he does. Each advisor working with President Johnson believes he has a winnable solution. It is all a terrible error in judgment on the part of his advisors--every one of them--especially the President."

Mc then asks Peter a very intriguing question, "But what about our Congress--could they not have stopped this madness? Our Congress backed the initiative for military action in March of 1967, in authorizing 4.5 billion for the war and why the Gulf of Tonkin Resolution in the first place?"

[And at the end of our war, Congress passed a law (Case-Church) that outlawed anymore military involvement in Southeast Asia ending the war.]

Buzz says most wisely, "Yeah, I hope that this war will not be in vain after so many people have died. But the war will be over when no one wants to fight anymore."

[As John Lennon of the Beatles said, "War is over if you want it."]

Guy then goes back to the subject of Generals, "Our military Generals want to fight this war because they believe we cannot lose it and that we'll win it for sure. And also many of our commanders did put a lot of blame on the South Vietnamese Commanders and their Soldiers for not fighting this war the way our Commanders thought it should be fought."

Buzz sympathizing for the South Vietnamese Army, "But who are we to dictate to the South Vietnamese military on how and when to fight this war when the South Vietnamese military know it cannot be won like this anyway?"

Peter responds to that with, "Yes, the South Vietnamese Commanders know this; but, our commanding officers are still making the South Vietnamese fight this war. We cannot blame the South Vietnamese military command nor can we blame their Soldiers." Mc then says, "Yeah but we cannot blame our commanders either because they truly and most foolishly believe they cannot lose this war no matter how it is fought." Peter says, "All of the options have been put out on the table and have been hashed and re-hashed over and over again by our commanders and our military advisors. The advisors in Washington had many theories on *winnable* strategies for this war. And many such strategies were presented because this is what they knew President Johnson wanted to hear."

Buzz says, "Yeah, but all the advice always fell on deaf ears because nobody had an agreement for a winnable strategy--no one had an agreement. Our military advisors were always jostling for position in Washington wanting to be first to present their winning military plans to the President. But truly the reality of mounting deaths with no ground gained was ignored by all."

[In the meantime the death toll eventually took 58,256 lives—KIA, 2,300 POW/MIA and 153,303 wounded all while deciding what to do with Vietnam. And add another 2,000,000 Vietnamese Soldiers both North and South who were killed in action and 2,000,000 civilians killed.]

Buzz then says, "*Everyone* loses when you lose life. No wonder they don't like us here." Mc says, "And let us not use the burnt-out excuse that this mess is part of the so called 'Cold War.' The 'Cold War' is cold--no fighting and no casualties--but our fighting here in Vietnam is very hot and the death is very real."

72

Buzz asks jokingly, "Have you ever heard the expression, *if it is not broken don't fix it?* We are fighting a war to prevent a future war from happening in this world. So *if it is not broken don't fix it.*" [Everyone laughs.]. We are fighting Russia and China in this 'Cold War' but with Vietnam we are fighting Vietnam's very real Civil War?" Peter comes in with some good reasoning, "In our own Civil War, we knew what we were fighting and why we were fighting. We fought brother against brother to save our Union and to purge it from a plague. It took a lot of prodding by President Abraham Lincoln to get his Military Generals to commence battle with each other. The same goes for the Vietnamese Commanders. Our military advisors really have to prod the South Vietnamese Generals to fight each other. I ask you who are we to interfere in their civil war because we want them to have our political ideologies?

"The Vietnamese people want a united country more than they want Democracy, Communism or any ideology. They are fighting brother against brother--not Democracy against Communism. Vietnam wants to be Vietnam."

Peter asks with a very sad question now, "Did our dead know or will they ever know what they had been fighting for or what they died for here in Vietnam? They are gone forever. But the war will still go on and no one knows why we are fighting. And also these Soldiers will never know anything ever again in their future that we-the-living still know and that we-the-living will always know about this war. Will our Soldiers ever know anything about anything ever again? The dead are now done with war. And one thing is for sure, the dead don't have to worry about death and dying anymore. It's over for them. As said by Plato, 'Only the dead have seen the end of war.'"

Guy then says, "And the dead do know one thing, 'it's better to be alive,'" [movie, <u>Full</u> <u>Metal</u> <u>Jacket</u>; screenplay authors, Gustav Hasford, Stanley Kubrick, and Michael Herr].

"Yes, that's for sure. It's better to be alive," adds Buzz lastly.

Chapter 8

Peter, Mc, Buzz, Guy, John, Think they
Know what this War is all About

Now the Soldiers hop into a Willis Jeep and drive on the way to Phu Bai. Peter takes the driver's seat. They get onto Highway 1 and try to head in direction to Phu Bai.

Peter asks, "Which way do we go?"

Buzz gives a rather cynical response, "There is only one way to go, and that is to take *the path of least mresistance*." [Everyone laughs.]. Mc says, "Or the path to hell." Guy says, "Hey if you want the path of least resistance, you are going in the wrong direction, man." [Everyone laughs.]

Mc adds his piece in agreement with Buzz this time, "Yeah, this time I agree with Buzz--*take the path of least resistance*. No just kidding with you. I know Vietnam is a scary place to be but I would rather be holding the hand of a beautiful woman. I'll tell ya' that. I want to find CaLu-- I think that's her name--and of course on the path of least resistance somewhere here in Vietnam. How am I going to find her again in this mess?"

Buzz then says to Mc, "Wake up man. You are not going to find her again in this mess—-not a living breathing chance of it. Sorry to burst-your-bubble. Don't you know where you are man?"

Mc answers "Yeah, man quite unfortunately, I do know where I am and I do know that it is not on the path of least resistance—-no man, it ain't."

Buzz continues, "No really, man, we are all in hell and not by our own choosing but by somebody else's choosing."

John lines up his side of the discussion with, "Don't blame someone else for your decision to come here. Blame it on the Bossa Nova," {ha, ha, ha].

Buzz now feels a bit irate with John's argument and feels that he wants to put John in his place, "You know, John, you have been real nice so far, real quiet and a real-nice-like guy, not opening your mouth about anything in all this mess; but, now I think that you are kinda opening your mouth just a little bit too much for my liking, man, so shut the f*ck up."

Guy sees a fight coming and responds to that with, "No let him alone, man. Can't you just see that we are all just *victims of circumstance* here, with no solution for nothin' anywhere around. Yes, we are all *victims of circumstance*."

Buzz is upset and responds crassly to John's ideas about war, "Well what do you want me to do about it, Guy—p*ss one?"

Peter sees a fight brewing between Buzz, John and Guy again.

Mc then tries to calm down Buzz a little bit with, "Come on you guys ... we are all in this mess together and we must try to get out of *all of this funk* together—and alive--somehow! Come on. Tomorrow is our day-of-reckoning and we will find out what this crazy war is all about so let us enjoy today. For today is *today*, yesterday was *yesterday* and tomorrow will be *tomorrow*."

Buzz cuts him off suddenly with, "Yeah, you are *the bright one*. Yeah, tomorrow will be tomorrow--and tomorrow I don't want to know about it, OK?"

Guy bursts in with, "Hey don't jump the gun on me now with this one. Everything will be OK. Not one of us knows shit about tomorrow. Tomorrow is our future. We can only hope that tomorrow will give us another tomorrow and that we can still have a future to hold on to."

Peter then says, "I will go to battle for my buddies and for my country to help us all."

John says, "Yes, this is our duty."

Buzz says, "Yeah, we are <u>our bravest young men</u> and don't you forget that."

Mc says, "Yes, we are the most powerful country on this planet and therefore we do these things for the betterment of humanity but if we are going to wield our power let us do it with reason and thought not with bold brash pride that gives us the false belief of a certain victory.

Peter stands up and says angrily, "Listen please understand one thing here and now. Our intentions for being here are totally honorable. We are neither 'bold nor brash' as so many accuse us!" Buzz says, "But now at last our government--our Senate--is questioning our purpose. We all have to know what we are fighting, don't we--finally? There is something very wrong here. Maybe it is I?" Guy thinks he really knows and wants to explain the problems with this war and why it is so hard to win it, "This is a war of attrition no matter which way you look at it because our enemy just keeps coming and coming. We can't go it alone. We'll run out. It's a world problem. Maybe the U.N. can help? Even President Johnson is just starting to see the light. He asked General Westmoreland, 'When we add divisions, can't the enemy add divisions ... where does it all end? At what point does the enemy ask for volunteers?' Westmoreland replied, 'That is a good question.'"

Buzz adds his comments about President Johnson's policies, "That quote did not sound too cool to me because it sounds like the decision-maker is not too sure about which policies to follow. No one really knows what the other one is doing. Civilians can't plan military strategy nor can the politicians. And there is no agreement in Washington. Peter then quotes, "Senator J. William Fulbright of the Foreign Relations Committee had a public hearing and said, 'Something ... is wrong or there would not be such a great dissent ... and whether or not the ultimate objective justifies the enormous sacrifice in lives and treasure.' Hey that is true. You know, Fulbright is really kinda right."

Guy says next, "I think this is a good idea. The Senate Armed Services Committee is having hearings concerning the influence of civilian advisors on military strategy planning."

Buzz says, "Maybe we need civilians in decision-making. Mc says, "Maybe there should not be a combination of politicians, military personal, civilians and advisors to the President. Buzz counters with, "Or better still we should just 'congressionally mandate a 10-member panel with civilians to consider what we could do to extricate the United States from [Vietnam] Iraq and Afghanistan including a phased troop withdrawal, a last ditch effort to stabilize the country and reaching out to U.S. adversaries in the region, including [Laos and Cambodia] Iran and Persia '... or somethin'. Can't we think of something?" Mc then says to that, "All of this should have been done a long time ago."

Peter changes the subject and says, "Yeah, but we just have to stop that trail that is going through the A Shau Valley and through Ap Bia."

Mc says, "The VPA has infiltrated 53,300 Soldiers and 86,000 North Vietnamese civilians across the borders and down the trails into South Vietnam. Our troops are outnumbered. We have tried everything to keep the enemy out. Robert McNamara knew we were in trouble back in 1963 with infiltration by land and sea. McNamara did not like the situation as it was unfolding in Vietnam and he believed the Communist would soon take control in Vietnam. McNamara said, 'The situation is very disturbing.' 'Current trends unless reversed in the next two or three months will lead to neutralization at best and more likely to a communist-controlled state.' Buzz then says angrily, "Then what the hell are we still doing here in Vietnam? Tell me--can anyone answer that question for me? Lives are being lost." Peter makes a statement, "Nothing is working to stop the flow of men and materials from coming-into Cambodia, Laos and North Vietnam and we just don't know enemy troops numbers."

Guy says, "So what has been decided as the plan to win?" Mc adds this important point, "They settled for 'graduated military pressure' and stuck with that plan until President Nixon came into office. This war is really about the restrictions that were placed on our troops throughout Southeast Asia. This is what this war is really all about."

Peter agrees, "Yes, I agree with you. That is what this war is all about--restrictions."

Mc adds again his important points about neutrality in Southeast Asia with Kennedy's plan, "Yeah, with our Neutrality Agreement, President Kennedy wanted Laos and Cambodia to be neutral so the people of Southeast Asia could have peace and self determination but in the end, it worked against us." Guy now says, "Now under President Johnson, we are prohibited from attacking MIG airbases in North Vietnam, so what the hell can we fight?" Peter says, "We tried many ideas to skirt around the issue of the Geneva Neutrality Accords. Neutral battlegrounds make it very difficult to fight a war like this. This neutrality stuff really messed us up for fighting war but I don't believe that Kennedy thought we would be fighting here in Vietnam anyway even though this neutrality idea was his." John says, "Yeah, President Kennedy wanted those neutrality accords because he thought it would make peace in Southeast Asia. But now these neutral areas are a stronghold for the enemy and it is used for infiltration of men and materials which is working against us." Mc adds, "President Kennedy was already setting up a plan with Secretary of Defense McNamara for U.S. troop withdrawal. But Kennedy did not live long enough to bring that to fruition."

Guy says, "But Governor Ronald Reagan had it right and said we should get out of Vietnam for this reason because '(...) too many qualified targets have been put off limits to bombing.'"

Peter then repeats this quote by John Prados, "Yes, but we are fighting this war is like we are 'firing at faces in the rain at night,'" [as said by John Prados, The Blood Road]. Peter then asks, "Have you ever tried to fire at faces in the rain at night, Guy?"

Buzz then answers, "Yeah, try it sometime—especially at night and of course in the rain, ha, ha, ha! You ain't going to hit shit in the rain at night--not in this lifetime. It ain't hap'nin'. So if you do fire at faces in the rain at night, it is either going to be the wrong target or you just ain't gonna hit anything. You can try real hard--all you want--but it ain't gonna happen any time too terribly soon--not in this lifetime or any other lifetime for that matter. As I said, with my *double* negatives, I always gotta be double *negatived* because I am *double negatived* anyway."

Mc wise-cracks in with, "Yeah, you got that one right. What's wrong with you bud—sounds to me like you are a *done deal*. You *are* truly double *negatived*. You have that one quite right." Buzz responds in anger to Mc, "Hey, what just bit you in the ass, crawled up it and died? Mc says, "It is none of your damn business? Buzz asks, "Was it CaLu?" Mc then takes a swing for Buzz's face and connects. Mc swings back and connects. Peter jumps in--stops the fight--and says, "Quite this shit. We gotta worry about this damn Trail. So ... way back before all of this death here in Vietnam, the New York Times reported that the U.S. is unable to stop the flow of North Vietnamese Soldiers and supplies coming into the South despite our extensive bombings---what happened?" Guy adds these ideas, "This war has become a stalemate. We have these choices: We can invade; we can do nothing or we can build an impenetrable barrier against infiltration of men and materials along the borders of South Vietnam. This barrier has been suggested by Robert McNamara and now it has become known in Washington, with the elites, as the *McNamara Line*. Various strategies were figured into possible plans for Vietnam: an invasion was one and the other was to create this barrier against infiltration as suggested by McNamara. This line was to cross the DMZ and Laos and run to the Thai border. This would be a technical solution combined with a military strategy but it never did come to a reality. The Joint Chiefs of Staff all agreed that this would not stop the infiltration." Buzz says, "No of coarse a wall won't work."

Peter adds his new idea about the war, "Then there is the weather war. We (U.S.A.) worked with the scientists at the Dow Chemical Corporation who helped to produce Agent Orange a chemical defoliant which may have helped to save many Soldiers lives but we really don't know. They also produced silver iodide to seed the clouds to make rain for the purpose of flooding; so, we can then therefore, flood out the enemy, make floods and mud him out. Then with an extra added boost, another chemical is laced to the clouds for a type of rain that creates a very slippery mud."

Buzz then says sarcastically, "You mean a real super slippery mud—no possible way! Yeah, real slippery mud for the Trail--sounds real good to me, man. But truly, how are they getting away with this? This sounds like a 'patchwork of muddled thinking that passed for strategy in Vietnam, everybody was right though everyone was wrong,'" [as said by John Prados, the Blood Road]. [Everyone laughs.]. Buzz repeats this quote, "Yes, truer words were never spoken about the strategy of this war—a--'patchwork of muddled thinking that passed for strategy in Vietnam, everybody was right though everyone was wrong.'" [They laugh.]

Mc says, "Yes, a lot of innocents are dying with a lot of *patchwork-of-muddled-thinking* going on!" Peter says to that, "Yes, you are right on that one, Mc." Mc then says most truly, "And you know who said it right ... Walter Cronkite said in the end 'The bloody experience of Vietnam is to end in a stalemate.' That's what's goina happen in this stinkin' war. And Mc then asks angrily, "Can't anyone stop this slaughter now?!" Guy then says a most provocative quote in a most determined voice, "We have to make up our minds on what to do now. Clark Clifford, U.S. Secretary of State said finally--and I mean finally--in March of 1968, 'The time has come to decide where we go from here.' He said there is 'no concept or overall plan anywhere in Washington for achieving victory in Vietnam.'" Buzz says, "So many have died with no plan!" Mc says, "The pity of all of this is the fact that we are not committed to this war doing little to stop enemy infiltration. Maybe let us get into the A Shau Valley for starters and on to that damn Hill 937 (Hamburger Hill) where we may be able to slow the flow?"

Buzz says, "And another problem: many times here in Vietnam after we won the ground that has been fought with blood, we give it back to our enemy."

Peter then says in agreement, "Yeah, it really doesn't make any sense to me and Time magazine put General Westmoreland on the cover and made him "Man of the Year"? I don't know. I don't think anybody knows." Buzz asks them, "Well, maybe he is in one way or another—-"Man of the Year"?

I don't know." Mc says, "But later Life magazine tried to give a balance of opinion by including photos 242 Americans killed the previous week on the battlefields of Vietnam. I don't know it all seems very confusing to everybody. But one thing for sure Soldiers are continuing to lose their lives here." Mc adds more ideas, "This country is not coordinating its efforts to formulate a sound strategy ... but our country must back-up our General and making him "Man of the Year" is not going to do it." John tries to set the record straight, "But really it is this, I 'sorta' agree with what Mc said before ... we need our country to back us up. How can our generals fight a war if their country is not behind them? General Curtis Le May always believed this." John adds some insight with another idea, "If our country is not behind us, how can we get troops needed to fight? Bottom line ... 'military intervention should enjoy congressional and public support.'" Buzz says most wisely to John's statement, "Or the best ... pull out of Vietnam, now!" Peter adds another idea, "We are fighting guerrilla warfare, and we should fight it with a counterinsurgency-type-of-strategy." {[And with another war in Afghanistan 2009--to fight counterinsurgency was "an all out counterinsurgency strategy, which includes an emphasis on protecting and wooing the [Vietnamese] Afghan population, and a more narrow focus on counterterrorism [anticommunism]}."

Peter changes the subject again to strategy, "The war in Vietnam does not allow us a front line of battle, but rather it is a perimeter defense. The United States is fighting a conventional war with front-line battle-strategy tactics. We must now try to fight this war in small groups that are maneuverable through helicopter insertion and extraction of troops in the dense jungles and on high steep mountain tops. Our troops had most of their major fire support from the air with the heavily armed Huey helicopter--Cobra and Hog--UH-1B Gunships, armed with 7.62 machine gun fire, 70 mm rockets and grenade launchers, F-4 Phantoms Jets and B-52 Stratofortress Bombers, F-105s and from the Landing Zones (bases) that fired 105 mm shells (M102s), M 101A1 (105), 105 SP (M108), 8 inch Howitzer (M 110s), 155 mm Howitzer (towed), from the bases, 175 mm guns (M 107s), M198s, Multiple Launch Rocket System (MLRS), TACFIRE and Battery Computer System (BCS) and then from ships off shore with Lance missiles also. We pumped 'em from every direction of the Landing Zone for up to several miles into the jungle or mountain-top areas at critical times in the battle. This did not have as much of an effect as it could have because of the steep incline of the mountains and the denseness of the jungles."

Buzz adds another idea on the war's strategy, "Yes but we have done this and even this does not deter the enemy or affect his maneuverability. However, fire support is not as effective as it could be on enemy troops. This is really a war of snipers, sappers, booby traps, ambushes, and pitched battles and retreats. Basically then with the enemy's strategy, we have decided to fight a conventional warfare on their guerrilla terms and most importantly, we insist on fighting it their way. That's it." Peter goes on with more of ideas, "Our commanders also insist on keeping the neutral battleground and fly zone areas off limits for our troops. How can we fight a war like this?

Guy then says, "The first part of the Vietnam War was primarily an 'insurrection by indigenous guerrilla forces and then later it has became more of an invasion by enemy regular army.' But General Westmoreland has his hands tied by politicians in Washington. We should let the Military Generals fight this war without interference from Washington. We gave Gen. Westmoreland a war he could not fight. 'The armed forces must be allowed to create the conditions for success.' The military is still going to fight it anyway. This is the mistake." Guy continues, "At one time in the war 'the heads of both the Marines and Air Force ... were vehemently opposed to ... large, mobile, search-and-destroy operations, wanting instead a kind of modified version of the enclave strategy first(...).' This way 'the allies could concentrate on protecting the lowlands and coastal regions.' And the enemy would take the highlands. General Westmoreland rejected that idea and 'believed passionately that the war had to be taken to the enemy, rather than waiting around for him to attack, and that it was better to do battle in the mountains than in the congested cities of the coastal plains.'" Peter says, "We should let the North Vietnamese Army attack us and get them on the offensive," (Douglas Pike, The Indochina Chronology).

Buzz has another idea, "Yeah, Westmoreland should tell Washington that we can't fight this war like this and that this war is not winnable for the Allies. But bottom line with all of this we need 'military goals that are clearly defined, decisive, attainable and sustainable.'" Then Buzz continues on with another idea about the A Shau Valley, "But Westmoreland has always been obsessed with taking control-- and rightly so--with the A Shau Valley because with North Vietnam, the A Shau Valley was the terminus for Base Area

611 which was a logistical stockpiling and stepping stone into South Vietnam."

They drive up Highway I and arrive at Phu Bai military base near the border of sea with flat landscape of dry scrub brush, dust with sand. As the Soldiers get to the base hundreds of sandbags are stacked everywhere around barracks and buildings. They are here now for their much deserved rest and continue their discussions on Vietnam and war in the base mess hall.

Guy now brings up his story on attrition, "Maybe we we're hoping that the strategy of attrition would work in our favor but it does not because the capacity of the enemy *to replace losses* is far higher than the losses that we the allies are able to inflict?"

"No, wait, stop--wait a minute--what you just said. We are not on the same wave length." And Buzz continues quite angrily and importantly, "You know, Pete, Guy, Mc ... I just don't like the sound of the last part of that statement you just made ... *to replace losses*?!"

Guy responds, "Yes Buzz but don't we have to get technical? I don't know." Buzz continues in anger, "What? Wait, wait, wait ... hold it, man ... *to replace losses* ... that is a strategy? It just does not sound too terribly right to me, man--*to replace losses?* How do you replace the loss of a parent's flesh and blood--the genes he carries and passes on for an eternity? A life born from their lives-- this one individual who would carry-on a part of the parent for an *eternity* for generations to come--and now he has just become a *replaced loss*--just a *replaced loss*? Is that all he is now--a *replaced loss*? Is that what all this boils down to--just a *replaced loss*? No, I just don't get it, Guy, John, Mc ... Pete. Is there something wrong with me? Life comes first! 'I don't want any part of this anymore. I choose human life over war, militarism, imperialism,'" [J. Bordeleau U.S. Veteran Iraq-Afghanistan War 2012].

Pete then drops his head down low, shakes his head from side to side with great sadness; he says and then quotes: "No man--nothing--nothing--can ever replace an individual--a life. 'War is a profane thing,'" [U.S. General Norman Schwarzkopf].

Chapter 9

**They Still Think they Know what this War is
All About and Mc Finds Her Again in Vietnam**

Joel returns from somewhere and says, "Hey men what's
wrong--lighten-up your load--you look like you just lost
your mother." Buzz says, "Well we all lost a little bit of
something here in Vietnam. Maybe we also lost a part of
ourselves. Look at all this mess this way. None of us asked
to be born but we were. We just come into this world to
perform our biological functions and hopefully we can *think-
a-little* and then we're goners forever." Guy says, "We don't
have to do this. We can speak-out against this war or any
war that we don't feel is right as did Bertrand Russell. He
did right with his mock-war-crimes tribunal in Stockholm,
Sweden to condemn us (U.S.A.). This brought attention to the
horror here. Our government told us *half-truths* and lies.
People were suspect about the outcome in Vietnam. News
reporters had an idea that we were being lied to as with G.
McArthur and Maureen Dunn. False numbers were reported with
enemy war dead. Also a lower casualty rate was being
reported for the friendly forces. It is like Aeschylus said,
'In war truth is the first casualty.' 'The Johnson
Administration had systematically lied to the public and to
Congress by expanding the war and lying about the subject of
transcendent national interests and significance,' [as said
Pentagon Papers, 1945-'67, "Pentagon Papers," Wikipedia.
Org. 14 Dec. 2010]. It is like we are winning one day and
loosing the next. General Abrams in one of his daily
situation reports to Saigon said, 'The enemy has the
determination and intention but is not capable at this time
to conduct sustained, all out *win or die* attacks on friendly
forces. The enemy is particularly vulnerable to AVRN sweep
operations, air strikes and detection by VR (visual
reconnaissance).' It all sounds a little bit sorta', kinda'
like *spin-doctoring* to me. I really don't know what's up."
Guy now says to his friends, "If you can figure this one
out, you are a better man than I. I don't know what is going
on here. I don't think anyone does."

Mc then wise-cracks-in with, "Yeah, none of us really
knows what is going on. All we know is that we have to fight
when-and-where we are told." Buzz then replies finally to
Mc's remarks, "You know somethin' I really wish I knew but I
don't." Peter quotes some good words of Karl Kraus, Austrian
writer and journalist (1874-1936), "'How is the world ruled

and how do wars start? Diplomats tell lies to journalists and then believe what they read.'"

Buzz clarifies the issue, "No you can't blame anybody in particular journalists, diplomats, politicians, military professionals, but you can blame everyone collectively for doing nothing." Peter says, "Yeah, I see you are right. I guess you can blame everyone together." Buzz changes the subject, "Yes, I have noticed your wording, Guy; if the reference has a negative inference to it then the wording becomes 'the' government--not 'our' government and the same with 'our' President. If it is a negative reference, we say 'the President'--not President Johnson or not 'our' President. Our country—-the U.S.A.-- will not attach *our* to a name of any negative reference about this war. It makes us seem less culpable with--'the government' and 'the President,' rather than *our* President or *our* Government. Why can't we accept our mistakes, blame ourselves, blame the people responsible, blame our government for having made a mistake and proudly say, *our* country--*our* government, *our* president?" Peter explains why we do this, "This is *the human condition*—-not necessarily *the American condition*—-but the human condition, I believe."

Mc asks a good question now, "Thus, can we really blame ourselves then for this horrible mistake in Vietnam? I believe we can."

Peter adds more ideas and clarifies this issue, "No bottom line, we do not want to blame ourselves but we should. There has been a lot of death because of the many lies propagated about this war. The real answer now lies with our future actions--with our future wars—-for our future generations to come. We just can't do this again. Even the Joint Chiefs of Staff had an idea of the infiltration coming through into South Vietnam; and, yeah, the Military Assistance Command (MACV) headed by General Westmoreland—-previously held by Williams, McGarr, Timmer, and later by General C. Abrams. They knew of the enemy infiltration throughout most all of this war. And the Central Intelligence Agency (CIA) was aware of the infiltration as well. The National Security Agency, the Army Military Intelligence, The Defense Intelligence Agency (DIA) and the Studies and Observation Group (MAC-SOG), the indigenous troops--the Civilian Irregular Defense Groups (CIDG's) which were the mobile strike forces of the Montagnard program—(strikers), the United States Information Agency and the Agency for International Development that helped aid South Vietnam are just some organizations that knew about what was going on in this war. Our government knew of the enemy infiltration into South Vietnam and said, 'There was nothing unusual or ominous about the NVA's re-supply efforts. Soldiers were moving South and most of the Soldiers were to replace *combat losses* of the past year.'"

Peter says, "Yeah, *combat losses* that was the excuse. We too (U.S.) had to replace our *combat losses* so we have the draft!" Buzz cuts-off Peter sharply as he is pissed off again. Buzz yells very angrily again on the subject of *combat loss* and most rightfully so. "What? What--*replaced loss*? Don't tell me we are going to go through this again. Is this what this shit all *boils down to* for mankind--his destiny for this world? We are nothing more than *combat losses*?! Aren't we each an individual with a mind and a soul with feelings and now we come here to this Vietnam--get killed--and become a *combat loss*--what--a *combat loss*?

Buzz turns to look at Peter in the face and asks, "Would you like being labeled a *combat loss*, Peter? If you should lose your life here in Vietnam, you would then become just a *combat loss*--just a damn statistic-of-war--of this war. Aren't we all living beings with feelings, hopes, wants, dreams, desires and who knows the meaning of the 'me'--the importance of 'me'--our souls--ourselves--and then we become a *combat loss*? Am I Sp4c. Buzz Jenkins Brule, *combat loss*--that's my name? Would that be a part of my epitaph--a *combat loss*? Should I say more--need I have to say anymore? Peter feels so sad about this and hangs his head down low and answers, "No." Buzz continues, "I'm a combat loss?! But ... if I do become a *combat loss* ... I can accept it for a cause for war--for a true cause. I can hang with that."

John disagrees somewhat, "If you are a Combat Soldier, and you are killed in battle then, therefore, you become a *combat loss*. That is just the way it is. It should not be but it is."

Peter answers to that with, "No. Life is life! Life is the utmost importance--anywhere, anytime, anyhow!!"

Mc now tries to calm-down Buzz who is very angry, "Listen, Buzz, you know we are not the only ones in this world who thinks this way. So don't go running off to look for some shoulder to cry on because there are no shoulders to cry on. Our enemy is General Vo Nguyen Giap who is a famous North Vietnamese General and who fought the French and now the U.S. He won the battle against the French at Dien Bien Phu in 1954. He did not think much about the loss of life but just victory for freedom. He said 'What are 45,000 for a battle? In war death doesn't count.'"

Buzz then says sarcastically, "Yeah, 45,000 in battle does not count when fighting for freedom, right? Isn't that what this war is all about––fighting for freedom?"

Peter then says again this most remarkable quote as said by Otto Von Bismarck, 'Anyone who has ever looked into the glazed eyes of a Soldier dying on the battlefield will think hard before starting a war.' Think about his eyes––yes his eyes! But maybe it is ... for a real cause—our freedom we will fight. But ... do you know ... looking into his eyes must be a horribly hard thing to do!"

Buzz then says, "Yes, you are right but not too many of us *Homo Sapiens* think like you do, Peter, or *Homo Erectus*. The meaning of the 'Erectus part' in the name does not represent us––our species--too terribly well––sorry to mention. As a species ... are we really *erect* in the true sense of the meaning *erect*? I wonder."

Then Buzz says as said by Mark Twain, "'Man is the only animal that deals in that atrocity of atrocities, war. He is the only one that gathers his brethren about him and goes forth in cold blood and calm pulse to exterminate his kind. He is the only animal that for sordid wages will march out ... and help to slaughter strangers of his own species who have done him no harm and with whom he has no quarrel ... and in the intervals between campaigns he washes the blood off his hands and works for the universal brotherhood of man—with his mouth.'"

Peter adds, "Oh, and by the way for our information guys ... I want you to know, 'Only two groups of animals men and ants, indulge in highly organized mass warfare,'" [said by Charles M. Maskins]. Buzz responds, "What a comparison?"

Then Mc asks a couple of intriguing questions, "Yes, Buzz, for once I agree with you. And Mark Twain is right on that--totally. Our species makes war and counts its casualties as *combat losses*. War is death, dying and being killed and yes it is a *combat loss* to anyone else except for that soldier who lost his life. What is it to him? What would he call his own loss of his life in an unnecessary war?" Peter answers sadly, "If he does not know then he will never know." Buzz says then so truly, "Any war is a horrific war whether it is a war that must be fought or whether it is an unnecessary war." Then Mc gives a quote from an eye witness on the horrors of war in Vietnam with this description of only one battle from the Easter Offensive--

the destruction of an American firebase--from a South
Vietnamese troop who lived to tell about it, 'the North
Vietnamese massed for the attack. The whole battlefield
roared-up.'" Peter adds another quote from an eye witness—a
first hand account--from a North Vietnamese officer,
'Barrage after barrage of artillery descended on [the South
Vietnamese]. The whole base quacked. Enemy artillery sites
were buried in smoke and flames. Clouds of smoke rose like
mushrooms.' This is another description from a diary of a
North Vietnamese Soldier, 'The hour for action has struck.
The boom of our artillery shakes jungles and hills. Shells
wiz over our heads. After a thirty-minute barrage, all enemy
guns emplacements on Highway 9 are paralyzed. Before us,
Firebase Dong Toan [Firebase Sarg] is engulfed in flames.
Four helicopters turn up: Two are immediately shot down and
the rest hastily turn tails. B-52s came for saturation
bombing all around the base. But our shelling becomes only
fiercer.'"

Buzz changes the subject, "But in November of 1967
General Westmoreland, Ambassador Bunker and President
Johnson told the American people on public T. V. that
'progress is being made.' Yeah, it does not sound like
progress is being made for anybody in war. What are these
guys thinking saying this to the American people—'progress
is being made?'" Peter responds with, "I quite sincerely do
not know how they can say *progress is being made*. It makes
no sense to me. But certainly it did make sense to some
Americans reading about this and watching this on TV at that
time. But unfortunately many Americans accepted this fact. I
think some people were fooled and they believed what they
heard." Peter says, "General Westmoreland did not report the
facts as they should have been reported in November 21,
1967, to news reporters, 'I am absolutely certain that
whereas in 1965 the enemy was winning, today he is certainly
loosing.' And [as said by President G. W. Bush with the U.S.
war in Iraq, 2006], 'Absolutely we're winning.' 'We're not
winning. We're not losing.'"

Buzz then says, "Double talk—isn't this when *one word*
has several meanings. Peter says, "No it's when words have
no meaning?" Buzz agrees and now discusses the importance of
lives, "I don't know but is there something wrong with me?
What is this? I don't like to be talked to--or fooled this
way--believe it or not--especially to the tune of over
58,000 lives gone in Vietnam."

[And in another war by 2013 6,374 lives for Iraq and
Afghanistan wars called Operation Iraqi Freedom and

Operation Enduring Freedom. 'Will (...) lessons be remembered 15 or 20 years from now? If history is a guide, don't count on it.' (Doyle McManus, reporter, LA Times, 2013)].

Buzz continues, "What is going on? And many billions of bucks later to boot ... and for what? It really ain't too terribly cool ... yeah ... believe it or not!" Mc wisecracks with, "But is this all gibberish talk, or are we all just discombobulated somehow?" Buzz then says. "No, I don't know." And Buzz asks, "Was he misleading the American people… or himself?" Can't our Congress figure this out-- that this war is not working? It is their responsibility. How 'certainly' is our enemy loosing? And how certainly are we winning? Congress needs to take a look at some of this information sometime." Mc says most sincerely, "No one knows anything about anything in Washington or in Vietnam. As Senator James W. Fulbright said about this war, 'The lesson I learned from Vietnam is not to trust government statements.'"

Now they hop in their jeep on their way to base.

Peter continues this conversation with, "Better still President Lyndon Johnson said in July 1966, 'I seek no wider war.'" Mc then added, "Yeah what is he talking about?"

Buzz says, "We knew his war was already wide enough. I think part of this mistake began when we gave full military powers to President Johnson to wage an undeclared war in Vietnam but even our National Security Council recommended bombing North Vietnam. I don't know." Peter says, "I know the Commander-in-Chief and our Congress have the power to declare war and to wage war." Mc says, "And all at a cost of two million dollars per day for this 'reckless, feckless misadventure,'" [as said by military correspondent, Joe Galloway, for Knight Ridder Press of President G. W. Bush with the U.S. War in Iraq].

Buzz emphasizes truly, "And the lives ... and the lives... "And then Guy talks about President Johnson's speech he gave to Congress, "President Johnson said in January 12, 1966 in the State of the Union Address, 'Yet finally, war is always the same. It is young men who are dying in the fullness of their promise. It is trying to kill a man that you do not even know well enough to hate ..., therefore to know war is to know that there is still madness in the world.'"

Buzz smartly adds, "I don't care if I ever have to hate my enemy enough to kill him. That is not the point. Whether we hate him or not; that's not the point. I can see there is enough madness in this world—-yes. But we don't have to hate to kill an enemy Soldier. We just have to know *why* we kill. We never become desensitized to killing. But the reality is ... the more we kill the harder it is to kill ... because we think. All I know is that we are killing and being killed left-and-right. Isn't that enough to know?" And Guy continues with this question, "And what was President Johnson referring to when he wrote a speech like this, with this quote ... 'dying in the fullness of their promise?'" Buzz explains the LBJ-quote further, "Yeah, but what was on our countryman's minds when they heard a speech like this and did nothing about it? Yes, 'dying in the fullness of their promise' and with no ground gained ... it is absolutely inexcusable! Stop this slaughter, now! I sincerely and quite honestly cannot imagine—-'young men are dying in the fullness of their promise'--for what? And do we know why? No, but we must! So many disagree with the American Veteran who had the guts to speak out against this slaughter in this war? Is there something wrong with my reasoning here? What is our country thinking? We must speak out against this war. As Martin Luther King Jr. said in his speech, Beyond Vietnam 'There comes a time when silence is betrayal.' Our country must speak out."

Then Guy decides to quote a part of President Johnson's speech to make another point, "But Johnson did believe he was doing right with Vietnam. President Johnson truly appreciates the Soldier's sacrifice and what he is doing in this war and said 'because brave men were willing to risk their lives for the nation's security and braver men have never lived than those who carry our colors in Vietnam this very hour.' President Johnson believes in his heart that his decision to stay and fight in Vietnam with *our bravest young men* is the right decision for America. I don't think he wants this war either. Maybe we give too much power to our President? Buzz adds, "Yeah, I guess so. We are here in Vietnam on the assumption that this war is being fought for our national security and for freedom in this world." John gives his own reasoning for fighting, "As Americans we have to ask ourselves *is this war fought for freedom and justice in this world? And I will tell you, yes, it is for freedom and for ... Vietnam.* Our Soldier is fighting for justice and freedom. This is why he fights."

Buzz says, "This is why he fights. But is this why he dies?" John then says, "Yes, he fights and dies for justice and freedom." Buzz then brings in another idea, "No, maybe you are wrong. Maybe it is the allure of war that drives courageous young men to war? As a Soldier said most truly with this most beautiful quote, 'And God help me when this war ends trust me, they all do end, I truly feel a part of me will die,'" [as said by a Soldier in the movie Under Heavy Fire].

Peter agrees, "Yes, there will always be someone who wants to fight war. The Soldier will fight if he thinks it is right. John says, "President Johnson believes that we must remain in Vietnam to fight for freedom and rid the world of Communism. The war in Vietnam is ongoing and will never end even if we do withdraw from Vietnam because Communism and anything-against-us [terrorism] is an ongoing threat to the Free World." Buzz quite defiantly and quite smartly says to that, "Well if we withdrew, the war would end for us—-the Soldier--that's for damn sure." Mc chimes in with, "Yeah, I guess you're right Buzz ... it would end for the Soldier."

Guy says, "President Johnson believes that he is making the right decision to fight in Vietnam. In January 1967, in another State of the Union Address before Congress President Johnson declares 'We will stand firm.'"

Buzz switches back with sarcasm, "Yes, everybody 'stands firm' when it is somebody else's life on- the-line."

John then changes the subject, "But I do truly believe that it is a tragedy that this country does not allow Nixon to bomb aggressively in enemy territory as he wants to do. When the United States is at war, we should fight with our mightiest—our best; otherwise, we will lose the war. And President Johnson believes that he is doing the right thing by 'standing firm' in this 'conflict'. John continues with an excellent idea—-perhaps a solution, "Yes, American Air Force General Curtis LeMay said it right and he said 'My solution to the problem would be to tell them frankly that they've got to draw in their horns and stop their aggression or we're going to bomb them back into the Stone Age.' Maybe this is the only way?" John says again, "But Johnson must be more aggressive to win this conflict quickly. Peter says, "Yes we must win this war quickly. It has to be quickly. As James Madison said "'No nation could preserve its freedom in the mists of continual warfare.' And that makes a lot of sense to me."

But then Buzz suddenly yells loudly in John's face, "Don't ever let me hear you call this horrible massacre a conflict, again. It is not a conflict or an experience--not with over 58,000 lives lost. It is a war! Men are dying--being butchered out there--and you call this a *conflict* with the length of the war and the amount of dead; it is a war! How many have to die to make this a war? Please give this war the respect and call it a war."

Mc then says, "The same thing happened with the Korean War. 'Not until long afterward was it even dignified by the name of war—-the governmental euphemism was Korean conflict,'" [Fehrenbach].

Buzz is pissed-off at John and asks, "This ain't no conflict. You talk about conflicts because you really don't know what you are talking about."

Guy agrees, "Yes, we should stop calling this war a conflict."

John changes the subject now, "Yeah, but President Nixon did it right by bombing Laos and Cambodia and allowing our ground troops to engage there, even though it was neutral territory. For the sake of *our bravest young men*, let us fight in North Vietnam, Cambodia, Laos or wherever we must commit ourselves to win and use our best strategy and arsenal which is our airpower! Let's do this war right if we are going to fight it. Let's win!" John quotes, "Well, with Nixon, this is the way the war should be fought for our Soldier. As President Ronald Reagan said, 'We should declare war on North Vietnam. We could pave the whole country and put parking strips on it, and still be home by Christmas.'"

Truman made this decision once--as horrific as it was. And aerial bombardment is a Soldier's best friend but I don't want bombing either. Civilians suffer horribly! As said by Prime Minister Sir Winston Churchill, 'It is probable that future wars will be conducted by a special class, The Air Force, as was by the armored knights of the Middle Ages.'"

Mc says, "But we all suffer in war. It is horrific that we as a nation have to praise bombing that is so wrong. But President Harry Truman said 'The Atom Bomb was no great decision. It was merely another powerful weapon in the arsenal of righteousness.'"

Buzz then says, "President Truman was talking self-defense, but it is truly a sad-state-of-affairs ... that mankind has to resort to the worst brutality to fight war. I don't know. None of this makes any sense to me. It is like looking at a face without a nose on it."

And Mc says most wisely, "But it had to be done."

Peter states in agreement, "Yes, it's truly horrible."

Mc says most truly, "President Truman took the defensive and the defensive in this case was righteous only because it ended the war that Japan had begun. It was terrible that we—-the U.S.A.--had to use the Atomic Bomb because we had to end the war with Japan."

Buzz adds, "And we did it. It was defensive."

Peter says, "But for us guys ... all of this was our world while we were lying in our mother's wombs and we just didn't know. With WWII, we had just come into a time which had no precedence in the annals of human history. We did not know as the *little ones*. Our innocence was our world of *little kids' games*, *make believe*, and *let's pretend times*. We just didn't know."

Buzz believes, "But now for these people here it is for their political beliefs and freedom. These people will fight for principle to be united if this is what they believe they have to resolve. They have to do it for themselves--to be a united Vietnam. We did it with our own Civil War. Maybe there can be a better solution? Yes but we are here now in Vietnam fighting their civil war."

Guy agrees and then continues his story about President Nixon's and President Johnson's war policies, "President Johnson was very careful not to bomb certain targets in neutral territory. He did not want to confront China especially with the bombing certain *off-limits* targets in Vietnam. Nixon however, opted to ignore the neutrality agreement and bombed neutral territory." Guy brings-up other ideas of another great statesman, Senator Robert Kennedy, with his quote, "Robert Kennedy said about President Johnson's course-of-action with the Vietnam War, 'The U.S. may be headed on a road from which there is no turning back, a road that leads to catastrophe for all mankind.'"

Buzz adds this quote again "Senator Kennedy is right-- it is a catastrophe. With man's destruction in an unnecessary war; it is the destruction for all of mankind." Peter says most appropriately with this quote, "We can't lose our lives to try to save the world *for freedom* because what may *be freedom* for me may not *be freedom* for you. It is not practical for us to dictate *our freedom* to the World. But truly the reality of it is ... it looks like we are fighting a war that does not have to be fought. As Walter Lippmann said 'The time has come that we stop beating our heads against stone walls under the illusion that we have been appointed policeman to the world.' *Nuf* said."

Buzz says, "We are not on the same wave length, John. We should not be here in-the-first-place to fight an unnecessary war, period." John interrupts Buzz, "But since we are here-in-the-first-place, let us kick ass and we will kick ass to show the entire world that no one can kick Uncle Sam's ass. We will prove a point."

Then Peter says quite appropriately, "But what point?"

Buzz says, "John does not know the point. But in the end, none of us really knows the point, do we? Because if we did, we would not be here in the first place, would we?"

John changes the subject and wants to piss-off Buzz somehow and asks him quite appropriately, "With all of your KP duty, how many dirty pans did you have to scrub today?"

Buzz shoots back an equally appropriate comment, "Oh don't you worry your pretty little head about it. The pans only get half done. I don't scrub the ass ends of my pans."

John mockingly says, "Maybe that is your problem. Maybe you should start cleaning more of the ass ends of your pans." [Everyone laughs.]

Buzz says, "Yeah, I will care about my 'ass ends' if you shut that mouth on your face."

John continues crassly and is very pissed off with Buzz right now, "Yeah, that's a good deal. I'll shut the mouth on my face if you take care of your ass ends of your pans. And also, I don't want to hear anymore of your mouth either, or see much more of it--around here--deal?"

Buzz says, "Yeah, but for you--your mouth and your ass-ends are really one-and-the-same, are they not?" [Everyone laughs.]. John has now calmed down a lot and changes the subject again, "This is not as funny as you think it is. We are all going out at 0500 tomorrow for our briefing! Let's be ready. We have a mission waitin' for us--a mission to kick some ass--and this is all you talk about--this shit? Let's go on our mission. Let's go kick-a-few. That is my philosophy—-always has been--always will be." Mc then comes in with a few words, "With your philosophy, John--the big shot--what do you mean *kick-a-few*? How do you kick only *a few*? I ain't kickin' the ass of just *a few*--believe me. That is not going to win this war. If I'm kickin', it's going to be an entire regiment, man, and if that ain't enough, I'll get out there and go kick a lot more if that is what it takes. Let's kick the hell out of 'em."

Peter now says, "But we gotta know what we are kickin' I mean how many are we kickin.' There's a whole lotta kickin' goin' on. And, yeah, not knowing that can destroy us. That is a bummer." John says to Mc and Peter, "Hey, listen, men, this all sounds to me like one big excuse not to fight and I am not ready to go off on some other tangent with you guys again, now. I have had enough of your melancholy blues about the I-don't-want-to-fight shit, OK man? I've had enough! So shut your face and quit your blubbering and your bullshit."

Mc says, "But wait, man, listen. We can't fight with each other anymore like this. We have a very real enemy out there who means business on the battlefield. This is not too cool because it is not going happen like our troops think it is. Our troops have to be ready and need support like with armored support. Some of these Armored Tanks or ACAV (Armored Assault Vehicles), Gun Trucks, a Quad 50 and a Duster are something. I mean these guys will back us up out there too and kick some ass. Listen to some of these names. They mean business. It is not too cool for our enemy to have to deal with those guys. These guys is what our enemy has waitin' for him and with these names--'Kontiki, Mad Man, Hired Killers, American Breed, A Whole Lotta Lead, Eve of Destruction, Good Luck Charm, The Widow Maker, The End, The Peace Maker and the Undertaker's Agent.' These Soldiers say, 'Find the bastards, then pile on.'"

John says, "Our Armored Infantry knew what they were doing with their armor. The North Vietnamese Army had massed tanks and heavy artillery. [As said by historian Dale Andrade], '(...) they handled them poorly with little coordination between armor and infantry.'"

Mc says, "I don't know but with those names it kinda' sounds like a game. But this is not a game? Our guys are fighting hard for their country--no more--no less!"

Buzz then says quite appropriately, "The problem is we just can't tell the difference between a game and dying?"

Peter then says "Hey, you are O.K., man, you said it right, none of us can tell the difference but we must try. Let us get ready for tomorrow."

John answers to that, "We just have to fight together and we have to take this fight to the *bad guys.*"

Buzz starts in again with more wise cracks, "Oh the *bad guys.* Who are the *bad guys*? How do you know they are *bad*? So assuming that they are the *bad guys*, does that then therefore, make us the *good guys*?

95

John quite appropriately bursts in with, "And yeah, I can call them the *bad guys* when they kill my buddy."

Buzz says, "But bottom line, it is unfair to draft a man, make him a soldier, and let him die when he is not too sure about what he is dying for ... or for a *war that does not have to be fought*. I mean Daniel Webster said it right with his speech at the House of Representatives in January 14, 1814, 'A free government with an uncontrolled power of military conscription is the most ridiculous and abominable contradiction and nonsense that ever entered into the head of men.' *Sobeit*."

Mc chimes in with, "Don't worry about *bottom lines*, or *bottom anything*, Buzz. This may be our last night anywhere."

John says, "No, it is not. We will make it back home--always have--always will--so shut your damn face."

Guy changes this conversation and says, "Well, this is our last day out on the town so let us get the hell out of here and go somewhere—-anywhere now. Tomorrow we have to report for a military briefing at COHQ for our mission so hit the road. Let's go."

Peter continues to drive.

Mc suddenly yells to Peter, "Stop. Stop the jeep here."

Peter says, "What the hell do you want, Mc?"

Mc says, "Look there's my girl! I met her there in that bar way back in Qui Nhon--remember? Remember the lovely thing I found there?"

Peter says, "Oh yeah, I do. You were in love. I mean you are in love."

Mc then yells above the sounds of bombs hitting just across the road and where a mass of pedestrians and troops are running fast from the bombing of the Phantom Jets.

Mc yells, "There she is." And Mc suddenly jumps out of the jeep and runs to a crowd of people and singles out this beautiful young woman. The two run into each other's open arms.

CaLu says with joy, "Oh I am so happy to see you. I never thought I would ever find you here again. I am so happy to see you."

Mc says, "I never imagined that I would ever find you here again in all of this madness. I have been looking for you forever ... ever since Qui Nhon. I haven't stopped looking for you--for a minute. Oh, beautiful one. I can't believe we are here together in each other's arms. Let's go somewhere together. Where are you going?" She replies, "I don't know--wherever you are going." Mc says, "Then, hop into my jeep here and let's go somewhere--anywhere--wherever you want to be alone with you. What is your name—like the song What's Your Name, Don &Juan (Claude Johnson, Roland Trone), [Big Top Records]. What do they call you--CaLu?" She says, "My name is CaLu Dejoui." He says, "Are you from around here?" She says, "No, I am from Qui Nhon--where we met. My Mom is Vietnamese; my Dad is French." Mc then asks CaLu ... unexpectedly ... and romantically, "If I Said You Had a Beautiful Body would you hold it against me?" (Bellamy Brothers), (David Bellamy), [Warner Bros]. CaLu is a beautiful woman with long straight black hair. She is petite of medium height. She has a Caucasian Asian nose—straight bridge and round tip—with beautiful bow-lips and Asian eyes. Mc then says, "I never thought I would see you somewhere here in this place--somehow again--in this terrible war."

CaLu explains, "This war is tearing our families apart. This war is leaving children without mothers and fathers to care for them. Our orphanages are overflowing with no more room to take in anymore. There is too much misery and suffering. Children are crying for their dead mothers; husbands crying for their dead wives and wives are left alone with families to rear by themselves. There isn't anybody here who has not been touched by this horrible war. Everyone is grief-stricken with overwhelming sadness. We cry and we cry. We all cry. Everyone is hurting desperately. We were happy here with our lives before the French came--and the Americans and the Communists. Vietnam has been fighting since the French came. With the French it was ten years of warfare. And now with the Americans, there's more misery and more war. We just can't do it anymore. What will it take to stop this? Vietnam belonged to the French, and now it belongs to the Americans and the Communists. This is my birth place--my homeland--but all I can think about is leaving this tragic country to get away from the terror and so much death. There is never any end to this fighting. My dad and my mom have seen so much death and misery with the French occupation and the French Indochinese War. Life can't be life here. There's never a smile and I can't be happy. CaLu continues her sad story, "My dream is that this horror will end soon. But now death and destruction is a way of life for us all."

Mc says, "Yes, I know. I hate this war. We don't belong here. If I had it in my power to end this war tomorrow I would-—somehow."

She says with sincerity and admiration, "But I never thought that I would ever see you again--ever again. I know that I am so happy now to see such a beautiful American Soldier like you." She asks him, "What is your name?" He replies, "Mc ... Chris Davison." Oh you are so American ... Davison! I love you ... American."

She grabs his hand hard with earnest and says let us go somewhere together ... please."

Mc sings her a song, Since I Met You Baby, (Ivory Jo Hunter): *Since I met you baby my whole life has changed*, *Since I met you baby my whole life has changed*, [Atlantic, Quality, Columbia].

CaLu begging with desperation, "Now, I am afraid for you--for your life, here in this war. I don't want you to get killed in this war. I don't want to lose you. I won't be able ... I can't live without you."

Mc now yells to Peter, "Stop. Drop us off somewhere—anywhere--where we can be alone together."

Within the next twenty minutes they find themselves alone together in a room somewhere in Saigon in pure happiness. He kisses her passionately. She undresses and he caresses her body with all the love in his heart. They are in love. He has wanted her for so long. Mc pulls her close and kisses her ever so passionately.

CaLu says with the greatest passion of love, "Oh, how I love you so much. You are so beautiful."

As he brushes his lips across hers he says, "The sight of your beautiful body, your beautiful face, your perfume is driving me mad for you. I want you and I need you desperately," [as he wraps his arms tightly around her bare waist]. She says with the most earnest of words on this planet, "Oh, yes, I love you, I need you, I want you. Please, Mc, don't ever let me go again--ever again!"

Mc reassures her, "I won't. I will never let you go again. I promise. I will never let you go--ever again--as long as I live!"

She says, "Please kiss me right now." She tenderly and ever so passionately touches her lips on his and he loves how she feels.

He says, "I love you. I have never wanted or needed anyone so much in my life. I've never seen anyone as beautiful as you." And then so overpoweringly he kisses her ... and she loves it so much! "Let me make love to you now, CaLu. There is nothing I want to do more in this world than to make love to you, right now!"

She says with tears of joy, "Yes, oh, yes, I want you ... oh, how I love you."

He is crazed with passion for her and says, "I love you more than my words can tell you."

Mc then says to her, "I kiss you like this and make love to you like this because I love you so much."

And CaLu agrees, "Oh, yes!"

And then the next day Mc and CaLu met up with Peter, Guy, Buzz and John. CaLu is at Mc's side. The two hop into the jeep together and they all head back to Camp Eagle.

"We have to report for duty tomorrow to be briefed on our mission. We will do it together, tomorrow," says Peter.

Everyone agrees.

Chapter 10

The Next Day

Guy says, "I have met some real cool people here in Vietnam but I am still tired of this place. I want to see Candice again. She is my life. I want to be with her for the rest of my life. We are good for each other."

Peter now reminisces now about Sherry also and how much he is in love with her. She will always have a place set deep in his heart, "Yes, I am thinking about Sherry now more than ever before as we get ready to go on this mission. I think about the things I would still like to tell Sherry and all of the things I want to do with my new son--and--us together--in Malibu—on the beach."

Buzz asks Peter more about his true love, Sherry, "Yeah, all of those 'Malibu Things' right on the beach, right, Peter? [They laugh.]

Guy asks Buzz this question but ... he knows, "*What things* on the beach Peter would be doing with Sherry—for real?"

Buzz says "No, I did not mean it that way. I meant your playing ball on the beach with Sherry although the other stuff would be nice also." [Everyone laughs.]

Guy jokes, "Now, let me tell you about Malibu Beach. It is neutral territory. It's for everyone."

Buzz jests, "It can't be too neutral at those prices?" [Everyone laughs.]

Peter says, "Yeah I know but I still love the place and Mc also loves Southern California--don't ya' Mc?" Mc agrees, "Oh, yeah, you better believe it. I love Malibu too and the southern coast of California as you do, Peter, but I like it more towards the San Diego side. That's my stomping grounds at San Diego State over there. I just gotta take CaLu there to show her."

Peter then starts to dream a little as his eyes gaze out to an illusion very far away, "Yeah, I like the coast more than you can imagine and with Sherry there by my side. That's my dream. Why should that be so much of a request?"

Buzz answers crassly, "Because you are here in his damn war."

Peter brings Mc's *CaLu* back into this conversation, "But Mc, you don't need Malibu to have CaLu. You have her already. And you would go anywhere in the world as long as you were with CaLu wouldn't you? Yeah, just Let Your Love Flow," Bellamy Brothers.

Mc says to Buzz, "Yeah, with CaLu I will go anywhere. Yeah, I wanna take her to Malibu and do on the beach all the things Peter wants to do with Sherry on the beach and that is not just play ball. CaLu is the most gorgeous woman I've ever known. I would make love to her all day long on that beach and never get tired of it. I know you don't believe me, Buzz, do you?"

Buzz says asininely to Mc, "No, it is not that I don't believe you, it is that I quite sincerely and quite honestly don't care."

Mc retorts back, "CaLu deserves that beautiful beach. I can picture myself making real passionate love to her on that beach. But really I could make passionate love with her anywhere on any beach anywhere this world. But right now, all I can think about is my being able to paint again. I love to paint. I am an artist. I'd like to paint a snow capped mountain surrounded by a pine forest because lately I have not seen any of that around here."

Buzz remembers his dad, "That reminds me of my dad Elmo Alfred Brule professionally known as Al Brule who is a well known fine arts painter and commercial artist. He is an American fine arts painter who paints early American genre, *Vanishing America*, and also paints reflections of his American Sioux Indian heritage. He painted a beautiful painting on our American Heritage—-the American Revolution-- called In Defiance of Kings. And he painted another called A Self Portrait which is representative of himself—-his life. But before his fine arts, he was a very successful commercial artist in New York City where he was best known for his Esquire Calendar paintings (pin-up girls, tastefully done), Brown &Bigelow, Burton-Shaw, his work for Doubleday Publishing, Dell Publishing, William Morrow & Company and many others. Many of his commercial illustrations were posted on billboards, sides of buildings, magazine covers, books, novels and newspapers of the 1950's. His style refects beautiful use of light and bright colors with his faces always most beautiful, handsome, and wholesome. His wife Betty modeled for him many times. She was a dancer in New York City. In Los Angeles in the early 1940's he worked in animation for Disney Studios and Warner Brothers Cartoons. He also painted a painting of Marion Davies with her poodles which is now hanging in the Hearst Castle in San Simeon, California. He also illustrated several children's books by Grosset and Dunlap--one is National Velvet and another is The Golden Stallion. He painted the cover of The American Magazine May 1953 and the cover of Master Detective magazine November 1958. Also, one of his paintings was painted for the Boy's Club of America and was presented to President Kennedy where it hangs in the White House."

Buzz continues, "And about his artwork--his life--my dad (Alfred Brule) always said, 'Keep the star shining.'"

As soon as Buzz finishes talking, the jeep swerves into a muddy bog and comes to a stop. They hear loud sounds and feel rumbling like thunder on the ground beneath them. It pounds every inch of their souls. It is the constant bombardment by the B-52's, the Phantom Jets and the Cobra Gunships on the ground in Vietnam.

Buzz then says about being struck by bombs, "This is a great mess in a mess."

Mc says, "Well don't complain. Do something."

Buzz says, "Oh you are so cute, Mucker, boy. You could surely run for The Little Miss America Beauty Pageant and with all of your cuteness, you would surely win. Let's just get outta this mess."

Mc says, "Oh, Little Miss--no--I would not compete in a contest like that. But if I did, I would really need you there to hold my pretty little hand, wouldn't I Buzz--for sure?"

Peter attempts to pull the jeep out of the mud hole by gunning the engine but the tires only dig deeper into the mud. The jeep cannot move forward nor can it move backward. They are stuck.

Buzz yells quite appropriately--yet maybe not quite so appropriately--with, "I thought you were a farm boy and you could deal with this type of stuff, Pete?"

Peter glares backward at Buzz and says nothing about the remark. But Peter then does say something in retaliation to that, "Let's get out and push this thing out of here before we get hit and Buzz you are first to push."

The Soldiers get out and push. The jeep does not move. Peter looks down at the tires and says, "This tire is full of star nails--no wonder."

Buzz now says stupidly to Peter, "Change the tire. You are good at that." [Everyone laughs.]

Peter snaps back, "No, I think you are better at it than I am," and hands Buzz the tire wrench. John then says to Buzz, "Yeah, you change it, big shot."

Just at this time a U.S. Military M548 unarmed cargo carrier--tracked cargo carrier--from another convoy, stops One Soldier salutes and says, "Hello, men. What is going on here?" The other Soldiers salute. "I am Pfc. John Ledbetter and here is Pfc. Tim Ferguson and Pfc. Steve Vale. Don't worry we will get you back to base."

Peter states, "We gotta be back at base and report tomorrow at 0500 hours at COHQ." Ledbetter responds, "Yeah, we have to be there too." Buzz says, "Well good. *We* have to be there too. I want to get to this mission because I feel like now I am just hanging in limbo. I'm not with it here. I can't hit top and I can't hit bottom--just floating, man-- just floating until I can get this mission done. I want to get it done."

Mc chirps in a good one, "Hey, man, you sound like you are on somthin.' [Everyone laughs.]. Buzz says, "Like what do you mean... dope? No, man, I am not on that psychedelic shit--no way—-not when I got to fight for my life out there on that damn battlefield. What are you thinkin' man? Besides I'm not a 'doper' anyway." John now says tersely and smartly, "Why I thought you hit bottom already by the way you complain about everything *left and right*. Anyway, be positive. Look at it this way, we are all together now, and together we'll kick some ass. The only way to go, now, is up." Buzz says, "Ya know somethin,' John, you are right. I did hit bottom being in this hell hole with you, I cain't get much lower than this. But I am a positive guy--always have been--from way back. My mom and dad had a lot of fun when they were making me—-that's why." Everyone laughs and Mc says, "Hey, yeah, what about my parents?" [Everyone laughs again.]. Buzz then says, "Well Mc, you are not such a positive guy so I don't think your parents had too much fun making you, ha, ha, ha. I'm sorry about that—-maybe they did?" But that is just my opinion maybe they did and maybe I'm wrong. Why not?" Peter then tells the other Soldiers in the cargo carrier, "Hey don't pay any mind to these idiots."

Now Peter looks out, sees, and hears two F-4 Phantom jets scream in, swoop down, and move up high in the distant northern sky. The jets swoop down deep to drop their bombs and they pull-up fast. Then bilious plumes of smoke with blazing balls of fire shoot upward blasting and lashing at everything in their pathway. Pete says, "Their meaning ... is death but ... I hope those guys up there can help us."

Buzz says, "Look at what those 'Mig Killers' are doing." Peter asks Guy sensibly, "How could anything live under that? I don't know why we are loosing this damn war when I see this type of total destruction? Our strategy is total destruction—-not to leave anything ... alive. That stuff looks like overkill to me."

John observes, "But it is still not enough bombing to win this war! And we especially appreciate those guys up there-—real-big-time--when we are out there on that battlefield. But right now it is the Viet Cong feeling those Phantom blows."

Guy says, "Yes, you are right. It will help us when we are out there on the ground fighting in this damn war while it's directed at our enemy." Buzz says, "Yeah, true but what about the others—-the civilians caught in this cross fire—- those poor tragic lives. Their only problem is that they were born in a country that was used as a pawn in the game of international chess—-a game the world is playing--poor things! They don't want to die. They're just caught in the way."

Mc then notes so wisely, "Yeah but aren't civilians always caught in the way--in some way--in war?"

Buzz reiterates, "Yeah, unfortunately, so, they are. I hate war--any war--with civilians--with Soldiers—-with anything. We are all just people caught in the way with our war games the world-over?"

Peter now says, "Let's get out of here and get to our job tomorrow morning where we will have a chance to play our war games again."

Mc says appropriately so, "Yes, these are our games we (Americans) are playing--this one big game-—this war game."

Buzz tops it with this, "'What a strange game. The only winning move is not to play,'" [WOPR, War Games].

Now Peter says very wisely this most appropriate quote, "Yes, the bottom line at the end of it all, as Sir Winston Churchill once said, 'The Americans will always do the right thing……after they've exhausted all of their alternatives.'"

"Yes, I believe that we Americans will always do the right thing. Yes, and in the end, we will," says Buzz to that.

Chapter 11

101 Airborne Reports to Camp Evans for a Pre-Mission Intelligence Briefing for Hamburger Hill In the A Shau Valley

Sp4c. McConnell reports for duty to Division Headquarters for a pre-mission intelligence briefing at 0500 the next morning as ordered at Camp Evans with the 101st Airborne, 3rd Brigade of the 187th Battalion (3/187th), the 1/506th, 2/506th and the 2/501st. Captain Kenner is Commander of Sp4c. McConnell's Company. Sp4c. Peter McConnell and Sp4c. Buzz Brule have been pulled out of their company for a RECON unit with Lieutenant Harper--the team leader/commanding officer (CO). Sp4c. McConnell attends this briefing with General Richard Wells Commander of the XXIV Corps and Lieutenant Colonel Coneycutt Commander at Camp Eagle and General Zain commander of the 101st. Peter and his buddies enter a room full of troops from Firebase Camp Evans. Sp4c. McConnell, Sp4c. Buzz Brule, Sp4c. Guy Von Bexin, Sp4c. Dion Johnson, Sp4c. Chris (Mc) Davison, Sp4c. John Kelsey and Sp4c. Joel Hammerstein are present with their RECON unit in their Company in the Army Airborne 101 Infantry. McConnell is with Captain Kenner and CO Lieutenant Harper leader for their LRRP/RECON unit which is getting prepared for their RIF mission for Hill 937 (Hamburger Hill, one of several hills) on Mt. Dong Ap Bia) in the A Shau Valley.

The commander turns to another commanding officer, "And this is Captain Brahm. Lieutenant Harper and Captain Brahm will be your commanding officers--leaders in your units for recon around the base before we go out onto Mt. Dong Ap Bia for Apache Snow. [From U.S. Supreme Court decisions, Goldman v. Weinberger], "'The military must insist upon a respect for duty and a discipline without counterpart in civilian life.' It is the 'subordination of the desires and interests of the individual to the needs of the services.' This is a basic principle of our constitutional law." Buzz then says, "Yes, and true but those two statements must be qualified somehow and we must know or define what is a *U.S. civilian,* a *U.S. serviceman* and a *U.S. citizen* when we offer life. But on another issue ... and with our Constutional rights such as our *right to bear arms*, we all make sacrifices as civilians for that right. American citizens are Soldiers in a way. We put our lives in the line of fire everyday so that others can have their Constitutional right to *bear arms*.

People die in order for a U.S. citizen to own a gun--*the few* must sacrifice for *the many*. The gun is respected more than life in America. A maniac can get a gun … believe it or not … he can get a gun. Can't we stop the guns … how many more innocent young children, people—-human beings--life, Robert Kennedy, Martin Luther King Jr. John F. Kennedy, John Lennon … are we insane?!"

Now the Commander explains the mission, "But now I will discuss your mission on Mt. Dong Ap Bia with Apache Snow. Captain Kenner introduces General Richard Wells, Commander of the XXIV Corps. Commander says, "Attention." General Wells walks into the room. Everyone stands up at attention, salutes and sits down.

General Wells says, "Good morning men. I am General Richard Wells at Camp Eagle--that is if some of you don't already know who I am." The roomful of Troopers cheer.

One Soldier yells out, "Yeah, we know you."

General Wells says, "At ease. Under the command from General Westmoreland we will try to secure our command in the A Shau Valley. General Westmoreland believes the A Shau Valley and the Central Highlands to be crucial in controlling Vietnam. He believes that controlling the Highlands is crucial in winning this war in Vietnam." By 1964 the North Vietnamese controlled most of the Central Highlands.

General Wells describes, ABOUT THE A SHAU VALLEY. "Now about this valley: 'This valley is on the far western edge of Thua Thien Province (...).' 'The valley ... is more than forty five kilometers long, mostly a flat stretch of land, covered with elephant grass and small trees' with a width of three hundred meters in one spot to three kilometers in another."

Then he explains the Hills on Mount Dong Ap Bia, "The enemy has built a network of roads and trials throughout the A Shau. Now the valley floor is covered with enemy division-sized base camps which are protected by hundreds of tanks, anti aircraft guns and heavy artillery. The mountains have concentric rows of deep bunkers and trench lines built into the mountains with ridges that are saturated with antiaircraft guns and mortars."

EXPLAINS BASE 611. He continues, "Base 611 used by the enemy in the A Shau Valley is an excellent avenue of approach that they use to get to Hue which is a major city in South Vietnam. Supplies from the Ho Chi Minh Trail are first stored at enemy Base Camp 611 and the supplies leave Base

611 before being transshipped further down the Trail or down Hwy 922 further into the Shau Valley. Enemy truck sightings had been seen at around a thousand trucks a day especially in the enemy Base 611 area in the northern A Shau Valley. The Marines with Dewey Canyon were able to take the enemy's huge cache of supplies that was stockpiled in A Shau Valley on the border near Base 611 and were able to open Route 9 to the Laotian border."

He continues, "But then with A Shau Valley, our enemy has a way of getting to Hue and the rest of South Vietnam. We must stop them. With the city of Hue we have seen our worst battles in South Vietnam. Many veterans compare the fighting in Hue city, known as the Citadel, with its ancient buildings, 'as the worst fighting since WWII,' [the Allies]. 'With tanks, recoilless rifles, Multibarrled Ontos, supported by a steady stream of fighter bombers and gunships ... the Marines and the ARVN moved with a steamroller attack that moved methodically through the city, house by house, street by street,' until every enemy Soldier in Hue was dead or on the retreat. And for this battle of Hue and the rest of Vietnam, '(...) the A Shau was the main enemy staging area.'"

PURPOSE OF MISSION. General Wells continues, "But now we have invaded the A Shau Valley and are trying to get it back again. At first 'the Marines were considered for the job of leading the initial assaults because of their shock value and ability to open beachheads.' But if sent it would jeopardize their [the Marines] places 'at the DMZ with their crucial blocking forces there.' So we can't do that. We need them there. So we then considered the Cavalry with 'their air mobility tactics' for Operation Delaware, the first assault on the A Shau Valley. General Tolson was the division commander. These troops were all well armed with the many helicopters in their fleet to do the job. The Air Cavalry are 'masters of the lightning like assault and the sudden decisive maneuver.' And their job was 'to pinpoint enemy antiaircraft positions' in the A Shau Valley but it was difficult to do because the enemy was everywhere and dug in deeply. Tolson was faced with 'intense flak and machine-gun fire over the central valley.' The 3/5th Cavalry with Operation Delaware Cavalry was pinned down and faced with 'a rain of mortar rounds coming in from enemy guns just across the border in Laos' and with the overcast sky and rain it became an insurmountable task. Then we sent in the 101st Airborne Division with the 2/327th, the 2/502d, the ARVN battalions with Operation Somerset Plains. They also met with tough resistance. And then again the Marines with the 1st, 2d and 3d Marine regiments went in to take enemy Base 611 with General Stillwell with Operation Dewey Canyon."

He continues, ABOUT OPERATION APACHE SNOW--THE MISSION. "But in the end General Abrams now in command of the MACV 'knew well that in past operations, it was one thing to drive the enemy from a base area and quite another to keep him out.' But now we have another chance at it--another mission to do it with you men. We will begin with Operation Massachusetts Striker, Operation Apache Snow and then Operation Montgomery Rendezvous. With Apache Snow, for Mt. Ap Bia you men will go in with five battalions from the 101st Airborne Division and spearhead this resistance with the 1/506th, 3/187th the 2/501st, the 2/506th, the 4/1 and the 2/1 ARVN--two ARVN battalions from the South Vietnamese 1st Division with what we call now Operation Apache Snow with the '3/5Cav, the 9th Marine Regiment and two other ARVN battalions in additional troop support for the operation.'"

BASE CAMPS IN A SHAU VALLEY. The General explains more about the A Shau Valley, "The northern end of the A Shau Valley was used as an area for stockpiling weapons (logistical stockpiling) for the NVA known at Base Area 611. As mentioned the enemy uses this camp to enter South Vietnam for combat." Now the General explains the base camps, "We now have secured these three enemy bases in A Shau Valley, A Luoi, Ta Bat, and Camp A Shau (Base 611). These bases were also formerly used back about four years ago by our CIDG Special Forces (indigenous troops trained by our U.S. Special Forces) but Victor Charlie (VC) seized them back again in a 1966 battle from our Special Forces." He continues, "Bottom line to this failure in our previous operations in the A Shau Valley was because we did not have enough troops, logistics and the firepower to fight it."

Buzz then tries to enlighten Peter, "Yeah, the real bottom line--the real problem--is we just don't have enough troops period because we do not a have a national commitment behind us for this war--no more, no less!"

Peter responds, "Yeah but ...? Yeah we really need a national commitment and if we don't have it, we should not be here in Vietnam in the first place--no more, no less. That is the reality of it all." Then Commander Wells continues, "Our mission now is to complete Operation Apache Snow where we will take Mount Dong Ap Bia," (with Hill 937/ Hamburger Hill). [Mountain Dong Ap Bia is comprised of several lesser hills. One such hill is known as Hill 937 or Hamburger Hill. Hills in Vietnam were generally first assigned numbers to identify them.]. The General explains a little about Reconnaissance Operations, "We will first go into Ap Bia with *reconnaissance in force* to RIF the mountain with Captain Harper. The object of riffing is to seek out any valuable information that our combat troops may need before going into battle. This is the 'intelligence preparation of the battlefield (IPB) process as well as by the commander in order to formulate confirm and modify his course of action (COA).'"

OPERATIONS IN A THE SHAU. Continues, "'These are operations undertaken to obtain, by visual observation or other detection methods, information about the activities and resources of an enemy or potential enemy, or to secure data concerning the meteorological, hydrographical or geographical characteristics and indigenous population of a particular area. Reconnaissance is a focused collection effort.'" General Wells continues, "As General George S. Patton Jr. said, 'You can never have too much Reconnaissance.'" The roomful of Soldiers hoots, hollers and whistles. General Wells summarizes, "Thus, now, we have successfully completed several missions under the approval of General Westmoreland in A Shau Valley with these military operations/missions: Operation Delaware in April 1968 with the 3rd brigade, the 1st Battalion 7th Cavalry Division, Operation Somerset Plains by the 101st Airborne which was a seventeen-day battle that cut-off enemy supply routes from the west with the 2/327th and the 2/502d and Operation Dewey Canyon also known as Lam Son 719, the Marines with three battalions of the 3rd Regiment took a 'regimental assault over land' [Zaffiri] and into enemy's Base area 611—-formerly called Camp A Shau. Camp Base 611 is also known as Muong Nong. It is an enemy base that sprawls on 'both sides of the Laotian-South Vietnamese border' at the head of the A Shau Valley. It had been our Special Forces camp before but now--bottom line--we just don't have enough combat troops to hold it."

Buzz then says, "Talk about our Special Forces? What the heck ... we give 'em green uniforms to wear with the green dye that runs or bleeds onto the Soldier's skin and turns their skin green. What the heck is that all about? Can't we give our men a good quality of uniform where the dye does not bleed? That is why the Cong calls them the Green Devils." Gen. Wells informs these troops further with, "Now we have three more planned operations for A Shau Valley. Each operation is targeted for a different part of the A Shau Valley to hit them hard and drive them out. The first is Massachusetts Striker with the 101st Airborne 2nd Brigade aimed for the capture of the southern valley where many cache discoveries have been found." [Later Operation Montgomery Rendezvous with the 101st Airborne Division built a new road and airstrip in the A Shau Valley and an additional two FSBs on the valley's edge.]. He continues, "With Operation Apache Snow, the 3d Battalion 101st Airborne, 9th Marines and 3rd ARVN Regiment we will begin to trace enemy infiltration routes on the Northern end of the A Shau and find his caches and destroy them. Thus, our purpose for Apache Snow is to make a direct challenge to the NVA troops in the Northern A Shau."

The Commander continues, "Operation Apache Snow must be completed with success and the only way to do that is if you men go in there and take that hill (Hill 937). It will help us in controlling the A Shau Valley which will put a big kink in their wire for the use of the Trail and especially if they try to stage any more offensives into South Vietnam. Operation Apache Snow will be a three-phased operation to destroy the NVA bases in A Shau Valley on Mount Dong Ap Bia. There we will send in five battalions to combat assault the hill and all under the double and triple canopy jungle in dense thickets of bamboo and waist high elephant grass." He continues to describe the plan to retake the A Shau Valley with a lot of enthusiasm as his voice gets louder, "We will block enemy escape routes into Laos along Highway 922 and interdict Highway 548 which runs the length of A Shau. But before we initiate Apache Snow, we will RIF Mount Dong Ap Bia for two days to pinpoint enemy hooch's and bunkers. We will RIF to find the enemy and his caches and then send in troops to destroy them." The General describes more, "Thus, with our missions going into the A Shau Valley, we will send in a total of ten battalions--three from the 101st Airborne which are the 1/506th, the 2/506th, the 3/187th, and the 2/501st. But with this, we will be faced with some problems. 'Heavy enemy antiaircraft fire' is a problem and so is the weather. The weather with continuous rain and dense gray drifting fog has already put us at a severe disadvantage in the A Shau Valley with Operation Delaware and Somerset Plains."

MATERIALS SUPPLY ROADS/ROUTES. Gen. Wells continues, "And then there is our supply of materials. We can do this by building a road through A Shau Valley which will provide us with a large steady stream of supplies by building a road from 'the 101st Airborne Division at Camp Eagle across the coastal plains, through the mountains and right into the

heart of the Valley.' And we have been able-to an extent--
disrupt the enemy supply routes in the A Shau Valley. We
uncovered huge caches of enemy supplies and munitions. We
also found enemy built Route Highway 614 which connected the
southern A Shau with Quang Nam Province. And we will build
Route 547 which will connect A Shau Valley to the Lowlands
and provide a route for our armored vehicles to connect to A
Shau Valley. This route will help us with our re-supply
efforts." The General continues, "Route 548 in A Shau Valley
has in the past been carrying tons of enemy supplies across
the length of the valley. The enemy has so far been able to
mask his flow of supplies and reinforcements into the
mountains every night." [The same problem—different war.
Will there ever be an end to this? As said by President G.
W. Bush with the U.S. War with Iraq. "We will disrupt the
attack on our forces. We will interrupt the flow of support
from Iran and Syria."]. The General explains further the
enemy truck routes in the Valley, "Now the enemy still
continues to use Route 922 in the A Shau Valley. This gives
him truck-transport from Laos to RVN (North Vietnam)
territory at the northern end of A Shau Valley where Route
548 is connected. 'Route 548 runs the length of the valley.
With these two routes, the enemy can accommodate heavy truck
traffic along the entire length of A Shau Valley. The enemy
moves in a southeasterly direction with the trucks full.
Then empty trucks move in a northwesterly direction to Base
Area 611 which is the enemy's staging area, for reloading.
Thus the trucks move in three stages: They move from Base
611 in Laos to the northern end of A Shau Valley, then, they
move southeasterly along Route 545 to around the area of A
Luoi Base Camp and then, they continue southeasterly to the
southern end of A Shau Valley.' The NVA are continuing to
use the A Shau Valley and Roa Nai Valley as major invasion
areas for South Vietnam. Strategically it is important to
them and to us. Thus the A Shau Valley is an arm of the Ho
Chi Minh Trail."

GEOGRAPHY A SHAU VALLEY. The Commander describes the
geographic of the A Shau again, "'A Shau Valley is a narrow,
steep walled gash running parallel to the Laotian border for
25 miles. Thick trees and brush cling to the slopes and the
valley floor. The valley floor and dark rain filled clouds
hover over the bordering mountaintops which go to a height
of 3,000 feet.' Its streams are leech infested, its dense
ridges and jungle cliffs are covered with rotted tree roots
on sixty-degree slopes, and it holds 140 different types of
poisonous snakes. The forest is so thick with growth that
you cannot see more than two feet in front of you."

He continues to explain, "Thus, basically this is the run-down on the A Shau Valley. The heart of A Shau Valley is about five miles from the Laotian border. It is a key to gaining advantage in the I (eye) Tactical Zone Corps area. The Valley is located in the far northwest corner just below the DMZ Line in South Vietnam. It is one of the two major enemy strongholds in the south. The A Shau Valley is the strongest enemy controlled area in South Vietnam and is protected by a complex of interlocked anti-aircraft batteries and is garrisoned by more than 5,000 enemy Soldiers. The enemy has built huge stockpiles of weapons and supplies. From here he is going down the Trail through Laos and then into A Shau Valley. The A Shau Valley is an important terminus of the Ho Chi Minh Trail. The Trail and its pipelines follow along the Chaine Annamitique Mountains that begin in North Vietnam and continue along the Laotian and Cambodian Border."

The General states, "So now we know what we are up against. [As said by Col. John Hoefling 2/17 CAV quoted by Samuel Zaffiri in Hamburger Hill], 'We are in for some tough fighting ahead, but I feel that we have never before been more capable of success than now. The NVA we are going to meet out there will be highly trained, well equipped, hard core troops who will stand and fight, especially when we get to his base camps and supply depots.'"

PLANS, DIVISIONS, BATTALIONS, REGIMENTS & CONDITIONS ON GROUND IN A THE SHAU VALLEY. The General continues, "We must have an established Airhead by the Sky Trooper of 1st Air Cavalry Division Paratroopers, the Screaming Eagle 1st Brigade, the 101 Airborne Division with the 3rd Battalion, the 3rd 187 infantry and 2nd Battalion from the 1st Army of the Republic of Vietnam ARVN Division, the 2nd 501 Infantry, the 1st Battalion 506th Infantry, 2nd of the 501, the 4/1st ARVN, the 2/1st (2 infantry battalions from 1st ARVN Division) and 3 battalions of the U.S. 9th Marine Regiment, the U.S. 3rd squadron and the 5th Cavalry."

PLANNED OPERATION. The General continues to talk, "Now Intel has found that they have a 'warehouse' in A Shau Valley where the enemy has been able to send troops and supplies into the lowlands from Laos. But we will counter with a combination of air assault battalions, combat assault battalions and RIF assaults (Reconnaissance in Force). But as for our tactics, we will go in with Air Force Fighters to bomb the jungle and open the canopy. We will use artillery (Howitzers/Big Guns) from nearby bases and we will prep the ground with our B-52's for our ground forces. With the enemy

underground bunkers, we will plot the targets--bunkers
locations--with our forward air controllers (FACs) and
RECON/RIF/LRRP teams so we can be accurate when we bomb
targets. The Special Forces and LuRRP units will also go in
to the battleground to pinpoint the location of enemy
bunkers." The General then recites a quote, "You
Paratroopers are going into A Shau Valley where you will
bravely fight for it. With your creed you say: 'I am a
Paratrooper. I save my country. If you tell me to kill the
enemy, they will die or I will die trying. I am a
Paratrooper. I will fight when others quit. No one can fight
as hard, march as far or endure as much pain as I. I am a
Paratrooper. I am at your command. Use me or lose the war.'"

Peter agrees, "Yes I will fight for my country and my
battle buddies. I will fight!" Peter then says with more
info, "But let us use all of our best technological
advantage and use it wisely. Because when we use artillery,
TAC Air support, Air Cavalry, fighter bombers, we have the
best advantage in fighting the enemy. And for our ground
troops, the lift helicopter works to our advantage for troop
insertions and extractions. But on Ap Bia, our battlefields
are on steep inclines and slopes on the mountains which
render our air advantage as being poor with little effect on
the bunkers." But Peter changes the subject, "In WWII, we
asked ourselves, *how do we end this war as quickly as
possible?* We answer: *we use our most lethal weapons.* I am
not at all proud of it-—Hiroshima--as we did with the Atomic
bomb. This is the game of war. I don't know."

Buzz then asks, "What do you mean, *I don't know.*

Buzz then reads from a paper he took out of his pocket
by Hermann Hagedorn from his book, The Bomb That Fell on
America: "'The bomb that fell on Hiroshima fell on America
too. It fell on no city, no munitions plants and no docks.
It erased no church, vaporized no public buildings, reduced
no man to his atomic elements but it fell, it fell.'"

ENEMY SUPPLY LINES/ROUTES--General Wells says, "Apart from A
Shau Valley, the enemy has also increased his arms and
personnel traffic along the Ho Chi Minh Trail into South
Vietnam in other areas along the border also. The
Communists' supply columns go into Laos and work their way
down the trails of the eastern side of the Laotian panhandle
and then into South Vietnamese territory. They are a threat
all along our neutral borders with Laos and Cambodia. But
the enemy has an inherent weakness in their logistical
systems because Hanoi's pipeline cannot adequately support
several divisions in one place or move from the base to the

battlefront fast enough to keep pace with their mobile units. They cannot stockpile the amount of supplies needed for a massive assault because it would be found by us. That is why the enemy needs the Trail and therefore he needs the A Shau Valley. In A Shau Valley the enemy has the supply lines and the storage depots all along the Mount Dong Ap Bia border with Laos and Vietnam and stores men and material in the mountain in his underground bunkers on both sides of the border. We have found 10 tons of rice and 75,000 individual and crew-sized rounds of ammunition and another 100,000 rounds of ammunition."

Buzz says resolutely and most sincerely, "Yeah, this is really the way to win this war--by taking their rice--that's the way to do it. Why don't we do it like that--just keep the food from 'em? They won't be able to fight without their rice. Like for example look at me--try to get me to pick up a rifle and start firin' at somethin' with it--anything-- without my C-rations of freeze dried ham and eggs--yeah-- just see how far I can get without the food. [Everyone laughs.]. That's kinda' the way of doin' it--isn't it?"

Another soldier over-hears the conversation--steps in quite angrily and says, "Yeah, but it is no fun that way-- just stopping their food supplies. Now by fighting like this, it is more fun; we can come-on in here and shoot-'em all up--all over this damn place--kill their men--and *ball* all of their bitches." [Peter laughs.]

Buzz then suddenly bolts-up out of his chair--giving the Soldier a daring look and says, "Bullshit on that crap! Get the hell out of my face, Bud--would ya? You are not going to screw anybody." General Wells is continuing in earnest, "We either go at it 100% or we don't fight it at all. You Soldiers as professional fighting men and we as commanders know one thing for sure, we cannot fight with our hands tied behind our backs. And the politicians have to stop fighting this war for us. They gave us the war and now we have to fight it. And as well, civilian advisors have to stay out of this war. They can't fight this war for us. We the military must fight this war. We need our politicians and our country to back us up and not fight this war for us. We either fight it at 100% our way or we don't fight it at all. [As said by writer Joe Galloway in his article in

2007], 'War may be too important to be left to the generals, but it damned sure can't be left to the politicians who have no experience of it.'"

TOPOGRAPHY HAMBURGER HILL. Buzz says, "But ... but ... With Hill 937 (Hamburger Hill) the Commanders must be sure also to fight the battle as well and must know what they are fighting before blaming anyone else. 'The mountain [Ap Bia] [is] covered with thick double and triple canopy jungle consisting of layers of vines, brushy trees, and stands of bamboo. The whole place [is] a network of trails and roads, and at night [one can] hear gas engines running and [that sound] like chain saws. During the day [one can watch] hundreds of enemy troops moving up the hill.' This piece-meal war we are fighting now is puttin' all our poor necks in this damn noose and its gettin' much tighter." But now Commander Wells gives a much different view, "We have launched our objective, and we are driving the enemy out. We are about to launch 'three of the biggest Allied operations of the Vietnam War (...)' '(...) to deliver a knock-out blow.'"

HISTORICAL BACKGROUND AND PERSPECTIVE. ["A battle raged up and down the A Shau for 167 days." "(...) two of the enemy regiments—-the 6th and the 9th-- would suffer terrible casualties, and the third—the 29th—(...) would be almost wiped out."]

PROBLEM OF NEUTRAL TERRITORY ON BATTLEGROUND. Buzz says angrily, "But the problem is, we have is a lot of neutral territory surrounding our battlefields. How can we fight a war like this? The enemy attacked the Marines with 122 mm Howitzers guns which were well emplaced into caves in Laos. The Marines of the 2d Battalion could not go in to Laos to finish them off. The enemy continued to attack the Marines killing 130 Marines. The enemy continued with their convoys of hundreds of trucks full of men and supplies heading into A Shau Valley South Vietnam. They were just a few hundred yards away but the Marines were unable to stop them because it is neutral territory. Look at what CG (a Soldier) of the 3d Marine Division said about this neutrality--that they were very frustrated '(...) to sit on this hill and watch those 1,000 (enemy) trucks go down those roads in Laos, hauling ammunition down south to kill Americans with,'" [as said by CG a Soldier in the 3d Marine Division from the website Home of the Heroes]. Peter says, "I agree and even more so, listen to this--what Major General John F. Freund-- a brigade Commander keeps saying. He says our albatross is that we have no flexibility to operate with U.S. ground forces outside the borders of SVN (South Vietnam) which is hurting our battle. A Marine master sergeant said '(...) my gunner kept yelling he had definite targets, people shooting at us but he couldn't fire back because there were unarmed people around them,'" (said by a Soldier in Afghan War 2009). And also a former 26-year Marine veteran also said 'Without reinforcement, denial of fire support and refusal to allow them to hunt and kill the very enemy we are there to confront are nothing more than sitting ducks,'" (John Bernard, Afghanistan 2009).

Buzz then leans over and whispers in Pete's ear and says, "'Ah shit Valley' you mean, and that is what it is going to do to us." Pete laughs and says, "Hey man, you are too damn disrespectful to all of those who have been killed in this war and in this valley." Buzz asks cynically, "Wouldn't you be like this too if your neck was just about to be tied into a damn noose like this and tightened some by someone?" Pete then begins a round of laughter that is almost out of control and says, "Well my neck is in this same damn noose as yours, bud." Buzz then says, "No. I am sorry and I don't want to be disrespectful to anyone who has ever fought or who has ever been killed in this war. That is not my intention at all." John then says in agreement to the General's plans, "What we do need in the A Shau Valley now [as said by Marine Corps Colonel Sullivan], is 'to neutralize enemy activities in the valley was [is] going to take more than occasional foray by a couple of battalions or even a couple of brigades. The failure of all such operations in the past could not be attributed to a lack of tactical expertise by the allied units, but to a lack of troops, logistics, and firepower. What it was [is] going to take to crack the valley was [is] not a brief raid or a large reconnaissance-in-force, but an all-out World War II-type invasion.'"

IN GENERAL--WAR STRATEGIES. Now the General explains strategy and his plan for neutralizing the A Shau Valley, "But first let me talk about military *strategy* in general. And I know that is what we need a lot of now. 'It is the planning and the conduct of warfare. It is the *art of the general*. It deals with planning and conduct of campaigns, the movement, and disposition of forces and the deception of the enemy. *Strategy* governs the conduct of warfare. It is the prelude to a battle and *tactics* controls its execution.' Today there are 'two types of strategy, *Grand Strategy* and *Military Strategy*. *Grand Strategy* is when we use the resources of an entire nation in the conduct of warfare.

Military Strategy is operational strategy and that is the planning and control of large military units such as corps and divisions.'" He continues to explain *military strategy,* "A *military operation,* then, is when we use deployed forces that involve the carrying on of combat with planning, calculating or the gathering of information as with Long Range Reconnaissance Patrol and Special Reconnaissance Forces. A mission can involve 'carrying out of a strategic, tactical, training mission or the process of carrying on combat, including movement, supply, attack, defense and maneuvers needed to gain the objectives of a battle or campaign' all with military operation code names. Buzz then leans over and says in Peter's ear, "Yeah but is there ever going to be any end to any of this?" Peter then says, "Yeah and I don't hear the word *Diplomacy* being bounced-around in here too terribly much. I think that should be fundamental to his *Grand Strategy.* With *Diplomacy* we can force or pressure another nation into compliance and in that way achieve victory without going to combat, yeah? Let's try for diplomacy and if it goes, we will reach the pinnacle of our greatness as Americans?"

Buzz then says, "Amen to that."

MILITARY STRATEGY PRINCIPLES. And the General continues to speak on military strategy. He says, "Today we see the main principles of military strategy with: 'the objective, the offense, cooperation, concentration (mass), economy, maneuver, surprise, security and simplicity.'"

General Wells says, "According to Field Marshal Count von Moltke, his view on strategy is this, 'Strategy is a system of *ad hoc expedients* by which a general must take action while under pressure.'"

General Wells says, "Bottom line to all of this for our military general is that 'the general should be flexible in formulating a strategy.'"

Buzz then says jokingly, "Yeah, we must always remember as Euripides once said, 'Ten Soldiers wisely led will beat a hundred without a head.'" [Peter laughs.]

SUN-TZU, NAPOLEON I, FREDERICK THE GREAT--STRATEGIES.
General Wells explains more, "The Chinese author, Sun-Tzu of the Art of War said about strategy, 'Do not repeat the tactics which have gained you one victory, but let your methods be regulated by the infinite variety of circumstances.' Frederick the Great used a '*strategy of exhaustion* to hold off his opponents and conserve his

forces.' He used 'geometric strategy which emphasized lines on maneuver, awareness of terrain and possession of critical strong points.' Napoleon I of France used the 'Strategy of Annihilation.' Napoleonic Tactics are 'offense at all costs.'"

TYPES OF WARFARE. The General continues his speech and describes warfare, "Now, let me explain to you the meaning of the different military tactics. There are several military tactics that are used in warfare: 'Guerrilla Warfare is an ancient form of asymmetric warfare which operates with small, mobile and flexible combat groups called cells without a front line. Attrition Warfare strategy is when the enemy is worn down to the point of collapse. Conventional Warfare is the use of conventional military weapons and battlefield tactics between two or more states in open confrontation. Fortifications Warfare is military construction and buildings designed for defense in warfare. Ground Warfare is infantry, amour and artillery. Hand to Hand Warfare is fighting unarmed combat in close quarters when the outcome is usually fatal. It is unarmed combat using improvised field expedient or muscle-powered weapons such as clubs and knives. Invasion Warfare is a military action consisting of armed forces of one geopolitical entity entering territory controlled by another such entity to conquer territory. Maneuver Warfare advocates defeat by an adversary by incapacitating their decision making through shock and disruption. Network-Centric Warfare is using technical advances in information technology. Siege Warfare is a prolonged military blockade and assault of a city or fortress with intent of conquering by force or attrition. Total Warfare combines the use of all resources. Trench Warfare is when both opposing armies have static lines of fortification dug into the ground facing each other. Unconventional Warfare achieves military victory through acquiescence, capitulation or clandestine support for one side in the conflict. Asymmetrical Warfare has a potential for optimal interaction between the respective strengths and weaknesses of two belligerents. Naval Warfare is naval combat on the seas and oceans.'"

He concludes, "But for us now, in order to get the job done, we must clear the enemy from Hill 937," (Hamburger Hill).

Buzz then leans over to Peter and says, "It all sounds like we are getting ready for the butcher house. Wouldn't it be something if a Soldier one day 'Edward J. Henry, Alpha Company, 2nd BN, 1969 decides to call that hill Hamburger

Hill' because of the human flesh butchered in battle resembled hamburger meat and was everywhere on the battlefield sticking to tree trunks and branches."

Peter then says on the spot, "Most horrifically ... and quite fittingly so."

Buzz then quotes, "Yeah, hah, as Ramman Kenoun so truly said 'The Soldier's main enemy is not the opposing Soldier, but his own commander.'"

General Wells says, "Now Lieutenant Col. Coneycutt will explain our Operation Apache Snow."

OPERATION IN A THE SHAU VALLEY CONCLUSION. Lt. Col. Coneycutt says, "Bottom line then and I repeat, *"Our bravest young men* are going to take Hill 937 which is a hill on the north side of Dong Ap Bia in the northern A Shau Valley. We will build Firebase Blaze and send three infantry battalions (about 1,800 men) into the A Shau Valley. Two will fight and one battalion will block enemy escape routes to push out the last vestige of the enemy presence in the northern part of the A Shau Valley--meaning Hill 937--Hamburger Hill--on Dong Ap Bia. Firebase Blaze will be our staging operation and PZ (pick-up zone). There will be 'three battalions from the 101st Airborne Division—the 1/506th, 3/187th, and 2/501st, the 2/506th --on the east end of the PZ and two South Vietnamese battalions—the 4/1 and 2/1 AVRN—on the west side.'"

Buzz then says derisively "Apache Snow? Back with the American Indians again, I just don't feel too good about naming all of these operations after the American Indians whom we (early settlers) treated so unfairly in taking their land and dividing it up for ourselves--that sucks. But who am I to say? That ain't too Kosher, man." Buzz continues, "But it is strange to name these battles after the American Indians whom we had treated so cruelly and so unfairly? And we name our helicopters Sioux, Choctaw, Kiowa, and Iroquois? Don't we have any shame on this issue? What is this? These tribes were beaten by the U.S. so badly. You know our longest war lasted for 46 years and it was with the Apache Nation. Does this make any sense to you? It seems almost ironic that we name our military operations after the American Indians. I don't know. Is there something wrong with me? We should have been negotiating contracts with the American Indians for land but instead we took their land from them *carte blanche* and displaced these people. But really here in Vietnam and there in America whose freedom are we really fighting? I don't know. Is there somethin' kinda wrong with my thinkin' here a little bit? Maybe it is I?"

Peter then answers with, "And I think these men here don't understand any of it—-Apaches, American Indians, Vietnamese--any of it."

Peter continues, "We should let these people here alone with their own country."

Peter says, "I know we should."

Buzz then says, "You know it is like the words to a song called Where Have All the Flowers Gone? Peter, Paul & Mary, 'Where have all the flowers gone' and 'when will they ever learn?'"

Peter then answers sadly, "I don't believe they ever will."

Peter then says [as said by Pope John Paul II], "'Humanity should question itself, one more, about the absurd and always unfair phenomenon of war.'"

Peter is with Guy, Mc, Buzz, Joel Hammerstein, Dion Johnson and John Kelsey together with their company. They are listening well to the Commander. They would rather be listening to Rock n' Roll music and their Country-Western music but nevertheless they are here at COHQ Camp Eagle and listening to their Commander.

Commander Coneycutt continues his discourse about Hill 937. The Commander then displays a huge map of the Mountain Dong Ap Bia in the A Shau Valley with several thick markings of grease-pencil lines that point to the enemy staging areas.

The Lieutenant Colonel informs further, "The enemy had the valley in their control and our balls were against the wall but now we are going to kick ass. He points to the map of Hamburger Hill. This is where you men will fight. We will kick their asses all the way back into Laos. This mountain must be ours if we want to win this war."

GEOGRAPHY--MT. AP BIA (HAMBURGER HILL). Commander Coneycutt now describes the geography of Mt. Dong Ap Bia, "The Montagnard Tribesmen call it the 'Mountain of the Crouching Beast.' It is tortuous terrain. It is a rugged jungle-shrouded mountain that is unconnected to the surrounding Annamite mountain range. It rises off the floor of the A Shau Valley to an elevation of 937 meters above sea level as it runs along the Laotian border. It is a huge, looming, wild, rugged, solitary mountain that is covered in double and triple canopy jungle with thickets of bamboo and elephant grass that grow as high as a man's head." He says, "Mount Dong Ap Bia has the appearance of having [as described by Samuel Zaffiri, historian and a Soldier in Vietnam], 'tendrils of some giant sea creature, a number of large ridges and fingers and a labyrinth of deep ravines and wide draws branch out in all directions. Two of these ridges—Hill 937 on the north and Hill 916 form mountains of their own, and like all the rest of Dong Ap Bia, lie under a thick, double-and triple-canopy jungle.'"

Commander Coneycutt continues, "And it is there that we will make our stand. You men will do your job. It is the determination and courage of the individual fighting man in the ranks who will win this battle on Hill 937."

[ACTUAL QUOTE BY COMMANDING GENERALS: As Colonel Conmy said about our Soldiers "This operation just proved again that the ultimate weapon is the infantry rifleman. Victory achieved by heroism of the rifleman going in and digging out the enemy." The rifleman lives by his job. "To seek out and close with the enemy, to kill or capture him. To seize and hold ground, and repel attack by day or by night, regardless of the season weather or terrain."]. [ACTUAL QUOTE BY COMMANDING GENERAL OF HAMBURGER HILL. Major General Zais later said of Hamburger Hill, "It was a tremendous gallant victory by a bunch of gutty guys."]

Buzz then says to Peter, "You better believe it. Here in all of Vietnam, we Soldiers are _our bravest young men_. He does his job as he is told to do for his country, for his battle buddies and for himself. _Our bravest young men_ are the best of the best."

Buzz then asks a hypothetical question, "What would you think if one day a young Soldier who fights on this Hill 937 (Hamburger Hill) asks the question about the loss of life on that hill with this question, 'Was it worth it?'"

Buzz continues with his hypothetical questions, "But even more so, wouldn't it be tragic if our commanders decided to walk away from Hill 937 (Hamburger Hill) with the loss of many lives? Tell me, wouldn't it be tragic?"

Peter then says, "I don't think that our commanders are capable of doing such a thing."

[NOTE: In the end The troopers who fought on Hamburger Hill (Hill 937/Operation Apache Snow) and had a very high casualty rate which took ten days to fight with 70 Americans KIA, 372 wounded, a total of five infantry battalions (1,800), ten batteries of artillery (big guns/Howitzers) battalions and the Air Force with 272 sorties with one million pounds of bombs and 152,000 pounds of Napalm. But ten days later, our Commanders ordered Hamburger Hill abandoned because they did not want a battalion to be tied down in a defensive role on that mountain.]

[ACTUAL QUOTE BY COMMANDING GENERAL HAMBURGER HILL. And many Commanders were happy with the job the Troopers had done in winning the battle at Hamburger Hill. Col. Joseph Conmy, Commander of the 3rd Brigade, 101st Airborne Division, later said of these fine Soldiers, "No matter how tough the job is, the American Soldier gets the job done (...). They eventually went up that hill and took it."]

John then counters as he overhears this conversation between Peter and Buzz and says, "Hey, our Commanders did not have the commitment from their country. It is unfair now to blame solely our military commanders?"

Buzz adds wisely, "Well that's the mistake then our commanders made. We should leave Vietnam. We do not have the national commitment and our Commanders know this."

Buzz continues, "This course is even more tragic for the fighting soldier! I am going out there to put my life on the line for my Commanding Officers and I trust nothing will be in vain. I trust our Commanders will have this all figured out for Hill 937--Hamburger Hill. I hope that the *intelligence* will be done and that we have an approximate idea of how many enemy troops we are fighting against. But it seems not to be so however. I know that any intelligence we can gather first on Ap Bia is crucial to saving the battle for our assault troops. But bottom line with this; whatever we gather first in intelligence, I trust our Commanders will analyze the strategy and not commit our troops foolishly ... so that we will go into battle to fight on the line for our country."

Peter asks honestly and quite prophetically, "Wouldn't it be something if our Commanders don't have an adequate strategy to win the battle on Hill 937 or if they commit our troops against an extraordinarily high number of enemy troops who are well dug in? We may just have to fight it and win it with blood and guts?"

[At the end of the Battle of Hamburger Hill, in May of 1969, Senator Stephen M. Young (D-Ohio) did question the strategy that was used at Hamburger Hill. (According to Zaffiri) "(...) Sen. Young questioned Gen. Zais' actual tactical handling of the battle."]

[And the Associated Press correspondent Jay Sharbutt asked why don't we have a battle strategy that might possibly help to save the lives of many American Troopers with his question in quote, "Why are you attacking this mountain with troops? Why don't you just pull back and hit it with B-52 strikes?" And according to Zaffiri, it was said that Honeycutt and Zais dismissed Sharbutt's report about the battle tactics on Hamburger Hill as "both distorted and sensationalized."]

REPEAT/SUMMARY OPERATION APACHE SNOW. But now the Commander summarizes how this battle of Apache Snow will be fought, "This how we will fight it for Operation Apache Snow on Mount Dong Ap Bia. We want to push the enemy back into Laos up along the northern slope of Dong Ap Bia Mountain heading west into Laos. We are trying to take out their underground bunkers which are loaded full with supplies. We are going to send Troops from *B, C* and *D* Companies in there with a three-pronged attack on the lower ridgeline of the mountain. Each company will go up the mountain in a different direction. But before we send in our assault troops out onto Mount Dong Ap Bia our RIF teams and LURRP teams will gather more intelligence on enemy movements, routes and installations. The LuRRPs will also be conducting detailed terrain analysis and on enemy bunker/hooch locations and lines of communication. As we have seen before on another hill Mt. Dong A Tay, our troopers have been faced with concentric rows of solidly built, well concealed bunkers around the entire hill mass. Enemy tactics has been to try to block our approach up these mountains. These bunkers are filled with explosives, booby-trapped satchel charges and the enemy waiting from within. Before we launch *Operation Apache Snow* with our assault troops, on Ap Bia, we will first have RIF in there by RECON to see if that mountain really has those great numbers of underground tunnels and bunkers systems built within. We have faced these underground bunkers on other mountains here with other battles but what awaits us on Mt. Dong Ap Bia, we don't really know yet? What awaits us up there ... we don't know? But I will tell you one thing our enemy is not going to slow us down no matter what he has up there on that mountain."

CONDITIONS OF ENEMY ON THE HILL. The Commander describes the hill, "As I have said, we have seen on Mt. Dong A Tay the NVA have built a system of deep bunkers which are all interconnected by tunnels and trenches. From aerial firepower, they are difficult to hit. 'Their bunkers are situated to thwart the accuracy and effectiveness of

American air and fire support. They are built into folds of the mountain. The dense jungle and sharp relief of the hill render our fire power less effective. The enemy may be securely sheltered there but with artillery, ARA and F-4 fire we will be able to prep the ground for our ground elements. These mountain ridges are heavily *jungled* and they are perfect for enemy concealment and infiltration. Just two miles away lay the shelter of the Laotian border sanctuary.' The bunkers well suited for the terrain of the terraced mountain contours and jungle covers. These bunkers have very good overhead protection and can resist a lot of pounding from air assault. But I will tell you, no matter what they have up there, we are taking the hill. We won 'em before and we will win 'em again."

Peter then says, "I see the Commander is hella determined to get this Hill 937--Hamburger Hill--on Dong Ap Bia but I hope it doesn't ruin us all."

Buzz says with hopelessness, "Yep, it looks like he is going to make us pay for it in blood." Commander continues, "We must bomb with napalm and bust bunkers with the recoilless rifle. You men will be inserted into the AO by helicopter. The enemy is formidable, tough and a well trained Soldier in well dug-in positions. Our best defense against the bunkers is the recoilless rifle."

The commander continues, "They are a very determined enemy. We have even found shirts before with 'sewn-on commands, *kill Americans, kill Vietnamese and stay and fight and don't run.*'" Buzz then says to Peter "I believe we will be faced with a highly skilled enemy in unexpected numbers who will display unprecedented determination to fight. 'This enemy has carefully chosen the battlefield terrain to neutralize the effects of our American technology while maximizing the remarkable light infantry skills of his own Soldier.' The NVA adapted their defensive tactics to maximize the terrain."

DESCRIPTION RECOILLESS RIFLE. [The recoilless is a lightweight weapon that fires heavier projectile. Two Soldiers carry the weapon to fire it and load it. It is rifled because it is made to make the projectile spin. It fires artillery-type shells with a range and velocity similar to a light cannon. Some versions are shoulder fired and carried. Larger/heavier versions are carried on chassis and are called Ontos. The lighter version—the 84 mm portable is called the Gustav or the goose after its inventor Carl Gustav—also known as RAAWS which stands for Ranger Anti Armor Weapons System.]

The Commander continues, "Our LRRP/RIF Teams can find the enemy units, squads or battalion-sized forces and their entrenched underground hooch's. Then our forward air controllers, at that point, can then call on Air Force fighter strikes with some bombing for 50 minutes. Then artillery (immobile big guns on the base) can fire for a 15-minute barrage. Finally we can send in more firing from our aerial rocket artillery helicopters and finally Cobra Gunships will insert elements into the AO that has all been well prepped. And other landing zones will be prepped as well for decoy to fool the enemy." Lt. Col. Coneycutt continues, "We have an enemy who is well dug into that hill with his bunkers in company-sized units and platoons. We have cleared a lot of the canopy with Napalm on that mountain so we can now have a more accurate idea on where those bunkers are located but we still need more of our RECON teams to RIF the area. You will be fighting on steep mud-covered slopes and dense tropical vegetation. Much of the terrain is still, yet, heavily forested but our air support should take care of that. This terrain still makes it difficult for helicopter landings, for artillery support (big guns/Howitzers located on bases or landing zones) and for B-52 strikes because of the close proximity of enemy troops with friendly troops. No news reporters can reproach us with that reasoning," [referring to news reporter Sharbutt who questioned just that during the Battle of Hamburger Hill]. Buzz interjects wisely and says to Peter, "There would truly be no bad news reports if there was no bad battle-command out here—bottom line—no *if, ands or buts* about it!"

U.S. AIR STRATEGIES ON THE HILL. The Commander then says to the troops, "Actually for us now in Vietnam our air support is in fact a way of life for most of our battles. 'The essence of air power is the offensive.'" Peter then says, "Yes, it all sounds fine but, with this battle also, 'we cannot take it for granted the artillery support of our ground troops as we have been doing with previous battles or our close air support with our F-4 Phantom fighter bombers (air strikes), FAC's/Forward Air Controllers (overhead surveillance), helicopter Gunships also known as Cobra Gunships (ARA/aerial rocket artillery or aerial rocket attack) and ARC light B-52 bombings with our air artillery (Big guns on base/Howitzers) because of these hills and steep slopes.'" Peter continues, "But our air support may not work every time. 'Troop transports/Slicks cannot land for insertion and extraction of troops on steep slopes and we will lack the artillery support that we will need. The

125

same problem applies for artillery fire from the bases because of the steep ravines and hillsides.' I can see we are in for a tuff one. We must be aware of all of problems we will have to our disadvantage with this battle of Dong Ap Bia with its Hill 937." Buzz adds, "Yeah, the problems are also going to be the jungle canopy, the weather, the terrain and the platoon and squad-sized units (because of jungle terrain and small trails). We will have a difficult time. This battle is going to be a battle with a well entrenched enemy on a hill in well protected bunkers where we must find them."

A SUN TZU WAR STRATEGY. Peter then says, "Yeah, we have to be sleuth--to do what we were trained to do as LuRRPs/RECON. There is a saying by the Chinese war strategist that describes these Soldiers best by Sun Tzu and it goes like this, 'Be extremely subtle, even to the point of formlessness. Be extremely mysterious, even to the point of soundlessness. Thereby you can be the director of the opponent's fate.'"

Buzz then leans over and tells Peter, I hope Commander Coneycutt is ahead of this game with his analysis of the upcoming battle on Hamburger Hill. He has to be aware of our disadvantages in battle or we will lose a lot of men."

U.S. AIR COMMAND--STRATEGY. Commander Coneycutt explains more, "Artillery, aerial rocket artillery and air strikes have been our aces-in-the-hole. As a matter of fact air power is a way of life here in Vietnam. U.S. Aircraft have been flying over the skies of Vietnam for the last ten years. It began with *Operation Rolling Thunder* [and ended with the Christmas Bombings]. All four of our military services are using air components including jet fighters, jet bombers and attack helicopters, Reconnaissance and observation of North Vietnam, search and rescue operations, troop transport, cargo and refueling missions. We have trained the South Vietnamese forces as well and now the South Vietnamese Air Force (VNAF) has a tactical air command center to help them coordinate air-ground cooperation. This is the way to do it."

Lieutenant Colonel Coneycutt gives a word of encouragement and hope for the troops with, "You have a job ahead of you. Even with our superior technological force, we have a very determined enemy but you men are highly trained troops and you will win. We will get quick victories by pinpointing the location of enemy's forces, isolating them from support, 'hamstringing their maneuver capability and finally smothering them with our overwhelming firepower.'"

Buzz says to Peter, "Our enemy is ready and waiting for us. For now, we really don't know for sure what destiny has in store for us up there on that hill, do we?"

Peter adds his wise ideas with this most important question, "It is the allure to battle. This is why we fight. It seems with all of this that we the U.S.A. just want to fight an enemy. We must let these people alone. It seems there will never be an end to this madness?"

Buzz says most wisely, "I don't think there ever will. I was talking to a Soldier today and he said to me with this most honest and truthful quote I have ever heard: 'And God help me when this war ends, trust me, they all do end, I truly feel a part of me will die,'" [quoted from motion picture Under Heavy Fire]. Or when war does end as said by George C. Scott, in the movie Patton; 'All glory is fleeting.'"

Buzz adds most sincerely, "And about the Trail, Operation Apache Snow, the neutral territory in Laos and Cambodia, enemy numbers and battle strategy, jungle terrain and underground bunkers."

"I hope it will all be O.K. for us but as for me, when all of this is said and done, when it is all over, after we have all lived-out this life's adventure here in Vietnam; I will hope that none of this will have been in vain—-that all of it will end well for *Our Bravest Young Men*," says Buzz once more.

Chapter 12

More Pre-Mission Intelligence

Briefings with Commander Coneycutt

Commander Coneycutt now changes the subject to explain more of the importance of A Shau Valley and the Trail.

HISTORY AND USE OF THE HO CHI MINH TRAIL "Now, I will discuss again the importance of A Shau Valley with its relation to the Trail. We have used advanced military technologies to monitor the Trail. We have target acquisition equipment, night observation devices and automatic data processing equipment, seismic sensors, surveillance and observational equipment. This equipment can provide us with very close coordination between intelligence activities and operational forces which we need here in Vietnam. Yes, these new advantages will do well for our troops." Now Commander Coneycutt asks, "But what is this Trail? It is 12,000 miles of roadway. The Trail begins in Hanoi and crosses into Laos at the DMZ and continues south. It is a combination of several roads--paved or dirt-- footpaths, bicycle paths, foot paths and truck routes. Where is the Trail? The trail is where many roads come into and go through to Cambodia, Laos and North Vietnam and into South Vietnam. The enemy keeps coming in here with his supplies through this network of trails which are well disguised."

The Commander explains further, "The Ho Chi Minh Trail is a complex web of pathways and roads and mountain passes. These passes are crucial checkpoints. There we have sensors placed that can detect sound, heat, and vibrations. But on the Trail we need more radio relay stations, communications posts and movement sensors to look for North Vietnamese infiltration levels."

He continues to speak, "The Ho Chi Minh Trail also called the Truong Son Road named after the mountain chain that runs through Vietnam. You know the Viet Cong Soldiers have taken an oath before embarking on the Trail, swearing not to return until the war is over. The enemy is taking supplies on the Trail--on old French and Russian-built bikes--on foot and on trucks and keep coming." [NOTE: between 1965 and 1975, a total of 1,777,027 tons of supplies had been moved down the Truong Route.]. He continues, "We use our infrared sensors to locate this traffic. But hot spots are made by our bombs from the day before so getting exact accuracy is difficult. The trail is charted and our Air Force is doing a good job of putting our enemy out of commission with our Stratofortresses and our Phantoms. Our enemy is also the thick cloud cover for which this part of the world is so well known. The enemy can hide under cloud cover. Cloud cover does not work for us when it comes to air support for our ground troops but we can use clouds so they can make mud and you know how we do this? We seed the clouds with silver iodide to make more rain for the Trail. We need floods to make mud. We can even make the mud more slippery with other chemicals added to the clouds. We can make a lot of mud."

Buzz leans over and says in Pete's ear, [as said by John Prados], "'Make mud not war!'" Pete laughs and can't stop.

Pete turns around laughing and says, "You idiot."

The Commander continues, "We make the clouds work for us. We even bounce search lights off of the clouds for more light at night."

Buzz leans over and whispers in Pete's ear again, "Yes I am for any advantage we can give to our troops but cloud cover--cloud cover? I was always told, my entire life that clouds are supposed to be good? Our commanders don't like it because it prevents air support of our troops." Peter adds, "No, clouds are not wanted here in Vietnam except by our enemy." [Peter laughs.]. Buzz says, "Well I was always taught and I always thought that ..." Peter interrupts him, "What now, idiot?" Buzz says, "Well, I am pissed."

Peter says, "No, don't do it here-—not now.

Buzz laughs and says again, "No I am pissed at this cloud-cover shit."

Peter says, "Pissed at what now? You are always pissed at somethin.'"

Buzz answers with, "Yeah but I always thought that clouds were good. What is wrong with cloud cover? It brings rain for plants and thus water for the rice crops to provide food for these people. Rice is important to these people. These people need food; therefore, they need clouds. By God, these were our first lessons in geography class in school…we had to know. I mean we had to know this stuff. From my first school days until now, it seems to have changed a lot. Did I miss something along the way—-or is it just I? What is wrong with cloud cover, Pete?"

Pete answers, "Ah, don't worry about that—-25 million acres of farmland so far have been destroyed in this damn war."

Peter says resolutely, "Ah, let's just sit and listen to the Commander speak. If we don't listen to him and learn somethin', we might--just might--possibly lose, not only our beating hearts, but we will lose our asses out there in this damn jungle somewhere--so just shut up and listen because I don't want to lose my ass out-there because I didn't get any of it."

Buzz then says, "Man, Pete, you are funny tonight. You are a man of my heart. Well, all I can say is if this is the case, all this shit going on with that trail, then we will lose our asses up there on Hill 937. With the trail and the neutrality working against us, then we must be careful and determined to fight to win this war."

Buzz changes the subject, "Let me tell you this *info*, well, a couple of years ago, a new variety of rice called the *Indica* variety was found in the Philippines that so far is boosting world production of rice and maybe one day it will boost world production of rice by about 20%. Isn't it good that one man can do something good for another? And also an American agronomist, Borlaug, who developed hybrid wheat called *dwarf wheat* in northwest Mexico that tripled wheat production. So let the Commander have his cloud cover."

Lieutenant Colonel Coneycutt continues, "The cover of the jungle canopy also leaves cover for the enemy. Our pilots have to follow radio commands. It is difficult to bomb targets that you don't know where they are located."

He continues, "But another problem is our neutrality--especially when we can't bomb near neutral territory. [Many Hawks amongst the politicians firmly believed that Washington ought to have ignored the 1962 Geneva Accords.]

Commander Coneycutt tells the Soldiers as he changes the subject of sensors on the trail, "We have sensors out there for many different uses. We have sensors to detect movement on the trail and we have them disguised as plants."

Buzz then leans over, gets closer to Pete's ear, and says, "That won't work. What happens when the batteries run out?" [Pete laughs.]

The Commander continues, "We also have seismic sensors out there."

Buzz then asks Pete, "What happens if they run a herd of Water Buffalo through there?"

The Commander speaks about it, "We have put sniffer sensors out there as well."

Buzz leans over near Pete and says, "Our Soldiers saw huge buckets of Water Buffalo urine hanging from trees and wondered what that was all about and now we know. It seems as if, 'The battle of the Trail became a contest between technology and ingenuity,'" [Prados].

Peter laughs out of control.

The Commander says, "The Viet Cong can't run from us anymore under the canopy of trees because we have Agent Orange that defoliates the trees."

Buzz then leans over to tell Pete quietly, "What happens if the enemy decides on night routes or new routes under the leafed canopies? I hope this is not a suicide mission like the rest of this damn war."

Peter responds with, "Yeah, well we will find out soon enough—-if we live long enough for it."

Buzz says, "You know what I heard about this Trail? "The enemy does not even bother to hide when he hears the spotter planes overhead. I heard that the Trail is beginning to look like a superhighway and one Ranger calls it 'Interstate Charlie.' One advisor said 'The only thing they don't have is stop lights.'" [Peter laughs.]

Guy says, "No. We are going to win this war. Mc says, "I want to win this war."

Buzz quips in, "We have to find those underground bunkers. We just need to kick some ass and fight it like a real war and bust bunkers on the way with our Recoilless Rifles. Yeah, we are going to go bunker busting on some hill out there somewhere."

HISTORY OF PAVN & TRAIL. Commander Coneycutt says Captain Kenner is an expert on early political Vietnam and he will tell you how this all came about. Commander Coneycutt then introduces Captain Kenner, "Captain Kenner will give you an historical insight or perspective on how this all began with the PAVN and the Trail in Vietnam."

A master sergeant who was standing by the door yells, "*Tension!*" Everyone in the room gets to their feet and snaps to attention. They salute.

Now Captain Kenner gives a lecture on the political history of Vietnam and the Trial.

Captain Kenner explains, "This Trail has existed for centuries as primitive foot paths set-up for trade routes that also run from North Vietnam to southern and western Vietnam. But it was improved to help tie Vietnam into a united country. Captain Kenner explains, "About the Trail itself ... the 559 Transportation Group 559 expanded and improved these small roads and foot paths. In September 1964 the Trail was still a one-lane dirt road that could only be used by jeeps and light trucks. This group is responsible for beginning the expansion of the Trail and they were called the People's Army of Vietnam (PAVN) and were created in 1959. They were responsible at the time for improving the road lines through Laos and Cambodia. In Vietnam the Truong Son system (the Trail) began with the 559 Transportation Group, Phan Tue, Dong Nguyen, Bui Phung, Nguyn Sinh, and the Military-Civilian Department of the VPA began a system of foot and bicycle traffic. Bicycles are known as the "steel horses." The favorite bicycle is the French made Peugeot or the Czech made *Czech Favorit* bicycles and they generally carry 300 pounds per bike."

Politics with the Trail began with the PAVN the group behind the movement of the liberation in Vietnam. The movement for unification and independence in Vietnam began not just with the Viet Cong and not just with the Viet Minh, but with the PAVN (People's Army of Vietnam)--a nationalistic movement. This group was formed by Ho Chi Minh and also General Vo Nguyen Giap who was the commander-in-chief of the PAVN. Group 759 and 959 was created to move supplies for the Pathet Lao in Laos into South Vietnam. This political network that attempted unification of Vietnam and the vehicle for unification was the Trail. The Trail was needed to achieve this end. A well known General for the Viet Minh, Le Trong Tan said about the Trail when asked: What would you have done to win the war if you were American? He said, 'If they (U.S.) had been wise, they should at a certain point in time have cut a specific section of The Trail and taken over that area. Then we would have been stuck. We would never have been able to fight and win as we did. If they had been brave enough to do so, they would at least have severely disrupted our strategic network.'" Captain Kenner explains further, "Now that I have explained the origins of the Trail, I will explain our Neutrality Agreement. You see--in the summer of 1962--the United States signed the international peace agreement with Laos. All foreign military forces had to leave Laos. This is why we cannot enter Laos. But the Communists in January 1963 did not hold up to their end of the deal. This basically put an end to the cease-fire/neutrality in Laos. They did not care one iota about the Neutrality Agreement with Laos. They did not follow the Peace Agreements."

A WALT ROSTOW THEORY (Kennedy Advisor). Captain Kenner continues, "As Dr. Walt Rostow once said to our advisors in Washington, 'It is difficult, if not impossible, to win a guerrilla war with an open frontier. (...) A cessation of infiltration would not end the war in a day; but I am confident that, without steady support, the strictly domestic aspects of the Viet Cong effort could be dealt with in a reasonably short period of time.'"

Buzz then says, "The trail into South Vietnam must be stopped here in A Shau Valley if we want to win this war."

Peter says to Buzz, Mc, Guy, and John, "Dr. Rostow is right."

HISTORY & USE OF TRAIL. Captain Kenner says, "The North Vietnamese Army and the Viet Cong occupy Cambodia's eastern provinces using those places as staging areas to fight the war in South Vietnam. The Trail is terminated through this border. It is considered a secret zone or War Zone D and with this area, Victor Charlie (Viet Cong) and NVA can launch attacks against targets in South Vietnam. The Viet Cong call it the 'Forbidden Zone' since they have almost complete control and freedom of movement within it. Captain Kenner continues to explain, "So here we are with all of this neutral territory that surrounds our battlegrounds and gives the enemy a place to escape. He can re-enter with any number of troops in a continuous flow across the border. I hope this information has been able to give you some insight on our situation here in Vietnam. Thank you."

Commander General Wells then steps over to the microphone and speaks again, "Thank you Captain Kenner for your information."

Buzz then says, "What I find most important in all of this is that our commanding officers (CO's) must be provided more information in some way that can coordinate our tactics and strategies on the battlefields and get enemy numbers. *RECON/RIF* teams will try to get this information. Our Commanders must estimate the enemy strength and know the terrain. Under jungle cover it is easy for the enemy to mask his numbers and his movements. The Commander has to know the terrain in order to 'visualize the successful conduct of the battle.'"

The Commander says, "You men have tough job ahead of you now. These are some of the tactics we have to deal with. Troops here can become 'ground bound' if we don't work around these disadvantages such as the flow of enemy supplies and reinforcements, the steep gradients of the slopes and the dense vegetation. Also enemy movement must be monitored and stopped by our command and intelligence and we must use a strategy that works to stop the enemy traffic on the Trail. And also fighting in this jungle, we must be sure to provide a 360-degree security around our bases here. Another thing we have to contend with are the Sapper Armies. Many are indigenous, highly skilled, daring troops that are sent into battle first by the NVA. These Soldiers are well prepared."

Peter then says, "Yeah, we do have to know who we are fighting to win this war. As Sun Tzu Wu in his Art of War said, 'Know thy enemy and know thyself and you will win a hundred battles.' We must know who we are fighting."

Buzz says to Peter, "Our Commanders do not follow that strategy. That is the problem. In fact we don't know who and how many we are fightin."

And then Buzz mentions the crucial problem again, "And who is running this war--the military Generals, the politicians or the advisors in Washington—-who?

Sp4c. McConnell says, "Yeah, I think this problem is in part because we are fighting on neutral ground. The enemy has his hooches, spider holes, bunkers and booby traps dug in deep and into their territory ... to boot. I believe that Rostow said it right when he said that ... it is very difficult to win a guerrilla war with an open frontier.

Commander Richard Wells continues, "But I just don't want to quote here. Let me give you more detail on Sun Tzu's ideas on war. 'Thus, we may know there are a couple of important essentials for victory: (1) He will win who knows when to fight and when not to fight, (2) He will win who knows both superior and inferior forces. (3) He will win whose army is animated by the same spirit throughout all the ranks, (4) He will win who prepared himself, waits to take the enemy unprepared and (5) He will win who has military capacity and is not interfered with by his sovereign.' Buzz then asks Pete, "Yeah, but you wanna know what Sun-tzu really said about war?" Peter then answers, "No, I don't know what Sun Tzu said about war." Buzz says, "He said that 'All war is deception' and maybe--just maybe—that is the way we are fightin' it here."

Peter then says truly, "You know, Buzz, truer words have never been said about this war."

Buzz says smartly, "But really war is really just all about *the hill* as Duke of Wellington said, 'The whole art of war consists in getting at what is on the other side of the hill.'"

Peter then says most smartly, "You know *getting to the other side of the hill makes* the most sense to me. I will fight my way there. I will do my job! I was asked to come here to Vietnam for my country and my battle buddies."

John then says, "Yeah, I agree--no doubt about it. I will fight and still try to get to the other side of the hill no matter what our disadvantage. It's our duty. We will fight and we will do our job as LuRRP's. We will win."

Buzz says, "Yes, this is a farce because there is wrong-in-that because if we don't question why we came here to fight in this war, then we may be doomed to fight and lose our lives for it and never know *why* we fought it. What draws us into this mystical spell to fight here in Vietnam? We had our lives back in the World. We had the world at our feet. Then we come here to fight. There are many reasons why we do it--maybe to prove something to ourselves—-maybe to prove our manhood to ourselves or to somebody else. Maybe it is boredom, unemployment, Democracy, Freedom, an adrenalin rush, or maybe a girlfriend. But it's a fight for self-defense for our country—-for our buddies? We can search our minds over and over again—forever and again--trying to figure it out but we still have no answer. We do know one thing though; we do come here to fight and to win."

Peter then says, "Many of us are just young--just out of high school and volunteer and really do not know. And some of us are drafted and do not know. But I can say one thing for sure many of us are allured to war."

Mc also says, "Yes, maybe that is part of it. Maybe we are allured to war, perhaps."

Guy then says, "But we *will* fight for each other, for ourselves and for our country—-we will."

Buzz then says jokingly yet quite sincerely, "We will fight. We will kick our enemy's ass all the way back into Laos and Cambodia and let them keep on coming even with all their neutrality shit. We will keep the enemy out but it's a difficult job to keep out anybody from infiltrating through a border--*any border*--but we must do it to save ourselves." [The Soldiers all agree.]

Buzz continues, "In the A Shau Valley we will cut-off the enemy supply routes. And Mount Dong Ap Bia is going to be our proving ground. We will turn it to powder."

Peter says, "Yes, we have to fight for it."

John agrees and says, "It is our duty. [As said by a Marine Soldier, from the war in Iraq 2006], "'In my eyes, it's not a burden. It's an honor to fight and protect my country.'"

Sp4c. Dion Johnson says, "Yes it is an honor to fight. But I still ask *how we got ourselves into this mess?* I mean, I love my gun—-my M-16--but it ain't worth getting my ass blown off by some Sapper shit who just wants his snakes in this snake infested hole with neutral ground all around us. He can have it all with my blessings. It just ain't worth it to me, man. It makes no sense, anyway, in the first place."

Joel says, "Yes, I agree here with Dion. I see it is no good to fight in a war with all this neutral ground around us with the enemy just coming down through the Trail with fresh troops."

Buzz says, "And Rostow said it right, 'Unless U.S. forces are located in the Laos corridor, below the seventeenth parallel, that corridor will continue to be used as a major route of infiltration.' Yeah, and to boot, we don't even have the manpower to cover all that ground."

Joel says, "The enemy will be back over across the border into their neutral sanctuary after we chased them out and kicked their asses back into Laos. He will just replace his lost troops with more troops and come back again across the border *fresh* once again. There's plenty more."

Joel continues, "But for me, my real problem is that I just hope my commander is smart enough to use me in my unit the way I have been trained as a sniper. So many times we snipers are placed out there without any *thought in mind* as to how to use us to our best advantage in battle."

Joel talks about sniper fire, "But with my sniper fire, I'll get them. And as far as weapons are concerned as I have always said, the only way to fight this war is to train our Soldier in sniper fire. The enemy is doing an excellent job of taking us out with his sniper fire. And even with their damn booby traps they are gettin' us. Many of our casualties are a result of sniper fire and booby traps--don't forget. And with your guys' automatic weapons fire you average 200,000 rounds spent for every enemy body count. With us-- the Army and Marine snipers we get one dead enemy for every round fired. Every one of our bullets produces a body count. Just call us the '13 cents killer' because the rifle cartridges cost Uncle Sam 13 cents for each."

Joel explains more, "Sp4c. Wolfing and I are a two-man team. He is the spotter and I am the shooter. But you know, Buzz, I don't want you to get pissed-off at me for equating life with money and body counts. Do you really think that I would be here in this mess if I really had the choice?"

Joel says again, "But no ... I can't believe we are fighting a war like this. Even our air defense is not allowed to get into Laos or Cambodia either. And we just don't know how many troops have infiltrated through the border the night before."

Commander Coneycutt gets up to the microphone.

Commander Coneycutt speaks, "Most of us are eager and restless for battle. We will use our superior technology anywhere we need some good old American TLC." [The-entire-roomful of GI's, laugh, hoot, holler and whistle.]

One Soldier yells out, "Yeah, way to go!"

Another Soldier yells, "You better believe it." [more laughter.]

Another soldier yells out referring to Coneycutt, "Don't listen to him. He's a damn lifer." [more laughter-whistles.]

Peter when seeing all of these Soldiers gathered together with so much enthusiasm in their hearts--in this room now--thinks for a moment about one of the wisest quotes ever said of any war. This beautiful most truthful quote is said by Captain Josh Rushing after seeing footage of casualties in war [in Iraq], '*It makes me hate war, but it doesn't make me believe that we're in a world that can live without war yet.*'"

Buzz says so wisely to that wonderful quote ... "Yes ... we are still living in a world that cannot live without war yet. But maybe ... just maybe ... one day we will walk away from war forever."

Buzz then wonders again, "But war really is perplexing because some wars must be fought but with this war, we don't really know for sure what it is all about or why we are really fighting it, do we? But ... however, finally, before blood is spilled in any war, anywhere, we must ask ourselves *why-are-we fighting this war?* But maybe it is not just our country, America that wants to fight in battle to prove something? Maybe it is mankind ... since his beginning of time? I don't know ... why!"

He continues, "With *all* of this organized war effort and planning--to fight--to kill another--to go into battle ... if only all of this effort was put towards a solution ... a solution for peace ... maybe someway ... somehow ... a solution? Eleanor Roosevelt once said with these true words, 'We have to face the fact that either all of us are going to die together or we are going to learn to live together and if we are to live together we have to talk.'"

Buzz continues with these wise words, "Yes ... we have to talk!"

Joel and Dion say, "We have to talk."

John then says, "We have to talk."

Peter says, "Yes, we have to talk."

Then their minds go back to the reality of their world.

Lt. Col. Coneycutt then says to Lt. Harper, "Sp4c. Peter McConnell you will be the Assistant Team Leader. Captain Kenner and Lieutenant Harper are your commanding officers (COs) for your RECON Unit. Tomorrow, Lt. Harper with your RECON Unit, you will report with Captain Kenner for a briefing on your mission in the jungle. I want you men to report on time. I know you men will do the job asked of you on this mission. We are all counting on you. Your country is counting on you. You are all brave men. You are our county's *bravest young men.*"

The Commander continues, "But first, Lt. Harper, you will report with your team in the jungle for two missions here around our perimeter at Da Nang Air Base."

He continues, "We must never relax our vigil for our principle."

He continues to address Lt. Harper, "And tomorrow your team will report at 0500 on the tarmac for your mission out in the jungle. That will be all."

Commander Coneycutt continues, "Now you men are not to repeat this mission, anywhere outside of these walls. Do you men understand? Do you have any questions? Thank you. That's all. You are dismissed."

The troops get up and begin to walk out.

Buzz then says, "Man that was some talk."

Dion says, "Wow, man what a session. I wanna fight their asses now all the way back to the Cambodian/Laotian Border on that mountain called Mount Dong Ap Bia, Hill 937. But I just don't want to stop at the Cambodian Border either, believe me."

Buzz says, "Yeah, you are right."

Mc asks Guy, "Don't you think this war makes a little more sense now that we know all of this stuff?"

Guy answers with, "Yes, I think so and we can fight it honorably." Mc says, "I know we will fight it honorably."

Peter says, "And we will go to *RIF*--to get the *info* and fight. Yeah, we will first do our job riffing (reconnaissance-in-force) Hill 937."

John says, "That's the way to go."

Dion responds to that, "Yeah, we can't let anyone down now. We'll fight."

Guy says with understanding, "Yeah, now this trail and neutrality bit all does make more sense to me, now. We must conquer a hill on Ap Bia to stop it."

Peter now enlightened with it all agrees, "Yeah, it sure makes more sense, now."

But Dion then says now with some skepticism, "But man like 'at the Cong will pop-up out of them spider holes and shoot our asses right off, [snaps fingers together, everyone laughs]. This ain't really goina' be too terribly cool."

Buzz then says, "Yeah, our Commanders have turned a blind eye to all of this. Just look at our struggle in the A Shau Valley so far. We just can't get a foothold in there."

Buzz continues, "I know holding the A Shau Valley is crucial for our troops. Our Special Forces Camp was booted out of the A Shau Valley by our enemy back in 1966 and now two years later, we are still trying to get it back."

[ACTUAL QUOTE OF COMMANDER--HAMBURGER HILL. At *too high of a price* with the battle on Mt. Dong Ap Bia--the Battle of Hamburger Hill the sacrifice was made. After the Battle of Hamburger Hill was fought a reporter questioned General Creighton Abrams (MACV Commander) about the high casualty rate of the battle of Hamburger Hill and he answered, "We drove them back into North Vietnam but I was criticized for the casualties that entailed. If they would let me know where they would like me to fight the next battle, I would be glad to do it there." That was General Abram's reasoning.]

[COMMANDER'S ACTUAL QUOTE. And Major General Zais (a Commander for Hamburger Hill) defended himself from a reporter's question about the outcome of the Battle of Hill 937 (Hamburger Hill) with this, "The Hill is my area of operations. That was where the enemy was where I attacked him. If I find the enemy on the other hills in the A Shau, I assure you, I'll attack him there also." He continued "I don't know how many wars we have to go through to convince people that aerial bombardment alone cannot do the job." But the important question is, if it is not going to work with airpower and the troops, who would be able to do the job? This is a decision our military commanders have to make. The Commander of the 101st said that the only importance of the hill was that the enemy occupied it and his (U.S. commanders) mission was to destroy the enemy forces and installations. He said that he found the enemy on Hill 937 and that is where he fought him but walked away shortly thereafter.]

Now the Soldiers step outside the COHQ and are hit with pouring rain in pitch darkness with only the perimeter lighting to see. They become completely soaked by the heavy downpour.

"Damn, it is always raining in this damn hole," says Buzz.

And now they proceed together in silence on their way to their bunkers for a good night's sleep but still thinking about everything. They learned enough for one good day. Peter turns on the radio which now plays a Hank Williams song sung by Conway Twitty and Loretta Lynne called I Can't Help It. *Today I passed you on the street (...)*. This song reminds him of Sherry. He thinks about Sherry. And another song came on the radio by country music singers, Carl and Pearl Butler with, Just Thought I'd Let You Know, *"Forgive me friend for buttin' in. But I'd like a word with you. Each night you're standin' at this bar (...)*, [Columbia].

Peter says, "I love this stuff. But now let's go. Tomorrow will be another day for another pre-mission briefing to go out into the bush around our perimeter here—near the base."

"Yes, they want us on practice runs around our base," says Mc.

"Yes, we will all be there tomorrow," says Dion.

"Yes ... we will," says Buzz.

141

Chapter 13

Lieutenant Harper's Squad from Base Da Nang out On Patrol in the Jungle

At COHQ, (company headquarters) the next day, Lieutenant Harper pulls a team from the company battalion. They are now going to be briefed on a mission to seek, intercept, and destroy enemy units that are on retreat in the jungle around Da Nang Air Base.

Lieutenant Harper says, "Before we hit the guerrillas out there in the bush, understand as General Alejandro Bayo stated, 'Feet and legs are the engine of the guerrilla.'"

Peter now says, "Yeah, the Vietnamese go out and gather up old discarded tires from our military vehicles, take this recycled rubber to make their sandals and then go to battle wearing them. How can you compete with that?"

Lieutenant Harper continues with, "You also have to know that the enemy may be well dug in and ready to defend their positions. Commo is all over here and it is heavily booby trapped."

Now Peter, Guy, Mc, Buzz, Joel, Dion, John and the rest of the team all load onto the choppers—the Slicks—for insertion to their destination into the jungle. Peter is ready to fight. The seventy-pound rucksack on his back feels like that and more. Peter slips his butt onto the skids of the chopper and sits as it hovers and blows over a maze of green canopy. He is a strong man--a large man with a large frame. Guy thinks as the hard wind blows against his face *how lucky he and Peter are to have Candice and Sherry.* But now Peter and Guy must let that-other-life go because now they must go into battle.

Pete leans over with a smile on his face and says jokingly to Guy, "In this slick, we move so fast above this maze of jungle, it seems like a movie placed on fast-forward speed. But I wish I could put my life on fast forward speed and be back home right now. I wish that I was looking down at a very different tree—my walnut tree back home." [They laugh.]. The pilot yells out suddenly, "This is your spot men—jump, jump now!" Peter looks down ready to jump. Peter leaps down and hits the ground. Peter lands hard but not harder than his training in boot camp and his AIT (Advanced Individual Training) at Fort Benning and Fort Campbell for which he was prepared.

But now his mind races to a faraway time--to a distant memory of time long ago in New York when *as a child he jumped to the ground from his tree house high in a tree.*

Lieutenant Harper shouts orders to Pete's squad, "Run your asses for cover."

The gunship inserts these Soldiers into an open field.

Buzz says, "I feel like a sitting duck here."

No sooner than the last man had jumped to the ground, did incoming start with AK-47 machine-gun bursts, incoming mortar, and grenade fire.

Lieutenant Harper shoots his orders, "Get to cover, fast, now, or you will never get there."

John is the first to the tree line. All squad members make it into the tree line. Just as they get into the cover of the jungle, intense gunfire and mortar rounds start again. The enemy is dug into position and begins to defend it heavily. A troop is hit and falls down--screaming loudly as he falls. He falls to the ground and moves no more. The medic says that there is no more to be done for him. Everyone knows no more can be done. From their left flank about twenty yards away, mortar rounds begin to fire around them. Pete feels one round whiz by his head with a flash and with the smell of cordite. The troops are digging-in frantically, at a frenzied pace and taking cover from incoming mortar.

Peter trying to be a smart ass, asks the Soldier sitting next to him, "You know our people back home would never believe that such a hell exists out here in this beautiful tropical jungle, would they?" But Peter does not hear the Soldier's response but feels the Soldier's warm blood hit him in the face. Peter turns to look at the Soldier and in horror, sees sitting upright, an unrecognizable form of mangled flesh which was once a man. What was once--a fraction of a second earlier--a young Soldier talking to Peter about the war, cannot answer Peter's question. A split-second-thought flashed through Peter's mind, *He heard my question, but I'll never know his answer. For an eternity my words were the last words he ever heard. My words were the last.*" Peter then says of the Soldier's wife that he left behind, [a U.S. Soldier killed in the U.S. War in Iraq on October 19, 2005], 'His loss in my life only grows as the months slowly become years and I begin to comprehend he is never, ever coming home.' She will wait forever broken-hearted."

Suddenly two Soldiers get up and start running fast to the cover of a fallen tree truck. As the two men run a two-yard dash in the midst of blazing gunfire, one Soldier is hit and falls in his tracks face down to the ground. The other Soldier who was running next to him stops to help his fallen comrade, but in so doing, he also takes a fatal hit and falls next to his dying comrade. One Soldier says to the other in his dying-whispering voice, "Hey, thanks. I appreciate it." The other Soldier says, "Yeah, any time, man," and they die together side by side in battle knowing of each other's fate. Buzz says to Peter sadly, "Hey, what a waste--those two Soldiers. I was just talking to one of them and he said he was looking forward to going state-side tomorrow to see his wife and his newborn. He was very happy with his life in this world especially after his *wife's giving birth* to their first child." Peter then says with much hurt in his heart, "Yeah, I have to talk to his wife and explain to her *that I was the last person to talk to her husband.*"

The jungle suddenly falls silent from the ravages of man's fury.

Peter says again, "You know Buzz, this is a beautiful jungle, but look at what man has turned this place into ... a hell-on-earth." Buzz says resolutely, "Yes, this jungle is beautiful but as long as we can keep this jungle at a reasonable distance." [They laugh.]. Those new Soldiers back in the World are prepping for war now with so much eager anticipation in boot camp somewhere and they don't have an idea of the hell they have waiting for them here in Vietnam."

The Medivac Dust-Off comes in to pick-up the men who lost their lives this day. The bodies are packed well and neatly sealed into the awaiting body bags with careful attention given to placing each piece of the body into the correct body bag. Their remains are now most dearly entrusted to the hands of another. These trusted people will take very good care of their remains and will be sure to give these remains an honorable burial and resting place that they so much deserve. As the Medivac takes off, Peter looks up at the slick with the body bags lying side by side and he says to Buzz, "All that is left is lifeless nothing-- no thoughts of their own with no life of their own. They are nothingness. These men went off to war as Soldiers looking to save the world but now the world must place their remains to rest--safely."

Buzz then says, "And yes ... I know there is *no return*."

The unit sets up camp with their perimeter of claymore mines and each Soldier takes a watch. Mc then says, "Let us be careful on our watch and not fall asleep because we don't know if this sleep tonight may be our last and follow us into an eternal sleep tomorrow."

Two Soldiers each at a time had a two-hour look-out duty and the off-duty Soldier took his rest. That very evening, Lieutenant Harper says, "Tomorrow we will forge further towards our goal and Sp4c. McConnell, you will take point. We will push these bastards all the way back to the border." He continues to address McConnell, "You are a good lookout and remember nothing passes by your eyes unnoticed. You got that McConnell?"

The next day in the early morning jungle, the sounds of the crickets, the cicadas and frogs could be heard. There are a couple of colorful birds hopping quickly and lightly from tree branch to tree branch and the platoon walks single file through the jungle with Peter as point. Point man must be alert to all signs of mines, booby traps and enemy and is the first in the line of fire. Peter has a very keen sixth sense with perfect hearing and vision which is required for the important position of point. The remainder of the unit follows behind him trusting in his keen senses and judgment.

Two Soldiers are talking quietly and reasoning it all in their *own way*... Private Al Decker says to Pvt. John Kastner, said by U.S. Soldier in war w/Iraq "'Well we are taking the fight to the bad guys.'" Pvt. Kastner then says, [as said by U.S. Soldier in war w/ Iraq], "'It's just bad people trying to stop us from doing our job.'" The Soldiers continue to speak that which is in their hearts. One says, "Here on the battlefield we have each other's backs. My motto is keeping your buddies safe and they'll keep you safe." Sp4c. Dion Johnson then says to Sp4c. Joel Hammerstein, "I like the way you popped that sapper out of the tree yesterday." John then says to Joel, "Well, we need more like you with your sniper fire in this war." Joel says rather angrily, "You know I really don't want to get my kicks from shooting men out of trees."

Aaah ... Aaah ... ear-defining screams from Sp4c. Kastner as he falls ten feet into a concealed--camouflaged, grass-covered pit—a booby trap—trapping the Soldier into a deep hole of sharpened bamboo spikes covered with feces. He slams face down onto the punji sticks and screams so loudly

that no man could do ... unless he was in the most horrific
of pain. The spikes puncture his face and his eyes. His eyes
are now pools of blood, pieces of eyeball, vitreous humor
that have been contaminated with bacteria. Pvt. Kastner
says, "I can't see, I can't see--my eyes, my eyes!" The
medic gives him a syringe of morphine. But the bacteria
moves quickly into his blood stream—-*septicemia*. Shrieking
and shivering--his head jolting backwards--his back arching
upwards—-his mouth gaping wide in a horrible silent scream
... as he dies.

Peter then says with such great sorrow in his heart, "I
was just talking with him and he was so happy to be going
home to be with his young son. When will it ever end for us-
-his son--and his son's son?"

Mc then says, "Well in a way he's lucky."

Buzz asks, "What do you mean *he's lucky?*"

Mc believes this, "Well he does not have to suffer
anymore of life's hardships."

"Guy says most sadly, "Well he is lucky that he is no
longer in pain."

John adds resolutely, "He knows death. It is something
us living will never know until it happens."

Buzz says, "Yes he now sleeps peacefully forever. His
life is over. His is gone." Guy says, "It is something… this
battlefield, here, is bringing the reality of death to us."
Peter then says with all *the sadness in his heart*, "He had
so much ahead of him in his life. He had so much waiting for
him. He was young-—too young. His life was waiting for him.
His whole life was yet ahead of him waiting. He is now a
statistic of war--for this war in Vietnam." Buzz then says
very angrily, "Oh those f*cking Gooks. I am so sick of it--
sick of them. Only a f*ckin' coward will kill a man like
this. Now, I will kill anything for doing this to my *battle
buddy*—-the f*cking Cong—-the f*cking gooks!" Mc then says to
John very sadly, "It is not so much fun out here in this
jungle, is it, John? Can you *feel the pain* as Robert Kennedy
said so well—-we must *feel the pain*." Buzz then interjects
another, "Or this quote from John Singleton Mosby, 'War
loses a great deal of romance after a Soldier has seen his
first battle.'" Peter then says sadly, "This quote is said
from another Soldier in war, [as said of a young Soldier,
Leon, in the War in Iraq 2006], 'They were young full of
life and in pursuit of a future they'll never know. ...'
They were young—-so very young." Peter continues with this
point, "Look at how much of their future they have lost.

While we are still walking on this planet, these dead Soldiers will be sleeping forever. Time stops forever for these dead. Everything that we *will* know, they will never know. Time is locked for them. They will never see a man walk on the moon or see supersonic space travel, unmanned aerial vehicle or a jet liner. They will never see the World Wide Web, computerized technology—-the iphone, the ipod, the ipad--the personal computer, the computer, ARPANET (connects 4 computers), integrated circuit (puts innards on one tiny chip), LED (light emitting diode), IEEE 802.16 (antenna transmits internet access), [Alex Hutchinson], TV remote control, microwave oven or ever know the concept of cell phone technology with its ease of use and its multipurpose functionality. They will never know the latest automobile technology such as forward drive, electronic ignition, three-point seat belt; rear-end posi-traction wheels, Ram Air with 366 hp under the hood, electronic fuel injection and electric windows. And on the dash a GPS (Global Positioning Satellite) system with simplified touch screen menus with voice and visual directions, programmed maps, voice prompted turn by turn directions which can take the driver anywhere he programs it to go. And communications satellites, fiberoptics and float glass (molten glass over molten steel), [Hutchinson]. The dead Soldier will never know organ transplants, coronary bypass surgery, angioplasty, the birth control pill, in-vitro fertilization, PROZAC, MRI scanning, DNA fingerprinting (with 30 billion units of DNA), scanning tunneling microscope (map surface of atoms, microscopic finger printing), genetic engineering, laser beam, pace maker, IV protease inhibitors, polymerase chain reaction (make DNA cheaply and quickly), genetic sequencing, [Hutchinson], polio vaccine, Digital X-Rays or any marvel of modern medicine. They will know nothing! Or do you think that these dead Soldiers could ever imagine the wireless telephone--cell phone where calls can be made from anywhere? Could they ever imagine *the age of technology* with the computer and the *World Wide Web* with its instantaneous access to anything anywhere in this world with the touch of a finger--or the magnificent ease-of-use of the computer keyboard with built-in programs that can do almost anything and easily erase an error with the touch of a button? Compare this to the typewriter with the rubber-type ink erasers? Or would these Soldiers ever experience running in waffle-soled running shoes and be able to wear Velcro, carbon fiber—-Kelvar--or experience the use of a cordless tool, smoke detectors, industrialized robots or superglue. Or would they experience wonderful listening to the clear and perfect sounds of digital music or a music synthesizer, a Sony walkman or an MP3 player? Or would they ever know about charged coupled devices (used in digital cameras) or be excitedly engrossed in a video game? Or be able to go directly to an automated bank teller without ever having to get out of the car? Any new technology today and tomorrow, they will never know. They will know nothing!" Peter continues about a *needless death* in a war, "Death in war for the Soldier ... he will never know what could have been in his life--a life gone forever (and for nothing). The dead Soldier is now only a memory to the living. 'They were all my age. I think of the good life I have lived and they never had a chance to live. They didn't give their lives. Their lives were taken,' [as said by Andrew Rooney].

　　And for a parent ... this puts life *out of its proper order*. The only consolation can be had when the parent can say *he had his time no matter how short it was* ... and he fought and he died. But for the parent this death is still *out of order*. How absolutely horrible it is to take sons away from their mothers and their fathers if it does not have to be. As I said before, 'Wrong is wrong no matter who does or says it,'" [said by Malcolm X]. Peter continues, "I cannot imagine their immense loss." Buzz interjects, "And back to the cell phone; what about the absolutely wonderful cell phone camera? The camera cell phone in which one can go into the inner-most execution chambers of a hanging (President Hussein Iraq 2006)--to see the horror of the true brutality of mankind's nature at its worst? This affords moments that one could never be allowed to see—-especially with the most eager look on the faces of the executioners and the look of *horrific fear of impeding death* on the condemned man's face? But most importantly, one can see the cruel nature of mankind at these otherwise most hidden moments. One is allowed this rare chance to see; albeit, the photos are grainy and amateurish but nonetheless—-yes the cell phone camera! These photos are available for us to see these fortunate glimpses of the barbarity of mankind. How awful! Sort of in this way ... we are reliving the *Old American West lynching* but with much greater detail. We can see the expressions on the faces--the hate and fear. It is absolutely essential to know of the capability of this type of brutality." Buzz continues with earnest but changes the subject about the invasion of another country, "But with regards to the invasion of another country and the hanging of its dictator, the United States should not get involved in providing its own justice by putting our noses into the political affairs of another country-—bottom line--because,

148

honestly, it is really none of our business. Most people the-world-over should question if we the U.S. should invade another country, topple its dictator and hang him." Mc then says most wisely, "But Sadaam Hussein went into villages in his country and committed mass murder—-genocide--on innocent people—-the Kurdish people in Northern Iraq--gassing them and killing thousands despite warnings from the world and from a U.S. Senator, Peter Galbraith. He had`warned us well."

Then a Soldier screams, "I have been hit. I have been hit." Peter looks over to the Soldier and sees the Soldier's entire uniform is splattered with blood. Buzz then runs over to the Soldier and asks him, "Where are you hit? The medic and Buzz attempt to work on the Soldier. They tear-off his uniform to look for his wounds. They find no wounds, lacerations or injuries of any type. Buzz asks, "Were you standing right next to Sp4c. Kastner when he was killed? Were you? You were, were you not?" The Soldier answers, "Yes, why yes, I was. Oh, then it is only is his blood. Oh, man, what a relief! It is only his blood. It's his blood and not mine. It is only Kastner's blood. It's not my blood? Man ... that was close. What a relief; I'm alive!"

Buzz suddenly bursts out very angrily to the Soldier and says to him, "You are acting like a coward. You just saw a man lose his life? You have his blood all over your uniform?! What the hell do you mean you feel relieved, *it is only his blood*? He was killed. What do you mean *it is only his blood*? This Soldier is dead. You have the dead Soldier's blood on your uniform and you are relieved? He just lost his life. What shit is this, man?" Buzz says nothing more and walks away in complete disgust.

Guy asks sadly, "Kastner got it. He is dead but what would Kastner have said if the situation was reversed?"

Peter then answers Guy's question sadly with a bit of truth, "Perhaps the same damn thing." Peter walks over to Buzz and sees that he is very upset and then says to him to try to calm him down a little, "You either feel-the-loss and stay behind or you move on quickly and try not to think about it any more." Mc then asks John about all of this death, "While training over there on that beautiful coast of Southern California at Camp Pendleton, did they prepare you for this here, did they, John?"

"No, they did not," answers John sadly.

The helicopter picks up the Soldiers and takes Peter's squad back to the Camp Eagle for a debriefing.

Chapter 14

Back at Camp Eagle and into the Jungle to Patrol Again

Back at their bunks, life does go on but it does not for the dead. All that is left for the deceased is the need to be put into an eternal resting place. The Soldiers are given orders this day to get to the target area above Bloody Ridge. Their mission is to get there tomorrow, but for tonight the Soldiers rest, relax and eat at Base Camp Eagle.

And for now, the Soldiers return to their bunkers to pack their gear.

Buzz continues, "Hey men it is pack-up time and we ain't goin' home any time too soon."

Such horror has passed into their lives these past hours. Peter now walks into the room.

Buzz then asks Peter, "Hey, man, what is wrong? You got the look like you are carrying the weight of this entire world on your shoulders?"

Peter responds with, "Well I guess I do. Battle is no fun."

Buzz then asks Peter crassly, "Why was it supposed to be fun?"

John then says to Buzz, "Shut up man. We don't need your brainy-ass comments around here, now--trust me." [Some laugh.]

The men begin to clean and load their weapons again and pack-up their gear for the bush.

Mc says, "Load your ruck. Let us get this gear straight, men. It has to be packed right."

Pete says, "I'm hearing you. I know."

Pete packs his gear--his weapons and ammunition.

John packs his gear as well. He packs a camouflage fatigue uniform, plastic poncho, floppy brimmed hat, jungle boots, twelve foot nylon rope, bayonet with scabbard, harness pistol belt, pistol belt, plastic canteen, snap link, ammunition, magazines, ammunition pouches, triangular bandages, lensatic compass, mirror for signaling, pen flares, insect repellant, pen gun flares, compress bandages, first aid pouch, extra pair of socks, rappelling gloves, toilette paper and water purification tablets and his own individual weapon.

Guy puts his rucksack down, opens it and begins to fill it. Guy quickly grabs Sherry's color photo that is sitting-out on the table and proceeds to fold it carefully and packs it into his rucksack. Guy now has Sherry's photo inside his rucksack--taken for Peter--with the rest of his gear. Mc also packs his girl friend's photo into his rucksack.

John then quizzes Guy with the photos, "Hey what is this mission all about--a damn photo contest? [They all laugh.]. We are going down to ..."

John is cut off by Buzz, "Out there, in that damn jungle man, we need all the space for our gear. We can't waste it on beauty contests. We don't have room." [Everyone laughs.]

John then continues to pack all of his stuff and agrees with Buzz for once. John adds C-rations, a CAR-15, Tiger Stripes (an extra uniform), extra bandoliers, sugar, razors, watch, several knives, band aids, shaving cream, tooth brush and tooth paste.

Buzz says suddenly and with surprise, "Oh man! Are you for real or are you just shittin' me, John?" [shaking his head from side to side]. "Talk about taking photos and stuff that we don't need out there on the battlefield; I don't believe this guy," [pointing to John]. "Look at him--tooth paste on the battlefield? No way, man! No way!" [Everyone laughs.]. "You know, man, the Viet Cong really don't give one holy damn if your mouth is brushed or not--that is--once they fill your gut with lead; they really don't give a damn about your mouth. And I bet you really wouldn't care much yourself, if your teeth were brushed or not if you had a couple of nice rounds of lead sittin' in your belly, would you, John? Once your gut is full of lead no one is going to care about your mouth--ever—believe me. Just give me a break, man, with that tooth-paste shit would you? We are not going out on a Girl Scout cook-out."

John retorts back, "Yeah, but you really must care about my mouth because you are always telling me to shut it." [Everyone laughs.]

John continues, "And you say you want a break? I'll give you a break right across your nose if you don't shut that damn mouth of yours. Here let me shut it for you, now, if you like?" John holds his fist right-up in Buzz's face gritting his teeth in anger. John says talking through his

151

clenched teeth, "Look—see—my teeth how white they are?" [John is pointing to his own teeth.]

Guy then steps in to try to slow these two men down.

Buzz then says to John, "You think you can shut me up? Try it! Go ahead and try. Take a punch." [Buzz holds a clenched fist up to John's face.]. You won't have anymore teeth to brush either by the time I'm done with you—-trust me." [Everyone laughs.]

John then asks Buzz now very sarcastically, "So you think that I should not take my tooth paste with me, then? [Everyone laughs again.]. If you say not to take it then, Buzz, I won't take my tooth paste with me but I am not a pig like you, with a bad mouth like yours."

John continues talking to Buzz rather sarcastically, "You know something; I know my enemy doesn't care about my teeth but I ain't gonna lose any sleep over it. But ... I think I just might cry right now just thinking about it. But I do know one thing for damn sure, I just want to shut *your* damn face for good. I have heard enough of your face for one lifetime--trust me."

John is very angry and grabs Buzz by his front collar and pulls him in closely to his face and says, "Listen, if I want to bring my f*cking tooth paste to the battlefield, I will bring my f*cking tooth paste to the battlefield, O.K-- understand--*capiche*? Shut your face up!"

Peter jumps in and says, "Hey men quit this, shit! We can't be fightin' each other like this. We fight Charlie but not each other. Now don't worry—don't fight--we will be out of here soon ... but I don't know how or when."

Buzz calms down and is very, very apologetic to John, "OK. OK, man. I am sorry."

Buzz then stops turns around and looks at Mc square the face and asks Mc very nicely, "Mc ... did you pack your box of tooth picks? I know you can clean your teeth pretty good with that shit. Come on Mc tell John about that shit."

Mc always uses tooth picks and everyone laughs hysterically. Guy then steps in and says, "Oh ... this is enough of this shit."

And in between Guy trying to stop this fight, Mc has a chance to try for a swing at Buzz's face and Guy says, "Listen men, why are we hating-on-each-other like this? What is wrong with you, guys? We don't know if this is going to be the last time we lace-our-feet into our boots. Come on," as he slaps Buzz on his back in a friendly gesture.

Peter at this point is going through a lot of stress because he wants to get the job done but he is afraid of dying. He wants to see Sherry again and he wants to hold his new son with joy.

Peter says, "God gave me life. I want to stay here for awhile longer in my living flesh. No, not yet, I don't want to be put to rest for endless eternity—-no not yet."

His friends ignore the comment as they could see Peter was hurting.

Guy says to Peter patting him on the back, "Everything will be O.K. Come on let's get something to eat."

They go on to the mess hall without a thought of battle in mind—-to eat--yes to eat--because life does go on for the living. Peter, Mc, Buzz, Dion, Joel, John and Guy all stroll by the buffet to enjoy a good and relaxing meal together. They get some joy in the mess hall sitting before full delicious plates of food. They are served mashed potatoes with gravy, sliced roast beef, cut green string beans, cherry-vanilla, Dutch Crunch pudding for desert. Peter has milk for his beverage.

Dion explains his story most wisely, "Joel, you want to hear why I cut out of my life way back--way back in the world, man? I got tired of seeing Momma goin' with nothing. I got tired of seeing the black folk get nothing. I got tired of loosing my dignity. I got tired of being turned down. ... *No boy, we don't need you here.* I just got tired of it, man. But ... too ... I came here was for the bucks and a job. And I have a good talent and they saw that. They need me here. I am indispensable."

Buzz then says, "Yeah but as Charles De Gaul once said, 'Graveyards are full of indispensable men.'"

Dion continues, "And I am good with my weapons. These steel babies got my interest real big-time and the army has trained me on how to use them right. You know whad' it means to be able to shoot? You know what I'm sayin'? I am "somebody" here in the military. The military needs me with my shooting skills. I'm good. Here I have some hope. The military knows my skills and they use it. Here I am given the respect I need because I know how to fight. I want to help my buddies. I know my weapons like nobody else does and I can shoot better than the best of us." Buzz now says, "I believe you are the best Soldier but when it is all said-

and-done, you go back to the world and do what you want. I
wanted to be a medic but they cross-trained me in weaponry
and a medic. I wanted to be trained only as a medic because
that's where my heart is. I am a premed major to be a doctor
of medicine--a physician. What pisses me off is they put a
f—kin' M-16 in my hands and I don't want it. I was going to
do something good for people but now I have to kill my
fellow-man. I was in my premed courses training to heal—-to
save the lives--which God has given to us. And now look at
what I must do here in Vietnam. My purpose on this planet is
to save lives not to take them. God gave us life and we
should respect it. It is my responsibility to do what I can
to save life—-not to take it. I don't want to take a life if
I can possibly help it, sobeit. When you go against life,
you go against God." John then says, "But you are wrong. God
wants us to *protect/fight* for our lives—-like the Bible says
in "Exodus", 'The Lord is a man of war.'' Buzz says, "I will
protect life too; yes I will fight!" Joel says, "Well what
about me? Look at me. I don't like this mess anymore than
the next man around here. But still all the same, I will do
everything possible to do the best job I can with my sharp-
shooting skills. Back in the world, I hung out at the
shooting range to shoot clay pigeons. Is this hobby of mine
supposed to make me a killer, now? Now tell me, is it? In
boot camp, they saw how good I was with a rifle; so, they
sent me to "Nam and put me in sniper school. I am here now
and I am at a point in my life where I will be able to make
a difference in battle by saving my fellow soldiers out
there on the battlefield and I will do it as a sniper." Then
Dion says to Joel, "Hey, no, man, you really don't belong
here in this war, man. If I could I would send your scrawny
ass back right now to the States but I know you want to stay
here and do your tour. [Everyone laughs.]. No, you should
not be fighting here in this damn jungle." Joel then says,
"I know man, if you could, you would send me back to the
World right now. I know you would. Dion, you too should be
back in the World with your life. You don't belong here—-
anywhere out here shooting-up anything—-anywhere--with an M-
16 in your hands." Peter says next, "I like guns, also, for
target practice. I am a good sharp-shooter but they have
also trained me to kill and to use my M-16 to fight for my
country." John says, "Well I am here to get those people who
are trying to destroy our way of life--our freedom around
the world. I am here to save our way of life for all of us
and to give freedom to others. Our troops have aided so many
people all around the world from 1775 to present according
to the Committee on Foreign Affairs. This has involved

boundary disputes, military invasions, political tyranny, civil/domestic unrest (uprisings, coups, riots), armed insurrections, natural disasters, (2010 disaster relief), state/national secession attempts, infrastructure collapse. Such as one example-in 1914 we sent U.S. Marines into Haiti and Santo Domingo to save citizens from civil unrest."

Buzz asks John, "But look at it this way, John--don't you think maybe—just maybe--we might be destroying these people's way-of-life here also—-the life that they want for themselves? Joel agreeing, "Yeah, I agree with you, Buzz. "Why can't we just let these poor people live as they want to live? Who in the hell are we to come into this small poverty-stricken—a third-world country--and dictate to them how to live life?" John says, "You are wrong! These people here don't want to lose their freedom. I'll show everyone how to fight a war--that I will win it for the South Vietnamese people. The North Vietnamese are trying to take freedom away from these people here in South Vietnam." And Joel says to that, "No, I disagree with you. I don't think they care about *freedom American style*. They would rather live with their own country as a united country without our troops here. Just because it is freedom and democracy for America, does not mean that it is freedom and democracy for Vietnam. It's a different country and a different culture which is not ready to change to our way of freedom and democracy." Buzz says, "They are not ready for our democracy but we are here to give them our democracy. The reality of it is we are fighting a war that does not have to be fought. [And what about when a country that we are militarily involved with--45 years after Vietnam--hangs an 8-year-old boy as a means of political defiance against their enemy, it is time for us--the U.S.--to bow-out gracefully ... now, wouldn't you think? (Afghanistan War, 2011)]. John plays the devil's advocate once again, "But if we leave these people alone here, their war will go on forever. They need our help." Capt. Brahm and Sgt. Cross then sit down next to the Soldiers. "Hello, my name is Captain Gene Brahm." The Soldiers salute and Capt. Brahm salutes. "I am your squad leader." The other officer introduces himself as Sergeant Cross. Captain Brahm says, "I could not help but over-hear what this good man [pointing to John] was saying about that is saving our country from our enemy and for our freedom. And you know something', he's right." Captain Brahm quotes, "As George Washington said, 'If we desire to avoid insult, we must be able to repel it; if we desire to secure peace, one of the most peaceful instruments of our rising

155

prosperity, it must be known, that we are at all times ready for war.'"

Captain Brahm then turns to look at Buzz and asks, "And what do you men think about all this? I don't know but I think you men are trying to think of every excuse in-the-book as to why you should not be here fighting this war. You will get yourselves killed out-there on a hill with that thinking."

Buzz then answers back--with a wisecrack, "What book are you reading? It sure ain't the same one I'm readin'?"

Then, Sgt. Cross is also pissed-off with Buzz's remarks and says, "You know somethin' Soldier ... you irk me. You can't just come on in here and talk like this around here within our earshot. I'd like to Court-Marshal your ass right now for that remark. We don't need *your type of thinking* around here. The number one thing that we all have to consider is to save lives and do it the best way we can ... we have to fight. And to save lives we must follow orders. To do the job right, we have to go out there together—-obey orders--cover each others backs--to show the enemy that we are well prepared, disciplined Soldiers who fight for each other, for our great country and for our freedom. We must stay a cohesive fighting unit. It's like this: 'Who would desire peace, prepare for war,'" [Flavius Vegetius Renatus].

Buzz looking directly at Sgt. Cross then says, [as said by Lt. General James Mattis, USMC], "But for some soldiers it is ... 'Quite fun to fight 'em, you know--it's a hell of a hoot. It's fun to shoot some people. I'll be right up front with you, I like brawling.' But I know in the end ... once you have me pissed-off you will be my best buddy out-there on the battle field. I know you will 'be with [me] every step of the way, teaching, cajoling, enforcing, bringing out the strength and confidence'" [Colin Powell].

Captain Brahm says back, "We fight for each other and for our great country. As Winston Churchill once said '(...)like his soldiers, sailors, and airmen who died side by side with ours and carrying out their tasks to the end all over the world. What an enviable death was his.'"

Buzz responds to that with, "The Soldier took his valorous death for his most fleeting chivalrous glory. As General Dwight D. Eisenhower said 'There is no glory in battle worth the blood it costs.'" Capt. Brahm continues, "My life will not be over until I go into battle where I can honor my country and my mission is completed. What happens after that, I don't care. I will have accomplished my purpose in my life! Then I know *I did what I needed to do for my country*. As General George S. Patton once said, 'I am a Soldier, I fight where I'm told and I win where I fight.'"

Buzz states, "'There is no honor in these wars. There's just shame,'" [A. Villatoro, U.S. Veteran War Iraq-Afghanistan 2012].

Buzz asks, "Yeah, true and as said by the poet Siegfried Sassoon, 'Soldiers are sworn to action; they must win some flaming, fatal climax with their lives. Soldiers are dreamers; when the guns begin, they think of firelight homes, clean beds and wives.'" Capt. Brahm recites, "As was said with *Band of Brothers*, 'We're all scared. You hide in the ditch because you think there's still hope. The only hope you have is to accept the fact that you are already dead. And the sooner you accept that, the sooner you'll be able to function as a Soldier is supposed to function: without mercy without compassion, without remorse. All war depends upon it.'" Captain Brahm says resolutely, "We will never back down. We have to show our enemy that we are the best trained men and the bravest men in the world. Like Lane Evans [U.S. Representative from Illinois] once said, 'Without the bravest efforts of all Soldiers, sailors, armies and marines and their families, this nation, along with our allies around the world would not stand so boldly, shine so brightly and live so freely.'" Buzz responds, "Yeah but is *this* war just? And as Benjamin Franklin said ... 'Without justice courage has little value.'"

Mc comes in with a *good one* now because he knows Buzz is *at the end of his rope* in talking with this officer and he will end up losing his cool and then perhaps get his ass court marshaled. So, Mc takes over this discussion. "My Battle Buddy and I see it one way and you see it another. Mc says this quote from D. Brandeis, Supreme Court Justice, "'The greatest dangers to liberty lurk in the insidious encroachment by men of zeal, well meaning but without understanding.'"

Captain Brahm is angry, "Are you trying to say I have *no understanding* of this war? I know the only way to win this war is to have strength from you--the fighting Soldier and to have support from our country. We have to show our enemy *who the boss is* because we--the U.S.A.--fight like no one else in this world. We are Soldiers, first and foremost. Our next mission is to go into the A Shau Valley to defend *our bravest young men* who have fought and won in this war, at other battles, at Firebase Blaze, Firebase Whip, Firebase Veghl--and all over 'Nam. It is your duty as *our bravest young men,* to defend this country. You know when I talk to you guys I think of this quote by Kahil Gibran, 'Safeguarding the rights of others is the most noble and beautiful end of a human being.' You know Sp4c. McConnell, Sp4c. Buzz Brule, Sp4c. Chris (Mc) Davison, Sp4c. Joel Hammerstein, Sp4c. Guy Von Bexin and Sp4c. Dion Johnson ... you men must understand that you are here to fight and defend. We will be there to push the enemy back to hell—-I mean clear back and win. As said by Douglas Jerrod, English playwright, 'We love peace, but not peace at any price. There is a peace more destructive of manhood of living man, than war is destructive to his body. Chains are worse than bayonets.'"

Peter now adds a good one, "No, but also understand that it is more like this. Listen to what Rosa Luxemburg said [Polish political theorist], 'Those who do not move, do not notice their chains.'"

Buzz is fuming fast-and-hard at Captain Brahm. He jumps to his feet in an instant ready to speak his part but decides not to do so and sits down. Peter still makes an attempt to hold him back.

Buzz then yells, "I am not listening to anymore of your words of wisdom. I'm sick of it. I'm not following you blindly into the battlefield. All I can say to you is, as said by Howard Zinn, American historian, 'Historically, the most terrible things, war, genocide and slavery have resulted from obedience, not disobedience.'"

Peter says, "Hey, Buzz calm down--apologize. You will end up in the brig for that one." Buzz apologizes reluctantly but asks, "What could be worse than a comment like that. I guess dying for it--that could be worse?"

Captain Brahm says, "We are American and we will win. We will win this war for freedom for Vietnam. We are the 'land of the proud' and 'land of the free.' As General Douglas Mac Arthur said, 'It is fatal to enter any war without the will to win it.'" Buzz then says, "But when you win ... 'The problem after a war is the victor. He thinks he has just proved that war and violence pay.'" (A.J. Muste, goodreads.com/author/quotes/3893807, 2013).

Captain Brahm says, "No, that is not true. John, you have it right. You want to fight and win. And Sp4c. Dion, you want to fight—-to use your guns to kill the enemy to win our freedom. Sp4c. Dion, I know you will come through fighting all the way. We will fight and die all the way to the end no matter what! As said by Karl von Clausewitz, 'Let us not hear of generals who conquer without bloodshed. If bloody slaughter is a horrible sight, then that is a ground for paying more respect to war, but not for making the sword we wear blunter and blunter by degrees from feelings of humanity, until someone steps in with one that is sharp and lops off the arm from our body.'"

Buzz replies to that quote very angrily and asks, "So then, therefore, you are saying; we must fight on brutal ground because if we do not, we are sure to lose the war that we are not too sure about? But you are wrong ... it is not the degree of humanity nor the brutality in war that permits its victory. It is about the war. It is simply having the cause with the will to fight and to win." Buzz continues, "If we have feelings of humanity in war and fight with our duller sword, we will lose the war but I think having a cause to go to war and fight is most important in war. We need the will to win. And we need the strategy."

Now Colonel Le Bo Dat (South Vietnamese Colonel) sits down next to them and retired from the ARVN (Army of the Republic of South Vietnam). He is a very handsome and dignified man. The Soldiers salute and introduce themselves.

Peter then cordially introduces the Colonel to Captain Brahm, "Captain Brahm, this is Colonel Le Bo Dat from the Army of South Vietnam--AVRN."

Captain Brahm salutes Col. Le Bo Dat and says, "Pleased to meet you Colonel Dat."

Col. Dat says, "Very *please* to meet you."

Buzz then asks Captain Brahm and Col. Dat an interesting question about the mercenary indigenous forces in Vietnam, "What do you think of the idea of sending-out a light infantry-type mobile force of Cambodian troops/volunteers/indigenous troops into War Zone D and into the Forbidden Zone? They are sent in and we have them operate without artillery support or a chance for reinforcement except for an occasional materials-drop every four days by parachute—-if that?"

Buzz answers his own question with, "I think that is not very good battle strategy for the Cambodian Troops or for the indigenous troops. I know they are volunteers and get paid for their work but ..." Buzz is cut-off by Col. Dat who says, "Yes, it is really impossible for a company-sized unit to conduct operations in War Zone D under those conditions. They could not hold-out for more than two days. It sounds more like a suicide mission instead. Those troops will be found by the enemy very quickly. But Capt. James

Gritz who is the executive officer and chief of the MACV Recondo School said, [the] 'boldness of such a venture is intriguing,'" [as quoted in Backjack-33 by James C. Donahue].

Buzz responds, "Intriguing?"

Buzz then says, "Yeah, but there is not enough precaution taken to protect those troops. How could that be too intriguing? That is not right no matter which way you slice it, War Zone D, man?"

Colonel Le Bo Dat asks, "'Intriguing'? 'Bold'? I think we need more of a criterion for the safety of troops—any troops--before putting a military idea into action. These indigenous troops are at a severe risk. It is what it is ... but still it does not excuse the fact that the fighting on these missions should be better planned for these troops."

Buzz then says, "I don't think any of it is too 'intriguing' or 'bold' especially if it puts you six feet deep into the ground. Everyone in this conversation is sick of War Zone D."

Col. Le Bo Dat says, "The Territorial Force Militias and the Vietnamese Special Forces (LLDB) have bolstered the numbers of troops working with the AVRN (South Vietnamese Army) and we are appreciative to these added Special Forces that put their lives on the line. I am sure Captain Gritz thought he was making the best decision at that time for these indigenous troops and ARVN troops to fight this war."

Col Dat explains again, "But the problem with this war is we Commanders have our own ideas about how this war should be fought and won and my problem is you can't dictate to our troops—the AVRN or anyone--on how to fight a war that puts lives at needless risk. You tell our troops when to fight and how to fight. You Americans pick the time, the battle, and the place. You can't. Our commanders don't have the flexibility to make instantaneous military decisions. Many times your choices are actually, in fact, the worst time for a battle." He continues and then recites a very intriguing quote, "This is our country and are our troops. You Americans can't dictate to us how to fight a war. Someday, history will prove that I am right. My enemy, General Vo Nguyen Giap said, 'Any forces that would impart their will on other nations will certainly face defeat.'" Captain Brahm says, "No, we are here to protect your country. You don't know what you are talking about and you don't know how to win this war without our U.S. forces. This

160

war is under our control and this is how it should be. If we leave now it will be a blood bath for all."

Col. Le Bo Dat disagrees and says, "What control? The Communists now hold 4,090 hamlets in South Vietnam. The Communists are in control."

Captain Brahm remarks, "No, we are keeping the Viet Cong Guerrillas and NVA (North Vietnamese Army) troops out of South Vietnam and also pacification is working in South Vietnam. Colonel, with all due respect to you ... you just don't know what you are talking about. If we leave your country to *fight it out* by yourselves, it will be a total loss for you. You may as well just hand your country over to the Commies on a silver platter. All we want to do for you is to keep your country free so you can live in freedom."

Buzz then says quite prophetically, "Maybe this war can never really be won by the South Vietnamese or by Americans. Maybe this war can't be won. Maybe Vietnam wants to be Vietnam."

John and Dion both disagree with Buzz.

Dion disagrees, "Maybe with our might we *can* save Vietnam for Vietnam for freedom. Yeah, this war can be won with my M-16. I want to use my gun to fight for freedom. All I know is one thing for sure; our dear Uncle Sam got us into this real good mess and it won't end any time too soon unless we help it along. This job has to be finished. But in the end, I think we should let the people decide for themselves on whatever freedom they want. If they want Communism, let them have it. If they don't want Communism, then don't let them have it. I don't know man. None of it sounds too terribly cool to me. I just want to show them that I can fight for somethin'. That is all I can say about this mess."

Peter then says most wisely, "Yeah man, I'm really goin' there with you and ... I know where you are coming from but so many of us don't know. We are comin' but we don't quite know for sure where we're goin.' And as General William Tecumseh Sherman, Union General in the Civil War once said, 'There is many a boy here today who looks on war as all glory, but boys it is all hell. You can hear this warning voice generations yet to come. I look upon war with horror.'" Peter continues most wisely to Sherman's quote, "A warning voice for generations yet to come—-generations to come. I hear his warning and I do know his reasoning."

Then Dion adds his part, "But then for our American freedom at home ... I thank all Americans who have fought and who have died in our Civil War and in all of our wars for freedom--for our country's cause!

Peter adds truly, "Dion, war is hell and all Soldiers everywhere will fight if they can right an unjust wrong—anywhere--for their principle."

Buzz continues, "I don't care about anything else here in this damn war except for my buddies and my M-16 that can save our butts out here." John now pipes in, "And how can our troops, as trained and prepared as we are, lose this damn war?"

Peter says, "We Soldiers are all trying our best to save your country, this country and ourselves. We are _our bravest young men_ but we also have to face the fact that it takes more than a brave young fighting Soldier to win a war. It takes good tactics, military planning, strategy, having the logistics and knowing who the enemy is to win the war. Our logistics is organized around our superiority in weaponry, artillery and airpower which gives us the advantage. We have supplies and the best troops. However, now I question the strategy and our numbers of troops to fight the enemy. Bottom line, with thenumb ers in this war, I don't believe that we are evenly matched."

Guy then says to that, "I agree. We are outnumbered. Our logistics is good but we need a decent strategy and more troops to win. And yes, _our bravest young men_ will do the job! We are the best fighting Soldier in the world. As U.S. General Westmoreland said, 'I don't believe that the men who served in uniform in Vietnam have been given the credit they deserve. It was a difficult war against an unorthodox enemy.'"

Mc chimes in with, "We really can't blame our Commanding Generals for their lack of military planning and strategy because their hands are tied by Washington."

Guy suddenly blurts in with, "Yes, politically no one wants this war. President Johnson does not want this war. He wants to focus on his 'Great Society.' He got stuck with this damn war. It is because he never wanted our country to be in Vietnam in the first place? He said in October 1964, 'We are not about to send American boys nine or ten thousand miles away from home to do what Asian boys ought to be doing for themselves.'"

Buzz quotes, "Yeah, LBJ got stuck with this war. I know the war in Vietnam is not what President Lyndon B. Johnson wants because he said, 'The guns and bombs, the rockets and the warships are all symbols of human failure.' Yeah,

President Johnson hates the Vietnam War. It is a thorn in his side and privately he has made derogatory words for the war—-referring to it 'as a *bitch mistress.*'"

Mc says, "However, our commanders should not be sending our troops out there to die--especially when they know their strategy is not for guerrilla warfare.

Buzz adds, "Yes, there is a failure in strategy. We are trying to fight a conventional, traditional war which we can't do here. Rather, we should be using 'counterinsurgency strategies' in this war but our commanders are insisting otherwise. That is what is wrong with this war!" Peter says, "Well in a way you can't blame our Commanding Generals because everybody and our advisors in Washington each have their own ideas on how to win this war. Each is vying for position to have "his" strategy "win-out" over the other strategy. These guys in Washington are civilians and they are dictating to the military how to fight this war. Let us keep our advisors--in D.C.--out of planning our military strategy." Buzz then says, "Again the real problem lies with the decision the Soldier has to make for himself at the very begininning--the decision to fight or not to fight the war. And as said so wisely by Lt. Col. Karen Kwiatkowski in the documentary movie, Why We Fight, 'Not enough people are standing up and saying *I'm not doing this anymore.*'" John says truly, "But when on the battlefield, it is too late to discuss politics and strategy because we Soldiers must obey our commanding officers." Peter agrees, "Yeah, we can't begin to question strategies once out in battle." Mc then so wisely asks, "Maybe it is our law-makers who bear the brunt of a lot of this responsibility? Why did they pass legislation to permit huge sums of money to be allocated for this war? Think about it. 'The U.S. spends nearly as much on military power as every other country in the world combined (...),'" [as said by Nicholas Kristof, "Time to Review Military Budget Taboo", Antelope Valley Press, 12/27/10, 7B.]

Buzz then answers honestly, "That is a good question."

Chapter 15

The Next Day on Patrol in the Jungle

They get to their slicks the next morning that are waiting to pick them up to take them out to battle. This is their last day out in the bush before embarking on the mission to the border in the A Shau Valley on the hill on Mount Dong Ap Bia (Hamburger Hill). The Soldiers load into the choppers. The putter-putter of the engine grows louder and louder as the chopper rises forward and upward into a thick layer of clouds. In the slick is a crew--a pilot, copilot, gunner, crew chief and bellyman. Buzz says in ear's-shot, "Ours is not to wonder why but what the hell are we doing in the A Shau Valley when we have the North Vietnamese troops entering South Vietnam at seven thousand per month. We're going out to slaughter Soldiers."

This is the world of obedience--the obedience to take orders--the obedience to die--to be killed--to do or to die. The helicopter screeches loudly as it moves skyward. Its huge hulk of steel-–its massive upward thrust took its filled hollow body with its most precious cargo out to battle. This mechanized piece of steel is ready to do its job-–to carry life to its awaiting death into the jungle below. As the troops jump into the jungle ready for battle, Peter says to Buzz, "We are not on the planet earth—a place that I know. This jungle here is beautiful. This jungle is different from anything I have ever known before back in New York. This is beautiful ... but ... beguiling." Buzz wisely remarks, "Yes, it is beautiful ... and beguiling and deadly it is. We got that one right." Peter then says, "It is difficult to forge a path of battle through this dense undergrowth and through nature's stoic and determined giants."

The trees loom high above--a wonderful place for life-if it could be. The birds sing for awhile in this beautiful place. But these trees haven't forgotten *the death*, *the destruction* and *the horrors* of a war from *a time before*. These trees have seen so much death that they have their own story to tell. And with another story to tell--in another war--a far away war--a long ago war--the American Civil War--the same *stand of trees* still lines the same country road in the Shenandoah Valley which runs along the crest of the Blue Ridge Mountains where many Civil War battles were fought and where many Soldiers died. But in Vietnam ... here ... in this jungle ... if the trees could talk about death and destruction in this war, they could talk of such horrible death and such sorrow ... but ... for now they'll just wait for man's wrath 'til tomorrow. And their message for man: *You are the guardians of our world and of this jungle. This is not a place for war. There is no place in this world for war!*

For the Soldiers outside the jungle... the light is sunny and bright ... but inside under the triple canopy of trees ... it is cool damp and dusk. The only light inside is caught by some tree branches that hold sway for beams of light that sparkle and dance with dark shadows on the jungle floor. It is soundless and still where thick fog drifts in circles as it swirls between giant trees ... where moss grows as thick carpets of deep green. The jungle is another world. As Peter looks up to the jungle canopy above; he cannot see the tops of the trees for they are too high but he does see coming from somewhere ... cool trickling water. He follows its *lead* downward into a clear rippling pool. Ah, the world of the jungle ... another *Wonder of God.*

Buzz then suddenly smart-mouths a good-one to John before sitting down to rest by the waterfall, "I have three questions for you John: Did you find your tooth paste? Is your tooth paste in your rucksack or did you leave it on a tree stump somewhere out here ... because this would be a good place to use it or maybe even to leave it ... for that matter?" [Everyone laughs.]. Mc Says, "Yeah, this is a good place to leave it for the Cong."

Bam ... John punches Buzz without any warning. He lays a hard fast fist on his face ... answering, "Yes, it is here. Do you want me to show you where?"

Guy then steps in between them and breaks-up the fight. You can't fight here. He says, "If Captain Brahm sees this, you guys are both going to get your asses court marshaled and there will be no cool fresh waterfalls where you will be going—trust me."

Buzz responds, "Yeah, good ... but in the brig, death won't be waitin' for me around the corner ... either ... will it?"

Guy then answers, "No, I really don't think it will."

Peter says angrily, "Oh, shut your faces, you guys. Looking at this cool water, I say, *let's get our asses in there*, now. I don't want this 70-pound rucksack on my back anymore nor do I want this M-16, nor do I want these combat boots. I'm tired of 'em. I want that water. What I really want is that damn waterfall with Sherry and me together in it." [He laughs.]

Buzz then says, "Yeah, it is none of my business but what would you be doin' with Sherry in that cool water pool?" Peter says, "Yeah, you got a natural dirty mind, Buzz. I'm convinced of it." Buzz says again, "Yeah, you are right and I am sorry for that remark."

Two Soldiers beat Peter into the pool. As they jump in, one Soldier says, "This is better than Requa Lake back home in the World—-back in New York--man--great."

Two more Soldiers climb up to the pool's source and sit on the rocky ledge where they hold look-out duty for the bathers below.

One of the look-outs says, "Let's watch these guys have some fun."

Eye-catching--Pvt. Joel Hammerstein sees a flickering shadow above, a dark silhouette of an enemy sniper perched high in a tree above and ready to aim. The enemy sniper aims but Pvt. Joel Hammerstein instinctively aims with his scoped M-40, sniper rifle--with its silencer--fires and hits an enemy sniper down.

Now the beauty of God's nature with the sounds of birds, crickets, cicadas ... in their fleeting moments ... of harmonious bliss is stopped suddenly on the left flank with more sounds of several rounds of incoming rocket propelled grenades, rapid machine-gun fire, and small arms fire on the troops. Buzz then throws a grenade, grabs his M-16 and begins firing in the direction of incoming. Peter jumps up and runs next to Buzz and throws a grenade into the direction of incoming fire. Buzz throws himself to the ground and pulls Peter down just in time to avoid a mortar round that shatters a huge tree trunk just behind the two of them.

Buzz then says to Peter, "That was close. That was a close one. That tree coulda'been us."

Peter says most wisely, "Yeah, none of us ask to be born, but since we are, we don't want to die."

Suddenly Captain Brahm goes over and angrily yells in Buzz's face very loudly, "Hey man. I did not give you orders to start volleying fire like that, do you understand? You wait for my orders."

Captain Brahm now yelling loudly, "Do you understand? You wait until I give the command to return fire. Do you understand, boy?"

Capt. Brahm continues yelling, "Now do you hear me? Do you understand me? Now get your asses pounding on these guys. Let's go get 'em. We won't take anymore fire from these bastards. Peter, get your ass on that machine gun and start firing on your left flank."

Peter jumps up and runs to the perimeter, gets down and begins rapid fire in the direction of his left flank. Buzz follows closely behind Peter. As soon as Peter begins firing enemy incoming stops suddenly. There is an eerie silence. Bang—-Boom ... more cracks of enemy fire through the silence--then mortar shells again and again from incoming. "Aahhh ..." Capt. Brahm shrieks aloud as he takes a hit.

Buzz quickly runs with the medic to Capt. Brahm's side and says, "Let me help you." Buzz and the medic tell Capt. Brahm, "You are going to be OK." But the medic knows that it is very hard to survive a wound like his.

Buzz helps the medic all that he can. Captain Brahm has a mortar blast injury that opened-up a hole in his abdomen. Blood and pieces of flesh are everywhere.

Buzz knows from his training that with a wound like this, it is impossible to survive it. Capt. Brahm is given morphine.

The medic says to Buzz, "If we can relieve some of his pain, he will be ahead of the game."

Peter feels such grief as he knows nothing can live with a wound such as this. Pete asks Mc, "How can one man do this to another? How can such weapons destroy human flesh with such ferocity and with such complete and thorough effectiveness? We are a very efficient species of animal, are we not?"

The medic says, "Get out of my way but make sure he gets that morphine, Sp4c. Brule. Peter looks on helplessly. The medic says, "I will put sterile water on his wound, clean around it and apply large battle dressing but there is really not much more I can do for him other than get him out of here and out of pain."

The medic continues, "We cannot do more than that. Sterile solution, morph and antibiotics are all that we can do for him now or until he gets airlifted out of here but he will probably die before that." The medic says to Captain Brahm, "Hang in there. You'll be OK."

Capt. Brahm then asks, "Am I going to make it? Help me. Please—tell me! Am I going to make it? I don't want to die!"

The medic says, "Yeah, you will not die," [But the medic knows otherwise].

By now the morphine is beginning to work and it is relieving some of his horrific pain. Captain Brahm now speaks in a low breathless voice, "Am I going to die? Do something for me, now, help me--the pain--the pain. Help me! Please!"

The medic again says, "You are going to be OK." [knowing otherwise].

The medic leans over to Spec. McConnell and says, "He won't make it but the morphine will make *what he has left* tolerable--until ..."

The medic continues speaking and says to Sp4c. Peter McConnell, "I can't give him anymore morphine or it'll kill him now."

The medic looks over to Captain Brahm and reassures him, "You are going to be alright, sir. Hang in there." Capt. Brahm then says with a stronger voice, "I am afraid to die but I can't take this pain anymore. It hurts bad. Stop the pain. Stop this pain!" [His voice grows stronger--louder and more forceful.]

Buzz says rather sadly to Peter, "Hey, I wish this Soldier to die fast, so he is no longer in anymore pain."

Sp4.c McConnell then says most sorrowfully-so, "Yeah, I never thought I would ever wish a man to die until now. His mother reared him so hard to give him life and make a life for him."

Captain Brahm now rests in his own deep pool of blood. Everywhere there are pieces of his flesh. Peter is kneeling next to Captain Brahm and wishing more than anything else in this world for help for him--from somewhere. Peter looks up and around and sees in horror, clinging all over the tree trunks--more pieces of Captain Brahm's flesh dotted everywhere on the bark and leaves of the trees. Peter knows that Captain Brahm has lost too much blood to survive. Nothing more can be done for him.

Captain Brahm now lies shivering in a deep pool of blood. Too much flesh and too much blood has been lost for any chance of survival. This blood was once Captain Brahm's most important tool for his life which carried oxygen and nutrients to every cell in his body so he could be a person of life but now it is waste and Vietnam will be able to live in freedom. His blood once served him well but now lies as a pools of waste on the jungle floor--or maybe not--maybe it will be used for another purpose much too horrible to say! Life in war is horrific especially for a war that does not have to be fought.

Buzz then asks Peter sadly, "How sad for a man to lose his life in a place like this and for a place like this? Does he realize what he has just lost for this? Will he ever know--probably not?!"

But Peter may have gotten his answer to that question because Peter just so happened to be looking directly into Captain Brahm's eyes as he lies dying. And his eyes were telling Peter: *No, it is not worth it at all.*

Chapter 16

Another Day, Back from the Jungle and

Meeting a New Recruit in the Mess Hall

Another day has come but it has not quite gone yet. There is a job still to be done for the living part of this planet and that is to fight Communism in Southeast Asia but the dead can rest now. They can rest--for them, time stops. Captain Brahm does not have to worry about Communism anymore.

Peter now says to Buzz, "I keep thinking about this very true quote after what happened today as was said by Mahatma Gandhi, 'What difference does it make to the dead, the orphans and the homeless, whether the mad destruction is wrought under the name of totalitarianism or the holy name of liberty or democracy?'"

Buzz then leans over toward a willing ear, reflects on the day, and says to Peter, "Yeah especially if we have to fight it for somebody else on the other side of the world."

Mc says emphatically, "And you too, Peter, you almost bought the farm, today. It is a good thing that tree was standing in your way!" [They laugh.]

Peter says, "I know, man, I am lucky and thanks, Buzz! I know you guys are always there for me and I owe you guys one."

Peter then repeats sections of the Ranger Creed, "'Never shall I fail my comrades, I will always keep myself mentally alert, physically strong, and morally straight and I will shoulder more than my share of the task whatever it may be, one hundred percent and then some. Energetically, I will meet the enemies of my country. I shall defeat them on the field of battle for I am better trained and I will fight with all of my might. Surrender is not a Ranger word. I will never leave a fellow comrade to fall into the hands of the enemy and under no circumstances will I ever embarrass my country.'" And Peter continues with respect, "We are here for each other."

Buzz now says quite sarcastically, "Yeah, you definitely don't want to 'embarrass' your country but what a day it has been and what a day it will be tomorrow in this horrible war but we just have to be tough and "hang in there" so we can get our job done."

Peter quotes, "Yes, I know, but think about the truth in this statement from Stanley Baldwin,

'War would end if the dead could return.' It is what we have been talking about all along, isn't it?"

Buzz says, "Yes, war would end. War is horrific. Who can we run to and where can we run?"

Peter answers, "Nowhere."

Then a young recruit walks into the mess hall and sits down at the table to join-in on a conversation with Peter and the Lieutenant. He is average height, lean and lanky Soldier with a light blonde crew cut--maybe 18. He has a glow--a naïve glow--of hope and of youth. He is naively happy about being here in this war.

The young Soldier salutes--introduces himself--as Pvt. Joe Wolfing and says, "They call me 'Surfer Joe' back home in L.A.--you know like the song by the Surfaris—Surfer Joe." Buzz thought of the song, Surfer Joe by the Surfaris,

Surfer Joe joined Uncle Sam's Marines today

They stationed him at Pendleton, not far away

They cut off his long blond locks I'm told...

(Bob Berryhill), [Dot, Decca, GNP Crescendo).

Pvt. Wolfing comes in with many questions like a newbie; "I just flew in here last night. I love to surf and I know that I will find a gnarly wave or two to hang lose on out there--totally—dude. So I won't even ask you guys but what about China Beach--Da Nang--the surf--what's it like? No, I'm like the Beach Boys, Surfin' U.S.A. (B. Wilson, C. Berry), [Capitol Brian Wilson, Mike Love, Dennis Wilson, Al Jardine, David Marks, Bruce Johnston,]. And how is the grub here in this place?"

Buzz busted in sarcastically, "Oh it is good--trust me. But this ain't gonna be a Southeast Asian surfing vacation for you over here on Da Nang Beach. It ain't hap'nin'. I guarantee you that! What shit man. It's really all about death. I can't stand seein' so much needless death."

Buzz whispers to Pete, "Man, that's queer. How naïve this Soldier seems to be but not more naïve than you or I or Mc or Guy or any of us, is it?" Buzz then says to Peter, "But he is 'new' here--a 'newbie'--and being 'new' keeps the glow in the eye. He does not know what terror lies ahead of him does he Peter? Should I tell him?" Buzz continues with this quote, "Oh it all seems so useless to try to tell him because 'War doesn't make boys men, it makes men dead,'" [as said by Major General Ken Gillespie].

Peter agrees, "Yes, it makes them dead."

Buzz continues talking as he leans over close to Peter, "I really can't talk to this guy. I really don't want to tell him what this f*kin' war is really all about. Can you blame me? And this *young one* is thinking about surfin.' Why shouldn't he be surfin' now on some beach somewhere back in the only world any of us ever knows? We all had not a care in this world except for being able to 'hang ten' on the next wave? This guy is right."

Mc steps in and begins a conversation with Pvt. Joe Wolfing and says, "Hey, let me show you were to get some cute girls around here. I found a girl here and you might be lucky and find one yourself too--I mean she is beautiful! It reminds me of this song: She is Just My Style by Gary Lewis and The Playboys," (Garrett, Caps, Lewis, Leslie, Russell), [Liberty Records].

Every time I see her she don't even look my way, Maybe she will notice me, but then what would I say?

Mc continues with, "I found my girl here. I could never have found a girl like her back home in the World. She is my life! I love her. Maybe you could get ..."

Buzz then interrupts Mc with these words,

"Why are you getting this Soldier's hopes all up when you know, damn well that there ain't nothin' out here but death? I mean ... life's a bitch here. Just because you were lucky and found one, doesn't mean ..."

Buzz with tears in his eyes, stops and then looks over to Guy hoping Guy could say something to this poor *young naïve.*

Buzz then says to Guy sadly, "Tell this poor Soldier what this war is really all about."

Buzz looking directly at this Soldier--Pvt. Joe Wolfing--most caringly and most earnestly says in a loud and angry voice, "Yeah, you are a much sought after commodity around here by our dear old Uncle Sam. That is the only way your body is wanted around here. They want your body real bad; man—real bad--but the dames don't want you. I am sorry to burst-your-bubble like this. The dames don't want you but they want your money. This place is not about the fun, the good, and the pretty. It's about the dead, the bad, and the ugly. There will be no hot babes comin' 'round after you here! You ain't going to get a taste of that surf stuff either. There will be no surfin,' no rollin'--no pokin' around in the sand and surf on that beautiful China Beach with that beautiful babe in your arms, with all the love you can give her--no way. It ain't ever 'goina' happen, around here, for you, not in this lifetime ... no ecstasy ... so, don't listen to this asshole," as Buzz pointing to Mc. Buzz continues with true disgust in his heart, "But here you will know one thing for sure and that is ... *what hell-on-this-planet-earth is all about*. So don't let this dumb punk-ass fool you," as Buzz pokes the young Soldier's chest with his finger. Buzz says again to Surfer Joe, "And take that surfer Joe smile off of your face because it is not going to last around here too terribly long."

The young Soldier starts to speak, "Well ..."

Buzz says, "You don't have to say more. Tears roll down Buzz's cheeks as Buzz pats the Soldier on the back. Buzz thinks of the young man in the song—-and all the young men in this war--with Galveston--as it comes into the mess hall--on the radio/intercom system. And with the song, the Soldiers all think of other places--far away—-like the Malibu beaches. Galveston, Glen Campbell and written by Jimmy Webb, [Warner Bros, Curb]:

Galveston, Galveston, oh Galveston,

I still see your sea winds blowin'

I still see her dark eyes glowin'

She was 21 when I left Galveston...

But suddenly and quite angrily Buzz stands up and turns around for everyone within an ear's-shot of his voice; he says it loudly for the entire mess hall to hear--a message for every Soldier.

Buzz says it well with this quote as said by Alfred Adler, "'Distorted history boasts of bellicose glory... and seduces the souls of boys to seek mystical bliss in bloodshed and in battles.'"

Peter then says despondently, "Tomorrow we have to report for our pre-mission briefing."

Chapter 17

Back to Camp Eagle with Lieutenant Strang

In their bunks Buzz says to Peter, "Sure I want to get Charlie more than anyone else here--believe me, I do. We are here, now. Let us do our tour. I overheard a Soldier say, who was injured in the war and wants to go back into battle after recovering from shrapnel wounds that sprayed his eyes, face and shoulders, 'I know I'm extremely lucky. None of my wounds are permanent. I just want to heal up and get back out there,'" [as said by a U.S. Soldier from U.S. War in Iraq].

Peter says, "Yes, I commend him for his bravery but I also keep thinking about Sherry back in the World and how I wish I was with her, now, on some 'dumb' beach somewhere--no not just somewhere, but in Malibu."

Buzz says, "Yeah, I know what you mean, Peter, but that beach in Malibu ain't so 'dumb'—-not at those prices."

Mc leans over into the conversation and says, "Yeah, I know what you mean, man. I love my girl and I love the beaches of Southern California. I love my girl with all of my heart. I met her here, believe it or not, here in this place. I want to take her back to the U.S. with me and I want to show her what life is all about back there in the World."

Peter then changes the subject, "Yes, but wanting to go back home does not mean that I don't want to do my job. I will fight for my country and for my battle buddies. I want to make the difference--to serve my great country honorably--to fight for my country in any way I can." Buzz says, "Yes, you are right--do your good deeds, Peter. I do believe, as well, in serving honorably and sobeit."

And then Buzz starts with his philosophy about military quotes most sarcastically, "And I am not too sure about what this quote means, '*deeds not words.*' *He tells me he is going to shoot me which is his deed.* He must shoot me but not talk to me about it. This is what this quote means to me. The Soldier believes that we really don't need words. But what I say is that we must try with *words* first and then if we have to do the *deeds, then we do the deeds.* With words we can talk--negotiate--come to some sort of a compromise ... an agreement or let's just talk before we fight. It sounds to me like someone does not want to talk here but we must talk. If we can't talk, there will never be a chance for peace.

[And as said by Jeanne J. Kirkpatrick], 'We have war when at least one of the parties to a conflict wants something more than it wants peace.'"

The Soldiers then walk to the mess hall for a relaxing and enjoyable meal but all the way there, they are caught in a downpour in deep slippery mud--slipping and sliding in the darkness. They get to the mess hall and there Peter, Buzz, Mc, Dion, John, Joel and Guy meet with Lieutenant Strang. The menu reads, sliced roast beef, French fries and kernel corn with chocolate pudding for desert and milk or Kool Aid for drinks.

Lieutenant Strang walks over next to them and sits down to eat. The Soldiers stand to salute Lieutenant Strang--a tall handsome man with a high forehead, piercing blue eyes and golden blonde crew cut. He speaks with a Southern drawl and a deep voice of slow careful intent.

Lieutenant Strang says, "At ease, men. How are you guys liking this war? Last time I spoke with you, you men were not very happy with it. Has that changed since, I hope, because we are going to win this crazy war." Buzz is angry and wise cracks in with, "How would my opinion of this war have gotten any better since we last met? I think we are all being bamboozled somehow; so, how am I supposed to be happy? Or am I just a fool," [Fools Rush In, (Rube Bloom, Johnny Mercer), Ricky Nelson]. Pete laughs hard at Buzz's nerve for saying such a thing to a higher ranking officer.

Peter then answers Buzz's question and tries to break the tension that Buzz has created and begins a long list. "We are not happy with any of this: General Westmoreland, Walt Rostow, Robert McNamara, General Paul D. Harkins, Edward Lansdale, CIA Director William Colby, JCS Chairman General Maxwell Taylor, National Security Advisor McGeorge Bundy, Ambassador Ellsworth Bunker, Ambassador Avril Harrimen, Ambassador Henry Cabot Lodge, General Victor Krulak, General Creighton Abrams and Lt. General C. Mc Garr, General Wallace Green Jr., Robert McNamara, Dean Rusk, Major General Melvin Zais (Commander of the 101st Airborne Division), General John Wright(replaced Zais as Commander of the 101st Airborne Division. Colonel Joseph Conmy (Commander 3rd Brigade of 101st Airborne), Lt. Colonel Honeycutt (Commander of Rakkasans on Hamburger Hill), General Jim Smith, the assistant commander of 101st Airborne, Maj. Kenneth Montgomery, operations of the 3rd Brigade, Maj. General John Wright replacement for Zais of 101st Airborne, Secretary of State William P. Rogers, Lt. General Richard Stilwell of XXIV Corps, Lt. Col., CO (Commanding Officer-

Corps Commander) of 2/506ᵗʰ, Major Collier and many other top military commanders and presidential/civilian advisors who make the decisions on this war. These are to name just a few. We are just not happy with any of it."

Lieutenant Strang responds to that with, "I know you are not happy with the war but we will win this war no matter what happens--we will win it." [As said by Navy Lt. David Rehmann, six-year POW Vietnam War], 'What's important today is that we defend the things we went over here [there] for in the first place.' 'It's really important that we pay attention to our freedoms and protect them.' Yes, we must save our freedoms. I love serving my country in any way that I can for that end. All of our Soldiers are willing to make the ultimate sacrifice for their country. What more do you want from a man?" Buzz answers crassly, "Yeah—the ultimate sacrifice--our lives! Lieutenant Strang says, "Yes, but as the Paratrooper's motto goes, 'Paratroopers die, but they are never beaten.'" And Peter questions that, "*Never beaten*? Losing a life is *never beaten*? I don't know about that but it sounds *beaten* to me." Lieutenant Strang says vehemently, "You know our Soldier must follow orders from his commanders. He can't ask questions now or later in battle or ever. When in battle an order is given by the commanding officer, the Soldier does not have time to question his Commander's orders! If he does not obey orders he will die and all of the Soldiers' on his unit will die! Fighting here, now, is the best thing we can do for our country--for any country. You can't change my mind!" Buzz then says with this quote, "But you see it only one way and that is *your* way. We must end war. And one thing would end war and that is as Ludwig von Mises once said, 'Only one thing can conquer war—that attitude of mind which can see nothing in war but destruction and annihilation.'" Lieutenant Strang says, "Yes, I do see it my way. Fight with all of your heart to win. You can't change the military way because it is here to protect you for peace and freedom the world over—tell Hitler about it. Just remember as said by President George Washington, 'To be prepared for war is one of the most effective means of preserving peace.' If the military way does not do it, who will? So don't try to come in here and try to change my mind. You are here now to fight—which ever way you came--to save Vietnam--and ultimately to save America. You listen, you obey and you follow orders to fight." Buzz then leans over to Peter and says resolutely and agreeing, "Yes, and we are here now—however we came-- and we will fight."

Peter says, "But now we can forget the war and all of its problems with this good food in front of us. We have a tray full of very delicious food to eat."

At their long dining table in the mess hall, trays of food line each side of the table and behind each tray, sits a very happy, smiling face eating earnestly. This is the Soldier's moment of happiness but it is ever so fleeting. The Soldiers are hungry, the food is good and they are happy! This is all they have!

Peter then says to Buzz sadly, "He will never change his mind. But now this is a good time to forget about the problems of 'Nam and I really find no need to think about any of it, now.

Buzz now leans over and says to Peter, "Yes you are right. His mind will never change. Let's not talk about it. I think that now we are ready to take our three-day stand-down before embarking on our mission into the A Shau Valley, to fight and to win ... don't you agree, Peter?"

"Yes, I do, Buzz. I really do," says Peter.

Chapter 18
Sp4c. McConnell Reporting
For Pre Mission Briefing with Captain Kenner

The next morning Sp4.c McConnell goes to the briefing with his--team/recon unit--for his mission to RIF for battle on Mt. Dong Ap Bia. Captain Kenner describes the importance of the mission to RIF the hill and explains, "Your team/recon unit will go in ahead of this assault on Mt. Ap Bia or Hill 937 (Hamburger Hill) to RIF the AO (area of operation) before battle to gather intelligence on locations of enemy bunkers. And you will be inserted to RIF the AO on Mt. Ap Bia. Your drop-off point is a couple of miles from your firebase by helicopter on a Slick Troop Transport.

DESCRIPTION OF OPERATION AND OF TERRAIN. Captain Kenner describes the mission which is in two phases one is RECON and the other will be assault, "You will RECON that is gather the information on enemy presence. Captain Kenner describes, "Mt. Dong Ap Bia runs along the Trung Pham River at the Laotian Border. It is covered with thick tropical double and triple canopied jungle. The land beneath the trees is covered with thick elephant grass and multi-stands of bamboo and vines—so thick you can't see more than two feet in front of you. It is hot and steamy in that jungle. There are steep hills and deep ravines and it is all controlled by our enemy who knows this ground like he knows the back of his hand. In addition to this terrain being difficult, he has built his well-fortified underground bunkers into the hills. He has booby traps, tunnels and his spider holes are everywhere. They are filled with his weapons, supplies and men. And don't get fooled. Just yesterday we lost fine Soldier who was tricked by a Vietnamese boy who wanted a handout and the willing Soldier searched his pockets for something but not but not before the boy put a live grenade in the Soldier's pocket. No ... this is his ground—-his land—-his place but for you ... you are the stranger. It is a strange unknown ground. He knows where he is and exactly what he is doing. You are the stranger in his land—-remember that!" Captain Kenner explains more, "With the assault phase, we will bomb—-prep-- the mountain for about an hour before we insert our assault troops. This will be followed by a fifteen-minute fusillade by artillery (from a nearby base). Also Aerial Rocket Artillery (Cobra Assault Helicopter) will pummel for another five minutes."

Peter then leans over and says to Buzz, "We go in before this. We are the Riffers (RECON). We go in before all the ground prepping, yeah." Buzz says, "And we have to get enemy troop numbers before we can make the assault on Ap Bia."

Captain Kenner explains, "We will provide for your RIF team with some TAC air support. You will be transported in and inserted by UH-IP lift helicopters and Cobra Gunships will give you fire support."

Captain Kenner continues, "Your RIF teams will give us some very valuable information that we will use to save lives on the battlefield. If we know where the bunkers are located, we can try to prep that area before sending our troops in there? Do you understand, men? You will report tomorrow with Lt. Lt. Harper and I will brief your team further on your mission in The A Shau Valley on Mt. Dong Ap Bia (on Hamburger Hill}. You are dismissed." [Note; Historically, McConnell's team did not RIF Ap Bia.]

Buzz answers his question, "Yes, I understand our purpose for our mission but I absolutely cannot forget this most true quote by Captain Josh Rushing (USM), 'It makes me hate war, but it doesn't make me believe that we're in a world that can live without war yet.'"

Chapter 19

Back to the Barracks and Report to

COHQ with Lieutenant Harper and Captain Kenner for

Another Briefing

The next day Pete, Mc, Buzz, Guy, Joel, John, Dion, and Joe report for the briefing at COHQ at 0600. The briefing room is almost empty because most of the troops are gone to the A Shau Valley for Operation Apache Snow. Pete's team from his Company and his Company Commanders Captain Kenner and Lieutenant Harper are present.

Captain Kenner from Peter's company says, "Good Day, men." They salute. "This is Lieutenant Harper." They salute. Lieutenant Harper will be your Commanding Officer for your team of twelve Soldiers (heavy team) which has been pulled from your company for your mission to *rif* Hill 937 in the A Shau Valley on Hill 937 (Hamburger Hill). On this mission you will work with an indigenous troop from the Montagnard Tribe." [NOTE: This is a fictitious military plan to RECON with LT. Harper's RECON team.]

SUMMARY OF MISSION AND CONDITIONS OF TERRAIN. The Soldiers salute and Lieutenant Harper salutes and says, "Good day men. I will be your Commanding Officer for your next mission." Captain Kenner then says, "Sp4c. McConnell, you will be Assistant Team Leader for your team. The enemy has several well-armed underground bunkers on Hill 937. You will be inserted as a RIF team on the mountain to find the fortified underground enemy bunkers and how many are out there. This will be done to find enemy strength, location and enemy infiltration routes from the border. By riffing that mountain our combat ground troops will gain valuable knowledge of where enemy bunkers are located which will help give our bombers something to hit. You may be working at a disadvantage with the weather--the high amount of rainfall, the excessive cloud-cover and the dense fog. We have intelligence from infrared readings, sniffer readings, sensor activities and agent reports which has told us that there are many enemy bunkers in there. A Company officer will make an overflight of the AO with your patrol leaders and insertion pilots to assess the terrain first. They will select the insertion LZ's and delineate your *RECON* zones. The intelligence sergeant will gather other intelligence information on the area and the operations sergeant will prepare the operations order with pre-plotted fire concentration areas and check your map overlays. Make sure

180

that before you go on your RIF mission, you are prepared with your immediate reaction drills and your team leader will give you a briefback."

SUMMARY OF MISSION AND CONDITIONS OF TERRAIN. And Captain Kenner then summarizes their mission once again, "We want to know where enemy bunkers are located. Your insertion points will be prepared and you will be working in dense triple canopied jungle. Surrounding that jungle is mountainous terrain with high rocky cliffs which makes your mission very difficult. The enemy has an advantage. He can crawl back into his sanctuary in Laos and return re-supplied with fresh troops and material--and all of it unhindered. Our line-ground--troops cannot go into Laos because of the Neutrality Agreement. This puts us at a severe disadvantage. And I want you to know that your mission, Operation Apache Snow, on Dong Ap Bia (Hamburger Hill) lies right on that neutral border. For your riffing mission, you will 'infiltrate through their escape routes, conduct surveillance, seek out the enemy forces and installations and collect intelligence.'"

Captain Kenner says, "Lieutenant Harper will give you more details on your mission."

Lieutenant Harper says, "Good day, gentlemen." They salute. "At ease. Let me give you a more detail account on our mission onto Mt. Dong Ap Bia. Our team will be inserted onto Mt. Ap Bia at last light by a troop transport slick— Huey--(Huey UH-ID) onto a well prepared Landing Zone accompanied by a Cobra Gunship. Three additional Huey's will accompany our slicks for decoy. The other Huey's will land briefly at the same time as decoy for your insertion. Many times the enemy will plant long bamboo poles upright or a lay out a blanket of punji sticks on our LZ's. We will leave at night and your return will be first light in the morning. As soon as we are inserted, we will secure our camp with the placement of claymore mines around a 360-degree security perimeter. That is all. You are dismissed."

Captain Kenner then says, "Well Soldiers back to your barracks and tomorrow for those of you who will report ... it is 0500 to the slicks on the tarmac and tomorrow we are to Firebase Blaze in the A Shau Valley. The enemy units in that area are dug in deep and are fighting hard and returning fire on their retreat back to Laos. Good luck and I know you men will do your job." Peter, Buzz, Mc, Guy, John, Dion and Joel step out from their briefing room into another massive downpour and into a sea of thick mud-- sloshing all the way in the dark back to their barracks.

181

Peter then throws his plastic poncho over his head. Mud
covers the ground several inches deep. Peter slips and
slides in the rain but his poncho keeps him dry. They enter
their warm bunkers have instant relief from the *cool damp*
and the wet air. The room provides the warmth they seek and
need. Plastic sheets hang over the window openings which
helps keep the rain out but the humidity is everywhere.

Dion then says, "Man, our Commander has me convinced we
will do it. The only way we will win this war is if we take
that damn mountain and we will do it together. I am ready to
fight it. I am going to run their damn asses all he way back
to the Laotian border and *then some*.

Guy says, "Yeah, don't worry Buzz. Tomorrow morning
will come soon enough and we are into the A Shau."

Mc says, "I want to find every damn hooch on that
mountain."

John says, "This is what I have been wanting to do all
of my life."

Peter says, "Yes, if I can help our troops do their job
and get our enemy *hide-outs*. I'll get it so that our enemy
has no place to hide."

John then says, "Then let's get on with it. We will
keep our enemy out in the open with no f*ckin' bunkers to
run to."

Buzz says, "I want to do my part for the same damn
reason—to get them off of that damn mountain. Nobody here
ever imagined that Buzz--crazy old Buzz--would ever say such
a thing would you?"

Guy then says, "Yeah, we will riff it then take that
f*cking mountain.

Peter says, "I agree whatever I can do to make the job
better for my battle buddies. [As said by an Army Sgt.
fighting in the U.S. War with Iraq], 'It would break my
heart to see one of my brothers in the military serving in a
place like this. I would much rather myself suffer than one
of them and they have kids to think about ... and it is good
serving with the men; it's good serving for this great
nation.'" [This quote was said by a Soldier who was killed
in the-U.S.-War-with-Iraq—-so very sad!]

Buzz then says, "Man, Yeah, we have been ranting and raging over this whole Vietnam War but now that I am here, I will do my duty for my country and for my buddies and I will go in somebody else's place so they don't have to go."

John says, "I was trained to fight and I will do whatever it takes for our country and for our buddies. If I have to I will put myself in his place."

Peter then says, "Yeah, I have a little one on the way but many of these Soldiers already have a houseful of kids who need a dad. I'll go for my buddies." [And as said by a U.S. Army Sgt. with the war in Iraq], "'They [the Soldiers] have kids to think about and I am a little young for [all] that right now. [So] I will go in their place.' [This quote came from the same Soldier who went in their place and was killed in the War in Iraq. He was young. He never had a chance to have a child of his own--to leave a part of himself behind]. Peter says again, "Yeah, this is all sad that it has to be this way and it shouldn't be."

Buzz then chimes in with, "This is all very heart-breaking ... it does not have to be this way? It really does not have to be like this ... no it doesn't!"

Mc agrees and says, "But at least we should know what hilltop we are going to die for, should we not? We must know what we are fighting for on that mountain so let's get outta here and RIF it."

Guy agrees, "We will fight and we will RIF it."

John then says, "We do our part like I have been telling you guys this whole time. I love the thrill of going into battle with the adrenalin rush." [Everyone laughs.]

Buzz then retorts back with, "But I hope our Commanders have it all figured out."

Peter then says, "I hope so. None of us wants to die. I really just want to have my life that is all I want is my life."

Buzz says, "Yeah, Peter, you are not asking for much. But now I'm starting to think like Jo. Maybe we just need to be happy--like *away from it all,* if not by the water in Malibu, maybe underwater somewhere-—maybe that is our world--like the song by the Frogmen, Underwater. [They all laugh.]

"Whaaat?!" Buzz looks at John in horror and asks him honestly, "What are you doing with that damn tape on that gun of yours?" John tapes his gun with green tape to camouflage it for the battlefield.

John answers, "I am camouflaging my gun."

Buzz then says, "Man, talk about war games—gee whiz! It's not your fault. I know this fight is in your heart, John. You are a good soldier, John, but gee-wiz. Like the song Gee Whiz, Carla Thomas." Buzz changes the subject and says, "And now we are going on a mission with the indigenous forces—the indigenous forces. And ... what are we making them fight our war for?"

Mc says, "We are making them fight our war for us and with us ... that is what we are doing here to these people." Guy says, "Yeah, I know these indigenous forces are being paid for it but it still does not make this war right."

Buzz continues with his ranting and raging, non-stop, "Our Commanders know that the indigenous forces don't want to fight ... except for the dollar. They don't want to fight this war because they don't care about Democracy and I can't honestly blame them. I mean I love Democracy but do these guys really love Democracy as much as we do ... no they don't and sobeit?" Mc then says, "No, they are here to be scouts for us because we are in unknown territory. We need them."

Buzz says irreverently, "Yeah, a Kit Carson Scout (indigenous troop) like from our 'Old West.' With these names—Kit Carson—it seems like we are actually trying to relive the days of the old American Western Frontier ... doesn't it?"

Guy agrees, "Yeah, totally. I agree. We recruit these indigenous forces to fight for us under the CIDG (Civilian Irregular Defense Group). And many times the indigenous forces are put into harm's way with company-sized units that are formed as Mobile Guerrilla Forces in Vietnam. If these guys are found they can be finished-off by the larger Viet Cong and North Vietnamese Army forces. Also, they do not get any artillery support or a chance for reinforcement for up to sixty days."

John mocks Buzz's talk, "But you know, man, you are laughing at us die-hard Soldiers ... but where were you when WWII broke out ... man ... really, come on? Many brave Soldiers fought and died for our freedom."

John then changes the subject to one that Buzz likes to talk about which is tooth paste, "You know, Buzz, about my tooth paste—remember? Ah, yeah, you don't care—do ya'? Yeah, anyway, I really did forget my tooth paste out there somewhere on some tree stump."

Buzz is ready for this one, "Yeah, but where is it now--that is the question--where? You would never know where it is with all of your razzle-dazzle shit going down with all that camouflage tape on your gun, would you? But your tooth paste, man, what a loss—-an entire tube gone—-just gone like that, as Buzz snaps his fingers. Your mouth, now, must be bad--real bad. I know your mouth is not the-cleanest-thing-in-this-world-to-fight-with is it, John, but ... but it's not your fault? A dirty mouth will not be too terribly cool for the Cong to deal with. They don't want to fight with that shit. Ah, but they don't care about your mouth ... too terribly much, anyway. They only care about your shootin' skills, man. All they really want is to pepper-up to your gut pretty well." [Everyone laughs.]

John retorts back with, "Talk about a dirty mouth. I have not heard a mouth as bad as yours since coming here to Vietnam."

Buzz then says to John, "Yeah, and you, John ... you are the one who never shuts up. If you keep-up your mouth like that, you may not have any more teeth to worry about by the time I get done with them. And definitely ... you won't need tooth paste." [Everyone laughs.]

John argues back, "But it really does not matter anyway because I don't bite when I fight. I really don't. But ... what can I do now because my tooth paste is still sitting out there on some tree stump somewhere? Ah ... I am not going to worry about it too terribly much anymore ... shit. I have too many other more important things to worry about like staying alive—-you know--like keeping my heart beating and winning this war that *can't be won*. And please, Buzz just don't worry *your* pretty 'little mind' too terribly much more about this tooth paste shit, OK?"

Mc chirps in with, "Yeah, 'little mind' ... you got that one right."

And Buzz keeps insisting about the tooth paste, "Is this *tooth-paste-tube-thing* of yours really going to bother you so much that it may keep you from fighting in the jungle somewhere, John? Because if it really bothers you that much, you can have my tube of tooth paste if you want it?" [They all laugh nonstop.] John then says back to Buzz with sarcasm, "Well I know now for sure that you are not *the-cheap-son-of-a-bitch* that I always thought you were. I mean are you really willing to give me your tube of tooth paste? No way! I can't believe it." [They all laugh.]. Mc adds with sarcasm to John, "Yeah, that is a good idea. Why didn't you

185

think of that before, Buzz? You could have saved us all of this fighting." Buzz says with sarcasm, "Well ... I didn't give him my tube before because ... really, I am a cheap son-of-a-bitch." Mc says to Buzz, "Just give him your tube now, Buzz, and shut up, already yet." Joel then says smartly, "No, don't worry about it. What we should do is this; let's just go do some *RECON* on that lost tooth paste tube and get it back, now." [Everyone laughs.]. Then Dion walks in and is confused with this tooth paste conversation and asks, "What are you guys talking about tooth paste ... in that jungle out there, man? Man, don't bug him. His teeth are all he's got. I don't take paste out there in that jungle with me either. I clean my teeth here at home in the barracks. But I think more important than keeping our teeth clean is keeping our guns clean." [Everyone agrees and gets serious.]. Joel adds, "Yes, I always take my gun-cleaning kit with me out there in the jungle. You guys are ridiculous—-making jokes out of shit like this--and we got to go out to fight somewhere? This is some serious shit. What's wrong with you?" Dion says again as he is disgusted with the whole thing, "Yeah that is ridiculous with your stupid ass jokes. This is really a damn big game, to you, isn't it--tooth brushes—-tooth paste--man? Come on, man." Pete answers, "Yes, it is one big game. Tomorrow we report at the tarmac at 0500 for the A Shau Valley. We are ready." Buzz says lastly, "We are all ready."

Buzz still thinks about this quote that he reads aloud from a folded and worn piece of paper that he pulls out of his pocket. He reads it to his friends ... this night before embarking into the A Shau Valley ... this true quote; he thinks deeply of its meaning and wonders what is this war really all about: "'Of course the people don't want war.... That is understood.... But it's always a simple matter to drag the people along whether it's a democracy, fascist dictatorship, a parliament or a communist dictatorship. Voice or no voice, the people can always be brought to the bidding of the leaders. That is easy. All you have to do is tell them they are being attacked, and denounce the pacifists for lack of patriotism and exposing the country to danger. It works the same in any country,'" [Hermann Goering in 1945 at the Nuremberg Trials from The Nuremberg Diary by G. M. Gilbert].

The war left these minds for the next eight peaceful hours of sleep but most importantly ... it's eight hours to forget everything.

Chapter 20

Fly into A Shau Valley with

Lieutenant Harper on their Way

To a Hill on Mt. Dong Ap Bia.

Sky Pilot by Eric Burdon and the Animals,

(Burdon, Briggs, Weider, Jenkins, McCulloch).

He smiles at the young soldiers

Tells them it's alright

He knows of their fear in the forthcoming fight

Soon there'll be blood and many will die ... [MGM].

This song is about the Military Chaplain who prays with the Soldier.

Sp4c. Peter McConnell is assistant team leader and Lieutenant Harper is the CO (commanding officer) of twelve men from Camp Eagle. They are ready on the tarmac at 0500 hours for pick-up by a troop transport slick to take Lieutenant Harper's Team to Firebase Blaze--one base among thirty American/Allied bases in the--A Shau Valley. This is the beginning of the first leg of their journey to their mission to take the Hill--to RIF Mt. Dong Ap Bia in the A Shau Valley with Operation Apache Snow. The trip will take a half hour from Camp Eagle to Firebase Blaze in A Shau Valley.

The pilot says, "Load up men. Are you ready?"

Buzz smart-mouths again to answer the pilot's question, "Why ... am I not supposed to be ready now for somethin'? [Everyone laughs—non-stop.]. Of course I am ready! Why shouldn't I be ready? I'd have to be an idiot if I was not ready to kill someone or something right now. My friend was just killed by a booby trap yesterday by a Victor Charlie (VC) or maybe by our cute little Victoress Charlene (VC) as I call her ass. She could be anywhere in that jungle under some crazy disguise—-dressed as a whore. I am ready to take her down—-and that is not lay her down but take that bitch down for good--once and for all! [Everyone laughs.]. I'm in the good mood to shoot anything right now, so don't get too near me because I just so happen to be in the mood. [Peter laughs under his breath.]. No coward booby-traps my friend and gets away with it."

John says to Lt. Harper, "Yeah, he is not too happy now because he just lost a *battle buddy* to a punji trap."

Lieutenant Harper says, "You men will be briefed again at COHQ (company headquarters) at Firebase Blaze and then tomorrow on the PZ at 0500 hours for the assault on the northern A Shau Valley."

Lieutenant Harper yells, "Hang on troops."

The sound of the strong engine gets louder and louder. Quickly, the ground grows distant as the transport veers to the right and climbs upward through the clouds to take them further away onto another destiny. A song comes on the radio and Buzz changes the subject and says, "Yeah, true, man, this song is true." The song sung by Martha and the Vandellas, Nowhere to Run, (Holland-Dozier-Holland), [Gordy Records]. Buzz starts moving and swaying to the music.

Nowhere to run, baby, nowhere, to hide

Got nowhere to run to, baby, nowhere to hide

"Nowhere to run, says Buzz."

Buzz says again, "No. Nowhere to run but for now let's Waltz Across Texas with Earnest Tubb and Willie Nelson."

When we dance together my world's in disguise it's a fairyland tale that comes true ... (Talmadge Tubb), [Decca Records].

Peter, Buzz, Mc, Guy, John, Joel and Dion are going into the A Shau Valley to Firebase Blaze. The valley is deep and runs between two 'heavily forested mountain ranges' 22 miles long and only six miles from the Laotian Border which is 'garrisoned by 5,000 enemy Soldiers.'"

Buzz says to anyone in ear's shot, "Ours is not to wonder why. Ours is to do or die, right?"

Joel answers, "No, not right."

Joel then continues his explanation, "Ours is to wonder why ... only."

The Lieutenant says, "We have some bases secured as of yesterday in the southern part of the valley but we still have a couple of snipers hanging around for a second serving of cooked rice 'A La Americana,'

Lieutenant Harper briefs the team again, "As soon as you men are choppered in, we will drop you off at LZ Blaze and you will RIF its perimeter. Be careful--the height of the elephant grass can be deceiving. The jungle has a false floor. Many times a Soldier will jump, not realizing the ground distance and break a leg."

"Ready to jump?" the pilot yells, "Get your asses off this chopper, now."

After what seemed an eternal time, the green light finally came on and the Lieutenant shouts, "All right you guys time to earn your pay." He motions for the line to start moving forward towards the exit. Peter suddenly thinks about Sherry--his intense love for her but--the cold wind hits him in hard and snaps him back into the survival mode. He jumps down ... into a cauldron of uncertainty and fear and onto the valley floor. Lt. Harper opted for a landing into the ten-foot tall elephant grass for a good camouflage. Surrounding the grass are numerous fifteen-foot-deep, water-filled bomb craters. But the troops are not interested in taking a swim at this time.

Before *the jump* the troops look down, feel the cold wind hit their faces and see a valley enshrouded in a blanket of dense white fog. The ground is covered with tall stands of tan-tipped elephant grass that makes movement to the blades of the chopper. The valley is surrounded by high green mountains with fog-filled gorges ... and where Mount Dong Ap Bia towers high above the rest. As they get closer, there's one narrow desolate dirt road meandering meaninglessly through the deep stands of elephant grass in this desolate valley of impending doom.

One after the other--Buzz, Peter, Guy, John, Mc, Joel, Joe and Dion with the remainder of the team are *CA'd* into the valley. The Soldiers are dropped into elephant grass taller than their heads and immediately the enemy begins incoming fire but Harper's team is backed up by artillery from Firebase Blaze. "The intense enemy flak and heavy machine-gun fire reigns over the valley floor with the enemy determined and still dug in the Central Valley and mountains. The enemy is well fortified with heavy guns—175 mm self-propelled Howitzers and a few 130 mm batteries." The Soldiers move single file with Peter walking point. Sniper Sp4c. Joel Hammerstein holds rear position. Now they are in the central A Shau Valley and tomorrow it will be H-Hour for Operation Apache Snow at 0500 hours and into the Northern A Shau Valley. "The NVA had nearly every mountain on both sides of the valley floor defended by antiaircraft guns. Most were the 12.7 mm heavy machine guns, but they also had a large number of 37 mm flak guns," [Zaffiri, Hamburger Hill]. John then wise cracks in with, "Man, these guys are packed." Buzz laughs now and says [pointing to Dong

Ap Bia], "That is where we will be tomorrow on that mountain. It is much bigger than I ever imagined." Peter says most astutely to that, "Yeah, you are right. How many enemy troops are waitin' for us? But we will find out tomorrow with our mission Apache Snow. Let's get back now."

Now they are back at the barracks and they settle into their bunks for a good night's rest.

The next day 0500 hours came all too soon for the execution of this massive assault onto the northern A Shau Valley to capture the hills. Operation Apache Snow will be conducted with five battalions of U.S. Military manpower. One of these Hills is Hill 937/Hamburger Hill--a hill on Mt. Dong Ap Bia. Three Battalions of the 3rd Brigade under Col. Conny (Col. Conmy) are with these troops—-"the 187th Infantry of the 3rd Battalion, the 501st Infantry of the 2nd Battalion and the 506th Infantry of the 1st Battalion" [Zaffiri]. It is an overcast day which does not deter anyone from the mission ahead. As explained by S. Zaffiri in his book Hamburger Hill: "Two-thousand Soldiers are waiting in the PZ Zone (pick-up zone) in nervous but eager anticipation in the northern A Shau Valley for the battles about to come. Phantoms high-five it overhead for the troops below as they streak past fast, suddenly zoom away and swoop down somewhere else over targets on distant hills that explode with violent repercussions and sounding distant thunders and rumbling the ground below them," [Zaffiri], [Studies in Battle Command]. "The entire NVA 29th Regiment from the 324B Division, the NVA 816th Battalion, two Companies of the NVA 806th Battalion, the 82 mm mortar battery, the 6th and 9th NVA regiments, and the K12 Sapper Battalion are waiting for them," [Zaffiri]. "But now these 2,000 Allied Soldiers are waiting in their PZ Zone to be picked up by a hundred Hueys with their jet engines roaring and coming in nonstop to pick-up their human cargo," [Zaffiri]. "These Hueys chopper-in with their ear-deafening noise ... with the smell of fuel and dust is in the air." These Soldiers go with uncertainty and bravery and are ready for battle--ready to back-up each other on the battlefield. Troopers are loaded onto the choppers. The choppers jerk then lunge forward taking these brave young men to a certain objective but to an uncertain destiny. They are *our bravest young men*.

Chapter 21

Riffing Mt. Dong Ap Bia (Hill 937)

Lt. Col. Coneycutt says, "Your first job, men, is to *recon* with your unit on Mt. Ap Bia (Hamburger Hill). Lt. Harper you will get our intelligence and then we will attack the mountain."

Lt. Harper, Sp4c. Peter McConnell and his team with Sp4c's Buzz Brule, Dion Johnson, Guy Davison, Chris (Mc) Davison, John Kelsey, Joe Wolfing, Joel Hammerstein and Vinh, and an indigenous troop (A Kit Carson Scout) from the Montagnard tribe are going in to RECON/RIF (reconnaissance in force) Mount Dong Ap Bia. They will be inserted by a Huey UH-ID slick transport. With the completion of this RECON mission they will combat assault the hill.

The song Eve of Destruction comes on the radio and it seems fitting for Sp4c. Peter McConnell's team now. This brings to Pete's mind all of his thoughts of this war as far back as he can remember to his training at Fort Benning and Fort Campbell.

The song, The Eve of Destruction, by Barry McGuire, written by Phil F. Sloan, Steve Barri, [Dunhill Records].

> *The Eastern world it 'tis explodin'*
>
> *Violence flarin' bullets loadin'*
>
> *You're old enough to kill but not for votin'*

Sp4c. Peter McConnell and his RECON/LRRP team are now in their slicks on their way into the jungles to their AO (area of operations) on Hill 937 (Mountain Dong Ap Bia). The team enters a jungle with Sp4c. McConnell who is most talented with tracking and riffing (reconnaissance-in-force) takes *point* (first). Peter can see things in the jungle that nobody else can see. Peter is *point* with Buzz *slack* (second) and Lieutenant Harper is *rear security*.

Dense jungle growth--the jungle appears from out of nowhere. It's a tree-line jungle at the base of a towering mountain coming from the depths of the forest above. With the mountain's ascent the forest grows deeper darker and denser--with tall trees, saw-tooth elephant grass, thick stands of bamboo and twisted and twined vines. But ... then ... with further ascent the jungle growth thins-out somewhat more at the very top. On most mountains the jungle trees rise to more than one hundred feet high. And these giants are even too big to wrap human arms around.

The valley brush is brown and dry ... but underneath this triple canopy of green ... deep dark and green inside ... there's a cool damp earth of muted hues with flowery blooms ... big green leaves on tall green stalks and twisted vines that grow wildly on the jungle floor.

This is the jungle world--a world shrouded in tropical beauty ... clad deep in mystery—-yes--with the mystery of-the-enemy-within. Peter then says, "I would like Sherry to see this beauty—-this mystique--this place--this color—-this jungle--the tropics. It's not all bad. ..." He pauses for a moment. "It's just that ... it's just that ... right now ... mankind has momentarily put-in a bad word ... here ... for awhile."

Buzz then wisecracks-in with, "Yeah, the jungle is nice but at a reasonable distance." [Everyone laughs.]

Lieutenant Harper says, "We will make camp here." They set a perimeter. Peter appears masculine with his wide square shoulders, strapped with his M-16 rifle across his back--dressed in his green uniform--his black leather boots and his Army Ranger helmet. Sherry is lucky to have a man such as him.

The Team makes their camp, checks their trail, sets their 360-degree perimeter with claymores and begins a twenty-four hour guard duty. For tomorrow the team will be again on its way up to the top of the hill--to find enemy camps--to get this Hill 937 on Dong Ap Bia.

But for now, this camp seems a *harbor site*. It is an area of thick vegetation where the team harbors during the night. And as said by Mike McCombs, Soldier who fought in Vietnam, "It is off the beaten track and which will provide cover and concealment to the team. An ideal harbor site is located in such inaccessible terrain that anyone approaching the site will make a lot of noise before reaching the site, giving the team ample time to leave or to react."

Sp4c. Peter McConnell then says resolutely, "This is the enemy's house. He is well entrenched here in his hideaway. This is his place--his country--but he does not belong here anymore than I do. We are all invaders from somewhere or another, are we not, and so goes war? But for now we have a mission to do--to find our enemy underground bunkers so we can get *Intel* on enemy numbers and RECON enemy terrain and enemy *whereabouts* ... yes ... then we will take this damn Hill.

Buzz asks Peter, "Man how did we get ourselves into this mess?"

Peter tries to answer Buzz's question. He cannot but he tries. But Peter really has no answer for Buzz or for himself. He says, "But we do what we must do and we must fight."

Peter says again--resolutely to Buzz, "I guess we would all be better off on some beach somewhere listening to our favorite tunes."

Peter in thinking *about it all, tries to turn back the hands-of-time*. All of his past has come together now and it makes him think *how he came here in this war. He wants to return to his life back home. He thinks about his football team—-the Tigers--and his home--Spring Valley. He thinks about Sherry, his mom and his dad and all the happiness in his life back home.*

He tries to rationalize this whole military mess with its international political entanglements with the Communist and which now has become his life. Peter is caught-up in something that seems to have no purpose for his life or for any life.

Peter quotes [as said by Secretary of State Colin Powell], 'War should be the politics of last resort, and when we go to war, we should have a purpose that our people understand' which we don't seem to have."

Peter says to Buzz [as said by Albert Harper teacher Highland High School], "'We should have planned this better. We should have anticipated this better by looking at what the French did here in this Vietnam; however, unfortunately, we took it with blind optimism.' We are now here with our job to find the enemy on Mt. Dong Ap Bia." Peter quotes again, "'The situation at home in the political arena, the Presidential directives and Presidential advisors all point to the fact that more studies should have been done. As far as stopping Communism in Southeast Asia, Vietnam is really only one of many fronts. Setting an example with Vietnam which seems to be our purpose should have been approached more directly by the inclusion of these Communist countries for our battleground--Cambodia, Laos and North Vietnam. Curtailing Communism in one country and not the other is pointless because it gives the Communist a sanctuary from which they can regroup and continue their aggression.'"

Peter continues to quote, "'Possibly had a formal declaration of war been instituted, maybe then, our entire country would be united behind this single cause. Maybe other Communists countries would have realized that this was not a mop-up operation but an absolute purging of Communism.

Possibly the Communist neutral countries would have declared war on the United States permitting our military to do whatever was necessary to win the war. The stoppage of aggression and support for the AVRN at the source instead of allowing neutrality would have stopped or slowed our armed offensive. However, this would have entailed escalating the war to the point where China and Russia may have gotten fully involved which would have amounted to nothing less than WWIII with the consequences of atomic warfare. We were carefully walking a thin line between stopping Communism in Southeast Asia without getting involved at it source which is China. Comparatively speaking it would be similar to trying to stop drugs after they have entered the United States with their thousands of distribution points instead of directly stopping it at its source (borders) through ultimatums and trade restrictions.'"

Sp4c. Brule says, "Yeah, but bottom line to all of this politics and stuff: War is war and Vietnam is a part of a place with war, which we don't need now or ever. Maybe, I might not be a Pacifist but truly I am against anything that takes a life without a reason. Why fight a war that does not have to be fought, why? I don't know. And it is for each of us to decide all of this before we go out into battle. I am not against all wars. I'm just against bad wars and this is a bad war."

Guy says, "Tomorrow we will climb the hill to find these hidden underground bunkers and then so we can call in our assault troops to the top that damn mountain. I have my M-16 and I am ready to kill my enemy."

Sp4c. Buzz Brule is strapped with his M72 Rocket Launcher and says, "Yeah, man, I am with you and this ain't no sex pistol." [Everyone laughs.]

Mc then says, "You better believe it." [Everyone laughs.]

Sp4c. Dion Johnson is with his M-60, Sp4c. Mc (Chris) Davison, Sp4c. Guy Von Bexin and Sp4c. John Kelsey are ready with their M-16s.

Mc then reiterates, holding up his M-16, "And this ain't no sex pistol either and CaLu knows that," [holding it up and looking at it.]

Buzz then 'smart asses' off with this one, "Maybe CaLu doesn't know that and that is why she likes you so much, ha, ha, ha! [They all laugh.]. Mc says, "And it ain't no *Ralph* for me either. I mean I ain't smokin' marijuana in that shit." {He laughs.]. Mc continues, "Yeah, she knows about my pistol and I know about her ... I'll have it all with her. I know she will be a good cook because she makes love to me so good." [Everybody laughs non-stop.]

Sp4c. Joel Hammerstein is ready with is M-40. Sp4c. Joe Wolfing carries his Colt, his M-40 and ammo for Joel. Lieutenant Harper, the Commander, and several other Troopers, with one indigenous troop (Kit Carson Scout) round-out the team.

In the deep of the night in the A Shau Valley white phosphorous flares light-up like shooting stars with brilliant white iridescent tails glowing against the black sky. And with their descent, they cast strange illusionary shadows on the canyon walls.

The next morning the troops begin to RIF up the mountainside. Normally RIF Teams or ground maneuver assault teams move in a single file at a distance between each team member of about five-to-ten-meters. Each man must be visible to the man in front and behind. As Peter walks point in the jungle and now pulling, he feels something wrap around the toe of his boot. He is horrified at what he sees. It is a string of commo wire. And then looks up and sees field after field of mines running up the mountain to the other side of the border. Peter is horrified with this sight.

Peter calls to his *battle buddy*, Buzz, and says, "Look at this shit as the points to the mountain ahead laced with mines and Peter then picks up the commo wire and unravels it from a twisted vine and says, "Come over here, Buzz, now Look at this shit. Then as said by a Soldier on Hamburger Hill, [from Zaffiri], 'They got fuckin' commo wire runnin' up here.'"

The team continues its trek up the trail stepping carefully. Peter pulls at the wire and finds it is securely attached to a tree. The wire is well protected and well insulated. The team follows the wire up the trail and they see that the wire runs all the way up to the top of Dong Ap Bia and crosses westward over into a ravine and runs up into Laos.

Buzz says, "We gottalotta Charlie up here."

And here on this mountain Peter knows that this territory is full of North Vietnamese Soldiers. But truly for Peter all he knows is that he has to do his job. Peter comes to a clearing. About one-hundred meters away he sees two 25-degree upward—sloped knolls on the North Slope. And in each knoll, Peter sees several rows of entrenched well fortified, well concealed underground bunkers that wrap around Hill 937.

The underground bunkers work complex labyrinths with underground tunnels, trenches, storage depots, underground shelters, hospitals and spider holes.

Sp4c. McConnell says, as he is looking through his binoculars, "I see it. Look at those dirt mounds around those knolls. That dirt has been moved. Those are mounds made by man. What is it? It does not look natural by the way those mounds sit on those knolls. I can't believe what I see—-look!"

Peter hands Buzz the binoculars and says, "Gooks up there. Look! Look at those underground bunkers all over the place on the far ridge—look--to your right on those knolls—those ridge-lines—that dirt--all around those mounds-—look! The Gooks have this entire mountain and we are surrounded. They are everywhere. I can't believe this! They are everywhere. We don't stand a chance. We have to get on the horn and tell Harper about this right now."

Buzz then says, "Those bunkers wrap all around that mountain. There must be hundreds of 'em up there and look-- they got tunnels going all the way around the mountain. There must be enough bunkers there to house a thousand troops at least. I see ridgeline after ridgeline with underground enemy bunkers wrapping all around the mountain."

Peter then says, "This does not look too good for us. Let's get on the horn. Let me radio Lieutenant Harper," with his radio in one hand and binoculars in the other.

And now Lt. Harper is very concerned about this discovery and Lt. Harper then says, "Let's call LTC Coneycutt now. This find is incredible. I can't imagine how many enemy troops must be holed up in those bunkers. Tomorrow we can RIF it again and find out how many more Sappers and Cong we got out there but there's a lot of 'em. There's a lot of Sappers."

Buzz says, "Enough of this Sapper shit."

And Peter looks over at Buzz--in horror and sees Buzz suddenly tearing off his clothes.

Buzz runs-out, stark naked, into the enemy line of fire armed only with wire cutters, a couple of bamboo strands that he is holding in his mouth, (this weapon—bamboo strands--was used by indigenous enemy Sappers to tie down the flares), and satchel charges hanging around his neck.

Sp4c. McConnell yells to Buzz, "Stop ... Buzz, get back here. You will be shot and killed. He has gone crazy."

Peter turns to Guy and says, "Buzz is going to get killed. He is on a suicide run. He won't be back."

Joel yells, "No that idiot is turning around—-look—see- [pointing to Buzz]. He is turning around! He's coming back and I hope he's back before he gets his ass shot off!"

Buzz returns.

Peter asks Buzz, "What in the hell was that all about?"

Buzz says, "I just had to do it. I had my ears burnt- out too much around here with that Sapper shit on how those damn Sappers can fight here in Vietnam with their K12 Sapper Battalion and their Bandoleer Torpedoes. I mean they can go out to battle nude or dressed only in loin cloths--resolute and determined--to accomplish their mission with the agility of a cat to pounce on enemy positions and all on *inside of a New York heart beat*. Man, this enemy can fight. These troops many times are the first teams sent out to battle by the NVA forces. The steel hand cutters they carry are used to cut enemy defense concertina wire."

Buzz argues back, "There's no harm done in my streaking out there for these Mothers. Don't worry about it." [Everyone laughs.]

Dion says, "Hey man, that's what you think. Now that our enemy sees that you have an ass that is no better than theirs or anyone else's. ... What are we going to do man, about that shit?! [Everybody laughs.]. Get your f*ckin' clothes on, man. You are half crazy! And by the way, as good as you look, you should have a woman by now--and I ain't no phag."

[Everyone laughs.]

Mc then says to Buzz, "All I can say, to you, Buzz, is ... you must like gettin' shot-at in the ass. And believe me I was tempted, ha, ha, ha." [Everyone laughs.]

Buzz responds to Mc with, "No, I really don't like gettin' *shot at in the ass* or anywhere, really, but I could un-tempt you, Mc, about shootin' me in the ass real fast if you let me."

Mc then says, "No I won't let you un-tempt me, idiot. You are the-dumb-one for doing a dumb shit thing like that."

Buzz says, "Yeah, I'm just dumb ... I guess."

Mc says, "Yeah, I guess ... dumb is right! And I know you don't like your ass too terribly much because I can see you are trying real hard to get your ass shot off by somebody. And I might try it if you let me." Buzz says, "No I won't let you Bud."

Then Buzz looks down in horror as he picks up his helmet. He sees that one of his battle buddies has pissed in it.

Buzz yells angrily, "So, which one of you 'sonsabitches' did this? This is the thanks you guys give me for showin' you my Sapper skills?" Whaaat the ...

Suddenly Surfer Joe says, "Hey, don't look at me. I didn't piss in it. Don't look at me like that. I didn't do it."

No one admits to it.

Mc then says, "Yeah, that is 'the thanks' we give you. That should 'learn' you boy for puttin' our lives at risk and alertin' the enemy with your streaking shit and scarin' the hell out of us, O.K?"

John says, "Yeah, you are lucky, man, if that is all you got is a *pissed-in helmet* and not *a-shot-in-the-ass*!"

"Or up the ass," as Mc suddenly *wise cracks-in* and laughs, ha, ha, ha."

Buzz is pissed off now and looking for a fight, yells in Joe's face to vent his anger on somebody--anybody.

Buzz says, looking right at Joe, "You know, Joe, I could punch somethin' right now but I won't because you've been real nice to me, lately. You are a real nice guy and so am I; so, that's why I won't punch-you-one."

In the meantime Sp4c. Joel Hammerstein keeps look-out high in a tree until Sp4c. Joe Wolfing relieves his watch duty. They are a team. Sp4c. Joe Wolfing carries the ammo most of the time and each one has the other's back. Sp4c. Wolfing is armed with a Colt .45 strapped at the hip.

Joel says to Joe, "You are a good Soldier and we are a team."

Sp4c. Joel Hammerstein does not climb too high into the canopy areas as it would block his vision near his lines of fire below. Joel feels invincible at such a height; but however, deadly fire has to be cautioned with anywhere in NVA (North-Vietnamese-Army) territory. No one is immune to enemy artillery fire. This jungle is the territory for the team to defend. They know this. But for now the jungle lies in silence waiting in the twilight with feared anticipation for the coming of the dawn light because light is needed for the human eye to see, to aim, to fire on target and to kill.

Buzz asks Joel, "Hey, Joel, where were you? Where did you just come from?"

Joel answers, "Out of the tree," pointing to the trees.

Buzz says sarcastically, "Oh that figures. I thought you just came down from the trees. Oh, what could be better? I guess we all came down from the trees sometime or another didn't we? So I can't fault you on that one, ha, ha, ha." [Everyone laughs.]

Mc says truthfully, "Hey, don't knock the monkeys too terribly much now. They don't shoot to kill each other in armed conflicts with such vast/huge and unimaginable numbers as we do. They don't do this. They are not that dumb to be running after each other all over this frigging jungle with AK's and M-16's in their hands set on automatic fire. It ain't *hap'nin*."

Buzz says, "No, the monkeys are not that dumb. They just want to live-out their lives--not necessarily in the absence of conflict--but definitely not in-hunting-down some type of *freedom*. I mean they might fight each other but they won't kill each other for *freedom*. But *we will* hunt-down and kill one another for *freedom*."

Peter wisely asks, "But if it is a matter of freedom-—a principle--can't we let the *principle of freedom* slack a little bit in the name of humanity? Like Dr. Borenstein said, 'Tis nobler to lose honor to save the lives of men than it is to gain honor by taking them.'"

Buzz answers most truthfully, "I don't know. The monkeys do it. The monkeys can give it some slack ... but man ... I don't know, maybe it is I whose head is not screwed on too tightly?" Jockingly Mc asks, "Which one?"

But now Mc gets serious and explains life, "But from a real point of view; and, Buzz you know this, all living animals--and monkeys included--everything on this planet-- must have aerobic respiration and ATP synthesis (the principles of life) which must be to carry on life. Look at it like this, there is the *principle of life* and the other is *the principle of freedom*. These two principles come into conflict with each other and sometimes one principle is lost for the other one. But which is more important?"

Buzz answers, "That is the question."

John then says, "Ok, enough of this monkey crap. You can't have both. So Buzz what do you want from me other than a swift kick in the ass because I am sick of your comments and complaints about everything and by the way so is everyone else around here." [Everyone laughs.]

Buzz then says it last, "Oh and yeah, the monkeys don't care about freedom—believe it or not."

Peter then asks Guy something quite interesting, "Could you ever imagine that an animal such as Buzz could possibly have ever existed in this world?" [Everyone laughs non-stop.]

Buzz then asks, "Why are you referring to me in the past tense as *ever existed?* That does not look too good for me and my future living status here, does it? So am I going to cease existing or what? I just don't like the past tense of existed."

Mc says, "We couldn't possibly be that lucky to have you *cease-to-exist,*" as Buzz swings one towards Mc's head but Mc ducks in time.

Buzz then says, "And yeah, you got that one right—*exist*--that's all we do around this hole is *exist*. It is *exist* in the present tense because we're not dead yet."

Guy looking over at Buzz adds fuel to the fire and answers Peter's question about Buzz, "No, I did not ever imagine that such an animal as Buzz ever existed—*ever*--either in the animal kingdom or in human kingdom. I did not—ever imagine it in my wildest dreams!" [Everyone laughs again non stop.]

Mc then wise cracks in with, "How would you know? I really don't give a shit which kingdom he comes from. He could come from *Kingdom Come* for all I care, so Buzz, just shut your damn face or I'll shut it for you."

Buzz then says, "Well let's not worry about the monkeys, the birds or the bees, because Sp4c. Peter McConnell just found a whole swarm of them up there on this mountain."

John asks jokingly with much cynicism, "Bees? Oh, no-- you found bees? Where? Oh, no I am scared of bees," as he makes trembling motions with his body and everyone laughs.

Peter changes the subject, "Quit this shit you guys. Let' try to get real here. No, we just found some more Gooks up in those hills over there--not the insect bees--but the human ones. Our asses are in the deep fryer now as we go into this Operation Apache Snow with all those damn Slopes up there on those slopes."

Dion quips in with, "Yeah, real good one McConnell with that play-on-words. I like 'at, man—real cool."

McConnell responds with, "Well I am real glad that you like my play-on-words but I really don't plan on loosing any sleep over it, even if you didn't like it—-and sobeit."

Dion responds to that with, "Good!"

The Soldiers are tense with this discovery of land mines and the underground bunkers everywhere and they have to get back to CP (command post)--to LTC Coneycutt.

And now Sp4c. Joe Wolfing comes over to explain more to Buzz about his look-out position high in the trees.

But then Buzz explains to Joe of the discovery of mines wrapped all over the mountain.

Surfer Joe says, "Oh, we gotta go to CP now and tell them what is happening out here with these mines and tunnels. This is some real deep serious shit up here."

Buzz says, "Yeah, there's no 'hanging ten' on that shit-—no Surfer Bird, Trashmen. We are already on the horn to LTC Coneycutt about all these hidden underground bunkers we have found. We told him everything." Buzz tells Surfer Joe, "This place is riddled with the enemy. This is not a fun game anymore is it? This jungle is a 'far cry' from that Surfer Joe in Malibu--isn't it?" Joe answers, "Yes, it sure is. Don't we all wish we were 'hanging ten' on some ocean wave out there somewhere—-anywhere and not worrying about any of this Gook shit up here in these hills! Our greatest worry back in California was catching a good ride at the Wedge at the extreme south end of Balboa Peninsula in Newport Beach, CA. Man when that south swell comes in, it makes a gigantic shore break wave. It is one of the toughest rides anywhere in the U.S. We would surf it in the summer and be listening to our surfer music like Misery by the Cordials or You Know I Do by the Crucibles or Surfin' Safari, Help Me Rhonda, Good Vibrations, Surfer Girl, Surfin' USA (Chuck Berry, Brian Wilson) by the Beach Boys (Brian Wilson, Mike Love, Carl Wilson, Al Jardin, Dennis Wilson, David Marks, Bruce Johnston) or somethin.' Yeah, you know we could all be havin' some real fun out there now on that beach. We could be surfin' and tannin' on some beautiful beach somewhere--out there--right now. But we are out here on these battlefields of Vietnam tryin' to prove somethin.' What...?" Surfer Joe continues, "What ... and

what it is? I really don't know—-our manhood maybe ... in
the middle of this quagmire? I really don't know, honestly,
I don't! But after all of this trouble and perhaps my life,
I would like to think this here, is all going to be worth
it--to fight and die here--to get this crazy mountain. But
anyway, I do know one thing for sure. I love to surf. I am--
for sure--the best surfer on the beach out there in Malibu—-
yes--Malibu. Our team was 1st in the national surfing
championship. I will never forget the surfing competition
over there and how our team won everything in sight. Our
music was blasting on the beach, such as the song Gear, Dave
Meyers, the Surf Tones and Time is On My Side, Painted
Black, the Rolling Stones;

And we beat-out our competition all the way. We rode the
most awesome waves—-the most perfect pipeline--right to the
beach. But then ... my team did not understand why they
drafted me in the Army and how I left them all behind to
come here to Vietnam. I love to surf, man. But I have lost
most of my surfer look and my surfing skills now. I forgot a
lot of my surfing skills."

Buzz then smart-mouths in with, "Yeah, first of all,
they cut-off all of your golden blonde locks. Shit ... what
a bummer!" And Surfer Joe continues, "And as each day
passes, I am more of a Soldier and less of a surfer."

With cynicism Buzz says again, "Man, that's a real
bummer, ha, ha, ha." [Everyone laughs.]

Dion says, "Yeah, we don't care about any of that beach
shit right now other than gettin' our asses off of this
f*ckin' hill alive so don't waste words on shit like 'at—-
all that beach-party-surfer-crap because I don't care about
it. I know there is nothing wrong with surfers and I respect
surfers because it takes a lot of technique and agility to
surf. And it takes a lot of stamina and guts. But now, I
just wanna get out of this rat infested hole and off this
f*cking mountain." [Everyone laughs but agrees.]

Now John smart-mouths in with, "It sounds to me like
you are scared of rats because you are *always* talking about
'em." [Everyone laughs again.]. Dion with a stupid comment,
"Yeah that is why I am so scared of you, ha, ha, ha."
[Everyone laughs.]. John rebuttals back, "Well, Dion, since
you are the *man-of-the-hour* and the *man-of-the-mouth*--who is
scared of rats--then don't talk to me anymore about how you
are going to take-out a whole damn platoon of Cong single
handedly. It aint happenin'. I'm tired of hearing it. You
are always bragging about shit like that. You won't be

gettin' out of this damn jungle in one piece with *too much of your bravery crap*--like that. One thing for sure, if you do decide to *take-it-all-on*, you will be leaving here in a body bag and maybe in-pieces in-that bag. I guarantee it." Buzz says sarcastically to Dion, "Oh, I love to hear this type of talk as we are about to go out into battle. Keep up the gory details--keep it up. What ass holes."

Peter then changes the subject, "Yeah, we gotta find out what those underground bunkers are all about so we can get to the top of this mountain and take it." Each Troop takes look-out duty until dawn. They break camp and walk a 20-meter line cautiously with stealth through the jungle floor to survey the camp area. Peter looks down and in surprise, again. He cannot believe what he sees--from out of nowhere--"a trail of blood," [Zaffiri].

Buzz walks over to look at it and says, "Hey, look at what the f*ckin' gooks left us here--a trail of blood."

Lieutenant Harper says, "Something is really wrong here! Where did this blood come from? The NVA never leave trails of anything behind. They take their dead away from battle and never leave a trail or hint of a trail, or a drop of blood, or a footprint or a broken twig behind. The enemy is always careful. So what is this then? This seems to me to be planted here deliberately on the trail. Why did they leave this stuff behind? Is our enemy throwing some clues our way to throw us off base? What is it? Maybe that's it."

"What?" says Peter. Peter suddenly stumbles on an enemy rucksack at the edge of the jungle floor--just before a clearing. This enemy ruck seems almost to be deliberately placed. Peter signals to Lieutenant Harper. Then he picks-up the rucksack which he should not have done because it could have been booby trapped. Peter then opens it and sees it's filled with small rice-sacks, has a "brand new AK 47 in a leather carrying case with banana clips, a Chicom grenade and an official North Vietnamese stamped document that reveals the numbers of North Vietnamese troops on the mountain," [Zaffiri].

The Scout says, "They left this here deliberately for us to see and to know. I believe we have an entire NVA regiment up here. We must clear out of here right now! I mean right now! 'There are hundreds of troops on this mountain of the 29th NVA Regiment known as The Pride of Ho Chi Minh.' 'They are big American killers' [Zaffiri]. You must stay away from them. 'You better clear out.' You are fighting against the 6th and the 9th North Vietnamese

Regiments. There is no way we can fight this. They are violent fighters. They fight violently for a short time and then withdraw. They hide and then they sneak behind enemy lines hitting our logistical support Landing Zones (LZ's) and Command Posts (CPs). 'NVA platoons and company-sized elements will flank your troops and come in on your rear.'"

The Scout continues, "We know now that by reading this document the enemy is waiting for our troops inside enemy perimeter [as said by Samuel Zaffiri], '(...) claymore mines have been emplaced and aimed skyward against the helicopters and the area is heavily booby-trapped.' Most of strategy that they have is to their advantage with their underground bunkers because they can fight under cover. We don't have that advantage. We are out in the open."

Lieutenant Harper gets on the horn to LTC Coneycutt and tells him of the find. "Blackjack, Blackjack, AperHarper calling Blackjack, Aperharper calling Blackjack, Over."

Boom--Crash! The team is rained down upon by a superior-sized enemy force with heavy artillery rocket and mortar fire and has hit, the Senior RTO operator with the company radio. He is down. The medic and Sp4c. Guy Von Bexin realizing the urgent necessity to get to the downed Soldier and get a hold of the radio, takes-off through a fusillade of hostile fire. The medic has a hard time getting to the stricken Soldier but finally gets to him and is able to pull him in and retrieve the radio.

Lieutenant Harper gets on the RTO in earnest and says to his Troops, "Let me call to Col. Coneycutt at Battalion CP ... "AperHarper calling Blackjack, Aperharper calling Blackjack, Over. There's enemy troops out there more than we thought—a *hellofa* lot more out there! The enemy has pushed us back down this mountain. We need immediate extraction. We are dealing with a numerically superior enemy who has us pinned down with automatic weapons, mortar, rifle, recoilless rifle and rocket propelled grenade fire. We need immediate extraction!"

Silence--radio contact is suddenly lost.

Lt. Harper attempts to re-establish contact with Coneycutt, "AperHarper calling Blackjack, Aperharper calling Blackjack, Over. Do you hear me? We are under heavy attack. Do you hear me? We are under heavy enemy fire. Our position is being compromised. We are being fired upon and need immediate extraction. We also have a document in our possession that needs translation. We need immediate extraction. We are heavily outnumbered. Over. Over and out."

There is more rain of small arms, automatic weapons, mortar, heavy rocket, artillery, and recoilless rifle fire from an *estimated-enemy-regiment*. Lt. Harper then fires several magazines of tracer ammunition to signal the gunships as he requests and needs more air support.

Choppering from out of nowhere, the gunships roll in. Lt. Harper adjusts air-strikes by base artillery fire for support of the incoming aircraft gunships. Then Harper and McConnell re-adjust fire for the offense by heavy artillery and helicopter gunship fire on the enemy.

"Oh—Look!" One Troop yells out, "Look, a man down, look," [pointing]. An American Soldier seems to have been placed in position against a tree by enemy troops. The Soldier appears to be in terrible extreme pain. He can't move. Two troops then move in towards him to help.

He appears to have several wounds through which he is loosing a large amount of blood. One wound seems to have partially torn the flesh on his leg.

The Soldier mutters something in an inaudible voice and appears to be in pain--lapsing in and out of consciousness. When he awakens his face shows twisted, contorted and the agonized expressions are done only by a man in extreme physical pain and suffering. Then two troops try to approach this stricken Soldier to help him.

"No, don't!" Lt. Harper yells out, "Don't get near him! He may be booby trapped. See those wires around his head? He is wired."

Peter then says, "But he needs our help now or he is going to die."

Peter approaches the Soldier more closely and sees that Lt. Harper is right. The Soldier is booby trapped. Peter can see a very small wire coming from just behind the stricken Soldier's ear. Peter says, "You are right he is wired but we can't just leave him here like this to die slowly?"

Peter can see the agony in this man's face and hear the pain and suffering in his voice. When the Soldier regains consciousness, he moans and ... he trembles in agonizing delirious pain.

He falls out of consciousness and awakens again and yells-out in excruciating pain.

Buzz says to Lt. Harper, "What can we do? We can't let this man continue to suffer?" Buzz begins to make a move toward the Soldier and Lt. Harper says, "I am ordering you,

Sp4c. Brule to stay put and don't move towards the Soldier! Stay away from him and that is an order. And if you don't obey my order, I will have you court marshaled if you live long enough. You will not only be putting your own life in jeopardy but you will be putting every Soldier's life here in danger, too."

Buzz then says, "We've got to do something for this Soldier. We can't leave him like this!" Lt. Harper insists. "Keep away from him and don't touch him. These guys specialize in setting booby traps for us."

Peter then says, "I can't stand to see my *battle buddy* suffering anymore. This Soldier here will die slowly if we don't do something for him as soon as possible. To witness a quick death of a buddy on the battlefield is tragic enough but to see a man suffer and die slowly like this, I cannot do? I'm going in to dismantle the explosives and get him out." Peter attempts to take a step towards the stricken Soldier.

Yelling, "Get back!", says a *battle buddy*, and bolting out forward a *battle buddy* pushes Peter backwards, knocks Peter down to the ground and runs forward yelling, "I will do it. I can do it. I will get it." He runs to the stricken Soldier and both Soldiers lose their lives. Peter gets up off the ground, realizing that this brave Soldier has just saved his life. For Peter a *tear of grief* says it all. Peter says, "This is beyond comprehension." Buzz then says understandingly, "No, it is not beyond our comprehension. We know, Peter, we know." Peter then says, "Yes, we do know why we fight." These Soldiers are *our bravest young men."*

"AperHarper calling Blackjack, Aperharper calling Blackjack, over--for immediate extraction."

Lieutenant Harper continues, "We have encountered and engaged the enemy and our position is compromised. But I have in my possession an enemy document that I want you to see." Lt. Harper's team is out-numbered by the enemy. Because of that, the Cobra AH-1C "Snake" (helicopter) comes in fast for extraction. The Cobra and the Huey appear suddenly from over the foothill avoiding enemy flak and 37 mm anti-aircraft gun fire. The sound of the helicopter engine with its rotors is pure glory to the ears of the awaiting Soldiers. It comes in hovering at tree-top level attempting to avoid incoming fire. The Huey is peppered by two rows of claymore mines that are pointing skyward and that go-off simultaneously with loud, ear-deafening blasts and blinding flashes of light. Hundreds of steel pellets shoot into the thin steel hull. The Plexiglas windshield is peppered but injuries are none and miraculously it continues on for its pick-up of troops. The enemy continues to target the Cobra at its LZ. Bam—Bam. There is a lull in the firing with only scattered small arms fire. But the Cobra stays airborne for protective fire. Then the Huey comes down low hovering over the ground momentarily before it slams down hard and fast for its pick up. Everyone in Lt. Harper's team manages to get aboard safely and then the Huey begins its lift upward while the accompanying ARA Cobra Gunship stays on the offensive and continues its directed gunfire on the enemy with mini-gunfire, HE rockets, fire from a 40 mm automatic grenade launcher, salvo or flechette rockets and the Huey pulls straight upward, banks to the left, races out of enemy range and disappears out over the next hill onto momentary safety to the great relief of the Soldiers inside.

Chapter 22

History of A Shau Valley, Back at Battalion CP

With Information on Intelligence and Col. Conny

With Another Briefing on Operation Apache Snow

Sp4c.McConnell knows he has found something important on the trail and explains it all to LTC Coneycutt back at Command Post. Then Lieutenant Harper with a Brigade Intelligence Officer and a Kit Carson Scout (indigenous troop) presents the enemy ruck sack that was found in the jungle. At this point Lt. Col. Coneycutt is very nervous and agitated about this news from this find and the news from the scout. Lt. Col. Coneycutt wants to know what the scout believes but really does not want to believe him. [NOTE: With this chapter some of the characters' discussions/points-of-argument in dialogue are fictitious.]

Lt. Col. Coneycutt (commander Hamburger Hill w/changed name) says, "Get that FT (f*cking Traitor), [who was a former North Vietnamese Soldier and now Kit Carson Scout] to tell me what he thinks about the enemy and this find on Ap Bia. I want to know what he says about it."

The Kit Carson Scout says, "The entire 29th NVA Brigade is on Mt. Dong Ap Bia and they are well dug into the mountain in underground bunkers with networks of tunnels in the mountain. I know what they have and what they are capable of. You cannot send your troops out there onto that mountain or you will be sending your men out to a certain death. Your troops will be out-numbered by the NVA out there on that battlefield."

Buzz then says, "We also found 'commo wire running all over' Dong Ap Bia [Zaffiri.]. This runs up to the crest and over to the other side into Laos." Lt. Col. Coneyutt snaps back addressing the Intelligence Officer and not wanting to believe any of this says, "Well, tell that gook (Kit Carson Scout) that is 'great news for us. He has made our day,' [Zaffiri, <u>Hamburger</u> <u>Hill</u>]. I am glad to hear about the enemy presence here all over this f*cking mountain. And why do you think we came here to Ap Bia anyway? Well, I'll tell you why we came here, we came here to kill us some North Vietnamese troops--to get them off of this mountain and that is exactly what we are going to do. This is what they will get. We will show them some Little Ol' American TLC. 'They're just doin' us a real big favor by hanging around this mountain,'" [Zaffiri].

At this point the Colonel is not reasonable. He does not believe the indigenous scout's story and now the Colonel asks the Intelligence Officer more about this Kit Carson Scout. The Colonel does not accept the indigenous scout's opinion of the discovery, [Zaffiri, Hamburger Hill].

Lt. Col. Coneycutt then turns to the Intelligence Officer and asks, "So tell me what he is all about?"

The Intelligence Officer explains the same situation, "There are a lot of gooks somewhere in bunkers out there on Dong Ap Bia and I mean a hell of a lot. We have reports from Lieutenant Harper's RIF Team that they are all over on that damn hill and more *intelligence* that we have gleaned from this document."

The document shows there are numerous enemy troops.

Lt. Col. Coneycutt (actual character--name changed) asks in anger, "If they are there ... as you say they are ... where in the hell are they on that damn mountain?!"

Lieutenant Harper (fictitious character) tries to make the Lt. Colonel understand that the Americans are outnumbered. "They are buried underground and holed up in those underground bunkers. Well with our last RIFs out there we have found the presence of many enemy troops in their underground bunkers and commo wired everywhere. Also and the mountain is wired with commo wire, enemy fire power, enemy trails, campsites, supply depots and now this document."

The Kit Carson Scout reiterates, "The enemy has enough supplies and tunnel networking for the 'entire 29th regiment.' We are looking at least 2,000 enemy Soldiers in number."

The Intelligence Officer then says, "I can't give you an exact number on enemy troop strength from our over flight of the area and from our maps of the enemy but we do know one thing ... there are a hell of a lot of them especially if we are dealing with the 'entire 29th NVA Regiment.' Our *Intel* can't say for sure but we have a pretty good idea and can expect their strength to be about twelve hundred to eighteen hundred men and reinforced with heavy weapons. The Scout says that they have been given orders from Hanoi to 'kick the shit out of the Americans,' [Zaffiri]. They are looking for a big fight up here on Mt. Ap Bia," [Hamburger Hill is Hill 937 on Mt. Dong Ap Bia]. Commander Coneycutt responds angrily, "'That's what we are looking for too—a big fight,'" [Zaffiri]. Lt. Col. Coneycutt still with anger, "Ah, tell that little bastard that he is full of crap. 'He does not know what he is talking about' and I just don't trust this little bastard as far as I can spit, [Zaffiri]. His numbers don't mean shit to me. We are going on with our plans for the assault on Mt. Dong Ap Bia."

Commander Coneycutt continues, "As said in another war--the Korean War--by Lieutenant Thomas Heath of G Company 23rd Infantry, Chipyong-ni, "'G*ddamit, get back up on that hill! You'll die down here anyway--you might as well go up on the hill and die there.'"

Buzz asks most truly and with some anger, "How many more f*cking hills do we have to climb and how many more men have to die on them? Huh, how many more men, eh? Life does seem to be expendable, doesn't it?!"

Buzz continues, "Sir, we can't just send men up that hill to die. You will be sending our troops to a certain slaughter."

Buzz says to Peter, "What is wrong with LTC Coneycutt? With existing intelligence and with previous experience in and the A Shau Valley this Operation Apache Snow is likely to encounter some serious resistance from the VPA (Vietnam People's Army/Quan Doi Nhan Viet Nam) and the NVA.

Peter then says, "And on top of it, the enemy is able to re-supply with fresh troops coming over from Laos. And he fights from his deep built-in bunkers up there." Now Peter says to Lieutenant Harper, "All of the *Intel* we've got now tells us our troops are far outnumbered by the enemy."

Lieutenant Harper then says, "Intelligence tells us that this is true but I have been given my orders to fight this battle." Peter turns to Buzz and asks in hopelessness, "Why are we fightin' this damn battle here? But we should have asked ourselves this question a long time ago. Now I see we must follow orders or die." Buzz responds hopelessly, "Yes, we fight this battle now because we have decided to fight this war. But we fight for each other more than anything else." Guy then says wisely, "But… yes we do fight for each other. And let's just *not* get our asses killed out there."

Buzz then says in his own sad way, "No, we have to go but yeah, why? It is a battle that must be fought." Buzz is resolute, "It will be a sacrifice in blood."

Now Buzz describes the HISTORY of the A Shau Valley,
(Zaffiri, Hamburger Hill). He says, "And I say this because
look at our track record here. Look at our history in the A
Shau Valley. These are some of the battles we fought here."
Buzz now begins a long list of past operations and battles
in the A Shau Valley to prove his point. Buzz explains the
history, "All we have to do is look to our past experiences
here in the A Shau Valley--our past battles here. Aren't
these battles enough proof that we have more enemy out there
than we can fight? 'The first attempt was with General Jack
Tolson with Operation Delaware of the First and Fifth
Battalion of the 7th Cavalry. They CA'd in on a rain of
mortar rounds from across the border from Laos. The 1/7th and
the 1/5th ran into rough resistance as they were riffing
(reconnaissance-in-force) across the valley floor. Weather
prevented any re-supply efforts for our troops. And General
Tolson did what every Commander in Vietnam should have done
because he knew A Shau Valley could not be taken. General
Tolson decided to halt operations in the Valley and ordered
a withdrawal.'"

Buzz continues, "Then the next operation was [said by
Zaffiri], 'With Operation Somerset Plains, the 101st
Fairborn's 2/327th and the 2/502nd maneuver battalions riffed
the A Shau and then went in with two AVRN battalions to open
the Ta Bat Airstrip.' They did not find a single cache. This
operation was also a failure. I mean what does it take for
our Commanders to understand this cannot work?" Buzz
continues with more, "The next operation, Dewey Canyon, [as
said by Zaffiri], '(...)the 1st, 2nd, and 3rd, battalions of
the Marine 3rd Regiment attacked enemy Base Camp 611 which
ran astride the Laotian Border to knock out the 122 mm field
cannons from the NVA which were well protected in the
shelter of caves inside the Laotian Border.' Now the Marines
were easy targets. 'The Marines continued a three column
march toward the Laotian Border to knock out the Big Guns.
The Marines were a success because they found huge supplies
of enemy materials: an arsenal antiaircraft guns, 122 mm
field cannons, thousands of AK-47s, grenades and rockets,
millions of rounds of small arms and millions of rounds for
machine guns and hundreds of thousands of pounds of rice and
in lives lost--1,700 of their best troops were killed and
three times more were wounded. The Marines suffered 130 KIA
and 400 WIA,'" [Zaffiri].

Buzz explains more HISTORY of the A Shau Valley, "The
Marines were a success but could not keep the enemy out.
This should have been a warning sign for our Commanders

because three days later across the Laotian Border by aerial reconnaissance, the NVA were moving back into 'Base Area 611 heading toward the valley down their Hwy 922'. How much longer can we permit this to continue?" Buzz explains further the battles that have been fought in blood in the A Shau Valley, "More problems were encountered in the [as said by Zaffiri], 'A Shau Valley with Operation Massachusetts Striker with the 2/17th (CAV) Cavalry under Col. Hoefling and the 101st 1/502 under Lt. Col. Davis.' They were to set up a staging area for attack on the A Shau at Firebase Whip but had to change plans and move on to establish firebase Veghel instead at the center of the valley. Then Lt. Davis was ordered to combat assault his 1/502 into the area that was a well fortified by the NVA's 816th with [said by Samuel Zaffiri, Hamburger Hill], '(...) rows of claymore mines pointing skyward and wired to detonate simultaneously.' The NVA 816th hit hard with a 'fusillade of rocket propelled grenades and rifle machine gun fire' and a 'torrent of RPG's and 60 mm mortar rounds' and knocking out helicopters. Hoefling ordered more air strikes but eventually 'Lt. Col. Davis 1/502 pushed the NVAs 816th out of the valley' but Davis faced tough resistance from the 816th on Mountain Dong A Tay with its deep underground enemy bunkers and tunnel networking. The Lt. Col. went up the ridge and was pushed back down again with sniper fire and machine gun fire. But the U.S. support from the air and the airbases with the 105 mm and the 155 mm fire power could not stop enemy resistance on the mountain. Lt. Col Davis sent in Charlie and Alpha Companies with a recoilless rifle to knock out some enemy underground bunkers. But then the NVA counter attacked and then withdrew again. The Americans called in air Napalm strikes, more air strikes for hours and with 'rifle and machine-gun fire and a shower of grenades' which all seemed to have little effect on the enemy. The U. S. Troops were fighting hard. [As said by Zaffiri, Hamburger Hill], 'Three companies from the 1/502 went up the ridge again but were thrown back down the mountain again from enemy satchel charges, exploding grenades and M-79 canister rounds and a barrage of small arms and machine gun fire,' [explained by Zaffiri], the 1/502 suffered 50% casualties on Bloody Ridge at Mountain Dong A Tay where the enemy refused to retreat and they were all over the mountain ridge. Thirty-five Americans were killed there."

Buzz says more about the HISTORY of the A Shau Valley, "This reminds me of his quote by T. R. Fehrenbach 'The inexorable law of combat is the disintegration and replacement of rifle companies.'" Buzz asks, "How much more can we stand? What more do our Commanders want? What does our country want?" Buzz continues his story with Operation Massachusetts Striker because it was seen plainly by the enemy's determination and through the 2/327ths back tracking that the enemy was there *en force* with a large dirt road, a fleet of Russian trucks, bulldozers and mechanical supplies and equipment. 'The 1/502 also found a large enemy hospital complex, trucks, 600 SKS rifles and thousands of rounds of recoilless rifle, mortar and howitzer fire.'" Buzz continues to explain this story of enemy will to fight. "Again on Mt. Dong Ngai with the NVA 6th Regiment, the NVA 806th and the K12 Sapper Battalion stayed to fight in their spider holes, their network of bunkers and tunnels. 'The enemy had many excellent food supplies with farms, thatched roof houses and gardens.' Buzz continues [And again as said by Zaffiri in his book Hamburger Hill], "'The 2/17 CAV suffered high casualties while trying to take a stand there.' And [Zaffiri] 'enemy caves were found with thousands of Chicom Rifles and grenades and many thousands of rounds of small arms ammunition and then on another ridge many tons of rice and hundreds of 122 mm rockets and RPG's (rocket propelled grenades) was found.' More air strikes by U.S. B-52s were called to pound the ground and also with ground artillery but it had little effect on the enemy underground bunkers. [And here as explained by Zaffiri], 'The enemy was always replaced coming down the Ho Chi Minh Trail.' The enemy had the tenacity with the numbers. [And here as said by Zaffiri in his book Hamburger Hill], "'The 217th was almost wiped out; the 2/501 replaced the 3/187th. Then U.S. Firebase Airborne was hastily built, lacked sufficient defense and a troop transport ship was shot down. Then this U.S. base became surrounded by bunkers and being hit by heavy mortar fire of the 6th NVA Regiment, the K12 Sapper Battalion, and two companies from the NVA 806th. With this 27 Americans were killed. More munitions were found in caves: 10,000 Chicom rifles and grenades, 20,000 rounds of munitions, RPG's (rocket propelled grenades) and 122 mm rockets, '" [said by Zaffiri, Hamburger Hill]. Buzz knows this story of the A Shau Valley all too well. And he truly knows that some people have to pay the price in blood to do the job as commanded to do.

Buzz makes his conclusion about HISTORY/battles [Zaffiri] in the A Shau Valley and comments to his *comrades in arms* about this impending battle on Hill 937 with Operation Apache Snow, "This will be certain death for all of us. The point--blood is being used as an expendable material of this war. I just don't know if we will ever be able to fight war like this?" He finishes his story on the history of the A Shau Valley!

And LTC Coneycutt ignores these comments and thoughts about the battles fought in the A Shau Valley, and he boasts of his successes in previous battles of the 3/187th on Mt. Dong Ngai. He continues with his ideas. The Colonel wants to fight this battle and ignores all other ideas. He continues to explain how his 3/187th relieved the 2/17th Cav. from Mt. Dong Ngai where his troops suffered many casualties. He has his mind made up.

LTC Coneycutt continues with his stubborn ideas, "I know you men disagree with me but other *RIF* teams have really proved that map reconnaissance and helicopter over flights were impractical in counting enemy numbers? We just don't know what's out there for sure. We just don't know for sure and we can't halt operations now because we are not sure. But we do know that we can beat 'em. No, I don't think it is going to be certain death for our troops." Sp4c. Brule says, "We can't go into battle like this. How can we go into battle and not be sure of strength?" The Commander continues, "We've proved it to ourselves that we *can* fight. The enemy is waiting for us but they don't know that *we* are waitin' for them. I would not send you men out there if I knew you were going to die." Buzz knows there is no way to explain his point to the Commanders.

Now LTC Coneycutt then introduces Col. Conny (Col. Conmy) (actual commander w/changed name) to explain the A Shau Valley and the mission on Hill 937--Hamburger Hill, Apache Snow briefing details again.

Col. Conny, (Col. Conmy) Commander of the 3rd Brigade (actual character--changed name) then begins to describe the mission, "We must continue with this fight. We have to clear out the enemy from the A Shau Valley with *Operation Apache Snow* on Ap Bia. And now with Lt. Harper's LRRP team which is about to be launched with Operation Apache Snow by the 101st Airborne Division airmobile infantry. [As said by Zaffiri in his book, Hamburger Hill]: 'Five battalions will combat assault as a reconnaissance (RIF) into the A Shau Valley. Each battalion will be inserted by helicopter into the valley and each battalion will search its assigned sector.' Lt. Harper your RIF team will form a company-size unit now and you will now combat assault Hill 937 with Apache Snow to capture that hill. It is a major part of this fight. This mountain with all of its little hills straddles the Laotian border and Hill 937' is one of them hills we gotta get. This is going to be our toughest battle ahead with Apache Snow.

We will do it. This operation then is the second part of our three-phase plan for this mission to rid the enemy from the A Shau Valley where we will fight the VPA." He continues, "Now for the A Shau Valley we start first in the A Shau Valley by sending units of the '3rd Brigade of the 101st Airborne Division which are the 3rd Battalion, 187th Infantry (3/187), the 2nd Battalion of the 501 Infantry (2/501), the 1st Battalion 506th Infantry (1/506), the second Battalion 506 Infantry 2/506th, the 2nd Battalion of the ARVN 1st Division, the 9th Marine Regiment of the 3rd Battalion and the 5th Cavalry and the 3rd ARVN Regiment into the A Shau Valley.'" Col. Conny (Col. Conmy) continues, "But for you now your mission now on Ap Bia, 'the 1/506 will attack from the South and our 3/187 will attack from the North.' Thanks to our RIF troops we have been able to try to figure our strategy for this mountain. LTC Coneycutt will go into [as said by Zaffiri], 'Ap Bia with multi company assaults by sending Alpha and Delta Companies to RECON in force and combat assault the north and the northwest fingers of Dong Ap Bia. Bravo and Charlie Companies will climb toward the summit on different routes.' Lt. Harper your company will be one of those companies now to combat assault the mountain."

Col. Conny continues [said by Zaffiri], "'With the 1/506th Infantry we will do probing attacks on the south slopes of Mt. Dong Ap Bia (Hill 916) with Bravo Company that will be heli-lifted in there.' The Alpha company--2/506-- will try to work with the 3/187 and the 2/506 to relieve the 3/187. We will try to relieve the AVRN 2/3 as well. Then we will send the 2/501 Infantry and the ARVN 2/3 to continue to fight the battle. 'The ground will be prepped with two hours of close air support fire and ninety minutes of artillery fire from ten nearby howitzer batteries.'"

Guy then says to Col. Conny, "It is not going to be that easy because our troops have to get into a position of assault on that mountain because our enemy is there waiting as he gets his reinforcements from Laos."

Col. Conny then responds with his opinion on Guy's idea on incomplete intelligence and incorrect information about enemy strength, "You are wrong. There is no more than a reinforced platoon or company enemy out there to fight. So what are you talking about? I know we can beat them! We have more than enough troops. That is all!" Sp4c. Buzz Brule then addresses Col. Conny before he leaves, "You are incorrect. We have already gathered intelligence on hills 900, 916 that there are gooks all over on those hills. Let's learn from these past battles on these hills that have given us a hard time such as with Dong Ngai, Dong A Tay and Doi Thong in the A Shau Valley. The enemy is not just limited to a few trail watchers (scouts) as we had first believed but they are NVA regulars who are well dug in and planning their revenge on our troops. And what about all that f*cking enemy commo wire, tunnels and land mines we found up there? It ran up the entire mountain on Dong Ap Bia. Can't the High Command see that we are dealing with a numerically superior enemy force, damn-it? I'm not gettin' my ass shot off for this shit." Now LTC Coneycutt comes in again with, "No. We don't know *exactly* how many troops the enemy has—-nor will we ever know—really. I don't believe that we are outnumbered! My battalion was able to win the fight on Dong Ngai and we can win it here again. On Ngai, we prepped the ground first with massive air strikes. I put my battalion on the attack from the lower LZ on Dong Nga--then we attacked up the mountain with Bravo, Delta and Charlie Companies. Our plan was perfect. We can do it again." Sp4c. Brule then says, [fictitious dispute. Lt. Harper's troops did not dispute fighting this battle], "Yes, you did win that battle there. You did good job out there but this one here on Ap Bia is a different battle. But the bottom line to all of this is that here we are outnumbered." Sp4c. Brule continues but brings up another battle that was fought, "Look at all of these other battles we have fought out here. But didn't you think that something was going on up there on Dong Ngai with all those secondary explosions after our B52 attacks? The whole southwest side of Dong Ngai was used as a huge enemy ammo cache? And you know about the three enemy caches that where found there on Dong Ngai?" LTC Coneycutt counters angrily, "No, you are wrong, we are going to kick the f*cking enemy off this f*cking mountain on his ass and all the way back into Laos! I'd never send my troops out there with the knowledge that my men would lose the battle. I am completely confident in what I am doing. My Troops are capable of fighting this battle a 100%. My troops are the best."

But Buzz retorts back by asking a good question but answers his own question, "But also General Creighton Abrams was not even sure about it. [As said by Gen. Creighton Abrams himself about the mountain, (actual quote by Commander)], 'We are not fighting for the terrain as such. We are going after the enemy.'" But Buzz asks, "But I ask *why then are we fighting for the mountain if we are not fighting for the terrain? This mountain--the terrain--is what we want.* Bottom line ... you are sending Soldiers out to win a battle that can't be won." Lieutenant Harper then says to LTC Coneycutt, "We will fight as you have ordered

with the mountain's four hills but it will be a very tough
job. We are fighting a formidable enemy. [As said by
Zaffiri, Hamburger Hill], 'The enemy is infiltrating into
South Vietnam at 5,000 per month with re-supply troops. And
the enemy forms small units that can maneuver easily around
our LZ's. All of these small trails however, work to our
disadvantage helping to make us down-size to squads and
platoon points of attack.'" Lieutenant Harper continues to
explain his story (fictitious character and argument) to
Commander Coneycutt and to everyone in earshot his most
important conclusion, "It has been now because our *RIF* team—
-RECON--our combat patrol--that have helped to put these
pieces of this puzzle together with all this information
here on Ap Bia. With my team ... we now have an idea of what
we are up against with this *data* and *intelligence* such as
enemy bases (installations), documents, prisoner-
information, our past battles here and with this
intelligence and our captured equipment etc. And also now we
do know the data on VPA *order of battle and disposition*.
Tunnels are everywhere and commo wire is strung to the top
of the mountain and into Laos. With another battle of Mt.
Dong A Tay our RIF teams also found commo wire, tunnel
networking and mines all over the place. What makes you
think Ap Bia is any different? The NVA also have [and as
said by Samuel Zaffiri], '(...) built a system of deep
spacious bunkers all inter connected by tunnels and trenches
and looking down ... on cut fields of fire.' The enemy sits
on carefully prepared fields of fire all over this valley.
All of this points to enemy saturation. We have more
information from a FAC plane which spotted some huts on a
ridge below the peak of Dong Ngai—the eastern side of A
Shau. Again what makes you think Ap Bia is any different? We
should re-plan our strategy and regroup if we want to
continue this fight. That is my conclusion. But we will go
as ordered by our High Commanders to fight this battle."

Buzz says lastly, "How much more proof of enemy numbers
do we need now? This tells me that this battle cannot be
fought but most importantly this tells me that this war
cannot be won."

Chapter 23

Lieutenant Harper's Company Unit Combat Assaults up Hill 937

Lt. Harper's Company is one of three companies to be inserted at dusk into the lower LZ for a mission to take the Summit, of Hill 937, (Hamburger Hill) on Mt. Dong Ap Bia with Operation Apache Snow.

LTC Coneycutt (actual character/commander but name changed) figures that with the 'three companies, each going up the mountain from different direction,' they could get to what was on that hill and the NVA would not be able to concentrate their fire on any one of them. Lieutenant Harper's Company is one of the companies assigned to assault the hill. LTC Coneycutt orders a massive air strike the day before to take out bunkers and to soften the ground for the troops. The three companies are to rendezvous at the upper LZ near the summit of the hill on the mountain.

Sp4c. Brule then says "But with these small units, our Troops are too decentralized which makes it difficult for a *unity of command.'* It will be much harder to take this mountain."

Lt. Harper says to his troops, "But I am here now to take command--to take this mountain from the enemy and that is what we are going to do because that is what I have been ordered to do so don't give me anymore excuses. We have a mission to do. We are going to rendezvous with the two companies at the summit. I have been ordered to take this mountain to its summit. Mount Dong Ap Bia is a mountain with several hills and one such Hill is 937 (Hamburger Hill), we must take to get to the top of Mt. Ap Bia and in so doing we have to knock out hundreds of enemy bunkers which are wrapped concentrically around this mountain. We are talking here about thousands of meters of underground bunkers all with complex tunneling networks all connected--full of enemy troops and booby traps. We will start with Hill 937."

He continues, "These hills have hundreds of underground bunkers and to get to them, we have to take out the main tunnels connecting these bunkers. Our company is going to assault the north side of the mountain to get to its summit."

The battle ground was prepped by air and ground artillery but the air strikes and artillery prep has had little effect on knocking-out enemy bunkers and their connecting tunnel systems. The troops are sent in to fight a very difficult battle.

Lt. Harper explains more of his opinion, "Those bunkers are a good place for the enemy to hide. The enemy is a master at camouflage. They know this jungle like the back of their hands and here we sit like with our thumbs up our asses trying to cover this ground. We are fighting a very determined enemy and we are fighting him on his turf. The NVA and the VPA (North Vietnamese Army/Vietnam People's Army) have concealed their bases completely from aerial surveillance. There are a lot of enemy troops out there but LTC Coneycutt, Maj. Gen. Zain, Gen. Wells, Col. Conny and LTC. Gorman keep turning a blind eye to the reality that we are facing a 'numerically superior enemy.'" Lt. Harper explains more, "The enemy moves at night under triple canopy jungle. Helicopter redeployment is almost impossible because we can't make LZ's (landing zones). We cannot suppress anti-aircraft fire because they keep their bases hidden under this triple canopy jungle." Lt. Harper continues his explanation of the theater of war on Ap Bia, "The jungle canopy covers the movement of the VPA and has created a non-linear battlefield because he moves in small units under this canopied jungle. They move around our LZ's and shoot down helicopters with small arms fire and rocket propelled grenades. He has his plan. He is meticulous, patient and very determined to keep the Yankee out of here."

Out on the mountain ready for battle, Lt. Harper says, "Let us make camp here in the cover of the jungle. Tomorrow we will move out--up the hill--in a northwest direction towards the ridge for an assault on the nearest rows of bunkers on our way to the summit. But now we will make camp, set the trip flares, make the perimeter and set the claymores."

At dusk the Soldiers set camp perimeter with claymore mines and set twenty-four hour guard duty and sleep only with their ponchos or their poncho liners (lighter and makes less noise). Each member in camp has a certain area for which he is responsible and which gives the team a 360-degree security. They make camp in the jungle in the dense bamboo thickets and brush. The brush is dense and it provides protective cover for the Americans. Their camp is a hundred meters away from enemy bunkers but still remains well concealed with its 360-degree perimeter.

At dawn, Lt. Harper's company assaults the bunker complex with 84 mm recoilless rifle fire, automatic weapons fire, hand grenades, and RPG's (rocket propelled grenades) onto the enemy position. The enemy launches in return, a savage well coordinated mortar attack.

Sp4c. Wolfing very enthusiastic about the battle ahead says, "We have to get out there and up this hill and blow the bunkers or we are all going to get our asses shot."

Lieutenant Harper gives a command for Sp4c. Joe Wolfing and Sp4c. Joel Hammerstein to run the hill to the next triple bunker complex and take it out. As Lt. Harper's company pushes forward, Sp4c. Hammerstein and Sp4c. Wolfing continue their drive forward as a two-man team up the hill ahead of the company. But suddenly Sp4c. Wolfing drops to his feet behind a log. He will not take another step forward. Sp4c. McConnell says to Dion, "Wolfing won't get up to move another foot. Do you see the panic and the absolute fear in his face? He believes he is going to die. He's shell-shocked. I mean this man is terrified. The Lieutenant can't make him fight this now."

Lt. Harper gives the order again, "Wolfing, get your ass up there and take out those bunkers, now, and that is an order. Get out and get those f*cking bunkers now! Do you hear me?" Wolfing is on the ground and won't get up. Wolfing says in fear, "I can't do it. I can't do it, anymore, man. Let me stay behind here to catch my breath for a minute." Buzz helps him to his feet but Joe collapses again. Buzz says to Peter, "Wolfing knows we are on a suicide mission and he is right." Sp4c. McConnell says to Lt. Harper, "This Soldier is in shell shock. He cannot move another step forward. You can't make him fight." Lt. Harper says, "Wolfing has to move out and get to those bunkers up ahead with us or he is going to die down here if we leave him. I gave him an order to do so and he is going to do it, understand?" McConnell then says to Lieutenant Harper, "Let me go in his place. I don't know what has happened to this guy but he can't move onto those bunkers now as you have ordered." Lt. Harper says, "He's a f*king chicken shit." McConnell then says, "No, I think he has been hit with battle fatigue or shell shock and he knows we are going to our slaughter." Lt. Harper understands then says to Peter, "OK go in his place but get him out of there."

Ka...Boom, a pair of Phantom Fighter-Bomber Jets, lay their defensive fire in the over above in the hazy sky to prep the ground for the line Soldiers (ground Soldier) on this mountain. The Soldiers look upward and see fleeting glimpses of two fighter jets darting between the jungle tree-tops in their suicidal dives to drop their 1,000-pound bombs on enemy bunkers.

Boom ... Boom ... huge balls of orange flames with huge black stacks of smoke shooting upward—-crackling--knocking-out everything in their path. When the two fighter-bombers finish their job, they climb straight upward together and bank to the left, head eastward towards the coast and disappear out of sight.

Lt. Harper says, "Many times for this reason our bombing won't work. Our fire support is restricted. We are too close to our enemy in proximity and our air support can't bomb effectively. Also our choppers are shot down by enemy rocket propelled grenades and enemy small arms fire hidden under the canopy of the trees."

Lt. Harper states, "But we got to get those bunkers and the only effective weapon against these underground bunkers now is Napalm delivered from our Phantoms. Our fighter-bombers are doin' their job for us with some good old Napalm. And for us with these underground bunkers, the weapon is the recoilless rifle. It takes-out the bunkers."

The Americans walk a single file through mountain slopes, down mountain crevices and ravines and up steep winding mountain trails in heavily controlled enemy territory. The jungle canopy now has gaping holes made by Allied bombs and artillery. The jungle green has given way to charred remains--burnt black and leafless with gaping holes in the canopy. Most is black and lifeless that has been burnt to cinders by napalm.

Sp4c. Joel Hammerstein as sniper proceeds ahead of the rest of his company with his scope and rifle. Sp4c. Peter McConnell takes point as senior scout. He is responsible for security on the front of the trail with early warning of enemy presence and keeping the compass direction for the company unit. Sp4c. Guy Von Bexin takes slack--is second in line--and the second team leader. Third in line is the senior RTO troop (radio and communications). This Soldier will maintain the paces taken and he will observe flank. Another Soldier Sp4c. Merjil takes rear position. If the troops stop for a short moment on their trail, point must face forward and rear must face forward and all team members in between alternate directions down the line.

Today the Americans do not gain ground because of intensive enemy fire from several enemy bunkers. The Americans maneuver through enemy territory taking out bunkers and then falling back into their well fortified positions for nightfall. And now they set a 360 perimeter.

At daybreak Lieutenant Harper says, "Today we're taking this hill. How many more times is the enemy going to push us back down this damn hill? McConnell and Brule go get your recoilless rifles and take out a row of bunkers just past that tree line."

Shining...flickering ... Sp4c. Hammerstein sees a muzzle flash and yells, "Snipers in the trees!" And in an instant Hammerstein brings down the sniper but a second later another muzzle flash and Hammerstein downed another.

Hammerstein says, "We gotta watch out for those trees with those snipers and they also got some claymores set in 'em too. These trees are wired real well with commo and snipers."

Buzz switches his M-16 on automatic and sprays the trees and still several more snipers fall to the ground. Peter sees another muzzle flash. Sniper fire gets heavier. Sp4c. Dion Johnson then comes in with his M-60 and mows-down some more snipers and takes some of the trees with them.

Buzz says, "That'll shut 'em up for a while. I think we got most those sonsofbitches hiding in those trees but there are still more of 'em up there."

Brule runs from cover to cover ducking more sniper fire from the treetops. The Americans hide in cover behind a boulder. Now there's a lull.

With a lull in enemy fire, the company unit starts out again into open ground. Bang ... Boom ... the unit is hit by enemy rifle, machine gun fire and small arms fire from five gunners in a cluster of one-man spider holes. The Americans run through 5,000 meters in a hail of fire in this heavily controlled enemy territory. But they take cover again behind some large scattered boulders and in a couple of B52 bomb shell craters.

Lt. Harper's company is fighting against a very determined, well fortified and well coordinated NVA battalion. The enemy is entrenched in his heavily fortified position. Enemy fire is ceaseless and the Americans are now caught in a voluminous hail of enemy grenades, heavy mortar, recoilless rifle, rocket propelled grenades, machine gun and automatic weapons fire. But Harper's company remains protected behind the boulders and the two bomb craters. The Americans return fire with their M-79 grenade launchers, a blizzard of rifle fire, machine-gun fire and mortar rounds. Then McConnell and Brule load aim and fire the recoilless rifle directly into the aperture of a bunker and knock-out five bunkers with one blast. Enemy Soldiers scream loudly as they are tossed high into the air.

Sp4c. Dion Johnson says to a Young Soldier next to him, "These guys are getting what they deserve for what they have done to these poor people here in South Vietnam."

The Young Soldier responds with, "Yeah, man you are right. Yeah, you are right. They deserve it. Let's go get 'em."

Sp4c. Dion Johnson and the Soldier jump-up from behind a bolder and run through a continuous hail of enemy fire, spraying their M-60s toward enemy position with effective suppressive fire--running side by side--cover to cover--boulder to bolder--avoiding enemy fire. They stop for a moment but run for another 20 meters to the next boulder and are now facing even more devastating mortar, recoilless rifle, automatic weapons and rifle fire that rains down on them. Miraculously Dion and the Soldier make it to the next bolder.

Feeling very proud of himself and now somewhat arrogant, the Young Soldier says, "We are the best. We're gonna' do it. We can't run much faster than this, can we?!"

This Soldier knows that he is going to show his battle buddies that he is going to win this war and that he is an important part of it. He is very eager to fight.

Sp4c. Dion Johnson then yells, "Yeah, and we can't shoot much straighter than this."

The Young Soldier yells, "Yeah, man, we are doin' it. We'll get 'em all. Hey, was that close enough for you, Dion," as shots ricochet off the bolder behind Dion's head?

Dion says, "Yeah, this is my lucky day."

The Young Soldier yells his battle cry very enthusiastically and he knows that he is going to make the difference in this battle, "Yeah! Come on; let's go get 'em. Yeah, come on, hey, let's go get 'em, as the two stand up and start their next sprint through a voluminous hail of exploding enemy grenades, machine gun and automatic weapons fire in this fusillade of enemy fire!"

The Young Soldier yells again, "Hey, come on let's go get 'em. Come on let's get 'em."

The two continue to run up the hill together side by side to the next bolder. Dion looks over to the Young Soldier and hears the Young Soldier's battle cry again, "Yeah, come on let's ..." as Dion feels the spray of warm flesh and warm blood splash from where the Young Soldier was standing. Now Dion sees nothing but mangled flesh and pools of blood. He hears no more sounds of a young man's voice-- nothing now from where the Young Soldier was standing--as he had yelled his battle-cries--moments before. This Soldier now ... will never *go get them!*

Then Dion thought as was said by Phillip Caputo (Vietnam Veteran) in Rumor of War "'*I guess every generation is doomed to fight its war... suffer the loss of the same old illusions, and learn the same old lessons on its own.*'"

His blood shed ... the young Soldier's blood was so important to him so he could be able *to go get* 'em. Blood is the body's most voluminous organ. His blood carried oxygen and nutrients to every cell in his body and his blood also carried-away his bodily waste products such as carbon dioxide, uric acid etc. Where once there was a young eager man, there now lays a pool of blood with mangled flesh on the floor of Mount Dong Ap Bia. But South Vietnam can have its *freedom* from someone. But ... again ... freedom from whom and freedom from what? What do we want to give to Vietnam? But Vietnam may not want it. God gave this young Soldier his life but somehow it was stolen away from him. ... *Yeah, come on let's get 'em*. No one really knows the meaning of any of this.

And now again Lt. Harper's company sets its night perimeter and plans for another day.

And ... again another day for the living. The next day the Soldiers begin their assault again to the summit. Caught off guard, Lt. Harper's company gets caught in ravine and becomes heavily engaged with a well fortified numerically superior enemy unit. There is a lot of intense small arms, automatic weapons, morter and rocket fire.

Buzz yells, "We are faced with a lot of enemy out there who is well fortified and well dug in and they ain't backing down for nothing. Let's go get 'em."

Lt. Harper yells, "Let's go.

Buzz says, "Yeah, let's go but we are outnumbered, here. Our enemy in the A Shau Valley keeps getting reinforcements of fresh troops from Laos."

The unit is met again with more machine gun fire--with a shower of exploding grenades. Boom—Bang--exploding through the tree line, the Americans are struck by a human-wave ground assault firing from the hip that penetrates the defensive perimeter. Lt. Harper and his company engage in hand to hand combat, return rifle fire and machine gun fire with a shower of grenades. Pc4. Dion Johnson throws a hand grenade and several enemy Soldiers go flying. Pc4. Brule fires his M-16 on automatic and says to McConnell, "I have you covered. Let's get out of here." The two take a dash forward. Dion and Peter throw their M-16's and take out their strapped Colts and shoot point blank into the enemy line. An enemy Soldier has Buzz in his line of fire to shoot and to kill but Peter pounces on the enemy Soldier just in time to divert the bullet's trajectory. Then Peter puts his Colt back into its holster and throws a hard punch into the enemy's face and knocks the enemy backwards but he comes back up forward again throwing a right hook to Peter's temple. This blow takes Peter back but Peter comes forward again very quickly with a hard fist to the face. The Enemy Soldier falls to the ground and Peter jumps on him and hits the enemy again with a strong hard Karate chop to the Soldier's left jugular and renders the enemy Soldier unconscious. The enemy Soldier is out and motionless. Peter then jumps up again with his gun and begins firing point blank. Another Enemy Soldier moves forward toward Peter with a gun in hand aiming at Peter point blank but Peter ducks down just in time to avoid the hit but pops back up again and slams his fist in the enemy's face and knocks-out the enemy. Peter then chases another NVA Soldier out to the perimeter line where the NVA Soldier with dozens of others gets shredded in a hail claymore-mine blasts and small arms fire set by the Americans. Boom—Boom-Bang--from the left flank, another NVA force comes around again on the American perimeter and the enemy is hit with an inundation with 60 mm rounds from the Americans and the Americans drive the enemy back.

Lt. Harper calls in for a napalm strikes. And air support comes in with Napalm strikes. Napalm strikes hit so closely to the American perimeter that the Soldiers could feel the intense heat singe their hair. These air strikes bought the American team enough time to move out and onto higher ground for cover near some boulders and closer to the main enemy bunker complex where the Americans can take them out. Peter and Buzz load and fire the recoilless and blast more enemy bunkers. Now the Americans move forward from their exposed position up closer to the summit to take cover in another group of boulders. McConnell throws two more grenades and busts five more bunkers. And now the team pushes even further up the ridge to a tree line bordering alongside a row of empty bunkers where the Americans take cover.

In the bunkers, the Americans are now faced with another rain of machine gun fire that begins another enemy assault and are again compromised severely. "I'm going," says Buzz as he leaps up and out of the bunkers, racing through the front line and "silences the emplacement with a grenade and kills four enemy troops (...)."

Peter thinks about what Buzz just did with his charging the enemy--and says to himself, *I guess each of us is a man in his own way.*

Buzz fails to silence the machine gun nest and the enemy continues to fire on the American position. McConnell wants to help his battle buddy and suddenly jumps forward firing his M-16 on automatic into two bunkers but then throws a grenade in one of the bunkers while still firing his M-16 at the same time, into bunkers silencing the machine guns. Peter is proud to be such an immense asset for his team. He is proud.

Buzz then says, "Hey, good job McConnell. That guy is not going to be talking or firing at anything again or to anybody too soon."

Lt. Harper yells, "Run for the tree line up the mountain past these bunkers."

Boom—Crash—Boom. The enemy Soldiers charge again for a frontal assault on the American front line of defense. The enemy appears from a large bunker complex which seems to be connected to a main tunnel line. The Americans are surrounded by a numerically superior enemy force with well coordinated infantry and mortar assault. And more enemy troops come emerging from their bunkers and spider holes everywhere. There is no end in sight for the Americans and the Americans receive another barrage of enemy fusillade as they make a run for the tree line under cover.

Lt. Harper knows the Americans must get some air support now. He gets on the radio and carefully adjusts the incoming air strikes.

Buzz then says to Harper, "Get on the horn to Blackjack (Lt. Col. Coneycutt) and let him know what is going on up here."

Lt. Harper says, "Aperharper calling Blackjack, Aperharper calling Blackjack, over. Call in the Snake and the Nape. We have to hit these tunnels with some 1,000 Pounders with delayed action fuses. Over."

Lt. Harper names the coordinates and a FAC goes in with his white phosphorous smoke to mark the enemy tunnel ridge to be bombed by the Phantoms. These tunnels connect networks of underground bunker complexes with a very determined enemy. Then the Phantoms (fighter bombers) come in to bomb the underground tunnel system. Then four American base artillery batteries pound the area for more than an hour but to no avail. The underground targets remain intact. The enemy has prepared his field of fire well and is fighting back hard on his suicidal mission and won't quit. Some tunnels are hit by American air fire but cannot knock-out the main connecting tunnels or bunkers.

Lt. Harper yells, "We must collapse those tunnels. We need a couple of good direct hits to knock them out."

Sp4c. Brule and Sp4c. Guy Von Bexin ... you men take the recoilless and assault those bunkers that connect to those tunnels. Sp4c. Davison and Sp4c. McConnell ... you men get firing the M-60's"

Boom... as Sp4c. Brule is running toward the bunker complexes, booming rocket and mortar fire burst at his feet and knocks him backwards where he falls near the enemy position in the line of fire ... motionless.

Lt. Harper yells, "We can't get to him, now, but continue to give protective fire so we can send someone in there to get him."

Peter then yells, "I'm going in to get him." Running ... Running ... and suddenly leaps forward through 'heavy raining rifle and automatic weapons fire.' And he falls.

Guy knows this battle is suicide for this entire team. Guy yells, "We can't lose our Soldiers. Those two are going to get killed out there."

Mc yells frantically, "We are going to lose both of them. They are gone. Let's go get 'em, now."

Sp4c. Mc Davison and Sp4c. Guy Von Bexin then make a mad dash to provide protective fire cover for Sp4c. McConnell with their M-60 and M-16 set on automatic. There is an intense volleying of fire between the enemy and the Americans in a 'mad minute.'

McConnell won't let Buzz die gets up and runs through open areas of heavy machine-gun fire to his fallen comrade. Without hesitation McConnell grabs a hold of Brule's leg dragging him over rocks and tree stumps to the cover of relative safety--near a boulder.

Mc continuously pounds protective fire for the Americans until they are back under cover and Sp4c. Buzz Brule regains consciousness.

Buzz then says, "What the f*ck?! Some gooks got me real good but not good enough." [Everyone laughs and everyone is relieved to be alive.]

Mc then says, "You see Brule ... I still like you."

Buzz then says, "Yeah, what would happen if you didn't like me? [They laugh together.]

Mc then says, "Well, this is like our kid's games, Buzz, they shot you down and you did get back up again. Buzz answers, "Yeah, I guess I did with your guys' help--thanks."

Sp4c. Joe Wolfing says, "Well you can thank Sp4c. McConnell, Sp4c. Von Bexin and Sp4c. Davison for saving it for you, man," [Joe patting Peter on the shoulder]!

Buzz says to Peter and Mc, "Hey, man, you guys did that for me? I can never thank you enough. I owe you guys one."

Sp4c. Dion Johnson then says to Peter, "Yeah, man, if you stayed out there any longer, you would have been a 'goner.'"

Boom-Crash-Boom. An enemy bunker complex comes alive with another rain of RPG's (rocket propelled grenades) and mortar fire that whoosh in and explode on the American position but Lt. Harper's team continues their assault to try to knock out more of the menacing bunker complexes and climb the hill. Then suddenly another Soldier in the unit, Pf4c. Merjil, as a one-man commando team crawls to the closest enemy bunker, leaps to his feet and charges the enemy bunkers. He knocks out three bunkers with a grenade launcher and partially collapses a connecting tunnel.

Lt. Harper yells out, "Good job Merjil."

And ahead are more concealed enemy forces occupying more bunkers. This enemy entrenchment halts the American advance and three Americans fall with a continuous barrage of intense enemy mortar, rocket propelled grenades, automatic weapons, and small arms fire. The Americans continue their push forward and upward without cover. There is no place--no ground cover or retreat for the Americans.

Lt. Harper yells back as loudly as possible to his company, "We got to take out that main tunnel system if we want to advance. I'm telling you men we got to do it and we won't retreat. We are not going back down this hill today. We won't retreat!"

McConnell and Brule know something has to be done. The team is severely compromised. Then the two-man team takes the lead assault on five more heavily fortified bunkers at the tunnel line and collapses them with the recoilless rifle. Sp4c. McConnell and Sp4c. Buzz Brule neutralize this threat and the team advances further. Then Sp4c. Brule charges again through a hail of enemy automatic weapons fire, destroying another bunker complex with hand grenades. Then McConnell and Brule fire the recoilless rifle and destroy a second enemy bunker. They feel proud and invincible.

John says enthusiastically, "Hey good job, men. We will get this hill if you keep this up." Buzz says, "Yeah, I know we will."

Lt. Harper orders, "Advance to the tree line!"

Lt. Harper knows his company has to take out all of the bunker complexes with their connecting tunnels to neutralize these key areas of enemy resistance before being able to get to the summit.

Lt. Harper yells orders to Mc, "Sp4c. Davison, take the assault on the way to next tree line. Knock out some bunkers and we will cover you."

Sp4c. Mc Davison takes his M-60 machine gun and launches a series of assaults against the fortified enemy emplacements and throws two hand grenades into the aperture of two bunkers. And Davison continues his assault, standing at the edge of a steep ravine. He is able to deliver accurate and suppressive fire on several more automatic weapons emplacements located near the tunnel system. And then Davison moves forward from one fortified bunker position to the next, stopping hostile fire.

Mc sees. Mc looks over and sees lying on the ground an enemy Soldier mortally wounded. As the Soldier looks up at Mc, the Soldier pleads with his eyes not to shoot. This enemy Soldier does not want to fight anymore. Mc can't kill a man who does not want to fight anymore. Sp4c. Mc Davison cannot shoot this enemy Soldier so he leaves the Soldier there. Mc has been trained to kill his fighting enemy but walks away from this Soldier taking his conscience with him.

As Erich Maria Remarque said in All is Quiet on the Western Front, "It was an abstraction I stabbed, But now, for the first time, I see you are a man like me….forgive me comrade. We always see it too late, the same dying and the same agony—-forgive me comrade." From the cover of the tree line, Sp4c. Mc Davison continues to move forward on his assault, spraying fire in enemy direction which gives his team the opportunity to advance to a more secure location to a tree line. Lt. Harper's company is now about two-hundred meters from the upper LZ and he knows that this next enemy bunker complex must be taken out before his company unit can get to the summit.

Lt. Harper yells, "Now, let's try it again. We must coordinate our ground assault with base artillery and air support to knock-out this damn tunnel and these damn bunkers."

Lt. Harper says, "Look over there—-you see--there is a long tunnel running down the center of that ridge that connects all those bunkers. If we can collapse that tunnel, it'll take the entire bunker complex with it. That is a tuff row-to-hoe but we must."

Lt. Harper skillfully adjusts once again ground artillery and air fire on the enemy position for the tunnel and the bunker complexes. He gives the coordinates and directs artillery and air strikes. The enemy fires back light antiaircraft assault weapons. But American artillery pounds back with tons of 105 mm, 155 mm and 8 inch artillery rounds. The fighter bombers pound the area for an hour but the air strikes seem to have little effect on the underground bunkers or the tunnel. The only alternative for the Americans now is to knock-out these bunkers by ground force and get to the tree line ready for a frontal assault on the bunker complex.

Lt. Harper says, "It looks like you men will have to do the job of knocking out these bunkers; so, let's get on to the recoilless rifle and the hand grenades, men."

Lt. Harper's team will not give up and continue their assault blasting out bunkers up the mountain to its summit.

Sp4c. Joe Wolfing (Surfer Joe) says to Buzz, "Man, now, it seems that besides just looking less like a surfer, I am definitely acting more like a Soldier." [They laugh.]

Buzz then says, "Yeah but you still have that surfer grin on your face. And all this killing and shooting has not wiped that smile off of your face yet."

Joe says, "Yeah, me Surfer Joe, the grinning surfer, and I'll continue to grin as long as we are all still walking. I am OK with this grin. But with all my surfing, my mom and dad told me that I have no future out-there on that beach as a surfer *hanging ten* on some wave somewhere. But now they would be proud of me--seeing me like this--being a-man-for-my country—-fighting here like this. They always told me to be a man—-that I was waistin' my life out there on those waves—-with no future with nothing and now I have a chance to prove myself. *Uncle Sam* has given me this chance here in 'Nam to prove it."

Buzz then asks, "Well, your parents are wrong because you have much more of a future out there on those waves than you do here fighting the Commies. You are better off on those waves." [The two laugh together.]

KA-BOOM—-KA-BOOM ... the enemy rakes a cascade of intense automatic weapons fire, Claymore mines, and a barrage of rockets and grenades from another concealed well fortified bunker complex. Lt. Harper's company races through a hail of fire wielding their weapons and firing back as they find cover briefly behind a large boulder. The Americans are pinned down with no escape. Then the American troops charge forward to the next tree line for cover. Oh no. Another Soldier is hit.

Buzz asks, "What happened?"

The medic says, "He was helping his *battle buddy* and got hit."

And the medic runs over to the aid of the stricken Soldier. The Soldier yells out, "Get out of here before you get killed."

This Soldier is hit by 75 mm mortar rounds. With this head wound he is losing cerebral spinal fluid and blood. The Soldier's head is covered in blood and with a piece of shrapnel that displaces his eye. This Soldier fought for freedom with honor as blood pours through his open skull. He gave everything he could for freedom. Yes, for freedom from something—-freedom from something--but not too sure yet—-but definitely for freedom.

"Aaaaahhh ..." A Soldier screams out ... in pain."

Lt. Harper takes his RTO and orders a Duster chopper (helicopter medical evacuation) to pick up the wounded. He says, "Roger. This is Aperharper. Over. I need a Duster in here now for a couple of WIA's. Over."

The Soldier screams out again, "Forget me. Move out and save your asses. Get the f*ck out of here, now!"

Guy then yells, "Get this wounded to cover, now."

As the Soldier lies wounded, Buzz cradles the Soldier's head in his hands attempting to comfort the Soldier as the medic administers first aid treatment--irrigating the

Soldier's wounds with sterile water and further attempting
to apply definitive coverage to the head wounds. Then Buzz
thinks of God for help. The Soldier is coherent and talking.
Buzz has hope for him. He hopes ... so very much ... that
the Soldier can survive his wound like this. Oh no. As Buzz
lifts the Soldier's head, the Soldier's head seems to fall
apart in pieces as a piece of skull bone sticks to his hand-
-like a cracked egg shell and part of his brain is open.
Buzz and the medic try everything in the world to save this
Soldier's life but the Soldier closes his eyes restfully. He
cannot seem to hang-on to life any longer. He dies in Buzz's
arms. Buzz feels so sad for him. He lost his life. Lt.
Harper then says, "The Duster will pick-up his body and take
him out of here."

Buzz says next and most wisely, "'Never seen so many
men wasted so badly,'" [as said by Clint Eastwood the movie
The Good, the Bad and the Ugly about Soldiers in another
war—the American Civil War]. Buzz then yells out in anger,
"But how many more? How many more? How many more?"

Now Sp4c. Wolfing feels he owes his team one with the
team's much compromised position. Suddenly Wolfing jumps
forward firing towards enemy positions with his M-16 on
automatic and throwing hand grenades at the enemy. He is
able to place his highly accurate suppressive fire on the
entrenched enemy bunkers. He succeeds in silencing several
enemy weapons but remains in his exposed position firing
all-the-while toward the enemy bunkers for a *mad minute*. For
a moment Sp4c. Wolfing has been able to successfully
disengage the enemy. And Joe continues to provide this
protective cover for his team as the team advances
cautiously up the hill. Sp4c. Joe Wolfing continues firing
his M-16 in sweeping motions toward the enemy position as
his team deploys to a more secure position. He continues to
fire until his rifle is damaged from an enemy hand grenade
but grabs another M-16 rifle in time--continues firing. Oh
God! No! Before Joe could take cover, mortar shells and RPG
rounds whiz by and fall onto Wolfing's very-compromised
position knocking him backwards. He is lying in pain on his
back with blood flowing profusely from a gaping wound to his
gut. The medic must stop this immense loss of blood now or
they *will lose* Joe. They must act fast to save him. Buzz
does the only thing he can do now. He closes the open wound—
-pulling it together with his hands--pulling and pressing
his fist onto the wound to close it. This action can save
Wolfing's life and it works as Wolfing's loss of blood slows
dramatically.

Buzz says to Sp4c. Wolfing, as the medic provides life-saving treatment and closes the wound, "Yeah, you are going to be O.K. You're going to make it. We have slowed your loss of blood. You will be getting out of here, back to the World, onto your surfboard again and to the beach."

Joe laughs and says in a whispered voice, "Yeah ... you know, I kept telling you, I look more like a Soldier and less like a surfer and you never believed me. [They laugh.]. But please do me a favor, Buzz, tell my friends—-my team back there in Malibu--that I never wanted to leave them." Buzz then says, "Yeah, don't worry about it. You are not going to leave them. I'll tell 'em. You are a real hero in my-book and a fine Soldier—-a real fine Soldier. ^You are the bravest Soldier anywhere. You are a real hero for saving our asses out here and gettin' us out of this mess. You are *our bravest young men*."

Joe seems to want to rest as he begins to close his eyes peacefully.

Buzz then says, "OK, man, I'll tell all of your surfer friends what a hero you are and we'll *hang ten*, together—in Malibu--don't worry."

Buzz then turns away and says, to Peter, "He has lost a lot of blood—-maybe too much."

Joe opens his eyes, looks up at Buzz and smiles through a trickle of blood coming from the corner of his mouth and says, "Thanks, man. You will tell my friends for me ... will ya? I know you will. I want them to know."

Buzz says, "Yes, I will tell them."

Joe says nothing more ... and just stares blankly at Buzz with his eyes open. He is dead.

Buzz then says, "To draft someone and make him give-up his life for it ... hell no?! All he wanted was a chance to live his life--to surf and do the things he wanted. Isn't that what everybody wants--their life--and to live it as they want? What's wrong with that? What is wrong with us? He could have had so much joy in his life surfing those waves in Malibu. War is hell ... especially if the war does not have to be fought!"

John says in tears, "But 'we started to feel bullet-proof since we haven't had any casualties. We felt a degree of invincibility. When it happens, it really hurts,'" [as said by a Major in U.S. Armed Services in war with Iraq]. Buzz continues, "Many Malibu waves will pass without Surfer Joe out there to ride them. He will never have his waves and the world will be without Surfer Joe! I will miss him. It will be hard for me to sit out there on that beach watching those waves crashing by and thinking about him. He's gone forever. It hurts a lot! I do know one thing for certain Joe will not have to fight war anymore."

Said by Buzz with a tear rolling down his cheek, "It is *most truly* like this quote by Plato ... 'Only the dead have seen the end of war.'"

Buzz then asks angrily, "How many more? How many more do we need to fight this war? Joe does not have to worry about fighting for freedom or Communism anymore?" Buzz continues, "He was just beginning his life. It was Joe with his life as he wanted to live it ... with his surfboard."

Buzz swallowing his words hard, says, "I can't believe he's gone. He had so much. [As said by Erich Maria Remarque in All Quiet on the Western Front], 'Oh God why did they do this to us? We only wanted to live you and I.'"

Joel says with sorrow and truth in his heart, "But he was so young and this is so true of us ... [as said by President Gerald R. Ford], 'All of us who served in one war or another knew very well that all wars are the glory and the agony of the young.'" Buzz says. "It's a f*cking trap. 'The trap that we have fallen into (...) will haunt us in every corner of this revolutionary world if we don't properly appraise its lessons.'" [Senator George McGovern, <www.wikipedia.org/wiki/George_McGovern>.]

Peter says with sorrow, "How horrible! We lost Wolfing but ... Buzz, Guy, Mc, Dion, John—-let's all try stay together for each other. Lieutenant Harper says, "We can't lose anymore men." Lt. Harper then gets on the radio to Coneycutt, "We need TAC air support in here, right now and a pick-up now for the KIA's."

Buzz then repeats and thinks, "KIA! We are surrounded and we are outnumbered." The company is pushed down the hill again by a hail of enemy machine-gun fire. John says, "Coneycutt is going to get his ass *fragged* if he keeps this up." Buzz says, "No man, that's wrong. We can't do that. We are here now and we have to fight. If we can't hang with our Commanding Officers, we should never have come here in the first place."

Brule grabs the radio--yells to Coneycutt, "How many more men are going to die for this f*cking hill? You know we are out-numbered. You have seen this before in previous battles out here. What we are up against here in the A Shau? Can't you figure this one out? Just the cache-of-enemy-

supplies alone, is enough to tell us everything. We can see
with that, there must be a lot of enemy out there." Brule
continues, "Our troops have found a [said by Zaffiri],
'Thousand AK-47s, thousands of recoilless rifles, 600 SKS
rifles, 10,000 Chicom Rifles and grenades with tunnel
networking for the entire NVA 29th Regiment.'"

["NATO forces uncovered 550 pounds of ammonium nitrate
and other bomb making materials while clearing a compound in
Marjah. Also found a weapons cache in Nad Ali that included
artillery rounds, pressure plates and blasting caps." (War
Afghanistan 2010).]

Brule continues, "How much more proof do you want?
Sending our numbers out there against their numbers is pure
suicide and I don't give a fuck how much technology we have.
We can't win this war like this!" Then over the horn, LTC
Coneycutt says, "We don't know how many troops we are up
against. And I will tell you one thing for sure these little
bastards are not going to push us off this mountain. Do you
understand that? We will stay and fight. We will stand our
ground and take this damn mountain. You men will start your
assault up that hill again tomorrow," [fictitious quote].

[U.S. Senator Edward Kennedy said of Hamburger Hill in
a Senate-speech, "Senseless and irresponsible ... madness
... symptomatic of a mentality and a policy that requires
immediate attention. American boys are too valuable to be
sacrificed for a false sense of military pride." And that
this was "(...) a sentencing to death of American Soldiers
who were ordered to win territory not related to winning the
war." He labeled the battle of Hamburger Hill as "cruelty
and savagery (...)." "(...) unjustified and immoral." Also
infuriated with the battle of Hamburger Hill was Sen. George
McGovern (D-SD) who praised Sen. Edward Kennedy "for raising
his voice ... eloquently ... in protest against a truly
senseless slaughter." Another voice said so well: Senator
Stephen M. Young (D-Ohio), "(...) they (Gen. Zais with other
military commanders) flung our paratroopers piecemeal in
frontal assaults. Instead of seeking to surround the enemy
and seeking to assault the hill from the sides and the front
simultaneously, there was just one frontal assault after
another, killing our boys who went up Hamburger Hill." As
said by Samuel Zaffiri, "Every Allied Unit that had gone
into the A Shau [Hamburger Hill location] in the last four
years had met disaster there (...)."]

"How many more times do we have to climb this Hill and
how many more men are going to die fighting for it? How many
more?" says Buzz loudly.

Chapter 24

The Americans Still Trying to Climb the Hill

The team takes another assault up the hill--riffing through the elephant grass and the jungle. Peter takes point and Buzz takes second/slack. Another Soldier in the team, Sp4c. Merjil, takes rear with the M-60.

Buzz looks up and says, "Those phantoms are pounding hard. I see those Cobra Snakes (AH-1G) with their M134 mini-guns and their M129 40 mm grenade launchers sweep down and open-up with machine gun fire by the door gunner and drop Nape to back-up our asses. We need 'em down here--their bombs, artillery mortar, napalm and rockets. Thank God for our air support."

An ARA Cobra Gunship passes overhead. Thap-thap-thap-thap-thap--the machine gun fire echoes across the valley, between the canyon walls and through the jungle tree-tops. The door gunner gives a thumb's-up with a smile while looking down at Buzz.

Buzz says, "Man ... those guys are for us. Our Snakes up there want the enemy's blood, real bad."

Joel yells, "We gotta get out of this elephant grass or we are all gonna die. I don't want to die in this shit. Believe me this elephant grass is no better than that triple canopy jungle over there unless I can shoot me some enemy out of those trees."

Lt. Harper yells his orders, "Sp4c McConnell and Sp4c. John Kelsey take the recoilless and go in after that first line of bunkers. And Sp4c. Sp4c. Brule you back him up with your M-16."

Then Sp4c. Peter McConnell and Sp4c. John Kelsey charge forward with the recoilless rifle and Sp4c. Brule runs alongside firing on enemy positions with his M-16. The two Soldiers blast 20 meters of underground bunkers and lob four hand grenades into the bunkers collapsing most of the bunkers with the enemy inside. Sp4c. Dion Johnson then pulls the pin from a hand grenade and throws it into another bunker. He repeats this action four more times on four more bunkers to finish them all off all while Brule is raining automatic gun fire on enemy position.

Lt. Harper says, "Let's go take cover at the next tree line and then continue up the slope to the northwest." Lt.

Harper yells orders again, "Go! Continue to the tree line and keep firing your weapons."

The team then runs for cover to the next tree line, 100 meters away and through open treeless terrain of dirt-covered hills that is pock-marked with B-52-bomb craters and charred trees from napalm.

Guy yells, "Hey, McConnell and Hammerstein fire at those f*ckin' bunkers. Look at that muzzle flash from that bunker complex on our right flank," [pointing into the direction of the bunkers].

Joel takes aim and silences the enemy. "I got that sonofabitch."

John says, "Good job. That sonofabitch ain't goina' shoot nobody no more."

Lt. Harper says, "Good job. I think we are going to take this hill."

And suddenly there is more "enfilading automatic weapons" and grenade fire coming from 100 meters away onto the American position from well camouflaged enemy fortifications. The Americans are surprised at this vicious attack from the enemy. McConnell then tosses two *well-thrown*" hand grenades into two more bunkers and the Americans continue to fire back through another hail of enemy fire.

John then yells, "Man this is addicting! I hate it but this shit is addicting. I am on an adrenalin rush right now. I am the best Soldier here. I am saving this war for freedom and for South Vietnamese people."

Mc then asks John, "I missed that. What's addicting?"

John then answers, "I don't like it, but this battle has me on an *adrenalin rush.*"

Buzz busts in with his words, "But bottom line to all of this--we know we gotta stop war somewhere—somehow--but I don't know how; otherwise, we will be condemned to live it again and again—-generation after generation so let's quit this adrenalin-rush shit, OK?"

John then responds, "Yeah, I know--but it's startin' to get addicting now, ain't it?"

Lieutenant Harper yells orders, "Stop and load your weapons. Sp4c. McConnell get that 60 firin', and Sp4c. Brule quit playin' with that hand grenade and throw it into the bunker. Get that recoilless goin' now, and start it firin'.

That recoilless is the only thing that is going to bust those f*cking bunkers."

Buzz and John are bracing the recoilless, loading, aiming and getting it ready to fire.

Lt. Harper yells, "Get it firin'."

Buzz yells back, "Of course I'm gonna fire it. What the hell do you think I'm holdin' this f*cking thing for--my looks?"

Buzz props the recoilless against a fallen tree trunk and says, "I knew that this tree would be good for somethin,' besides just standin' pretty for shade."

Mc then says, "Yeah, it ain't standin' too pretty now thanks to all this shit!"

Buzz fires to his left flank into the direction of fire from the enemy bunkers and he hits the bunker's aperture, collapsing and knocking out a two-man machine-gun nest.

Buzz yells out--rejoicing, "I got 'em. Hey I got a couple of 'sonsabitches.' Those 'mothers' will never see the light of day again. I guarantee it."

Guy then says, "That seems to work. We are on our way to the top."

Sp4c. Guy Von Bexin then teams-up with Sp4c. Buzz Brule, takes the recoilless again and props it up against a small boulder and then they aim again into enemy bunkers from several meters away and fire with accurate hits collapsing several of the underground bunkers and killing all-of-the enemy inside.

Guy yells, "I got 'em." Joel rejoicing at the hits yells out, "Hey, man, good! Good job! I can see by the look in your eyes, Guy that busting those bunkers makes your day." Sp4c. Von Bexin says, "Yeah I guess it does."

Lt. Harper yells, "Shut up. We really don't care about the celebration of Von Bexin's good feelin's or what he gets his kicks-off-of or the-look-in-his-eyes, right now, man. So get your asses movin' out there now! All we care about is that we silence this enemy for good--once-and-for-all--and get to the top of this f*ckin' hill. Do you understand me, men? Let's get out and get up that hill over there and get those bunkers on the northeast slope, now," [pointing up to the tall hill ahead].

Buzz then says, "Lt. Harper is really pushin' us up this hill. Yeah, he wants blood."

Peter then wisecracks in with, "Yeah, as long as it ain't my blood." [They laugh.]

Mc says laughingly, "Yeah, McConnell--no one's gettin' any McConnell blood here, ha, ha, ha."

The enemy is firing from interlocking automatic weapons and rocket propelled grenade fire from two enemy bunkers. The American team now fires back with small arms, machine guns, M-79s, light antitank weapons and an 84 mm recoilless fire.

Peter then says, "Man, these guys are hell-bent on killing us all."

The team moves forward firing all the way but then the Soldiers move down into a ten-foot ravine to take a short break to reload their weapons. The rear comes in with Joel but he stays behind up on the crest to take a-couple-of-more last-minute shots at some muzzle flashes before descending into the cover of the gulch.

Joel says, "I'm up here aimin' and shootin'. Someone cover my back."

Sp4c. Chris (Mc) Davison yells, "They ain't goina' get you, Bud. I got your back, man. Let one of them gooks try somethin'. I just wanna kill me another few."

And Mc leaps up and takes protective fire for Joel's back aiming in enemy direction with his M-16 set on automatic. The Americans feel like they are on a roll today.

They now believe in their invincibility except for the tragic loss of their *battle buddy* Wolfing. They momentarily seem to forget about him but they really know and they will never forget. But maybe while in battle they have to forget. We don't know.

Sp4c. Dion Johnson jumps up and out of the ravine with his M-60 and says, "I got your ass covered, man--ain't no one's gonna get 'ya, man. I'll see to that personally," as he holds up his 60 and aiming.

And Sp4c. Peter McConnell with his M-16 aims toward the enemy and says, "I got your back, man. I see now why they trained us and worked our asses off back there in boot camp. I have your back—don't worry. You'll make it. I know you will. I have confidence."

Buzz then yells sarcastically to Peter, "Man that is your problem, Peter. You have confidence. You have too much confidence."

Joel yells, "Yeah, McConnell, "I know you got my back. You always have someone's back covered in this damn war-- thanks!"

Sp4c. Mc Davison suddenly bolts up and out of the ravine with his M-16 and with a couple of hand grenades and tosses them directly into two enemy bunkers ahead, blows them up and then dives back down, head first, into the soft dirt of the ravine for cover.

McConnell yells, "Good job, Davison. You're always there."

Lt. Harper yells out, "Come on let's get out of here." And the team grabs a fast foothold on their leap up and out of the gully to the outer edge--up and out into the open flat ground--into enemy view—-and through another devastating rain of enemy fire. The Americans continue to assault forward through this "enfilading machine-gun fire" across an open field for a tree line a hundred meters away.

Rockets and grenades explode and toss Sp4c. Mc (Chris) Davison into the air. With these repercussions Sp4c. Davison is knocked-out and lies motionless and helpless in the field of fire. Suddenly Sp4c. Peter McConnell makes a dash-out under heavy fire risking his own life to get to Mc, grabs a-hold of Davison and carries him to the safety of cover through withering machine-gun, small arms, and mortar fire. Peter saves Mc's life.

Davison comes-to and yells, "Hey man, "I owe you one."

McConnell yells, "Yeah, don't worry about it. Pay me back later with a drive through Malibu beach." [They laugh.]

McConnell yells again, "They got us with incoming fire on our left flank. And let's just make sure they don't try to flank us or double-up back on us from our rear position. That's their favorite game around here."

Joel says, "Yeah, the enemy is known for that--coming-up back around on to our rear."

Peter yells, "Let's just keep assaulting this hill forward. Let's go! We'll get outta here sooner or later. Let's roll. We will do it!"

Peter fires his M-16 set on automatic onto the determined enemy assault on the left flank hoping to slow-down enemy fire so the team can dash for cover. He yells, "Come on men. Let's go for it or we won't make it out of here, alive." Guy yells, "Cover me I am going in to blast a bunker or two--to fire on that mother."

And then Von Bexin *one-mans-it* returning grenade and machine-gun fire on another bunker through a hail of enemy gun fire. This provides more cover for his team.

The team continues in open ground through withering automatic machine gun fire and finally the troops make it to cover ... deep into the Indochina Jungle.

In the jungle, Lt. Harper's Company forms a night defensive perimeter. They set up claymores, put-up listening posts and perimeter guards. They then form a 360-degree defensive perimeter. This is important because American companies/units/platoons cannot mutually support each other because of terrain and jungle. The Americans here are generally just small decentralized units at battle.

There is a lull in the *firing of arms* because it is near nightfall. These Soldiers take a rest in a small gulley where they had set up camp that is out of firing range and under the canopy of the jungle ... as nightfall approaches. And their conversation begins.

Buzz says, "These guys are out for blood and we are outnumbered 2 to 1. Ain't that cute? Can't you men see this mess we are in right now?" Lt. Harper says, "Yes, but we must follow orders from our higher-up command. We are not here to argue 'the rights' and 'the wrongs' of this war, here, right now, on this battlefield. It is too late for that, now! We are here to fight and we must follow orders or we die. If you don't like this battle, you should have said something a long time ago--before you got out here. Now you have to finish this job and then if you want, go fight somewhere else in another war—-a war that maybe--you can agree with--and under different circumstances or conditions. You should have protested to your government when the time was right—-when you had the chance--but don't do it here on this battlefield, now! My Dad volunteered in World War II. He was Chief Master Sergeant Robert E. Harper in the Mighty 8th Army Air Force. He was a proud Soldier who performed his duty as translator/interpreter for the *Casablanca Conference 1943* (codenamed Operation Symbol) with President Franklin Roosevelt, Prime Minister Churchill, General De Gaulle and General Henri Giraud. The subject at the conference was what to do on the overall future global military strategy for the Western Allies and for the military invasion of Sicily and Italy during WWII. He was truly a proud Soldier and we are very proud of him." Peter says, "Yes, I am sure you are proud of your dad. We are all proud of him. Our bravest young men performed their duty for love of country and with honor. They are truly brave men. We are all brave men."

Lt. Harper continues, "These Soldiers here are all proud too but all we can do, now, is just get this job done and be out of here and back home as soon as we can. Now we are here to fight--to do our duty like all great Soldiers in wars past—-to do our duty for our country. 'Cpl. Henry F. Warner knocked out two German tanks. General Eisenhower did a remarkable job organizing troops, logistics and supplies. Gen. Patton had great discipline with his troops to fight hard and move rapidly over difficult terrain in winning the Battle of the Bulge to save freedom for us. (...),' [as said Arthur I. Cyr, "Remembering the Battle of the Bulge," <u>Antelope</u> <u>Valley</u> <u>Press</u>, 12/27/10: 6B]. So, now, I don't want to hear anymore of this bunk about not-liking this battle or any other battle out here now, understand? I know you guys are all committed to this cause and to each other. I know you men will do your job as the proud Soldiers you are. We are now counting on each other to complete our mission and to just save our lives." Buzz retorts back, "Yeah, and you are right but I beg to differ with you ... I was drafted and we are outnumbered. This all should be understood. We lost a couple of nice people out here on this battlefield for naught--just trying to bust some f*ckin' bunkers so that we can take this damn hill for which we really do not have much hope of conquering. Did we forget about Surfer Joe already? He's not even a memory anymore, is he--not even a damn memory anymore?! Nobody remembers and nobody cares. And a disabled veteran told me this and this is how this veteran believes: *I have come to realize that our mental and physical wounds are of no interest (...). We were used. We were betrayed. And we have been abandoned,* (Tomas Young, wounded Iraq Veteran, 2003)." Peter agrees, "So many don't care. But *a Soldier will die for a war that should never have been fought. He will die for the lies of politicians. He will die for war profiteers. He will die for the careers of generals. He will die for a cheerleader press. He will die for a complacent public that made war possible. He took all this upon his body. He was crucified, and there are hundreds of thousands of crucified bodies like his in Saigon [Bagdad], and Hanoi [Kandahar] and the Delta [Peshawar] and Walter Reed Medical Center in Maryland, bodies and corpses, broken dreams, unending grief, betrayel, corporate profit, these are the products of war* (Chris Hedges, writer 2013)." Buzz then says, "But as I said ... let us never forget and hold compassion always. *The lost* and *the suffering* will be with us always. 'With friends and family who have known love and loss, [there is] awful sadness and joy in memory (...)' (Anderson). And we will always remember." Buzz says more but

argues, "We will. But I guarantee you one thing for sure,
Surfer Joe ain't surfin' any more waves over there in that
Malibu place but he *is* wrapped-up in a body bag somewhere in
cold storage getting ready to be shipped-out on his way
back." Mc says, "Yeah, for once, I agree with Buzz on this
one—totally. He is absolutely right! And so far in this
battle, we have lost many precious lives for something we
are not too terribly sure about or why we are fighting for
it." John then asks, "Yeah, but what about all of *our fine
bravest young men* who have fought and lost their lives in
our-battles-past--for our country-fighting against Nazism
and Fascism? Buzz says, "Yeah but we can't let any of these
Dinks get us like this here, now. They are *all about* the
annihilation of anyone they don't like or anyone they don't
agree with ... or anyone who is American. Can't you men
figure that one out?"   Mc says jokingly, "Yeah, the reason
... they are jealous because we are the greatest country on
earth!" Buzz then says, "You know with every joke there is a
little bit of truth in it, ha, ha, ha! I mean the Nazis were
jealous of the Jews? The English were jealous of the Irish?
Yeah, the greatest country on earth ... but that is a whole
other issue and I ain't goin there right now on that one—
maybe some other time, maybe." Joel then says, "No, just
because WWII was a *right* war to fight, let's not get
paranoid and somehow think that this war is also right."
Peter agrees, "I know none of us believes this is the right
war—no war is right—especially this one. None of us wants
to die up here on some lonely hill in the middle of Vietnam.
We want to be back with our wives or our girls--like right
now. We dream to go back home." Buzz then says, "No, it's
like yesterday that we want back home." [Everyone laughs.]

   Buzz continues, "I don't know. This is all wrong. Or
maybe ... maybe there is something wrong with me. Maybe
there is." John says, "Yeah, in WWII--it was
Totalitarianism/Nazism we were fighting and now it is
Totalitarianism/Communism." Peter states, "Yes it was
Totalitarianism/dictatorships and where people had no
freedom. And now we are fighting Communism for these people
who have no freedom. But they really have no freedom with
our tearin' up their country like this." Buzz asks, "Yeah,
to say the least ...so basically then, we have to go around
this world fighting any country that does not have Democracy
or freedom? Is that what is happening? That is a tall order
for us Americans to fill--especially by ourselves to fight
the-world-over for freedom and Democracy. We send our
country's Soldiers out there to fight this-world-over;
giving up their lives to give these countries *the freedoms*

that *we want them to have*, true--if this is what they want?"
Mc then says agreeing with Buzz, "Our country--the USA--is
living in freedom by the ideals that our Founding Fathers
gave to us. We are living in freedom because we have the
most advanced defensive technology in the world to fight for
it. And yes ... it should always be defensive technology
that we use to keep that freedom--don't you think? But as
for defensive technology ... I don't see it used here. All I
see here are American Soldiers dying--yes dying--for
something that we are not too sure about. But we don't want
to die up here for nothing!"

Peter says, "Yes, we should always use defensive
technology and I know we--the U.S.A.—will always make the
right decision in the end--to do what is the best for
everybody." John says, "Yes, we do know what we are fighting
for in Vietnam. It is for Democracy and so let's fight it
the way it should be fought with our most advanced
technology. But maybe the problem is that we ... as a
country ... are not really committed enough to Vietnam to
fight for it? We are fighting this war like a giant without
a head. We must know--and most important—as a country we
must back-up our Soldiers!" Peter agrees, "Yes, but [as said
by Henry Fosdick American Justice of the Peace—County
Commissioner, 1922], 'The tragedy of war is that it uses
man's best to do man's worst.' Congress should put an end to
it. But now our job is to get up this hill. Then I can get
back to Sherry. I will be with Sherry again and I will see
our new baby. We will be happy together." Buzz then says to
that, "I know you can't wait to see her, Peter. You want
back home like yesterday, already yet. You are a lucky man
to have beautiful woman waiting for you at home—and then a
beautiful son!"

Dion wise-cracks-in with, "Yeah, but we are here now to
fight a battle so let's get on with it."

And Peter says, "And we're stuck. And back to Kennedy's
ideas: as I always say, I don't think that President Kennedy
wanted this war to be a long and as is happening now."
Buzz says, "So we are now back to 'Square One' as Peter
believes, President Kennedy would never have put us in this
war for as long as it is happening now—or ever. Why do we
fight a war like this?" Peter suggests an answer, "This war
is not right for us or for anyone. All I see is death and I
don't want to see anymore Soldiers dying. It is like what
Bertrand Russell said, 'War does not determine who is right—
only who is left.'"

Buzz says, "Yeah, this war is not right but for some Soldiers it will always be right because the Soldier feels that this is his duty. It is the Soldier's duty—-his duty to fight for his country." Peter says, "But for us, we must know *why we are fighting?*" This is what my wife Sherry has been asking all of this time."

Buzz then says, "Oh, Peter, you are one of those 'lucky ones' who has a *beautiful one* waitin' for him on his return home from battle with all the love in this world."

Dion says, "Yeah, make love—-not war. [They laugh.]. Yeah—not war. Can't we just see—-I mean open our eyes a little bit--that this shit is just all wrong—-just wrong, man, wrong! Just make me the President for one day. I'll show 'em."

Guy then says, "No. You deserve more than just one day to be President of the United States ... to say your word."

Dion says, "Yeah, I guess I do. But I really don't care about all the fanfare of being 'the President of the U.S.' I just want to see all people--white, black, brown all live together in peace and harmony with one another--to be free—- to be free from want and to have freedom. I mean not just always dreamin' about it--but having it and with no scraping-by or hookin' up with something in the streets for it. I mean I just want *what is a fair share* for everyone including the Black Brother. That's all I want. It's about people and it's about my country that takes care of its people—-all people. It's about respect in a symbiotic relationship with everyone. Yes, my country gets my respect and I show my respect whenever I can and yes, I fight for my flag. For America, it is about respect for my country. In America everyone should get what is a fair share for everyone and equal opportunity. And not just for some people for somewhere else but for everyone in America."

Dion changes the subject, "But this war. What is this all about? This war isn't fair. It takes people away. It just takes people away, period." We have to know where we fight, why we fight and how we fight."

Peter then says most wisely, "Yes, it does. It does take people away but this has to stop--somehow—-sometime! It has to stop."

Dion agrees and repeats, "Yeah, man--somehow—-sometime. It has to end. There has to be an end to this madness! I don't know--over 58,000 lives. ... That's a lot. I don't know. *Someother* robbed them to sleep."

Buzz agrees, "LIFE is most important--no matter what! Maybe there is something wrong with me to see it like this?" Peter then says, "Yeah, sometime--somehow but I don't think man will end it for a long time. I still remember this quote--the wisest--most truthful quote I've ever heard."

Peter says this quote again, "You see I do believe most truly [as said by Marine Capt. Rushing a U.S. Pentagon spokesman, after viewing war film footage of dead American Soldiers killed in the war in Iraq], 'It makes me hate war, but it doesn't make me believe that we're in a world that can live without war yet.'"

And the next day comes. Guy says sadly and most resolutely to Peter as they prepare for battle, "Well Peter, we learned the hard way that the world really doesn't live happily ever after, does it? And that when we are shot down ... we really don't get back-up again, do we, Peter?"

Peter then answers sadly, "No, I guess we don't ... really ... live happily ever after ... and we don't ever get back up again. But I will get back up again--like you and I did way back a long time ago in that school yard. I will get back up again to see Sherry and my little son. I will be back home. We just have to get this damn hill now and then we are back home. Sherry and I will have our life together once again." Lt. Harper says, "Look at the enemy over there. We got a hundred more meters to go up that f*ckin' hill. The top of the hill is full of fortified underground bunkers that honeycomb this mountain. So far on this mountain we have found and neutralized several tunnels all interconnected with deep bunkers, 'a subterranean hospital, many spacious storage areas and a regimental CP which is all underground and hidden from view. We have found [Zaffiri, Hamburger Hill] '152 individual and 25 crew served weapons, 75,000 rounds of ammunition, thousands of mortars and RPG rounds and over 10 tons of rice.' We have destroyed much of that tunnel networking and we should be able to get to the top of this hill today. You have done a good job, men, and you should all be proud of yourselves. We are almost there!"

John says, "But the reality of this battle is that there's still a lot more of 'em out there. There must still be a couple of hundred more bunkers dug in up there in them thar hills." Lt. Harper says, "We have more war to go but we are almost there." Peter says, "Yes, more war to go then we can go home. That's right, almost there!" Buzz says it right, "Yes, that is it--to the top."

Lt. Harper says, "We must call in for more air artillery. We just don't have enough firepower on the ground to do it ourselves."

Lt. Harper then gets on the horn to CO to call in artillery. Then from Allied bases tons of Allied artillery rounds are fired--500 hundred and 1,000 pound bombs with delayed-action fuses hit the enemy positions and make gaping holes in the tree canopy and more bunkers collapse--left and right--leaving everything in smoldering ashes. Unfortunately, the fire power cannot wipe out the entire bunker complex. There is still a couple of hundred meters of bunker rows left yet to be destroyed. The ARA Cobra Gunships and base artillery fire more rounds to soften the ground for the ground forces but to-little avail.

Buzz then says, "I see so much utter destruction here. I can't believe I am a part of this horror." Peter then responds to Buzz's statement, "Yeah, Buzz you got that one right!"

Lt. Harper then petrified with fear asks [as said in Zaffiri's book, Hamburger Hill by a Soldier fighting on Hamburger Hill], "'What in the hell is it going to take to get those bastards off of this mountain?' I believe there's a lot more of 'em out there. We got to get 'em. I don't know." But the enemy continues sweeping the hill with a fusillade of mortar and machine gun fire on the American position. The Americans continue their assault. The enemy is resilient, determined and well dug into their well-fortified enemy positions. Enemy mortar rounds then explode in a rain of fire and shrapnel. RPG's (rocket propelled grenades) explode cutting down everything in their path as the Americans desperately try to fight back the summit.

Dion says, "I can't believe how determined these guys are--fighting for this damn rat infested jungle."

Aaahh ... Sp4c. John Kelsey takes a-shrapnel hit.

His leg is shredded flesh from the knee down—-pieces of shredded flesh dangle from his bone.

John screams, "My leg! My leg!" His screams echo, horrifically, throughout the canyon walls—-screams ... "My leg! My leg!"

The medic runs to him giving him medical aid before he bleeds to death. The medic says, "He has lost his leg but I can stop his massive blood loss to save his life. His leg is gone. There is nothing we can do to save his leg." The medic stops John's hemorrhaging wounds. "I can save his life but I can't save his leg."

In the meantime the unit is subjected to a concentrated "bombardment of heavy mortar, rocket and rocket propelled grenade fire." Their position is severely compromised. They are under a continuous rain of fire. The troops must continue to fight for the top of the mountain.

The medic says, "He is a lucky man. I have been able to stop his bleeding and I have him stabilized now. He is going to make it. Let's call in for the Dust-Off (medical airlift, air ambulance--Duster) and get him to a trauma field unit/hospital (a MUST unit/Medical Unit Self Contained) as quickly as possible." Sp4c. John Kelsey has lost his leg.

And Lt. Harper's company continues on.

Lt. Harper yells, "Here we go men. Come on," He is swinging his arm around in a *come-on-let's-go motion*.

The company rushes through another heavy barrage of automatic weapons and mortar fire with no let-up in sight from a very determined enemy which sends Lt. Harper's company reeling back down the Hill once again. But now the team sets a night perimeter.

Lt. Harper says, "The enemy is very determined." Buzz then tells Dion, "I see we are condemned to climb this hill one more time, aren't we?" Guy answers, "Yes, I guess we are to get pushed back down this hill again."

Peter says, "Yes, more war to go until we get to the top, to save our country, and then we can go home."

Nightfall begins and another sad day ends.

The next day the Americans are hit with "a torrent of heavy small arms fire", continuous "enfilading machine-gun" and mortar fire. This barrage keeps pounding at the very determined American position.

Peter then says, "These guys can get relief from the border at Laos and Cambodia in their well armed underground bunkers."

The team has to take out several more meters of enemy bunkers before they can make a try for the top of the hill. It is still a fight upward.

Suddenly, another Soldier, Sp4c. Fred Bermejo-Lopez is shot with a piece of shrapnel to his leg and falls to the ground. Sp4c. McConnell pulls him to safety behind a rock emplacement. The medic administers first aid. Sp4c. Bermejo-Lopez talks with McConnell for moment, "Hey man, you just

saved my ass out there. Thanks much, man. I owe you one."
Sp4c. McConnell then says, "Hey, don't worry about it. We
are all getting out of here soon. Everything is going to be
OK." Sp4c. Bermejo-Lopez then says, "I don't like going back
to the World now until my job is done but mostly, man, I
just don't like leaving you guys out here to fight this shit
yourselves. I want a taste of these guys real bad, man. Am I
gonna be Ok, do you think--I mean with my leg? Am I gonna
lose it?"

The medic administers medical treatment and says to
Peter, "He will probably lose his leg." But McConnell tries
to give the Soldier hope and says, "You may not lose your
leg. You are going to be OK."

Bermejo-Lopez says, "I hope I don't lose it. My old
lady ain't gonna want nothing to do with me. I mean bein'
half of a man ..." McConnell says, "No man, you are not half
a man. She married you for you, not your leg. Sp4c. Bermejo-
Lopez says, "No, really man, tell me the truth. Am I gonna
lose it? If I lose it, my woman is done with me. I don't
want to be half a man." McConnell says, "I had a friend who
was an athlete and 'who was paralyzed when his spinal chord
was severed in a roadside bombing (...),' [by a claymore
mine blast] and another friend 'where a bomb blast shattered
part of his face, broke his arm and three bones in his back
and caused him to lose his left leg below the knee.' These
guys with their wives have accepted it all ... as they are
our bravest young men. You both have to lean on each other.
That is a symbiotic relationship." McConnell continues,
"Yes, and don't worry about other people. People will point
and stare because people are like that." You will have some
good days and you will have some bad days, but there will be
more good days than bad days if you let it. Don't let your
physical condition control you. You must control it! Anyway
you and your wife will lean on each other in this world. You
must ... if you want to survive."

[Many veterans return home disabled for life. Gary
Sinise is one person who is backing a project called
American Veterans Disabled for Life Memorial which is a
"public tribute to the legions of men and women who are
living with, and often still suffering from wounds that they
sustained while fighting in the nations wars." Another
Soldier ... Kovic, a Vietnam War Veteran told his story.]

Chapter 25

Another Battle in Vietnam

Dion is completely disgusted with the outcome of this operation. He is fed-up with loosing his battle buddies so dear to his heart and climbing this mountain only to be pushed back down again--and again. And losing his battle buddies.

Sp4c. Dion Johnson yells out loudly, "I ain't climbing this mother-f*cker one more time," and suddenly Dion bolts up from out of the safety of cover with his M-60 in hand, spraying fire in every direction, as he yells for everyone to hear, "'Fuck this bullshit!'" Dion charges forward. He pulls his M-60 up to his chest, sprays bullets from side to side--in every direction--as he runs up the hill with the fastest speed a man could go--running for his life--200 meters, then another 200 meters and then another, [Zaffiri]. Then 'Johnson (Dion) falls down into the enemy foxhole' and begins firing his M-60 at anything that moves inside. He then back-jumps up out of the foxhole and fires his M-60 back down into the foxhole killing two enemy troops inside. Johnson then pulls the pin from his hand grenade and tosses it into an enemy bunker next to him. Because of his brave actions, the Americans are now able to follow Dion up the hill closer to the summit where the troops find an empty bunker for cover. Dion panting and out of breath says to his team inside the cover of a bunker, "Well, I told you I'm tired of climbing this damn hill and that I was not going to climb it again and you guys just didn't believe me, did ya'? Now we are 400 meters closer to the top of this f*cking mountain," [Zaffiri, Hamburger Hill]. Peter yells to Dion, "Great job, man! You're doin' it. We will get to the top, today," [as he slaps Dion on the back]. Buzz then states emphatically, "I guess you mean what you say, don't ya', man? You don't like climbing this f*cking mountain day after day--time after time? I think that you just don't like this mountain and the Gooks in it, do ya'?" Dion answers, "No, I really don't. You guessed that one right. I want to get the hell out of here. Fighting for this damn place just somehow don't seem to be worth it to me, anymore. They are going to put us all in an eternal sleep if we keep this up. And in the end we ain't winnin' nothin'." Dion Johnson continues, "So with nothin', I'm not givin' what I have for nothin'-- somethin' that I never really have anyway--and that is this f*ckin' hill--this f*ckin' hill. I can't have it and I don't want it! And believe it or not, I really don't want to go into an eternal sleep for this hill. There is too much out there in this World waitin' for me. I don't wanna to get outta this life yet." Dion continues, "But for you guys, my battle buddies, I'll do it!" The company continues to come under a "hail of withering automatic guns and rifle fire." The company is cornered. The enemy is everywhere. Sp4c. Peter McConnell realizing that his team is compromised runs forward firing his M-16 into the enemy bunkers. Sp4c. Buzz Brule runs alongside McConnell firing his 60 into the bunkers. McConnell takes his grenade launcher and fires it directly into an aperture of a bunker knocking out more bunkers. Brule throws two hand grenades killing three NVA Soldiers inside. A "torrent of rifle and machine-gun fire, rains back" on the Americans with the enemy trying to push them back down the hill once again. Mc and Guy then set the recoilless in aim for the bunker complex and fire several more rounds which collapse several more bunkers. Sp4c. McConnell quickly reloads his weapon and suddenly bolts out from his perimeter and charges up the steep side of the mountain, yelling, "Come on men," [taking his team several hundred more meters up the hill]. Lt. Harper and Johnson follow closely behind McConnell firing their weapons as the enemy returns fire. Sappers fire a round of Bangalore Torpedoes with more intensive enemy machine-gun fire that rakes the American's position again and again. Lt. Harper and Dion are pushed back down the hill into a severely compromised position. Then McConnell turns back down the hill to the two compromised Troops (Johnson and Harper). And realizing his team's danger, Peter single handedly fires the grenade launcher into the enemy bunkers wiping out the threat and providing some protective cover for his Commander, Lt. Harper and Sp4c. Dion Johnson so they can get back to cover. Dion says to Peter "Hey, man, thanks for giving me that cover. You saved us out there." The company continues to move up the hill and Brule takes the lead with McConnell firing their weapons as the company moves forward. Buzz yells, "I like the way you fight, McConnell. We are going to take this damn mountain today and I mean today! There's no holdin' us back! We will be up there!" Sp4c. McConnell and Brule continue their brutal climb upwards as a two-man team toward the summit. The two Soldiers assault a two-man enemy bunker-complex with rifle and grenade fire. There is insurmountable weapons' fire. McConnell sees the menacing bunkers ahead and neutralizes two more machine gun nests with two perfectly placed hand grenades. McConnell and Brule continue their move up the hill ahead of their company. They feel good with the job they are doing. Peter

then says, "We are doin' it, Buzz! We are doing it! Let's
go! Let's go!" McConnell moves out ahead of Brule as a one-
man team from bunker to bunker with a grenade launcher and
silences four more, two-man bunkers. Then an enemy Soldier
appears from out of a concealed position and catches
McConnell by surprise but Sp4c. Guy Von Bexin warns
McConnell just in time, "Watch out, McConnell!" McConnell
hears Buzz's warning and moves just in time, missing enemy
rifle fire. Von Bexin (Guy) then kills the enemy Soldier
with his pistol and at the same time throws two hand
grenades into two bunkers "neutralizing this intervening
bunker emplacement." Sp4c. Guy Von Bexin then asks Sp4c.
Peter McConnell, "I never thought we would be playing this
game for 'real' when we were runnin' around back there in
that school yard--way back there in another world, did ya?"
McConnell answers sadly, "No, I didn't think so either. It
is really quite unfortunate that everything had to come to
this." But McConnell really wants to get his team to the
top. And now establishes security for his team in the cover
of some large boulders and several tree stands. As McConnell
is heading for covered defense, an enemy Soldier throws a
hand grenade toward McConnell but McConnell avoids the enemy
fire by diving headfirst into a nearby ravine. The American
team now takes cover behind some boulders in a ravine. Lt.
Harper then yells, "Good job men but we are not out of the
woods yet!" Enemy fire continuously sweeps the hilltop with
a "volleying of nonstop grenades" as the Americans continue
their assault up the hill. But the Americans are now
compromised because many of their troops have been killed or
injured. Lt. Harper's company now is unable to sustain
effective fire against the well armed camouflaged
underground bunkers but is still optimistic about taking the
hill today and continues on. Lt. Harper yells, "We still
have to rendezvous with our troops on the summit. Let's go."
The team moves out from the cover of the boulders into the
open on their way further up to the summit--firing all the
way. Now they must maneuver themselves out from their
exposed position for cover to the next tree line. They
continue their very determined upward climb without any
thought of retreat. Peter says, "We will climb this hill to
the top. Yes, more war to go until we get to the top--then
we are home free." The company continues its assault. These
Soldiers are determined. Sp4c. Peter McConnell is leading as
point element and has gained a lot of ground for his team as
has Sp4c. Dion Johnson moments earlier. Johnson attacked the
hill as a one-man assault team towards the top. Now
McConnell is proud to be out in front of his company--ahead

of his troops. This team is under continuous heavy automatic weapons fire from well emplaced and well fortified enemy bunker positions. Sp4c. Buzz Brule now takes the lead again to relieve McConnell--charges ahead as a one-man-assault team toward the next row of enemy bunkers. Brule throws his hand grenade at another enemy machine gunner and silences him. Brule then secures the enemy weapon and directs his team forward up the mountain closer to a tree line--further up and closer to the hill's summit. Then Sp4c. McConnell yells out with hope, "Good job Brule. We are gettin' closer to the top! I know were gonna make it today." [They laugh together.]. Sp4c. Buzz Brule feels real good now about leading the assault and covering his team. He continues to provide protective fire with his one-man-assault against the enemy defensive position. Sp4c. Peter McConnell feels he wants to do something more for his team and pulls up his M-16, switches it on automatic and fires his entire 20-round magazine in an instant *mad minute* into the incoming hail of enemy automatic weapons fire. McConnell fires into the first bunker with accurate rifle fire and then secures another enemy machine gun. He feels very proud of himself for backing-up his team. Sp4c. Buzz Brule and Sp4c. Peter McConnell now charge together upwards to the next bunker with their weapons and continue to silence more bunkers. Brule looks over to McConnell and yells, "Hey, today, we're an unbeatable team?" McConnell yells back, "Yeah, we are right on! We are going to make it up this hill." The company follows behind Sp4c. McConnell and Sp4c. Brule as the two troops lay down covering arms fire for their team. Sp4c. Joel Hammerstein then notices a muzzle flash and he fires one burst of fire and knocks out another enemy Soldier. Joel says, "I got that one. I got that one fine and dandy." Sp4c. McConnell feels invincible and so proud to be forging ahead with his battle buddies and now moves out ahead to provide for more protective fire head-on into another line of enfilading machine-gun fire as a "one-man assault team" knocking out yet another bunker. Peter then continues on to the next bunker himself in a horrendous hail of fragmentation from bursting enemy rounds and from a fusillade of rocket propelled grenades. McConnell knows he will make it up this hill, today. It's out. McConnell runs out of ammunition but reloads his weapon in an instant with an ammunition magazine. He continues to provide protective cover for the forward advance of his team. Then Brule comes-in and fires-in and knocks out another threat of machine gun-fire with his grenade launcher. McConnell says, "Good job Buzz we are doing it! And besides I like Sherry too much to leave her now. [They laugh together.]. I want to get back to Malibu to play in that surf. [They laugh.]. And besides if we don't fight our way out of here now, we'll never get out of this hell hole." Buzz says reassuringly, "Yes, we will fight it, Peter--we'll fight it together." McConnell and Brule move on ahead of the company as a two-man assault team working together to establish forward security that this team needs. Peter wants to do more for his team and then decides to one-man-it ... and ... steps forward but ... oh no ... what just happened to Sp4c. Peter McConnell? He is knocked backwards by a-shrapnel hit to his upper torso and falls to the ground. McConnell is down.

Buzz rushes to Peter's side--yelling. Guy rushes to Peter's side. Mc, Dion and Joel rush to his side. Buzz can't believe this. For a flash in Buzz's mind, he wishes he could turn back *the hands of time*--retrace Peter's steps for Peter. Buzz asks himself and God: *Please can we just retrace our footsteps in seconds--God--please God--a couple of seconds?* God sees this horrific moment and can't do anything to stop it, change it or reverse it. God can't request Buzz's prayer.

The medic rushes over.

Peter has been hit with a severe fragmentation wound to his chest. This is a severe shrapnel wound. Peter is loosing massive amounts of blood and air. Blood is everywhere! Peter needs a miracle. Peter has an enormously high velocity fragmentation wound by explosive munitions from a fragmentation weapon that does a lot of damage to tissue. This wound has opened Peter's chest, cutting and lacerating tissue all the way through with the missile's (fragments') path—radially tearing and stretching all of his tissue around this missile but...

Peter is now gasping for his words with each labored breath and he asks, "What has happened and my Sherry?" Peter says, "Please tell Sherry, I love her with all my heart. I want to see Sherry again." Guy runs to his rucksack and takes out Sherry's photo, unfolds it and then holds it up near Peter's face so Peter can see Sherry again. Peter smiles and says so reassuringly, "There's Sherry!"

Buzz is now in total fear for Peter's life and does what he can by putting his hand over Peter's sucking chest wound to stop the entrance of additional air into his lungs. The medic now listens for audible breath sounds that may perhaps show signs of hope for survival. Buzz says to Peter,

"You're going to do it. You gotta' make it. You gotta' make it, for Sherry. Hang on. You're going to make it."

But this wound can be fatal from hypoxia and severe hemorrhaging with hypovolemia. Peter is now fighting for each breath he takes. The medic places an appropriate cover to his sucking chest wound with adhesive medical tape and secures it with a pressure dressing and an IV. Peter seems to be breathing much more easily now. Everyone is hoping beyond hope for Peter's life. His air has to be allowed to exit. And air coming in through the wound must be prevented from being sucked-in during inspiration. And also now his blood must be restored. But even if his blood volume is restored, he still has to deal with hypoxia with atelectasis (collapsed lung) and chest decompression. This wound is extraordinarily difficult to address in battlefield conditions. But medics are doing it. Peter needs immediate extraction. Lt. Harper calls in for a Duster. Peter now has an immense accumulation of blood in his lungs and in his thoracic cavity creating pneumothorax—hemopneumothorax. Peter must get help now if he is going to make it! Yes, maybe. Maybe there is hope for Peter-—a miracle, maybe. And once again, Peter's breathing has improved. Buzz then says, "Let's get him out of here. We must get him out on to a Duster if he is going to have any chance of making it."

Surrounding his external wound, his blood appears frothy and bubbly (oxygen entering through the wound). With an open chest wound, outside air gets into the pleura cavity through the open chest wound. Air accumulates with each difficult breath Peter takes causing his lungs to collapse. His skin begins to be a cyanotic blue. The medic tries everything and places a chest tube with a huge bore needle for intubation through his chest wall that releases the trapped air through the tube. This might work. But there's no improvement. And once again, Peter is having great difficulty breathing but ... there's still a chance for him to live! The medic says, "It will be a miracle if we can save him--maybe we can—maybe!" Buzz now asks the medic for more help, "We gotta get him out of here, now!"

Peter is gasping. And his eyes begin to close sleepily then open and stare then close.

Buzz's heart pounds fast. Buzz screams to Peter, "Don't go! No, no, don't go, Peter! Stay with me! Hang on Peter! You can make it! Hang on! Don't go! Don't die! Do it for me! Do it for Sherry! The Duster will be here!"

Buzz says, "'It is only those who have neither fired a shot nor heard the shrieks and groans of the wounded who cry aloud for blood more vengeance, more devastation. War is hell,'" [as said by Gen. William Tecumseh Sherman].

The medic continues his frantic efforts to save Peter's life. Guy is holding Sherry's photo above Peter. Now Peter sees Sherry's face. Peter's eyes begin to open again. He stares at Sherry. His eyes are now locked on Sherry. Buzz says, "Hang on Peter. You're doing it! Hang on ... for your son, for Sherry and for me!"

Peter is looking at Sherry. He's looking at Sherry ... staring. Peter says nothing but his eyes *say it all with sadness* as Peter looks at Sherry's face. Gasping ... Peter's chin moves up. His lips turn blue ... his mouth gapes open ... struggling for air. Peter is struggling hard with each breath. He can't get air! Peter is struggling! Then Peter's eyes close. Peter's respiration stops. Peter dies.

Peter must see Sherry one more time--to be sure Sherry is there right next to him. He opens his eyes in an instant ... for a last look at Sherry. Then death closes his eyes forever. Peter does not see Sherry anymore! Vietnam takes Peter far away!

Buzz is helpless--in tears--in total despair--and with anger he yells out, "Peter's gone! He's gone! This sucks, man. Peter is dead! He punches the ground hard with his fist." Buzz yells-out again as loudly as his voice can carry him, "Nobody ... absolutely nobody ... takes my friend ... takes my generation ... and gets away with it ... absolutely nobody!" Buzz asks, "Why ... why make a man fight in a war that does not have to be fought? What's wrong with us?! Peter just wanted his life!"
Then Guy says with horrible grief and tears—-his voice breaking-up--yells out, "He was my best buddy. He's gone! This is all I know. He's gone! This is all I can say about Peter--this war--this battle. He was my best friend. I knew him my entire life. We played together back there in that schoolyard and he's gone with only a memory-of-a-man-who-once-was--who died in a battle. We played war together as kids and Peter *always got back up again!* We always rode off into the sunset. We had so much fun back there on that school playground. We just didn't know! We just didn't know! We were kids! These were always just play-times--just fun-war-games. I don't know how my life is going to be without Peter. God, I will miss him so. His mother will grieve for him and Sherry will grieve. And he died for Vietnam.

Mc says, "We will always grieve for Peter and for this war." Buzz says, "I will never forget Peter! I can remember way back in that little tavern by the sea, near Qui Nhon, when Peter pulled back the curtain to look out at the beautiful sea—-it was to another sea--to that distant sea far away. That's when I saw a tear roll down Peter's cheek. Sherry is going to have a horrible time. It will be hell for Sherry. Peter is never ever coming home again." Buzz says, "Peter told me a-while-ago ... *I will fight for my country because I am proud of it but I hope my country has tried for peace. I will do my duty for my country as I am told. I am glad to be born—-to be alive--to have my life. But I hope my life does not end too soon or in vain in a battle somewhere because I want to hang around some more—-to be with Sherry and my son. If I go, I know that my God and I have been good together. I will always be with my God and he will always be with me but I still want to be around here in my life.*" Buzz in tears, continues to remember Peter, "I can say five things about Peter. He was honest, faithful--loyal to his wife and to his country. He loved Sherry with all-of-his-heart; he loved Malibu. He will never know his son. And he never wanted this war. He was a real nice guy who just wanted to live-out his life with Sherry but his chance to live it was *taken away* from him--for this battle—-for this war. He talked about death in this war; he asked about death in this war and now he *is* death in this war."

Mc asks, "But what have we done? Buzz asks once again, "Why draft a man ... make him die for a war that does not have to be fought--why?!" Mc quotes U.S. Senator Gruenig with his most eloquent quote, "This quote came straight from the Senator's heart; Senator Gruenig warned us all too well at the beginning of this war but not one of us listened, 'All of Vietnam is not worth the life of a single American boy.'"

Buzz remembers these songs, "I will always remember Peter and what Peter loved the most and what we have done here in Vietnam. When I hear Peter's favorite songs I will always think of Peter: Floyd Cramer, It's Only Make Believe (Twitty, Jack Nance); Morton Downey Jr. &Terrytones, I Beg Your Pardon (Burnette; DeVorzon; Cogswell); Paul Pace, I May Fall Again; Clyde McPhatter, Treasure of Love (J. Shapiro; L. Stallman); Tommy McClain, Sweet Dreams (Don Gibson); J. Paris & P. Tesluk-Johnny &the Hurricanes, Red River Rock; Turtles, It Ain't Me Babe; Richard Blandon, Cleveland Still, Billy Carlisle, James Miller, Thomas Gardner, Grate-Dubs, Could This Be Magic (Johnson; Blandon); Bobby Austin & Johnny PayCheck,

Apartment Number Nine; Bo Diddley, Road Runner; Dave
Somerville, Bill Reed, Kowalski &Levitt-Diamonds, Little
Darlin' (M. Williams; D. Carroll); Earl Lewis & Jack Brown,
Aziz, Rivera,III, Coleman-Channels, That's My Desire; Procol
Harum, Whiter Shade of Pale; Barry McGuire, Eve of Destruction
(J. P. Sloan); Hank Williams, You Win Again; Dale & Grace, I'm
Leaving It Up To You; Aubry Jones, Holding Things Together
(Totten/Haggard): Frankie Laine, That's My Desire; Joey
Canzano; Arnone; Sontollo; Salvado; Bialoglow (G. Paxton-
Duprees, You Belong to Me (P. W. King; Chilton Price; R.
Stewart); Percy Sledge, When a Man Loves a Woman (A. Wright;
C. Lewis); Bobby Hatfield, Bill Medley-Righteous Brothers,
Unchained Melody (Alex North; Hy Zaret), You've Lost That
Lovin' Feeling; Eddie Holman, Lonely Girl (L. Carr, E.
Shuman); Troy Shondell, This Time; Elvis Presley, There's a
Honky Tonk Angel; Jerry Lee Lewis, You Win Again; Jack Scott,
Burning Bridges; Tom T. Hall, Back When Gas Was Thirty Cents a
Gallon; George Lanius-Crescendos, Oh Julie; Sahm, Meyers,
Fender, Jimenez-Texas Tornados, Mendocino; Kendalls,
Pittsburgh Steelers; Donna Fargo, Don't Be Angry; Richard
Bourque, Louis Cormier, Hank Williams Medley; George Strait $
Alan Jackson, Murder on Music Row (L. Cordel, L. Shell);
Johnny Lee, Looking for Love (Mallette; Morrison; Ryan);
Charley Pride, All I Have to Offer You is Me (D. Frazier, A.
L. Owens; Mike Ness-Social Distortion, Making Believe (Work);
Andy Tielman, Blue Byou (Hillman, Parsons); Randolph Michaud,
Soldiers Last Letter; Hank Williams Jr., Living Proof; John
Anderson & Emmylou Harris, Just Someone I Used to Know
(Clement); Aaron Neville, The Grand Tour; George Jones, I'm
Not Ready Yet (Hall); Jamey Johnson, Lonely at the Top (K.
Whitley); Ronnie McDowell, It's Only Make Believe (live);
Peter's most favorite: Davis Sisters or Skeeter Davis, I
Forgot More (Cecile Null); Tommy Collins-Country Life 13 or
Mel Tillis or Mick Flavin, New Patches; Vernon Oxford, Country
Singer; Paul Dwayne, Oh Papa; Earl Thomas Conley, Heavenly
Bodies; Moe Bandy, Picture in a Frame; Stonewall Jackson,
Don't Be Angry (Wade Jackson); Porter Wagoner & Dolly Parton,
Making Plans (V. Morrison; J. Russell); Ned Miller, From a
Jack to a King; Wynn Stewart & Johnny Paycheck, Wild Side of
Life (A. Carter; W. Warren); Conway Twitty & Loretta Lynn,
Making Believe; Jay Black, Cara Mia; Dan Paisley-Southern
Grass, Tennessee Waltz; Carl Butler &Pearl Butler, Don't Let
Me Cross Over (Penny Jay Moyer); George Jones & Johnny
Paycheck/Lytle, Things Have Gone To Pieces (Leon Payne); Don
Gibson, Woman Sensuous Woman (Gary Paxton); Dan Fogelberg,
Stewball (Woodie Guthrie); LaLa Brooks-Crystals, Then He
Kissed Me; Keith Whitley, I Never Go Around Mirrors (L.

Frizzel; S. Shafer); Buck Owens & Don Rich-Buckaroos, Together Again; Conway Twitty, Georgia Keeps Pulling On My Ring (D. Marshall; T. Wilkins); Brian Wilson, Mike Love, Carl Wilson, Al Jardine, Dennis Wilson-Beach Boys, Surfin' USA; Freddy Weller, Bar Wars; Rheal LeBlanc, Drinking Again (Schneider; Southhall); Hert LeBlanc, All I Want for Christmas Dear is You (B. Owens); Yvon Collette, Ensemble Avec Les Anges; Roy Head Treat Her Right (Head; Kurtz; Gibson); Johnny PayCheck, If You Think Your Lonely (Buell; Rupp; Johnson); Conway Twitty-Twitty Bird Band, To See My Angel Cry (Twitty; L. White; C. Haney); Vince Gill, Which Bridge to Cross (V. Gill; Bill Anderson); Vern Gosdin, If You're Gonna Do Me Wrong, (Vern Gosdin, Max Barnes); Gene Hughes-Casinos, Then You Can Tell Me Goodbye.

the best: Steve Wariner or Bill Anderson, Tips of My Fingers (Anderson); Raul Malo, I Still Miss Someone, (J. &R. Cash); Waylon Jennings, I've Always Been Crazy (Jennings); Narvel Felts, Somebody Hold Me (A. and R. Aldridge, S. Richards); Mick Flavin, The Old Side of Town (Tom T. Hall); Mick Flavin Table in the Corner (Conway Twitty); Mick Flavin, Afraid of Losing You Again (D. Owens, D. Frazier); Brady Clark, Drinking Whiskey Straight, My Marriage is on the Rocks; Gene Watson-Farewell Party Band, Farewell Party (Lawton Williams); Uncle Kracker/Matthew Shafer or Conway Twitty, Window Up Above (George Jones); Vince Gill, Dawn Sears, When I Call Your Name (V. Gill; Tim DuBois); Carl Butler, Don't Let Me Cross Over; Pascal Bessette, Mama Si Tu L'Aimes (Gerald LeBlanc); Vernon Oxford, Shadows of My Mind; Paul Dwayne, Je T'Aime; Victor Wood, A Tear Fell (Eugene Randolph; Dorian Burton); Gary Puckett, Woman, Woman (J. Glaser; J. Payne); the best of best: Gene Hughes, Then You Can Tell Me Goodbye (J. D. Loudermilk).

It is true ... we are allured to war—to a war that we don't have to fight and not one of us knows why ... oh ... not one of us knows why a man has to die for it--not one of us knows. But for now we do know one thing for sure; we can truly say--and ever so truly say--that *Peter does not have to fight war anymore.*

Buzz is grief-stricken ... helpless ... oh so helpless ... ever so helpless ... beyond control. Buzz grieves. He grieves. Buzz will always grieve. Buzz looks down at Peter as Peter lies motionless in silence. Buzz knows nothing more can be done for him and yells-out loudly ... and ever so loudly ... that even the dead could hear ... "Oh, God please ... God ... tell me ... is there ever going to be an end to this madness?!"

And that's how it rests.

Bibliography Volume II

Our Bravest Young Men

"101st Airborne (Airmobile) during Vietnam." Militaryphotos.net. 20 August 2006 <http://www.militaryphotos.net/forums/archives/index.php/t-15131.html>.

25th Infantry Division Association. 25thida.com. Sept. 2005 <http://www.25thida.com>.

"25th Aviation Battalion." 25th Aviation.org. 7 July 2006. <http://25thaviation.org/history/id908.html>.

"A Shau Valley." En.Wikipedia.Org. 16 March 2006. Feb. 2006 <http://en.wikipedia.org/wiki/A_Shau_Valley>.

"Abrams Defends Fight For Peak." Washington Star, May 21, 1969.

Ace Pilots. "Air War in Vietnam." Sept.2005 <www.acepilots.com/vietnam/main.html#top>.

"Aircraft of the Vietnam War."240thahcfl. Feb.2006 <http://240thahcfl.www1.50megs.com/aircraft.html>.

Amazon.Com. 14 July 2006 <http://www.amazon.com/gp/reader/1880684314/ref=sib_dp_top_cr/102-0623746-7404963?ie=VTF8&p=55006#reader-link>.

Andrade, Dale. Trial by Fire. New York: Hippocrene Books, 1995.

Anti War. Antiwar.com. October 2005 <http://antiwar.com/quotes.php>."Apache Snow Ends." *The Srceaming Eagle*, June 23, 1969.

"Apache Snow Ends." The Srceaming Eagle, June 23, 1969.

Army.Mil. Feb.2006 <http://www.army.mil/cmh-pg/books/vietnam/north/nprovinces-_ch6.htm#ashau>.

"Battle of Hamburger Hill." En.wikipedia.org. 12 September 2006. <http://www.en.wikipedia.org/wiki/Battle_of_Hamburger_Hill>.

Bellamy, Col, U.S.A. Ronald, F. (Walter Reed Hospital) "The Nature of Combat Injuries and the Role of ATLS in their Management." Homestead.com. 29 September 2006 <http://www.homestead.com/reactdoc/chest.html>.

Borders, Robert Spec.5, "Dong Ap Bia." Summer 1969 Rendezvous With Destiny Magazine. Summer 1969. Feb. 2006 <http://www.Lcompanyranger.com/Ashau/ashauarticle1.htm>.

Brotherswar.com. October 2005 <www.brotherswar.com/civil_war_quotes_4b.htm>.

"Casablanca Conference Jan. 14-24 1943." History.sandiego 11 January 2007 <http://history.sandiego.edu/gen/WW2Timeline/Casablanca-images.html>.

Chambers, Larry. Death in the A Shau Valley. New York: Ivy Books. 1998.

"Chapter Seven." Robertcorman.com. 4 August 2006 <http://www.robertcorman.com/chapter_seven.html>.

Childress, Sarah. "Vets on the Street." Newsweek Magazine <http://www.msnbc.msn.com/id/17316437/site/newsweek/?GT1=903 24 February, 2007.

"Cicero." En.wikipedia 4 February 2007 <http://en.wikipedia.org/wiki/cicero>.

Combat Studies Institute. "Studies in Battle Command." Ehistory.osu. 20 March 2006 <http://ehistory.osu.edu/Vietnam/essays/battlecommand/index.cfm>.

Conboy, Ken and James Morrison. "Early Covert Action--the Ho Chi Minh Trail," Vietnam, August 2000. 28 Jan.2006 http://www.thehistorynet.com/vn/blearlycovertaction/index.ht

"Conway Twitty", by Shawn Mather. Rockabilly.com. 15 February 2007 <http://www.rockabillyhall.com/conwaytwitty.html>.

Conway Twitty Web Site. 30 July2007 <http://www.conwaytwitty.com>.

"Decent into the A Shau Valley." Randygreenart.com. March 2006 <http://www.randygreenart.com/a_shau_valley.htm>.

Denise Bostdorf and Steven Goldzwig, "Idealism and Pragmatism in American Foreign Policy Rhetoric: The Case of John F. Kennedy and Vietnam." *Presidential Studies Quarterly*, vol 24. 30 April 2006 <http://mcadams.posc.mu.edu/goldzwig.htm>.

Dobbs, Lou. "Dobbs: Our Leaders are Ducking Reality on Iraq." Cnn.com. 6 December 2006 <http://www.cnn.com/2006/us/12/05/Dobbs.Dec6/index.html>.

Donahue, James C., Blackjack-33. New York: Ivy Books, 1999.

Donovan, Melissa, "Writing Forward." <www.writingforward.com/grammer/punctuation>.

Dr. Simon Appleby. Symbol. "The Casablanca Conference." Casablanca Conference.com March 11, 2007 <http://casablancaconference.com/default.asp>.

Drake.edu. Oct. 2005 <http://drake.edu/artsci/PolSci/pols124s02/strategy.html>.

Earl Lewis. Mypages.blackvoices.com. 2 September 2007 <http://mypages.blackvoices.com/channels>.

Earthlink.Net.Feb.2006 <http://home.earthlink.net/~cmarsz/piros.html>.

EHistory. "Vietnam War.' Oct. 2005 <http://ehistory.osu.edu/vietnam/index.cfm>.

EHistory. Ehistory.osu. 16 March 2006 <http://ehistory.osu.edu/vietnam/essays/battlecommand/index.cfm>.

EHistory.Osu.Edu. Faculty of Combat Studies Institute. April 2006 http://ehistory.osu.edu/vietnam/essays/battlecomand/index.cf

Esper, George "Enemy Back in Control of Ap Bia." New York Times. 17 June 1969.

Fact Sheet: Hamburger Hill, A Shau Valley, Operation Apache Snow, prepared by U.S. Army J-3, Pacific Division, n.d.

"Fiction Writing." About.Com. 19 July 2012 <http://aboutwriting.about.com>.

Ford, Harold P. The CIA: and the Vietnam Policy, Three Episodes 1962-1968. Pittsburgh: Government Printing Office, 1998. <www.cia.gov/csi/books/Vietnam/index.html>.

Galloway, Joe from Knight Ridder press, "Reporter Halberstam Spoke Truth to Power." the Antelope Valley Press 4 May 2007:B6.

Global Security. Org. "Military, Vietnam War." Dec. 2005 <www.globalsecurity.org/military/ops/vietnam.htm>.

Global Security. Org. Globalsecurity.Org. 3 May 2006 <http://www.globalsecurity.org/military/ops/vietnam.htm>.

Graduateshotline.com. Graduateshotline.com 3 October 2007 <http://www.grduateshotline.com/list.html>.

Prof. Grinker, Mark A., "The Legal Writing Teaching Assistant, The Law School Guide to Good Writing." <www.kentlaw.edu>.

Gruntonline.com. Nov. 2005 <www.gruntonline.com/US_Forces/us_Helicopters/us_helos.htm>.

Hair, Frank Lt. "Massachusetts Striker." Summer 1969 Rendezvous With Destiny Magazine. Summer 1969. February 2006 <http://www.Lcompanyranger.com/Ashau/ashauarticle1.html>.

"Hamburger Hill, The Real Story." Historyinfilm.Com 5 October 2006 <http://www.historyinfilm.com/hamhill/real7.htm>.

"Hamburger Hill, The Real Story." Historyinfilm.com. 8 October 2006 <http://www.historyinfilm.com/hamhill/real7.htm>.

"Hamburger Hill." Angelfire.com. 7 October 2006 <http://www.angelfire.com/pahotshot_478/HamburgerHill.html>.

"Hamburger Hill." Angelfire.com. Dec.2005 <http://www.angelfire.com/pa/hotshot478/HamburgerHill.html>.

"Hamburger Hill." Historyinfilm.com. 30 September 2006 <http://www.historyinfilm.com/hamhill/real7.htm>.

Harper M.D., Chris J.E. (medical student at Karol Marcinkowski University of Medical Sciences), Personal interview. 29 September 2006.

Historical Summary of the Battle of Dong Ap Bia (Hamburger Hill) May 1969, 101st Airborne Division, n.d.

Hitchhiking Vietnam, Letters from the Trail. PBS. Org. December 2005 <http://www.pbs.org/hitchhikingvietnam/>.

Hitchhiking Vietnam, Letters from the Trail. Pbs.org. 18 March 2006 <http://www.pbs.org/hitchhikingvietnam/places/index.html>.

"Ho Chi Minh Trail." En.Wikipedia.Org. 21 April 2006. Feb.2006 <http://en.wikipedia.org/wiki/Ho_Chi_Minh_trail>.

Horvath, Major Richard L. "Mystique of the Valley." Rendezvous With Destiny Magazine. Fall 1968. Dec. 2005 <http://wwwLcompanyranger.com/Ashau/ashauarticle1.htm>.

"Intelligence Analysis of the 29th NVA Regiment, 101st Airborne Division, no date.

IPedia, Internet Encyclopedia, "Military Science."
IPedia.com. 5 October 2006
<http://www.ipedia.com/military science.html>.

IPedia, Internet Encyclopedia, "History." IPedia.com.
10 November 2006. <http://ipedia.com/history 2.htm>.

IzSally. Izsally.com. Jan. 2006
<http://www.Izsally.com/stories/hamurger.html>.

Izsally.com. 21 march 2006
<http://www.Izsally.com/stories/hamburger.html>.

"Jonathan Swift." En.Wikipedia 1 February 2007
<http://en.wikipedia.org/wiki/jonathan swift>.

Karlin, Wayne; Minh, Le; Vu, Khue and Truong. The Other
Side of Heaven. Williamantic: Curbstone Press, 1995.

Linderer, Gary. Phantom Warriors, BKI, LRRP's and
Rangers in Vietnam. New York: Ballantine Publishing Group,
2000.

"Long Range Reconnaissance Patrol, LRRP."
Diddybop.demon. 3 July 2006
<http://www.diddybop.demon.co.uk.lrrps.htm>.

Long Range Reconnaissane Patrol. Wikipedia.Org. 23
August 2009 <http://en.
Wikipedia/wiki/Long_Range_Reconnaissance_Patrol>.

Magary, Alan Spec. 5. "Montgomery Rendezvous." Summer
1969 Rendezvous With Destiny Magazine. Summer 1969.
March 2006
<http://www.Lcompanyranger.com/Ashau/ashauarticle1.html>.

Medal of Honor Recipients. "Vietnam War (M-Z)."
Army.mil. 23 August 2006 <http://www.army.mil/cmh-
pg/mohviet2.htm>.

Medal of Honor Recipients. "Vietnam War, (A-L)."
Army.mil. 22 September 2006
<http://www.army.mil/cmh.pg/mohviet.htm>.

"Medical, Integrated Publishing, Chest Wounds."
Tbub.com. 30 September 2006
<http://www.tbub.com/corpsman/149.htm>.

"Military Footholds." En.Wikipedia.Org. 2 May 2006.
Feb. 2006 <http://en.wikipedia.org/wiki/airhead>.

Militaryhistory.about. March 2006
<http://militaryhistory.about.com/gi/dynamic/offsite.htm.?si
te=http%3A%2F%2FHome.earthlink.net%2F%7egt3d%2FPage_Diary_HH
.html>.

Misty. Mistyvietnam.com. Sept. 2005
<http://www.mistyvietnam.com/history.html>.

"Module4-Citing Your Sources with MLA Format."
Ollie.dcccd.edu. 25 August 2006
<http://ollie.dcccd.edu/library/Module4?M4-
V/examples.htm#interviews>.

MSNBC.com. "Newsweek, Politics, He Only Saved a Billion
People, by Jonathan Alter." 25 July 2007.
<http://www.msnbc.msn.com/id/19886675/site/newsweek>.

Nastasi, Mike. "The Role of Airpower in the Vietnam
War." Militaryhistoryonline.com. 12 May 2006
<http://www.militaryhistoryonline.com/vietnam/vietnam/airpow
er/default.aspx>.

Natasi, Mike. "The Role of Airpower in the Vietnam
War." Militaryhistoryonline.com. September 2005
<http://www.militaryhistoryonline.com/vietnam/airpower/defau
lt.aspx>.

"Naval Gunfire." En.Wikipedia.Org. 3 May. 3 May 2006
<http://en.wikipedia.org/wiki/naval_gunfire_support>.

NBCSandiego.com. "Vic Salazar, Anchor, NBC 7/39
Reporter." Nbcsandiego.com. 12 August 2007
<www.nbcsandiego.com/meetthenewsteam/1287945/detail.htm>.

O'Reilly, Bill; TV news anchor, Fox News, O'Reilly
Factor. "Commentary, What's Ahead For Iraq?" Antelope Valley
Press 14 January 2007:A13.

"Operation Massachusetts Striker Information for 2 BDE
101 ABN." Flyarmy.org. 20 August 2006
<http://www.flyarmy.org/panel/battle/69030102>.

Operational Report, 1st Cavalry Division, April 1969.

Operational Report, 2nd Brigade, 101st Airborne Division,
April 30, 1969.

Oyler, Harry Lt. "Apache Snow." Summer 1969 Rendezvous
With Destiny Magazine. Summer 1969. March 2006
<http://www.Lcompanyranger.com/Ashau/ashauarticle1.html>.

Oyler, Harry, Lt. "Apache Snow." Lcompanyranger.com. 11
July 2006
<http://www.Lcompanyranger.com/Ashau/ashauarticleL.html>.

Parker, Kathleen; Orlando Sentinel, "Clicking on
Death." the Antelope Valley Press 10 January: B6.

PBS. Hitchhiking Vietnam, Letters from the Trail.
Pbs.org. 19 March 2006
<http://www.pbs.org/hitchhikingvietnam/places/index.html>.

Phillips, Donald T., Lincoln On Leadership. New York: Time Warner Company, 1992.

Prados, John. The Blood Road, The Ho Chi Minh Trail and the Vietnam War New York: John Wiley and Sons, Inc., 1999.

Prints and Photos, Vietnam War. Printsandphotos.com. 30 June 2007 <http//printsandphotos.com/prints_photos/vietnam_war.html>.

Robert E. Lee. En.Wikipedia. Sept.2005 <http://en.wikipedia.org/wiki/Robert_E._Lee>.

Rosenfeld, Harry, writer Albany Times Union. the Antelope Valley Press 10 January 2007: B7.

Scalard, Lieutenant Colonel Douglas P. "The Battle of Hamburger Hill: Battle Command in Difficult Terrain Against a Determined Enemy." Ehistory.osu.edu. Faculty Combat Studies Institute. April 2006 <http://www.ehistory.osu.edu/Vietnam/essays/battlecommand/index.cfm>.

Show Case Home. Showcase.netins. September 2005 <http://showcasenetins.net>.

Martinez, Reynel. Six Silent Men. New York: Ballantine Publishing Group, 1997.

McElwaine, Sandra; Albright, Madelaine; Clooney, George; Cohen, William; Bipartisan Genocide Prevention, Not On Our Watch, "Obama Hires a Clooney Confide." The Daily Beast; Yahoo News; <http://news.yahoo.com/s/dailybeast/20100414/ts_dailybeast/7589_obamahiresaclooneysidekick>.

"Stabilization of Trauma in the ER." Madsci.com. 29 September 2006 <http://www.madsci.com/manu/trau_che.htm>.

Static.Cc. March 2006 http://www.static.cc.gatch.edu/fac/thomas.Dilsch/AirOps/AShau-3.html.

Sudanreeves.org. Reeves, Eric. "Sudan Research Analysis and Advocacy." Sudanreeves.Org. October 2011 <http://sudanreeves.org/2009/06/re-writing-of-the-darfur-narrative/>.

Summers Jr., Colonel Harry G. (U.S. Army, ret.). "Hamburger Hill Revisited." Vietnam. 25 May 2006 <http://www.the historynet.com/vn/blhamburgerhill/index.html>.

FROM:
B&T Pub Services
30 Amberwood Pkwy
Ashland, OH 44805

TO:
DATAMATION IMAGING SE
BOOKS RECEIVING
7700 GRIFFIN WAY STE B
WILLOWBROOK, IL 60527

(420) 60527

BTC
   STANDARD

B/L #:

PRO #:

Purchase Order : MOM4013405

Department #:

Carton Qty:

Sales Order #: M1620299

Carton #:

Shipping Lane:

SSCC – 18
   (00) 1 0082952 003472310 1

Talking Proud. "How Did So Many Intelligent Guys Make Such a Mess of Vietnam?" 1 October 2006 <http://www.talkingproud.os/historylbjvietnam.html>.

Techize. Techize.com. 5 April 2005 <http://www.techize.com/articles/military_strategy>.

Techize. Technize.com. 1 May 2006 <http://www.techize.com/articles/militarystrategy#fundanentals_ofmilitary_strategy>.

"The Civil War." Sonsofthesouth.Net. Sept. 2005 <www.sonofthesouth.net>.

The History Net. Com. thehistorynet.com. Jan. 2006 <http://www.thehistorynet.com/vn/blearlycovertaction/index.html 28 Jan.2006>.

The History Net. Com. Thehistorynet.com. Nov. 2005 <http://thehistorynet.com/vn/blhamburgerhill/indexX2.html>.

The History Place. Com. Thehistoryplace.com March 2005 <http://www.thehistoryplace.com>.

"Music of the Vietnam War Era." Members.aol.com. 30 may 2007 <http://members.aol.com/vetschoice/1965-75.htm>.

"The Vietnam War, Under Fire, Soldiers Preparing to be Evacuated." Vietnampix.com. September 2006 <http://www.vietnampix.com/fire5g.htm>.

"The Vietnam War, Under Fire, Marines, Operation Starlight." Vietnampix.com. September 2006 <http://www.vietnampix.com/fire9a.htm>.

"The Vietnam War, Under Fire, U.S. Soldiers, Operation Thayer II." Vietnampix. Com. July 2006 <http://www.vietnampix.com/historyfire9al.htm>.

"The Vietnam War, Faces, Soldier in Vietnam 1968." Vietnampix.com. September 2006 <http://www.vietnampix.com/faces2b.htm>.

"The Vietnam War, Faces." Vietnampix.com. September 2006 <http://www.vietnampix.com/fire2c.htm>.

T.J. Lubinsky, "PBS Television Series", Doo Wop 50 1998. More Doo Wop 50, 1999. Doo Wop 51, 1999. More Doo Wop 51, 2000. Rock Rhythm and Doo Wop, 2000.

Tyson, Ann Scott. "In a Volatile Regime of Iraq, U.S. Military Take Two Paths." The Washington Post 15 September 2006. <http://www.washingtonpost.com/wp-dyn/content/article/2006/09/14/AR2006091401900_pf.html>.

"U.S. Helicopters, The Airborne Army." Jan. 2006 <http://www.gruntonline.com/US_Forces/US_Helicopters/us_helos.htm>.

"Unconventional Operations." Army.mil. March 2006 <http://www.army.mil/cmhpg/books/vietnam/90-23/90236.htm>.

Veterans for Peace. Veteransforpeace.org. 21 February 2007 <www.vetransforpeace.org>.

"Vietnam picture Tour." Feb. 2006 <http://namtour.com/ripcord.html>.

"Vietnam War." En.Wikipedia.Org. 3 May 2006. December 2005 <http://en.wikipedia.org>.

"Vietnam War." Feb.2006 <http://www.casahistoria.net/vietnamwar.htm>.

"Vietnam War, Under Fire." Vietnampix.com. Feb. 2006 <http://www.vietnampix.com/fire5g.htm>.

Weisman, Jonathan and Lyndsey Layton. "Veterans Group Speaks Out On War." The Washington Post 8 February 2007. <http://www.washingtonpost.com/wp-dyn/contest/article/2007/02/07/AR2007020702317.html>. 22 March 2007.

Wikipedia. "A Shau Valley." En.wikipedia.org. 11 July 2006<http://www.en.wikipedia.org/wikipedia.org/wikipedia.org/wiki/A_Shau_Valley>.

Wikipedia. En.wikipedia.org. 23 May 2006 <http://en.wikipedia.org/wiki/Declaration_of_war_by_the_United_States>.

Wikipedia. Wikipedia.org.7 may 2006 <http://en.wikipedia.org/wiki/jitterbug_stroll>.

Wpafb.af. Jan. 2006 <http://www.wpafb.af.mil/museum/ac/vw.htm>.

Wu, William, City Editor of the Antelope Valley Press, Telephone Interview, 12 December 2006.

Www Watson. Org. Watson.org. Sept. 2005 <http://www.watson.org>.

You Tube. "You Tube, Conway Twitty, *To See My Angel Cry*." 22 July 2007 <www.youtube.com/watch?v=4Ut829NMRwO>.

Zaffiri, Samuel. Hamburger Hill. New York: Ballantine Books, 1988.

Endnotes Volume II

Our Bravest Young Men

page 3

Bryan A Peterson. Lance Cpl., "Elite Honor Fallen AV Marine." Okinawa Marine 1 December 2006: page 14.

Bryan A. Peterson, Lance Cpl., "Elite Honor Fallen AV Marine." Antelope Valley Press 12 December 2006: 1A.

page 4

Nicholas Kristof, "What About Afghan Women in This War?" Antelope Valley Press 25 October 2010: 5B

Valley Press Staff. "Ex-Valley Man Killed in Iraq." Antelope Valley Press 12 December 2006: 1A.

Rahim Faiez; Jason Straziuso, "Afghan Police: More Foreign Troops Not the Answer." Antelope Valley Press 22 September 2009: 2B.

Miranda Leitsinger, "Life Over War: U.S. Veterans Return Medals at NATO Summit." USnews.msn.com. 21 May 2012 <http://usnews.msnbc.msn.com/_news/2012/05/20/>.

Diana West, "New U.S. Rules of Fighting." Antelope Valley Press 15 September 2009: 9A.

Dale Andrade. Trial by Fire (New York: Hippocrene Books, 1995) 537.

page 5

Byron York, (The Washington Examiner). "Restrictive Rules Put Troops in Danger." Antelope Valley Press 7 October 2009: 6B.

John Prados, The Blood Road, The Ho Chi Minh Trail and the Vietnam War (New York: John Wiley and Sons Inc., 1999) 34.

Joe Galloway, Knight Ridder press. "Leave Iraq now—Don't Wait Until 2008." Antelope Valley Press 8 December 2006: 5B.

George Will, "In Afghanistan Genius is Knowing When to Halt." Antelope Valley Press 3 Sepember 2008: 6B.

page 6

Bill O'Reilly, "Meanwhile in Afghanistan." <u>Antelope Valley Press</u> 26 November 2007: 11A.

John Prados, <u>The Blood Road</u> (New York: John Wilely and Sons, Inc., 1999) 52.

John Prados, <u>The Blood Road</u> (New York: John Wilely and Sons, Inc., 1999) 39.

John Prados, <u>The Blood Road</u> (New York: John Wilely and Sons, Inc., 1999) 70-71.

John Prados, <u>The Blood Road</u> (New York: John Wiley and Sons, Inc., 1999) 36.

page 7

John Prados, <u>The Blood Road</u> (New York: John Wiley and Sons, Inc., 1999) 72.

John Prados, <u>The Blood Road</u> (John Wiley and Sons, Inc., 1999) 208.

John Prados, <u>The Blood Road.</u> (New York: John Wiley and Sons, Inc., 1999) 20.

John Prados, <u>The Blood Road.</u> (New York: John Wiley and Sons, Inc., 1999) 208.

page 8

John Prados, <u>The Blood Road.</u> (New York: John Wiley and Sons, Inc., 1999) 76.

John Prados, <u>The Blood Road.</u> (New York: John Wiley and Sons, Inc., 1999) 77.

John Prados, <u>The Blood Road</u> (New York: John Wiley and Sons, Inc., 1999) 77.

John Prados, <u>The Blood Road</u> (New York: John Wiley and Sons, Inc., 1999) 7.

John Prados, <u>The Blood Road</u> (New York: John Wiley and Sons, Inc., 1999) 7.

John Prados, <u>The Blood Road</u> (New York: John Wiley and Sons, Inc., 1999) 7.

John Prados, <u>The Blood Road</u> (New York: John Wiley and Sons, Inc., 1999) 77.

page 9

John Prados, <u>The Blood Road</u> (New York: John Wiley and Sons, Inc., 1999) 77.

John Prados, The Blood Road (New York: John Wiley and Sons, Inc., 1999) 7.

John Prados, The Blood Road (New York: John Wiley and Sons, Inc., 1999) 70.

John Prados, The Blood Road (New York: John Wiley and Sons, Inc., 1999) 70, 77.

MSN, Famous War Quotes, Msn.com. 11 November 2007 <http://encarta.msn.com>.

Anti War. Com. "Quotes." Antiwar.com. 31 may 2006 <http://www.antiwar.com/quotes.php>.

Mike Nastasi, "The Role of Airpower in the Vietnam War." Militaryhistoryonline.com. 12 May 2006 <http://www.militaryhistory online.com/Vietnam/airpower/default.aspx>.

page 10

Ben Feller. "Korea: Obama Contrasts North and South." Antelope Valley Press 26 March 2012: 3B.

Mike Nastasi, "The Role of Airpower in the Vietnam War." Miliaryhistoryonline.com. 14 May 2006 <http://.militaryhistoryonline.com/vietnam/airpower/default.aspx>.

page 11

Mike Nastasi, "The Role of Airpower in the Vietnam War." Miliaryhistoryonline.com. 14 May 2006 <http://.militaryhistoryonline.com/vietnam/airpower/default.aspx>.

Dale Andrade, Trial by Fire (New York: Hippocrene Books, 1995) 520.

Dale Andrade, Trial by Fire (New York: Hippocrene Books, 1995) 524.

page 12

Dale Andrade, Trial by Fire (New York: Hippocrene Books, 1995) 524.

Dale Andrade, Trial by Fire (New York: Hippocrene Books, 1995) 520.

Dale Andrade, Trial by Fire (New York: Hippocrene Books, 1995) 520.

Dale Andrade, Trial by Fire (New York: Hippocrene Books, 1995) 524.

Dale Andrade, Trial by Fire (New York: Hippocrene Books, 1995) 520.

Dale Andrade, <u>Trial by Fire</u> (New York: Hippocrene Books, 1995) 524.

Techize. Techize.com. 26 April 2006 <<u>http://www.technize.com/articles/military_strategy</u>>.

page 14

Fortune City. Members.fortunecity.com. 12 August 2006. <<u>http://members.fortunecity.com/city/citymidi/LYRICS/before_the_next_teardrops_falls</u>>.

Marty Lloyd. Com. Martylloyd.com. <<u>www.martylloyd.com/artist_c/conway_twitty_lyrics/desperao_love_lyrics.html</u>.

MCA Nashville, UTV Records, division of UMG Recording, Inc. <u>Conway Twitty, 25 Hits</u> (Tennessee: Nashville 2004) CD.

page 17

MCA Nashville, UTV Records, division of UMG Recording, Inc. <u>Conway Twitty, 25 Hits</u> (Tennessee: Nashville 2004) CD.

page 18

Just Oldies. "Sincerely." Just-oldies.com. April 2005 <<u>http://www/just-oldies.com/</u>>.

page 21

"<u>Oh What a Night.</u>" Vee Jay Records and Cadet. 29 September 2008. (1956 1969)

page 24

"*Wasted Days and Wasted Nights.*" Elyrics4u.com. 11 August 2006 <<u>http://www.elyrics4u.com/f/freddy_fender.html</u>>.

page 26

MCA Nashville, UTV Records, division of UMG Recording, Inc. <u>Conway Twitty, 25 Hits</u> (Tennessee: Nashville 2004) CD. 2004) CD.

page 26 & 27

MCA Nashville, UTV Records, division of UMG Recording, Inc. <u>Conway Twitty, 25 Hits</u> (Tennessee: Nashville 2004) CD. 2004) CD.

page 29

Wikipedia, the Free Encyclopedia. "Phoenix Program." En.Wikipedia.com. 20 June 2007.

<<u>http://en.wikipedia.org/wiki/Phoenix_Program</u>>.

Wikipedia, the Free Encyclopedia. "Phoenix Program."
En.Wikipedia.com. 20 June 2007.
<http://en.wikipedia.org/wiki/Phoenix_Program>.

Wikipedia, the Free Encyclopedia. "Phoenix Program."
En.Wikipedia.com. 20 June 2007.
<http://en.wikipedia.org/wiki/Phoenix_Program>.

Joe Troiano's Blog, "Keeping Music Alive." 17 June 2012
<http://joetroiano.wordpress.com/2011/01/08/ea>.

page 31

Anti War. Com. "Quotes." Antiwar.com. 31 may 2006
<http://www.antiwar.com/quotes.php>.

page 32

Singul Artists. Singulartists.com 13 March 2007
<http://singulartists.com/artists_m/marvin_gaye>.

T and J Enterprises Lyrics Database. "Alley Oop."
Lyrics.tandj. Feb. 2006
http://lyrics.tandj.net/index.cgi?song=The_Hollywood_Argyles
_Alley_Oop

page 34

Lyrics Vault. Lyrics vault.net. 7 July 2006
<http://www.lyricsvault.net/songs/10935.html>.

Launch Cast. music.yahoo.com. 7 July 2006
<http://music.yahoo.com/launchcast/stations/stations.asp?i=5
05>.

Able2Know. Com. Search.able2know.com. 7 July 2006
<http://search.able2know.com/About/7897.html>.

page 40

Anti War. Com. "Quotes." Antiwar.com. 31 may 2006
<http://www.antiwar.com/quotes.php>.

The Muppet Show by Jim Henson, Disc 1-4, 1977.
Trademark, The
Muppet Holding Company, Department C-5, Burbank, California.
Distributed by Buena Vista Home Entertainment, Inc. and Walt
Disney Studios.

page 41

Ralph S. Brax, "Fresh Look at African Slave Trade."
Antelope Valley Press 29 July 2006: 4B.

Ralph S. Brax, "Fresh Look at African Slave Trade." Antelope Valley Press 29 July 2006: 4B.

page 42

Chris Carola, (Associated Press) "150th Anniversay Prompts New Look at War Between States." Antelope Valley Press 29 May 2012: 7B.

Jeff Gray, Far and Away Studios, Inc., Goshen, N.Y. Norman Brahm, Fire in the Ramapos. 1998. Distributed by Rockhouse Mountain Music, Palisades Interstate Park Commission Press, Bear Mountain, New York, CD

page 43

"John Wayne Quotes." En.thinkexist.com. 20 May 2006 <http://www.enthinkexist.com/quotes/john_wayne/2.htm>.

"Famous Peace Quotes, Anti War Quotes-4." Toppun.com. 26 October 2006 <http://www.toppun.com/Great-Quotes/famous-peace-quotes-anti-war-quotes.htm>.

"Chief Joseph." En.wikipedia.org. 26 October 2006. <http://en.wikipedia.org/wiki/Chief_Joseph.htm>.

"Mass Holocaust Grave Found in Ukraine." Peoplepc.com. 5 June 2007<http://home.peoplepc.com/psp/newsstory.asp?cat=TopStories&referrer=welcome&id=2007>.

Verena Dobnik and Randy Herschaft, (Associated Press) "Details on Jewish Ghettos Excruciating." Antelope Valley Press 12 May 2012: 3B.

page 45

Showcase.net. September 2005 <http://showcase.net/web/creative/lincoln/speeches/gettysburg.htm>.

Show Case Home. Showcase.netins. September 2005 <http://showcase.netins.net>

Show Case Home. Showcase.netins. Sept. 2005 <http://showcase.netins.net>.

Show Case Home. Showcase.netins. Sept. 2005 <http://showcase.netins.net>.

page 46

Show Case Home. Showcase.netins. Sept. 2005 <http://showcase.netins.net>.

Show Case Home. Showcase.netins. Sept. 2005
<http://showcase.netins.net>.

AOL Hometown. Members.aol. Sept. 2005
<http://members.aol.com>.

Show Case Home. Showcase.netins. Sept. 2005
<http://showcase.netins.net>.

Www. Watson. Org. Watson.org. Sept 2005

<http://www.watson.org>.

page 47

Show Case Home. Showcase.netins. Sept. 2005
<http://showcase.netins.net>.

Show Case Home. <http://members.aol.com>.

Showcase.netins. Sept. 2005 <http://showcase.netins.net>.

Show Case Home. <http://members.aol.com>.

Showcase.netins. Sept. 2005 <http://showcase.netins.net>.

AOL Hometown. Members.aol. Sept. 2005

National Park Service. Nps.gov. Sept. 2005
<http://www.nps.gov>.

The History Place.Com. Thehistoryplace.com. March 2005
<http://www.historyplace.com/civilwar/index.html>.

"Historic Quotes." Presidentlincoln.com. 26 October
2006 <http://www.presidentlincoln.com/quote7-war-
historical.html>.

page 48

Donald T. Phillips, Lincoln On Leadership. (New York:
Time Warner Company, 1992) 108.

Donald T. Phillips, Lincoln On Leadership. (New York:
Time Warner Company, 1992) 120

Donald T. Phillips, Lincoln On Leadership. (New York:
Time Warner Company, 1992). 126.

Donald T. Phillips, Lincoln On Leadership. (New York:
Time Warner Company, 1992). 121.

Donald T. Phillips, Lincoln On Leadership. (New York:
Time Warner Company, 1992) 129.

Donald T. Phillips, Lincoln On Leadership. (New York:
Time Warner Company, 1992) 129.

Donald T. Phillips, Lincoln On Leadership. (New York:
Time Warner Company, 1992) 129.

Donald T. Phillips, <u>Lincoln</u> <u>On</u> <u>Leadership</u>. (New York: Time Warner Company, 1992) 110.

Anti War. Com. "Quotes." Antiwar.com. 30 May 2006 <http://www.antiwarquotes.com/quotes.php>.

Brotherswar.com. October 2005 <www.brotherswar.com/civil_war_quotes_4b.htm>.

"The Civil War." Sonsofthesouth.Net. Sept. 2005 <www.sonofthesouth.net>.

Robert E. Lee. En.Wikipedia. Sept.2005 <http://en.wikipedia.org/wiki/Robert_E._Lee>.

page 49

Donald T. Phillips, <u>Lincoln</u> <u>On</u> <u>Leadership</u>. (New York: Time Warner Company, 1992) 110.

Donald T. Phillips, <u>Lincoln</u> <u>On</u> <u>Leadership</u>. (New York: Time Warner Company, 1992) 114.

Donald T. Phillips, <u>Lincoln</u> <u>On</u> <u>Leadership</u>. (New York: Time Warner Company, 1992) 133.

Donald T. Phillips, <u>Lincoln</u> <u>On</u> <u>Leadership</u>. (New York: Time Warner Company, 1992) 135.

Donald T. Phillips, <u>Lincoln</u> <u>On</u> <u>Leadership</u>. (New York: Time Warner Company, 1992) 135.

"War Quotes." Chatna.com. October 2005 <http://wwwchatna.com/theme/war.html>.

page 50

Show Case. Showcase.net. Sept. 2005 <http://showcase.netins.net>.

David Brooks, (New York Times). "Afghanistan Fight an Illusion for U.S." <u>Antelope</u> <u>Valley</u> <u>Press</u> 28 September 2009: 6B.

The Heritage Foundation. "American Military Intervention: A User's Guide," John Hillen. 24 January 2010 <www.heritage.org/research/nationalsecurity/BG1079.cfm>.

page 51

Robert E. Lee. En.Wikipedia. Sept.2005 <http://en.wikipedia.org/wiki/Robert_E._Lee>.

page 52

Show Case. Showcase.net. Sept. 2005
<http://showcase.netins.net>.

page 55

Misty. Mistyvietnam. 9 June 2005
<www.mistyvietnam.com/history.html>.

Misty. Mistyvietnam. 9 June 2005
<www.mistyvietnam.com/history.html>.

Misty. Mistyvietnam. 9 June 2005
<www.mistyvietnam.com/history.html>.

"Chapter Seven." Robertcorum.com 3 August 2006
<http://www.robertcorum.com/chapter_seven.html>.

page 56

Dale Andrade, Trial by Fire (New York: Ballantine
Books, 1995) 465.

Dale Andrade, Trial by Fire (New York: Ballantine
Books, 1995) 465.

En.Thinkexist.Com. Thinkexist.Com. 1 May 2006
<http://www.thinkexist.com>.

page 57

Zaazdzbeta. Zaazdz.com. 3 May 2006
<http://www.aazdz.com/quotes/topics/war>.

"War Quotes." Chatna. Com. Sept. 2005
<http://chatna.com/theme/war.htm>.

page 58

"Quotes and Pictures of War." Krishnaland. Com. October
2005 <http://Krishnaland.com/WAR.html>.

"Quotes and Pictures of War." Krishnaland. Com. October
2005 <http://Krishnaland.com/WAR.html>.

Think Exist. "War Quotes." Thinkexist. Com. September
2006 <http://en.thinkexit.com>.

Brainy Quote. Brainyquote.com. Oct. 2005
<www.brainyquote.com>.

Brainy Quote. Brainyquote.com. Oct. 2005
<http://www.brainyquote.com>.

page 59

Wild Guns 'C' Troop, 11th Cavalry. Wildgun5.tripod. 12
May 2006 <http://wildgun5.tripod.com>.

page 60

Joe Galloway, (Knight Ridder press). "Reporter Halberstam Spoke Truth to Power." Antelope Valley Press 4 May 2007: 6B.

"Reporting America at War, David Halberstam, The Saigon Press Corps." PBS. Org. 7 January 2007 <http://www.pbs.org/weta/reportingamericaatwar/reporters/halberstam/presscorps.html>.

page 61

Julian E. Barnes, "A Shift to Protect the Afghan People." Los Angeles Times 26 July 2009: 20A.

page 62

"Vietnam War." En.Wikipedia.Org. 3 May 2006. December 2005 <http://en.wikipedia.org>.

page 63

John Prados, The Blood Road, The Ho Chi Minh Trail and The Vietnam War. (New York: John Wiley and Sons, Inc., 1999) 245.

John Prados, The Blood Road, The Ho Chi Minh Trail and The Vietnam War. (New York: John Wiley and Sons, Inc., 1999) 245.

page 64

Mike Nastasi, "The Role of Airpower in the Vietnam War." Militaryhistoryonline.com. 12 may 2006 <http://militaryhistory.com/vietnam/airpower/default.aspx>.

Mike Nastasi, "The Role of Airpower in the Vietnam War." Militaryhistoryonline.com. 12 may 2006 <http://militaryhistory.com/vietnam/airpower/default.aspx>.

page 66

Misty. Mistyvietnam. 9 June 2005 <www.mistyvietnam.com/history.html>. (not exact quote)

Misty. Mistyvietnam. 9 June 2005 <www.mistyvietnam.com/history.html>. (not exact quote)

Misty. Mistyvietnam. 9 June 2005 <www.mistyvietnam.com/history.html>. (not exact quote)

Misty. Mistyvietnam. 9 June 2005 <www.mistyvietnam.com/history.html>. (not exact quote)

Misty. Mistyvietnam. 9 June 2005 <www.mistyvietnam.com/history.html>. (not exact quote)

Misty. Mistyvietnam. 9 June 2005
<www.mistyvietnam.com/history.html>. (not exact quote)

Misty. Mistyvietnam. 9 June 2005
<www.mistyvietnam.com/history.html>. (not exact quote)

"Chapter Seven." Robertcorum.com 3 August 2006
<http://www.robertcorum.com/chapter_seven.html>.

page 67

John Prados, The Blood Road, The Ho Chi Minh Trail and
the Vietnam War. (New York: John Wiley and Sons, Inc., 1999)
41.

John Prados, The Blood Road, The Ho Chi Minh Trail and
the Vietnam War. (New York: John Wiley and Sons, Inc., 1999)
41.

John Prados, The Blood Road, The Ho Chi Minh Trail and
the Vietnam War. (New York: John Wiley and Sons, Inc., 1999)
47.

page 72

Anti War. Com. Antiwar.Com. 4 May 2006
<http://www.anti.war.com>.

page 73

Anti War. Com. "Quotes." Antiwar.com. 30 May 2006
<http://www.antiwar.com/quotes.php>.

Natant Films, (Producer), Kubrick, Stanley, (Director)
(1987) Full Metal Jacket. U.S.A. Warner Home Video.

John Prados, The Blood Road, The Ho Chi Minh Trail and
The Vietnam War. (New York: John Wiley and Sons, Inc., 1999)
210.

page 76

John Prados, The Blood Road, The Ho Chi Minh Trail and
the Vietnam War. (New York: John Wiley and Sons, Inc., 1999)
210.

John Prados, The Blood Road, The Ho Chi Minh Trail and
the Vietnam War. (New York: John Wiley and Sons, Inc., 1999)
225.

Warren P. Strobel, "Bush, Iraq Study Group Seek
Solutions." Antelope Valley Press. 14 November 2007: 1B.

page 77

John Prados, The Blood Road, The Ho Chi Minh Trail and
the Vietnam War. (New York: John Wiley and Sons, Inc., 1999)
78.

John Prados, The Blood Road, The Ho Chi Minh Trail and the Vietnam War. (New York: John Wiley and Sons, Inc., 1999) 78.

John Prados, The Blood Road, The Ho Chi Minh Trail and the Vietnam War. (New York: John Wiley and Sons, Inc., 1999) 47.

"Counter Offensive Phase III." Feb. 2006 <http://www.ichiban1.org/html/history/1965_1969_american_war/05_counteroffensive_phase3_1967_1968.htm>.

page 78

Think Exist. "War Quotes." Thinkexist. Com. September 2006 <http://en.thinkexit.com>.

Brainy Quote. Brainyquote.com. Oct. 2005 <http://www.brainyquote.com>.

John Prados, The Blood Road, The Ho Chi Minh Trail and The Vietnam War. (New York: John Wiley and Sons, Inc., 1999)

page 79

John Prados, The Blood Road, The Ho Chi Minh Trail and The Vietnam War. (New York: John Wiley and Sons, Inc., 1999) 219.

John Prados, The Blood Road, The Ho Chi Minh Trail and The Vietnam War. (New York: John Wiley and Sons, Inc., 1999) 219.

John Prados, The Blood Road, The Ho Chi Minh Trail and The Vietnam War. (New York: John Wiley and Sons, Inc., 1999)

"History of the Vietnam War, Part I American Engagement, 1960-1964." Ichiban1.Org. 2003. Jan. 2006 <http://www.ichiban1.org/html/history/bc_1964_prewar/america_engages_1960_1964.htm>.

"History of the Vietnam War, Part I American Engagement, 1960-1964." Ichiban1.Org. 2003. Jan. 2006 <http://www.ichiban1.org/html/history/bc_1964_prewar/america_engages_1960_1964.htm>.

page 80

The Heritage Foundation. "American Military Intervention: A User's Guide," John Hillen. 24 January 2010 <www.heritage.org/research/nationalsecurity/BG1079.cfm>.

Bob Herbert, "Americans Fed Up With War in Afghanistan." Antelope Valley Press 30 September 2009: B8.

page 81

Global Security. Org. "Military, Vietnam War." Dec. 2005 <www.globalsecurity.org/military/ops/vietnam.htm>.

The Heritage Foundation. "American Military Intervention: A User's Guide," John Hillen. 24 January 2010 <www.heritage.org/research/nationalsecurity/BG1079.cfm>.

Samuel Zaffiri, Hamburger Hill (New York: Ballantine Books, 1988) 38.

Samuel Zaffiri, Hamburger Hill (New York: Ballantine Books, 1988) 38.

Samuel Zaffiri, Hamburger Hill (New York: Ballantine Books, 1988) 38.

"The Battle for Hamburger Hill." Time, May 30, 1969

page 82

The Heritage Foundation. "American Military Intervention: A User's Guide," John Hillen. 24 January 2010 <www.heritage.org/research/nationalsecurity/BG1079.cfm>.

page 83

Mary Wisniewski (Writer), Greg McCune & Stacy Joyce (Editors), Reuters, "Veterans Symbolically Discard Service Medals at Anti-NATO Rally." Newsyahoo.com. 20 May 2012 <http://news.yahoo.com/veterans-symbolically>.

Zaadzbeta. Zaadz.Com 7 May 2006 <http://www.zaadz.com/quotes>.

page 84

Quotations About War. Quotegarden. 5 October 2008 <www.quotegarden.com/war.html>.

Dale Andrade, Trial by Fire. (New York: Hippocrene Books, 1995) 426.

Dale Andrade, Trial by Fire. (New York: Hippocrene Books, 1995) 25.

Eric Lewan, "Hangar Flying, Historic Military Quotes." Members.cox. 8 June 2006 <http://www.members.cox.net/milreform/milquote2.html>.

page 86

Dale Andrade, Trial by Fire. (New York: Hippocrene Books, 1995) 36.

Quotations About War. Quotegarden. 5 October 2008 <www.quotegarden.com/war.html>.

page *87*

Dale Andrade, Trial by Fire. (New York: Hippocrene Books, 1995) 53.

Dale Andrade, Trial by Fire. (New York: Hippocrene Books, 1995) 53.

Anti War. Com. "Quotes." Antiwar.com. 30 May 2006 <http://www.antiwar.com/quotes.php>.

Anti War. Com. "Quotes." Antiwar.com. 30 May 2006 <http://www.antiwar.com/quotes.php>.

Quotations About War. Quotegarden. 5 October 2008 <www.quotegarden.com/war.html>.

page *88*

Dale Andrade, Trial by Fire. (New York: Hippocrene Books, 1995) 53.

Global Security. Org. "Military, Vietnam War." Nov. 2005 <www.globalsecurity.org/military/ops/Vietnam.htm>.

Global Security. Org. "Military, Vietnam War." Nov. 2005 <www.globalsecurity.org/military/ops/Vietnam.htm>.

The History Place. "The Vietnam War, America Commits, 1961-1964." Thehistoryplace.com. Feb. 2005 <www.thehistoryplace.com>.

The History Place. "The Vietnam War, America Commits, 1961-1964." Thehistoryplace.com. Feb. 2005 <www.thehistoryplace.com>.

Terrance Hunt, "Bush Not Satisfied with War in Iraq." Antelope Valley Press 26 October 2006: 1B.

Terrance Hunt, "Bush Not Satisfied with War in Iraq." Antelope Valley Press 26 October 2006: 1B.

page *89*

Doyle McManus, "Iraq War: Lessons Learned?" Los Angeles Times 17 March 2013: 28A.

Anti War. Com. "Quotes." Antiwar.com. 30 May 2006 <http://www.antiwar.com/quotes.php>.

The History Place. "The Vietnam War, America Commits, 1961-1964." Thehistoryplace.com. Feb. 2005 <www.thehistoryplace.com>.

Joe Galloway, Knight Ridder press. "Bush Gets Desperate." Antelope Valley Press 15 December 2006: 5B.

The History Place. "The Vietnam War, America Commits, 1961-1964. Thehistoryplace.com Feb.2005 <www.thehistoryplace.com>.

page 90

The History Place. "The Vietnam War, America Commits, 1961-1964. Thehistoryplace.com Feb.2005 <www.thehistoryplace.com>.

The History Place. "The Vietnam War, America Commits, 1961-1964. Thehistoryplace.com Feb.2005 <www.thehistoryplace.com>.

The History Place. "The Vietnam War, America Commits, 1961-1964. Thehistoryplace.com Feb.2005 <www.thehistoryplace.com>.

YouTube. "Beyond Vietnam." Martin Luther King Jr. Youtube.com 18 Jan. 2010 <www.youtube.com>.

The History Place. "The Vietnam War, America Commits, 1961-1964. Thehistoryplace.com Feb.2005 <www.thehistoryplace.com>.

page 91

Sydney J. Furie, (2001) Under Heavy Fire U.S.A. 20th Century Fox.

The History Place. "The Vietnam War, America Commits, 1961-1964. Thehistoryplace.com Feb.2005 <www.thehistoryplace.com>.

Walter J. Boyne, "Le May." Air Force Magazine, On-Line March 1998. http://www.afa.org/magazine/Marh1998/0398lemay.asp. 20 March 2007>.

World of Quotes. Com. Worldofquotes.com. 4 November 2006 <http://wwwworldofquotes.com/topic/war/1/index.htm>.

page 92

T.R. Fehrenbach, This Kind of War (Washington, D.C.: Brassey's, 1963) 452.

Eric Lewan, "Hangar Flying, Historic Military Quotes." Members.cox. 8 June 2006 <http://www.members.cox.net/milreform/milquote2.html>.

Eric Lewan, "Eric Lewan's Air Force Page, Historic Military Quotes." Members.cox. 8 June 2006 <http://www.members.cox.net/milreform/milquote2.html>.

Eric Lewan, "Eric Lewan's Air Force Page, Historic Military Quotes." Members.cox. 8 June 2006 <http://www.members.cox.net/milreform/milquote2.html>.

page 93

"Town Meeting of the World: The Image of America and the youth of the World with Robert F. Kennedy and Governor Ronald Reagan." Town Meeting of the World with Charles Collingwood, CBS TV and Radio Network, New York, May 15 1967. 2005 <www.jfk.library.org>.

Anti War. Com. "Quotes." Antiwar.com. 30 June 2007 <http://www.antiwar.com/quotes.php>.

page 95

My DD. Com. Dec.2005 <http://www.mydd.com/story/2005/5/5/91240/41560>.

15th Field Artillery Regiment 1917-2004. "The Guns in Vietnam." Oct. 2005 <http://www.landscaper.net/theguns.htm#dusters>.

"Vietnam War, Under Fire." Vietnampix.com. Feb.2006 <http://www.vietnampix.com/fire5.htm>.

15th Field Artillery Regiment 1917-2004. "The Guns in Vietnam." Oct. 2005 <http://www.landscaper.net/theguns.htm#dusters>.

"Vietnam War, Under Fire." Vietnampix.com. Feb.2006 <http://www.vietnampix.com/fire5.htm>.

Dale Andrade, Trial by Fire. (New York: Hippocrene Books, 1995) 18.

page 96

Anti War. Com. "Quotes." Antiwar.com. 30 May 2006 <http://www.antiwar.com/quotes.php>.

page 98

House of Lyrics. Houseoflyrics.com. 10 July 2006 <http://www.houseoflyrics.com/lyrics/ivory_joe_hunter/since_i_met_you_baby.html>.

Launch Cast. Music.yahoo.com. 9 July 2006 <http://music.yahoo.com/launchcast/stations/stations.asp?i=505>.

page 104

About. Quotations.about. 30 May 2006 <http://www/quotations.about/gi/dynamic/offsite.htm>.

"One-Liners and Quotes Page." Winc.TV. 6 October 2008 <www.winc.tv/artman/publish/article_116.shtml>.

page 105

Cornell University Law School. "Supreme Court Collection." Lawcornell. 10 April 2008 <www.lawcornell.edu>.

. About. Com. "United States Military Enlistment Standards," by Rod Powers. 1 July 2008 <http://usmilitary.about.com/od/joiningthemilitary/a/enlstandards.htm>.

page 106

Samuel Zaffiri. Hamburger Hill. (New York: Ballantine Books, *1988) 11.*

Samuel Zaffiri. Hamburger Hill. (New York: Ballantine Books, 1988) 11.

page 107

Samuel Zaffiri, Hamburger Hill (New York: Ballantine Books, 1988) 35.

Samuel Zaffiri, Hamburger Hill (New York: Ballantine Books, 1988) 35.

Samuel Zaffiri, Hamburger Hill (New York: Ballantine Books, 1988) 37.

Samuel Zaffiri, Hamburger Hill (New York: Ballantine Books, 1988) 38.

Combat Studies Institute. "Studies in Battle Command." Ehistory.osu. March 2006 <http://ehistory.osu.edu/Vietnam/essays/battlecommand/index.cfm>.

Samuel Zaffiri, Hamburger Hill (New York: Ballantine Books, 1988) 39.

Samuel Zaffiri, Hamburger Hill (New York: Ballantine Books, 1988) 39.

Samuel Zaffiri, Hamburger Hill (New York: Ballantine Books, 1988) 40.

Samuel Zaffiri, Hamburger Hill (New York: Ballantine Books, 1988) 41.

Samuel Zaffiri, Hamburger Hill (New York: Ballantine Books, 1988) 51.

page 108

Combat Studies Institute. "Studies in Battle Command." Ehistory.osu. March 2006 <http://ehistory.osu.edu/Vietnam/essays/battlecommand/index.cfm>.

Samuel Zaffiri, Hamburger Hill (New York: Ballantine Books, 1988) 61.

page 109

Combat Studies Institute. "Studies in Battle Command." Ehistory.osu. March 2006 <http://ehistory.osu.edu/Vietnam/essays/battlecommand/index. cfm>.

"101st Airborne (Airmobile) during Vietnam." Militaryphotos.net. 20 August 2006 <http://www.militaryphotos.net/forums/archives/index.php/t- 15131.html>.

"Military, Ch. 13 Reconnaissance Operations." Global security.org. 4 July 2006 <http://www.globalsecurity.org/military/library/policy/army/ fm/3-30/ch.13.htm>.

page 110

"Operation Massachusetts Striker Information for 2 BDE 101 ABN." Flyarmy.org. 20 August 2006 <http://www.flyarmy.org/panel/battle/69030102>.

Samuel Zaffiri, Hamburger Hill (New York: Ballantine Books, 1988) 48.

Samuel Zaffiri, Hamburger Hill (New York: Ballantine Books, 1988) 47.

"Operation Massachusetts Striker Information for 2 BDE 101 ABN." Flyarmy.org. 20 August 2006 <http://www.flyarmy.org/panel/battle/69030102>.

Combat Studies Institute. "Studies in Battle Command." Ehistory.osu. March 2006 <http://ehistory.osu.edu/Vietnam/essays/battlecommand/index. cfm>.

page 111

Terrance Hunt, "Bush Sending More Troops." Antelope Valley Press 11 January 2007: 4A.

Combat Studies Institute. "Studies in Battle Command." Ehistory.osu. March 2006 <http://ehistory.osu.edu/Vietnam/essays/battlecommand/index. cfm>.

"Decent into the A Shau Valley." Randygreenart.com. March 2006 <http://www.randygreenart.com/a_shau_valley.htm>. Static.cc. March 2006 <http://www.static.cc.gatch.edu/fac/thomas.Dilsch/AirOps/ASh au-3.html>.

"Hamburger Hill." Chs.helena.K12. 5 December 2006 <http://www.chs.helena.k12.mt.us/faculty/hhill/juniors 2001/rreinier2.htm>.

Lt. Frank Hair, "The Summer Offensive in the A Shau Valley." Rendezvous With Destiny Magazine. Summer 1969. Dec. 2005 <http://Lcompanyranger.com/Ashau/ashauarticle1.htm>.

"A Shau Valley." En. Wikipedia.Org. 16 March 2006. Jan. 2006 <http://enwikipedia.org/wiki/A_Shau_Valley>.

Colonel Harry G. Summers Jr., (U.S. Army, ret.) "Hamburger Hill Revisited." Vietnam. 25 May 2006 <http://www.the historynet.com/vn/blhamburgerhill/index.html>.

Lower Jumper, Usparatroopers.org Jan. 2006 <http://www.usparatroopers.org/paratrooper.htm>.

"Military, Ch. 13 Reconnaissance Operations." Globalsecurity.org. 4 July 2006 <http://www.globalsecurity.org/library/policy/armyfm/3-30/ch.13.htm>.

Lieutenant Colonel Douglas P. Scalard, "The Battle of Hamburger Hill: Battle Command in Difficult Terrain Against a Determined Enemy." Ehistory.osu.edu. The Faculty Combat Studies Institute. 23 May 2006 <http://ehistory.osu.edu/vietnam/essays/battlecommand/index.cfm>.

Samuel Zaffiri, Hamburger Hill (New York: Ballantine Books, 1988) 47.

Dale Andrade, Trial by Fire. (New York: Hippocrene Books, 1995) 177.

page 112

Samuel Zaffiri, Hamburger Hill (New York: Ballantine Books, 1988) 54.

Lower Jumper, Usparatroopers.org Jan. 2006 <http://www.usparatroopers.org/paratrooper.htm>.

"Military, Ch. 13 Reconnaissance Operations." Global security.org. 4 July 2006 <http://www.globalsecurity.org/military/library/policy/army/fm/3-30/ch.13.htm>.

Lieutenant Colonel Douglas P. Scalard, "The Battle of Hamburger Hill: Battle Command in Difficult Terrain Against a Determined Enemy." Ehistory.osu.edu. The Faculty Combat Studies Institute. 23 May 2006 <http://ehistory.osu.edu/vietnam/essays/battlecommand/index.cfm>.

"Studies in Battle Command," the Faculty Combat Studies Institute and LTC Douglas P. Scalard. Ehistory.osu.edu. 9 June 2008 <http://ehistory.osu/vietnam/essays/battlecommand/index.cfm>

"Hamburger Hill, Vietnam, Remembering Those Who Served." 9 June 2008 <http://angelfire.com/pa/hotshot478/Hamburger Hill.html>.

page 113

Lower Jumper, Usparatroopers.org Jan. 2006 <http://www.usparatroopers.org/paratrooper.htm>.

"One-Liners and Quotes Page." Winc.TV. 6 October 2008 <www.winc.tv/artman/publish/article 116.shtml>.

page 115

Jo Galloway, "Let's Not Loose Sight of the Bloody Mess in Iraq." Antelope Valley Press 21 July, 2006: 12A.

Samuel Zaffiri, Hamburger Hill (New York: Ballantine Books, 1988) 53.

Larry Chambers, Death in the A Shau Valley (New York: Ivy Books, 1998) 11, 12.

Samuel Zaffiri, Hamburger Hill (New York: Ballantine Books, 1988) 53.

Samuel Zaffiri, Hamburger Hill (New York: Ballantine Books, 1988) 53.

Home of the Heroes. Homeoftheheroes.com. Feb.2006 <http://www.homeofheroes.com/westeyfox/3 mystery.html>.

page 116

Diana West, "You Can't Win Afghan Hearts." Antelope Valley Press 19 January 2010: 9A.

Byron York, (The Washington Examiner) "Restrictive Rules Put Troops in Danger." Antelope Valley Press 7 October 2009: 6B.

"Vietnam Picture Tour." Feb. 2006 <http://namtour.com/ripcord.html>.

"Vietnam Picture Tour." Feb. 2006 <http://namtour.com/ripcord.html>.

Samuel Zaffiri, Hamburger Hill (New York: Ballantine Press, 1988) 48.

Techize. "Military Strategy." Techize.com. 5 March 2006 <http://www.techize.com/articles/military_strategy#Principles_of_military_strategy>.

Technize. Technize.com. 1 May 2006 <http://www.techize.com/articles/militarystrategy#fundanentals_ofmilitary_strategy>.

page 117

Techize. "Military Strategy." Techize.com. 9 March 2006 <http://www.techize.com/articles/military_strategy#Principles_of_military_strategy>.

Technize. Technize.com. 1 May 2006 <http://www.techize.com/articles/militarystrategy#fundanentals_ofmilitary_strategy>.

Technize. Technize.com. 1 May 2006 <http://www.techize.com/articles/militarystrategy#fundanentals_ofmilitary_strategy>.

Technize. Technize.com. 1 May 2006 <http://www.techize.com/articles/militarystrategy#fundanentals_ofmilitary_strategy>.

Brainy Quotes. Brainyquotes.Com. 3 May 2006 <http://www.brainyquotes.com>.

Techize. "Military Strategy." Techize.com. 8 March 2006 <http://www.techize.com/articles/military_strategy#Principles_of_military_strategy>.

Techize. "Military Strategy." Techize.com. 8 March 2006 <http://www.techize.com/articles/military_strategy#Principles_of_military_strategy>.

page 118

Techize. "Military Strategy." Techize.com. March 2006 <http://www.techize.com/articles/military_Strategy#Principles_of_military_strategy>.

Techize. "Military Strategy." Techize.com. March 2006 <http://www.techize.com/articles/military_Strategy#Principles_of_military_strategy>.

Techize. "Military Strategy." Techize.com. March 2006 <http://www.techize.com/articles/military_Strategy#Principles_of_military_strategy>.

Home of the Heroes. Homeoftheheroes.com. Feb.2006
<http://www.homeofheroes.com/westeyfox/3_mystery.html>.

Home.swipnet. 20 march 2006
<http://home.swipnet.se/longrange/usmc SNIPERS VIETNAM.htm>.

page 119

Anti War. Com. "Quotes." Antiwar.com. 30 May 2006
<http://www.antiwar.com/quotes.php>.

Home of the Heroes. Homeoftheheroes.com. Feb.2006
<http://www.homeofheroes.com/westeyfox/3_mystery.html>.

Samuel Zaffiri, Hamburger Hill (New York: Ballantine
Books, 1988) 4.

page 120

Anti War. Com. "Quotes." Antiwar.com. 30 May 2006
<http://www.antiwar.com/quotes.php>.

Homeoftheheroes.Com. Jan. 2006
<http://wwww.homeofheroes.com/wesleyfox/3_mystory.htm>.

"The Infantry Rifleman." Defense.gov. 25 May 2006
<http://www.defense.gov.au/army/2549RQR/rifleman.html>.

"The Infantry Rifleman." Defense.gov. 25 May 2006
<http://www.defense.gov.au/army/2549RQR/rifleman.html>.

Lt. Frank. Hair, "The Summer Offensive in the A Shau
Valley." Rendezvous With Destiny Magazine. Summer 1969. Dec.
2005
<http://www.Lcompanyranger.com/Ashau/ashauarticle1.htm>.

page 121

Samuel Zaffiri, Hamburger Hill (New York: Ballantine
Books, 1988)2.

Gatech.edu. 12 March 2006
<http://www.cc.gatech.edu/fac/Thomas.Pilsch/Airops/AshauSFCC
amp.html>.

Army.mil. 12 March 2006 <http://www.army.mil/cmh-
pg/books/vietnam/northern/nprovinces-chp.6.htm#ashau>.

"A Shau Valley." En.wikipedia.org. 11 July 2006.
<http://en.wikipedia.org/wiki/A Shau_Valley>.

Homeoftheheroes.Com. Jan. 2006
<http://wwww.homeofheroes.com/wesleyfox/3_mystory.htm>.

"Hamburger Hill, The Real Story." Historyinfilm.com. 8
October 2006
<http://www.historyinfilm.com/hamhill/real7.htm>.

page 122

George Esper, "Enemy Back in Control of Ap Bia." <u>New York Times</u>. 17 June 1969.

Samuel Zaffiri, <u>Hamburger Hill</u> (New York: Ballantine Books, 1988) 277.

Sen. Stephen M. Young, Senate Speeches, May 29, 1969.

Samuel Zaffiri, <u>Hamburger Hill</u> (New York: Ballantine Books, 1988) 197.

page 123

Samuel Zaffiri, <u>Hamburger Hill</u> (New York: Ballantine Books, 1988) 198.

Samuel Zaffiri, <u>Hamburger Hill</u> (New York: Ballantine Books, 1988) 197.

Jay Sharbutt, "Allied Troops Capture Mountain on Eleventh Try in Ten Days." <u>New York Times.</u> 20 May 1969.

Lt. Frank Hair, "The Summer Offensive in the A Shau Valley." <u>Rendezvous With Destiny Magazine.</u> Summer 1969. Dec. 2005 <http://Lcompanyranger.com/Ashau/ashauarticle1.htm>.

"A Shau Valley." En. Wikipedia.Org. 16 March 2006. Jan. 2006 <http://enwikipedia.org/wiki/A_Shau_Valley>.

Lt. Frank. Hair, "The Summer Offensive in the A Shau Valley." <u>Rendezvous With Destiny Magazine.</u> Summer 1969.Feb. 2006<http://www.Lcompanyranger.com/Ashau/ashauarticle1.htm>.

"A Shau Valley." En.Wikipedia.Org. 16 March 2006. Feb.2006 <http://en.wikipedia.org/wiki/A_Shau_Valley>.

Samuel Zaffiri, <u>Hamburger Hill</u> (New York: Ballantine Books, 1988) 197.

page 124

Lt. Frank Hair, "The Summer Offensive in the A Shau Valley." <u>Rendezvous With Destiny Magazine.</u> Summer 1969. Dec. 2005 <http://Lcompanyranger.com/Ashau/ashauarticle1.htm>.

"A Shau Valley." En. Wikipedia.Org. 16 March 2006. Jan. 2006 <http://enwikipedia.org/wiki/A_Shau_Valley>.

Lt. Frank Hair, "The Summer Offensive in the A Shau Valley." <u>Rendezvous With Destiny Magazine.</u> Summer 1969. Feb. 2006 <http://www.Lcompanyranger.com/Ashau/ashauarticle1.htm>.

"A Shau Valley." En.Wikipedia.Org. 16 March 2006. Feb.2006 <http://en.wikipedia.org/wiki/A_Shau_Valley>.

Combat Studies Institute. "Studies in Battle Command." Ehistory.osu. 17 March 2006 <http://ehistory.osu.edu/Vietnam/essays/battlecommand/index.cfm>.

Samuel Zaffiri, Hamburger Hill (New York: Ballantine Books, 1988) 197.

Samuel Zaffiri, Hamburger Hill (New York: Ballantine Books, 1988) 198.

page 125

"Giulio Douhet." En.Wikipedia.Org. 16 April 2006. Jan. 2006 <http://en.wikipedia.org/wiki/Giulio_Douhet>.

Combat Studies Institute. "Studies in Battle Command." Ehistory.osu. 17 March 2006 <http://ehistory.osu.edu/Vietnam/essays/battlecommand/index.cfm>.

Samuel Zaffiri, Hamburger Hill (New York: Ballantine Books, 1988) 198.

page 126

Techize. "Military Strategy." Techize.com. March 2006 <http://www.techize.com/articles/military_Strategy#Principles_of_military_strategy>.

Techize. "Military Strategy." Techize.com. March 2006 <http://www.techize.com/articles/military_Strategy#Principles_of_military_strategy>.

Combat Studies Institute. "Studies in Battle Command." Ehistory.osu. 17 March 2006 <http://ehistory.osu.edu/Vietnam/essays/battlecommand/index.cfm>.

"Quotations by Author." Quotationspage.com. 11 July 2006 <http://www.quotionspage.com/quotes/Sun-Tzu/>.

Lieutenant Colonel Douglas P. Scalard, "The Battle of Hamburger Hill: Battle Command in Difficult Terrain Against a Determined Enemy." Ehistory.osu.edu. The Faculty Combat Studies Institute. 23 May 2006 <http://ehistory.osu.edu/vietnam/essays/battlecommand/index.cfm>.

Combat Studies Institute. "Studies in Battle Command." Ehistory.osu. 17 March 2006 <http://ehistory.osu.edu/Vietnam/essays/battlecommand/index.cfm>.

Samuel Zaffiri, Hamburger Hill (New York: Ballantine Books, 1988) 198.

page 127

　Sydney J. Furie, (2001) Under Heavy Fire U.S.A.

　Caffey, Frank, McCarthy (Producer), Frank and
Schaffner, Franklin J. (Director) (1970) Patton. U.S.A.
20th Century Fox.

page 129

　John Prados, The Blood Road, The Ho Chi Minh Trail and
the Vietnam War. (New York: John Wiley and Sons, Inc., 1999)
221.

page 131

　John Prados, The Blood Road, The Ho Chi Minh Trail and
the Vietnam War. (New York: John Wiley and Sons Inc., 1999)
220.

　Dale Andrade, Trial by Fire. (New York: Hippocrene
Books, 1995) 232.

　John Prados, The Blood Road, the Ho Chi Minh Trail, And
the Vietnam War (New York: John Wiley and Sons, Inc., 1999)
325.

page 132-

　John Prados, The Blood Road, The Ho Chi Minh Trail and
the Vietnam War. (New York: John Wiley and Sons, Inc., 1999)
220.

page 132

　"Central Intelligence Agency, The World Factbook."
CIA.Gov. 2006 <http://www.cia.gov/library/public/>.

　"Vietnam Peoples Army." Wikipedia.Org 2006
<http://en.wikipedia.org/wiki/PAVN/>.

page 133

　John Prados, The Blood Road, the Ho Chi Minh Trail, And
the Vietnam War (New York: John Wiley and Sons, Inc., 1999)
64.

　James C. Donahue, Backjack-33. New York: Ivy Books,
1999.

page 134

　Techize. "Military Strategy." Techize.com. March 2006
<http://www.techize.com/articles/military_Strategy#Principle
s_of_military_strategy>.

Techize. "Military Strategy." Techize.com. March 2006 <http://www.techize.com/articles/military_Strategy#Principles_of_military_strategy>.

Combat Studies Institute. "Studies in Battle Command." EHistory.osu. 19 March 2006 <http://ehistory.osu.edu/vietnam/essays/battlecommand/index.cfm>.

Wikipedia. "A Shau Valley." 11 July 2006 <http://www.en.wikipedi.org/wiki/A_Shau_Valley>.

Lt. Frank Hair, "The Summer Offensive in the A Shau Valley." *Rendezvous With Destiny Magazine.* Summer 1969. Feb. 2006 <http://www.Lcompanyranger.com/Ashau/ashauarticle1.htm>

"A Shau Valley." En. Wikipedia. Org. 16 March 2006. Jan. 2006 <http://en.wikipedia.org/wiki/A_Shau_Valley>.

About. Quotations.about. 30 May 2006 <http://www.quotations.about.com/gi/dynamic/offsite.htm>.

page 135

About. Quotations.about. 30 May 2006 <http://www.quotations.about.com/gi/dynamic/offsite.htm>.

"Famous Peace Quotes, Anti War Quotes-4." Toppun.com. 26 October 2006 <http://www.toppun.com/great-quotes/famous-peace-quotes-anti-war-quotes.htm>.

About. Quotations.about. 30 May 2006 <http://www.quotations.about.com/gi/dynamic/offsite.htm>.

page 136

Christopher Amico, "Valley Marine Wins Silver Star." Antelope Valley Press 28 July 2006: 8A.

Dale Andrade. Trial by Fire (New York: Ballantine Books, 1995) 66.

page 137

Home.swipnet. 20 March 2006 <http://home.swipnet.se/longrange/usmc_SNIPERS_VIETNAM.htm>.

Wikiquote. "War." En.wikiquote.org. 3 June 2006 <http://www.en.wikiquote.org/wiki/War>.

page 138

Quotations About War. Quotegarden. 5 October 2008 <www.quotegarden.com/war.html>.

All Great Quotes. Allgreat quotes.com. 7 October 2008 <www.allgreatquotes.com/war_quotes.shtml>.

page 140

Home.swipnet. 20 March 2006
<http://home.swipnet.se/longrange/usmc SNIPERS VIETNAM.htm>.

Colonel Harry G. Summers Jr. (U.S. Army, ret.).
"Hamburger Hill Revisited." *Vietnam.* 25 May 2006
<http://www.thehistorynet.com/vn/blhamburgerhill/index.html>

Home.swipnet. 20 March 2006
<http://home.swipnet.se/longrange/usmc SNIPERS VIETNAM.htm>.

Colonel Harry G. Summers Jr., (U.S. Army, ret.).
"Hamburger Hill Revisited." *Vietnam.* 25 May 2006
<http://www.thehistorynet.com/vn/blhamburgerhill/index.html>

Home.swipnet. 20 March 2006
<http://home.swipnet.se/longrange/usmc SNIPERS VIETNAM.htm>.

Colonel Harry G. Summers Jr., (U.S. Army, ret.).
"Hamburger Hill Revisited." *Vietnam.* 25 May 2006
<http://www.thehistorynet.com/vn/blhamburgerhill/index.html>

Home.swipnet. 20 March 2006
<http://home.swipnet.se/longrange/usmc SNIPERS VIETNAM.htm>.

Home.swipnet. 20 March 2006
<http://home.swipnet.se/longrange/usmc SNIPERS VIETNAM.htm>.

Colonel Harry G. Summers Jr., (U.S. Army, ret.).
"Hamburger Hill Revisited." *Vietnam.* 25 May 2006
<http://www.thehistorynet.com/vn/blhamburgerhill/index.html>

page 141

MCA Nashville, UTVRecords, division of UMG Recording,
Inc. Conway Twitty, 25 Hits (Tennessee: Nashville 2004) CD.

OneBarton. Just Thought I'd Let You Know. You Tube,
Broadcast Yourself, 1 February 2008
<www.youtuibe.com/watch?v=th9RXauwzVw>.

page 142

Diego C2C Wendt M., "Using A Sledgehammer To Kill A
Gnat." Airpower Journal Summer 1990.
<http://www.airpower.mawell.af.mil/airchronicles/apj/4sum90.
html>.

All Great Quotes. Allgreat quotes.com. 7 October 2008
<www.allgreatquotes.com/war_quotes.shtml>.

page 143

MSNBC-on-line. "Honoring the Fallen." MSNBC. Com. 28
May 2007. <http://www.msnbc.msn.com/1d/18338428/?GT1=9951>.

page 145

   Rick Jervis, "Fighting the Wounds of War." <u>Chicago Tribune</u> 26 October 2004. <<u>http://www.notinourname.net/troops/wounds-26oct04.htm</u>>. 6 September 2004.

   Rick Jervis, "Fighting the Wounds of War." <u>Chicago Tribune</u> 26 October 2004. <<u>http://www.notinourname.net/troops/wounds-26oct04.htm</u>>. 6 September 2004.

page 146

   "Famous Peace Quotes, Anti War Quotes-4." Toppun.com. 26 October 2006 <<u>http://www.toppun.com/great-quotes/famous-peace-quotes-anti-war-quotes.htm</u>>.

   "Taps for an Only Son." <u>The Antelope Valley Press Magazine</u> November 2007: p. 18.

page 147

   <u>Popular Mechanics</u> "The Top 50 Inventions of the Past 50 Years,"(Dec. 1, 2005), Hutchinson, Alex. Popular Mechanics.com. 8 March 2012 <<u>http://popularmechanics.com/technology</u>>.

   <u>Popular Mechanics</u> "The Top 50 Inventions of the Past 50 Years,"(Dec. 1, 2005), Hutchinson, Alex. Popular Mechanics.com. 8 March 2012 <<u>http://popularmechanics.com/technology</u>>.

page 148

   Andrew Rooney, <u>My War</u>. New York: Perseus/ Public Affairs, 1995, 2000. p. *xiii*.

   Quote Garden. QuoteGarden.com. 2 May 2006 <<u>http://www.quotegarden.com</u>>.

page 153

   About. "About War." Quotations.about. 30 May 2005 <<u>http://www.quotations.about.com/gi/dynamic/offsite.htm</u>>.

page 154

   Wikipedia. "Timeline of United States Military Operations." en Wikipedia.com 24 January 2010 <<u>www.en.wikipedia.org/wiki/List_of_United_States_military_history_events</u>>.

page 155

   Quote DB. Quotedb.com. 6 June 2006 <<u>http://www.quotedb.com/authors/george-washington</u>>.

Rahim Faiez, (AP). "Afghanistan Insurgents Hang 8-year-old Boy." Antelope Valley Press 25 July 2011: B1.

page 156

Wikiquote."War." En.wikiquote.org. 3 June 2006 <http://www.en.wikiquote.org/wiki.War>.

Zaadzbeta. Zaadz.Com 4 May 2006 <http://www.zaadz.com/quotes/topics/war>.

Colin L. Powell, "Views, Kindness Works." Parade 20 May 2012: 12.

Anti War. Com "Quotes." Antiwar.com. 30 May 2006 <http://www.antiwar.com/quotes.php>.

Zaadzbeta. Zaadz.Com 5 May 2006 <http://www.zaadz.com/quotes/topics/war>.

page 157

Think Exist. Com. Thinkexist. Com. 4 May 2006 <www.thinkexist.com>.

Mary Wisniewski(Writer), Greg McCune & Stacy Joyce (Editors) Reuters, "Veterans Symbolically Discard Service Medals at Anti-NATO Rally." Newsyahoo.com. 20 May 2012 <http://news.yahoo.com/veterans-symbolically>.

Zaadzbeta. Zaadz.Com 5 May 2006 <http://www.zaadz.com/quotes/topics/war>.

Quoteland. Com. Quoteland. Com. 4 May 2006 <http://www.quoteland.com>.

Think Exist. Com. Thinkexist. Com. 5 May 2006 <www.thinkexist.com>.

Arthur I. Cyr, "Taylor's War Crimes Conviction Way Overdue." Antelope Valley Press. 7 May 2012: 4B.

Anti War. Com. Antiwar. Com. 5 May <http://antiwar.com/quotes.php>.

QuoteLand. Com. Quoteland.Com. 5 May 2006 <http://www.quoteland.com>.

page 158

Zaadzbeta. Com. Zaadz.Com. 5 May 2006 <http://www.zaadz.com/quotes/topics/war>.

Anti War. Com. Antiwar. Com. 5 May <http://antiwar.com/quotes.php>.

Anti War. Com. Antiwar. Com. 5 May <http://antiwar.com/quotes.php>.

Wikiquote. "War." En.wikiquote.org. 3 June 2006
<http://www.en.wikiquote.org/wiki/War>.

Zaadzbeta. Com. Zaadz.Com. 5 May 2006
<http://www.zaadz.com/quotes/topics/war>.

Anti War. Com. "Quotes." Antiwar.com. 30 May 2006
<http://www.antiwar.com/quotes.php>.

page 159

James C. Donahue, Blackjack-33. New York: Ivy Books,
1999.

page 160

Anti War. Com. "Quotes." Antiwar.com. 30 May 2006
<http://www.antiwar.com/quotes.php>.

page 161

About. Quotations.about. 30 May 2006
<http://quotations.about.com/gi/dynamics/offshoot.htm>.

page 162

Anti War. Com. Antiwar.Com. 2 May 2006
<http://www.antiwar.com>.

Eric Lewan, "Hangar Flying, Historic Military Quotes."
9 June 2006
<http://www.members.cox.net/milreform/milquote2.html>.

Sees Sharp Press. Seessharppress.com. 25 October 2006
<http://www.seesharppress.com/warquotes.html>.

Wikiquote. "War." En.wikiquote.org. 3 June 2006
<http://www.en.wikiquote.org/wiki/war>.

page 163

Global Security. Org. Globalsecurity.Org. 3 May 2006
<http://www.globalsecurity.org/military/ops/vietnam.htm>.

Susannah Shipman and Eugene Jarecki, (Producer) and
Jarecki, Eugene (Director) (2004) Why We Fight. U.S.A. Sony
Pictures.

page 170

Think Exist "War Quotes." Thinkexist.Com. November 2005
<http://www.en.thinkexist.com/quotations/war/2.html>.

About. "U.S. Army Ranger Creed." Usmilitary.about. 23
march 2006
<http://usmilitary.about.com/od/army/a/rangercreed.htm>.

page 171-172

Brainy Quote. Brainyquote.com. Oct. 2005
<www.brainyquote.com>.

Anti War. Com. Antiwar.Com. 4 May 2006
<http://www.anti.war.com>.

International Lyrics Playground. Lyricsplayground.com.
8 July 2006
<http://lyricsplayground.com/alpha/songs/s/surferjoe.shtml>.

International Lyrics Playground. Lyricsplayground.com.
8 July 2006
<http://lyricsplayground.com/alpha/songs/s/surferjoe.shtml>.

page 173

Anti War. Com "Quotes." Antiwar.com. 30 May 2006
<http://www.antiwar.com/quotes.php>.

Houseoflyrics.com. 23 march 2006
<http://www.houseoflyrics.com/d/artists/gary_lewis_and_the_p
layboys/songs/shes_just_my_style.html>.

Risa Song Lyrics Archive. Galveston. Risa.co. Jan.
2006 <http://www.risa.co.uk/sla/song.php?songid=13675>.

page 174

Rick Jervis, "Fighting the Wounds of War." Chicago
Tribune 26 October 2004.
<http://www.notinourname.net/troops/wounds-26Oct04.htm>. 5
September 2004.

Anti War. Com "Quotes." Antiwar.com. 30 May 2006
<http://www.antiwar.com/quotes.php>.

page 175

Home.att. Feb.2006 <http://home.att.net~gkozdron>.

Quote DB. Quotedb.com. 2 June 2006
<http://www.quotedb.com/authors/george-washington>.

Leoslyrics.com. March 2005
<http://leoslyrics.com/listlyrics.php?hid=7obdZP4dy3W%3D>.

page 176

Charles F. Bostwick, "History, Surviving Six Years as
Vietnam POW." Antelope Valley Press 2 April 2012: 8C.

Charles F. Bostwick, "History, Surviving Six Years as
Vietnam POW." Antelope Valley Press 2 April 2012: 8C.

Anti War. Com. Antiwar. Com. 4 May 2006
<http://www.antiwar.com/quotes.php>.

Home.att. Feb.2006 <http://home.att.net~gkozdron>.

Wikiquote. "War." En.wikiquote.org. 3 June 2006 <http://www.en.wikiquote.org/wiki/war>.

Anti War. Com. Antiwar.Com. 4 May 2006 <http://www.anti.war.com>.

page 179

Wikiquote. "War." En.wikiquote.org. 3 June 2006 <http://www.en.wikiquote.org/wiki/war>.

page 181

"Unconventional Operations." Army.mil. March 2006 <http://www.army.mil/cmhpg/books/vietnam/90-23/90236.htm>.

page 182

Arawa Damon, CNN.Com. "Behind the Scenes, After his Death, Sgt. Mock's Words Mean Even More." Cnn.com. 10 November 2006 <http://www.cnn.com/2006/world/meast/11/10/btsc.damon/index.html>.

page 183

Arawa Damon, CNN.Com. "Behind the Scenes, After his Death, Sgt. Mock's Words Mean Even More." CNN.com. 10 November 2006 <http://www.cnn.com/2006/world/meast/11/10/btsc.damonb/index.html>.

page 186

"One-Liners and Quotes Page." Winc.TV. 6 October 2008 <www.winc.tv/artman/publish/article_116.shtml>.

page 187

Sky Pilot, Eric Burdon and the Animals. Getlyrics.com. February 2006 <http://www.getlyrics.com/lyrics.php/Eric+Burdon+&+Animals/Show+Lyrics/SKY+PILOT>.

page 188

No Where To Run. Smartlyrics.com. March 2006 <http://www.smartlyrics.com/song376467-Martha-And-The-Vandellas-Nowhere-to-run-lyrics.9spx>.

Waltz Across Texas. Lyricandsongs.com. 13 August 2006 <http://lyricsandsongs.com/song/278604.html>.

Classic Country Lyrics, "Waltz Across Texas." Classic Song Lyrics. Com. <http://classic-song-lyrics.com>.

Blu.org. March 2006
<http://www.blu.org/b2227th/paye5.html>.

Blu.org. March 2006
<http://www.blu.org/b2227th/paye5.html>.

page 189

Samuel Zaffiri, Hamburger Hill (New York: Ballantine Books, 1988). (direct quote from book)

Samuel Zaffiri, Hamburger Hill (New York: Ballantine Books, 1988). (direct quote from book)

page 190

Samuel Zaffiri, Hamburger Hill (New York: Ballantine Books, 1988). (not direct quote)

Studies in Battle Command, Combat Studies Institute. XXIV The Battle of Hamburger Hill. 4 April 2008 http://ehistory.osu.edu/vietnam/essays/battlecommnd/index.cf

Samuel Zaffiri, Hamburger Hill (New York: Ballantine Books, 1988). (not direct quotes)

Studies in Battle Command, Combat Studies Institute. XXIV The Battle of Hamburger Hill. 4 April 2008 http://ehistory.osu.edu/vietnam/essays/battlecommnd/index.cf

Samuel Zaffiri, Hamburger Hill (New York: Ballantine Books, 1988). (not direct quote)

Studies in Battle Command, Combat Studies Institute. XXIV The Battle of Hamburger Hill. 4 April 2008 http://ehistory.osu.edu/vietnam/essays/battlecommnd/index.cf

Samuel Zaffiri, Hamburger Hill (New York: Ballantine Books, 1988). (not direct quotes)

Studies in Battle Command, Combat Studies Institute. XXIV The Battle of Hamburger Hill. 4 April 2008 http://ehistory.osu.edu/vietnam/essays/battlecommnd/index.cf

Samuel Zaffiri, Hamburger Hill (New York: Ballantine Books, 1988). (not direct quotes)

Samuel Zaffiri, Hamburger Hill (New York: Ballantine Books, 1988). (not direct quotes)

Samuel Zaffiri, Hamburger Hill (New York: Ballantine Books, 1988). (not direct quotes)

page 191

Leoslyrics.com. March 2005
<http://leoslyrics.com/listlyrics.php?hid=7obdZP4dy3W%3D>.

page 192

"The Harbor Site." Grunt.space. 7 February 2006 <http://grunt.space.swiri.edu/harbor.htm>.

Michael D. McCombs, "A Shau." Grunt. Space. Jan.2006 <http://grunt.space.swri.edu/ashau.htm>.

page 193

Anti War. Com. "Quotes." Antiwar.com. 30 May 2006 <http://www.antiwar.com/quotes.php>.

Albert S. Harper, (French Teacher, Highland High School), Personal Interview. 10 January 2006.

Albert S. Harper, (French Teacher, Highland High School), Personal Interview. 10 January 2006.

Albert S. Harper, (French Teacher, Highland High School), Personal Interview. 10 January 2006.

page 195

Samuel Zaffiri, Hamburger Hill (New York: Ballantine Books, 1988) 82.

page 199

Anti War. Com. "Quotes." Antiwar.com. 30 May 2006 <http://www.antiwar.com/quotes.php>.

page 203

Samuel Zaffiri, Hamburger Hill (New York: Ballantine Books, 1988). (not direct quote)

Samuel Zaffiri, Hamburger Hill (New York: Ballantine Books, 1988). (not direct quotes).

Samuel Zaffiri, Hamburger Hill (New York: Ballantine Books, 1988) 77.

Samuel Zaffiri, Hamburger Hill (New York: Ballantine Books, 1988) 78-79

Samuel Zaffiri, Hamburger Hill (New York: Ballantine Books, 1988) 78-79.

Samuel Zaffiri, Hamburger Hill (New York: Ballantine Books, 1988) 78-79.

Samuel Zaffiri, Hamburger Hill (New York: Ballantine Books, 1988) 78-79.

Lt. Frank Hair, "The Summer Offensive in the A Shau Valley." *Rendezvous With Destiny Magazine.* Summer 1969. Jan. 2006 <http://www.Lcompanyranger.com/Ashau/ashauarticle1.htm>.

"A Shau Valley." En. Wikipedia.Org. 16 March 2006. Dec. 2005 <http://en.wiki/A_Shau_Valley>.

page 208

Samuel Zaffiri, Hamburger Hill (New York: Ballantine Books, 1988) 82-83. (not direct quotes)

Studies in Battle Command, Combat Studies Institute. XXIV The Battle of Hamburger Hill. 4 April 2008 http://ehistory.osu.edu/vietnam/essays/battlecommnd/index.cf

Samuel Zaffiri, Hamburger Hill (New York: Ballantine Books, 1988) 82-83. (not direct quotes)

Samuel Zaffiri, Hamburger Hill (New York: Ballantine Books, 1988). (not direct quotes)

Samuel Zaffiri, Hamburger Hill (New York: Ballantine Books, 1988). (not direct quotes)

Studies in Battle Command, Combat Studies Institute. XXIV The Battle of Hamburger Hill. 4 April 2008 http://ehistory.osu.edu/vietnam/essays/battlecommnd/index.cf

page 209

Studies in Battle Command, Combat Studies Institute. XXIV The Battle of Hamburger Hill. 4 April 2008 http://ehistory.osu.edu/vietnam/essays/battlecommnd/index.cf

Samuel Zaffiri, Hamburger Hill (New York: Ballantine Books, 1988) 82.

Samuel Zaffiri, Hamburger Hill (New York: Ballantine Books, 1988) 83.

Samuel Zaffiri, Hamburger Hill (New York: Ballantine Books, 1988) 55.

Samuel Zaffiri, Hamburger Hill (New York: Ballantine Books, 1988) 55.

Samuel Zaffiri, Hamburger Hill (New York: Ballantine Books, 1988). (not direct quote)

Studies in Battle Command, Combat Studies Institute. XXIV The Battle of Hamburger Hill. 4 April 2008 http://ehistory.osu.edu/vietnam/essays/battlecommnd/index.cf

Samuel Zaffiri, Hamburger Hill (New York: Ballantine Books, 1988) 55.

page 210

T.R. Fehrenbach, This Kind of War (Washington, D.C.: Brassey's, 1963) 251.

page 211

Samuel Zaffiri, Hamburger Hill (New York: Ballantine Books, 1988) 55.

Studies in Battle Command, Combat Studies Institute. XXIV The Battle of Hamburger Hill. 4 April 2008 http://ehistory.osu.edu/vietnam/essays/battlecommnd/index.cf

Samuel Zaffiri, Hamburger Hill (New York: Ballantine Books, 1988) 83, 55, 57, 93.

Samuel Zaffiri, Hamburger Hill (New York: Ballantine Books, 1988) 83, 55, 57, 93.

page 212-213

Samuel Zaffiri, Hamburger Hill (New York: Ballantine Books, 1988) 83, 55, 57, 93.

Studies in Battle Command, Combat Studies Institute. XXIV The Battle of Hamburger Hill. 4 April 2008 http://ehistory.osu.edu/vietnam/essays/battlecommnd/index.cf

Samuel Zaffiri, Hamburger Hill (New York: Ballantine Books, 1988) 55. (not exact quote)

Medal of Honor Recipients. "Vietnam War (M-Z)." Army.mil. 23 August 2006 <http://www.army.mil/cmh-pg/mohviet2.htm>.

Medal of Honor Recipients. "Vietnam War (A-L)." Army.mil. 23 August 2006 <http://www.army.mil/cmh-pg/mohviet2.htm>.

Studies in Battle Command, Combat Studies Institute. XXIV The Battle of Hamburger Hill. 4 April 2008 http://ehistory.osu.edu/vietnam/essays/battlecommnd/index.cf

"Studies in Battle Command," the Faculty Combat Studies Institute and LTC Douglas P. Scalard. Ehistory.osu.edu. 9 June 2008 <http://ehistory.osu.edu/vietnam/essays/battlecommand/index.cfm>

Samuel Zaffiri, Hamburger Hill (New York: Ballantine Books, 1988) (not exact quotes)

T.R. Fehrenbach, This Kind of War (Washington, D.C.: Brassey's, 1963) Title Page.

Samuel Zaffiri, Hamburger Hill (New York: Ballantine Books, 1988) 55.

Samuel Zaffiri, Hamburger Hill (New York: Ballantine Books, 1988) Title Page.

Samuel Zaffiri, Hamburger Hill (New York: Ballantine Books, 1988) 55, 57, 93. (not exact quotes)

Studies in Battle Command, Combat Studies Institute. XXIV The Battle of Hamburger Hill. 4 April 2008 http://ehistory.osu.edu/vietnam/essays/battlecommnd/index.cf

Samuel Zaffiri, Hamburger Hill (New York: Ballantine Books, 1988) 55, 93.

Samuel Zaffiri, Hamburger Hill (New York: Ballantine Books, 1988) 57, 55. (not exact quotes)

Samuel Zaffiri, Hamburger Hill (New York: Ballantine Books, 1988) 57, 55. (not exact quotes)

Samuel Zaffiri, Hamburger Hill (New York: Ballantine Books, 1988) 57, 55. (not exact quotes)

Studies in Battle Command, Combat Studies Institute. XXIV The Battle of Hamburger Hill. 4 April 2008 http://ehistory.osu.edu/vietnam/essays/battlecommnd/index.cf

page 214

Studies in Battle Command, Combat Studies Institute. XXIV The Battle of Hamburger Hill. 4 April 2008 http://ehistory.osu.edu/vietnam/essays/battlecommnd/index.cf

Samuel Zaffiri, Hamburger Hill (New York: Ballantine Books, 1988) 55.

page 215

Samuel Zaffiri, Hamburger Hill (New York: Ballantine Books, 1988) 93, 55, 57. (not exact quotes)

Samuel Zaffiri, Hamburger Hill (New York: Ballantine Books, 1988) 93, 55, 57. (not exact quotes)

Studies in Battle Command, Combat Studies Institute. XXIV The Battle of Hamburger Hill. 4 April 2008 http://ehistory.osu.edu/vietnam/essays/battlecommnd/index.cf

Samuel Zaffiri, Hamburger Hill (New York: Ballantine Books, 1988) 93.

Samuel Zaffiri, Hamburger Hill (New York: Ballantine Books, 1988) 93.

Samuel Zaffiri, Hamburger Hill (New York: Ballantine Books, 1988) 93.

page 216

Samuel Zaffiri, Hamburger Hill (New York: Ballantine Books, 1988) 93.

"Studies in Battle Command," the Faculty Combat Studies Institute and LTC Douglas P. Scalard. Ehistory.osu.edu. 9 June 2008 <http://ehistory.osu/vietnam/essays/battlecommand/index.cfm>

page 217

Samuel Zaffiri, Hamburger Hill (New York: Ballantine Books, 1988) 93.

Samuel Zaffiri, Hamburger Hill (New York: Ballantine Books, 1988) 93.

"Studies in Battle Command," the Faculty Combat Studies Institute and LTC Douglas P. Scalard. Ehistory.osu.edu. 9 June 2008
<http://ehistory.osu/vietnam/essays/battlecommand/index.cfm>

page 218

Samuel Zaffiri, Hamburger Hill (New York: Ballantine Books, 1988) 57.

page 219

"Medal of Honor Recipients, Vietnam War (A-L)" Army.mil. 4 September 2006 <http://www.army.mil/cmh-pg/mohviet.htm>.

page 224

Anti War. Com "Quotes." Antiwar.com. 30 May 2006 <http://www.antiwar.com/quotes.php>. (source: Philip Caputo, A Rumor of War)

Brainyquote.com 12 September 2006 <www.brainyquote.com>. (source: Philip Caputo, A Rumor of War)

Fruitfromwashington. Com. Quotataionsabout.com. 12 October 2006
<http://quotationsabout.com/gi/dynamic/offsite.htm>. (source: Philip Caputo, A Rumor of War.)

All Great Quotes. Allgreat quotes.com. 7 October 2008 <www.allgreatquotes.com/war_quotes.shtml>.

page 226

"Medal of Honor Recipients, Vietnam War (A-L)" Army.mil. 4 September 2006 <http://www.army.mil/cmh-pg/mohviet.htm>.

"Medal of Honor Recipients, Vietnam War (M-Z)" Army.mil. 4 September 2006 <http://www.army.mil/cmh-pg/mohviet.htm>.

page 227

"Medal of Honor Recipients, Vietnam War (A-L)" Army.mil. 4 September 2006 <http://www.army.mil/cmh-pg/mohviet.htm>.

"Medal of Honor Recipients, Vietnam War (M-Z)"
Army.mil. 4 September 2006 <http://www.army.mil/cmh-pg/mohviet.htm>.

page 229

Carl Laemmle, (Producer) and Milestone Lewis (Director)
(1930) All Quiet on The Western Front Universal Studios,
U.S.A.

page 232

Alberto Grimaldi, (Producer) and Leon, Sergio
(Director) (1966) The Good, the Bad and the Ugly.
Italy/Spain. Arturo Gonzalez Producciones Cinemetograficas,
S.A.

page 233

Lance Cpl. Bryan A. Peterson, "Elite Honor Fallen AV
Marine." Antelope Valley Press 12 December 2006: 4A.

Lance Cpl. Bryan A. Peterson, "Elite Honor AV Marine."
Okinawa Marine 1 December 2006: page 12.

page 234

Anti War. Com. "Quotes." Antiwar.com. 30 May 2006
<http://www.antiwar.com/quotes.php>.

World of Quotes.Com. Worldofquotes.com. 4 November 2006
<http://www.worldofquotes.com/topic/war/1/index.htm>.

Thinkexist.com 10 October 2006
<http://en.thinkexit.com>.

Samuel Zaffiri, Hamburger Hill (New York: Ballantine
Books, 1988) 93.

page 235

"NATO Rockets Miss Target, Kill 12 Afghan Civilians,"
Yahoo News, AP Press. News Yahoo.Com.
<http://news.yahoo.com/s/ap/20100214/ap_on_re_as/as_afghan>.

Theo Lippman Jr., Senator Ted Kennedy (New York: W.W.
Norton and Company, 1976) 65.

Samuel Zaffiri, Hamburger Hill. (New York: Ballantine
Books, 1988) 275.

Samuel Zaffiri, Hamburger Hill. (New York: Ballantine
Books, 1988) 276.

Samuel Zaffiri, Hamburger Hill. (New York: Ballantine
Books, 1988) 276.

Samuel Zaffiri, <u>Hamburger Hill</u>. (New York: Ballantine Books, 1988) 276.

Samuel Zaffiri, <u>Hamburger Hill</u>. (New York: Ballantine Books, 1988) 277.

Samuel Zaffiri, <u>Hamburger Hill</u>. (New York: Ballantine Books, 1988) 7.

page 240

Medal of Honor Recipients. "Vietnam War (M-Z)." Army.mil. 23 August 2006 <<u>http://www.army.mil/cmh-pg/mohviet2.htm</u>>.

Medal of Honor Recipients. "Vietnam War (A-L)." Army.mil. 23 August 2006 <<u>http://www.army.mil/cmh-pg/mohviet2.htm</u>>.

Medal of Honor Recipients. "Vietnam War (M-Z)." Army.mil. 23 August 2006 <<u>http://www.army.mil/cmh-pg/mohviet2.htm</u>>.

Medal of Honor Recipients. "Vietnam War (A-L)." Army.mil. 23 August 2006 <<u>http://www.army.mil/cmh-pg/mohviet2.htm</u>>.

page 242

Chris Hedges, *The Crucifixation of Tomas Young*, Truthdig truthdig.com 3-10-13 <<u>www.truthdig.com/dig/item/the_last_letter_20130318/</u>>.

Phil Donahue. <u>Body of War</u>, Ellen Spiro, Beradine Colish, Karen Bernstein, Eddie Vedder, Jeff Layton Film Sales Company 2007.

Bill Moyers, <u>The Journal</u>, Pbs.com, 3-21-08 <<u>http://www.pbs.org/moyers/journal/032/2008/watch2.html</u>>.

Dylan Stableford, <u>The Lookout</u>, *Iraq War VetPens Last Letter to Bush and Cheney*. Yahoo News, Yahoonews.com 3/17/13 <<u>http://www.yahoonews.com</u>>.

Dennis Anderson (Editor), "Big Three-Day Week-End's Shift in Meaning." <u>Antelope Valley Press</u> 27 May 2012: 13A.

page 244

Quotations About War. Quotegarden. 5 October 2008 <<u>www.quotegarden.com/war.html</u>>.

Wikiquote. "War." En.wikiquote. 4 June 2006 <<u>http://www.en.wikiquote.org/wiki/war</u>>.

page 246

Wikiquote. "War." En.wikiquote. 3 June 2006 <<u>http://www.en.wikiquote.org/wiki/war</u>>.

Samuel Zaffiri, <u>Hamburger Hill</u>. (New York: Ballantine Books, 1988) (not a direct quote).

Studies in Battle Command, Combat Studies Institute. XXIV The Battle of Hamburger Hill. 4 April 2008 <u>http://ehistory.osu.edu/vietnam/essays/battlecommnd/index.cf</u>

page 247

Samuel Zaffiri, <u>Hamburger Hill</u>. (New York: Ballantine Books, 1988) 13.

page 248

Medal of Honor Recipients. "Vietnam War (M-Z)." Army.mil. 23 August 2006 <<u>http://www.army.mil/cmh-pg/mohviet2.htm</u>>.

Medal of Honor Recipients. "Vietnam War (A-L)." Army.mil. 23 August 2006 <<u>http://www.army.mil/cmh-pg/mohviet2.htm</u>>.

Medal of Honor Recipients. "Vietnam War (M-Z)." Army.mil. 23 August 2006 <<u>http://www.army.mil/cmh-pg/mohviet2.htm</u>>.

Medal of Honor Recipients. "Vietnam War (A-L)." Army.mil. 23 August 2006 <<u>http://www.army.mil/cmh-pg/mohviet2.htm</u>>.

Medal of Honor Recipients. "Vietnam War (A-Z)." Army.mil. 23 August 2006 <<u>http://www.army.mil/cmh-pg/mohviet2.htm</u>>.

Medal of Honor Recipients. "Vietnam War (A-Z)." Army.mil. 23 August 2006 <<u>http://www.army.mil/cmh-pg/mohviet2.htm</u>>.

page 249

Bob Herbert, (NYT). "Support Wounded Heroes." <u>Antelope Valley Press</u> 4 April 2007: 5B.

Bob Herbert, "Support Wounded Heroes." <u>Antelope Valley Press</u> 4 April 2007: 5B.

Bob Herbert, "Support Wounded Heroes." <u>Antelope Valley Press</u> 4 April 2007: 5B.

page 250

Samuel Zaffiri, <u>Hamburger Hill</u>. (New York: Ballantine Books, 1988) 261.

Samuel Zaffiri, <u>Hamburger Hill</u>. (New York: Ballantine Books, 1988) 261 (not direct quote)

page 251

Medal of Honor Recipients. "Vietnam War (M-Z)." Army.mil. 23 August 2006 <http://www.army.mil/cmh-pg/mohviet2.htm>.

Medal of Honor Recipients. "Vietnam War (A-L)." Army.mil. 23 August 2006 <http://www.army.mil/cmh-pg/mohviet2.htm>.

page 252

Medal of Honor Recipients. "Vietnam War (M-Z)." Army.mil. 23 August 2006 <http://www.army.mil/cmh-pg/mohviet2.htm>.

Medal of Honor Recipients. "Vietnam War (A-L)." Army.mil. 23 August 2006 <http://www.army.mil/cmh-pg/mohviet2.htm>.

Medal of Honor Recipients. "Vietnam War (M-Z)." Army.mil. 23 August 2006 <http://www.army.mil/cmh-pg/mohviet2.htm>.

Medal of Honor Recipients. "Vietnam War (A-L)." Army.mil. 23 August 2006 <http://www.army.mil/cmh-pg/mohviet2.htm>.

page 256

Anti War. Com. "Quotes." Antiwar.com. 30 May 2006 <http://www.antiwar.com/quotes.php>.

page 257

The History Place. Com. "Vietnam War, 1961-1964." Thehistoryplace.com. March 2005 <http://www.thehistoryplace.com>.